Forging the World

Forging the World: Strategic Narratives and International Relations brings together leading scholars in International Relations (IR) and Communication Studies to investigate how, when, and why strategic narratives shape the structure, politics, and policies of the global system. Put simply, strategic narratives are tools that political actors employ to promote their interests, values, and aspirations for the international order by managing expectations and altering the discursive environment. These narratives define "who we are" and "what kind of world order we want."

The first part of the book lays out the theoretical framework for the use of narratives in global politics and addresses methodological and ethical issues raised by the study of strategic narratives. The volume then proceeds with case study chapters on the European Union's narrative of integration, U.S.-Russian narratives about the post–Cold War global system, China's foreign policy narrative, narratives of international development, narratives surrounding the Arab Awakening, the narratives and counternarratives advanced by al Qaeda and the players in the War on Terror, and the role of narratives in managing crises and constructing global order. The book concludes with a discussion of conceptual and methodological insights and points to areas for future research.

Alister Miskimmon is Reader in European Politics and International Relations and Co-Director of the Centre for European Politics at Royal Holloway, University of London.

Ben O'Loughlin is Professor of International Relations and Co-Director of the New Political Communication Unit at Royal Holloway, University of London.

Laura Roselle is Professor of Political Science and International Studies at Elon University and Visiting Professor of Public Policy, DeWitt Wallace Center for Media & Democracy, Duke University.

Forging the World

Strategic Narratives and International Relations

*Edited by Alister Miskimmon,
Ben O'Loughlin, and Laura Roselle*

UNIVERSITY OF MICHIGAN PRESS

Ann Arbor

Copyright © by the University of Michigan 2017
All rights reserved

This book may not be reproduced, in whole or in part, including illustrations, in any form (beyond that copying permitted by Sections 107 and 108 of the U.S. Copyright Law and except by reviewers for the public press), without written permission from the publisher.

Published in the United States of America by the
University of Michigan Press
Manufactured in the United States of America
♾ Printed on acid-free paper

2020   2019   2018   2017   4   3   2   1

A CIP catalog record for this book is available from the British Library.

Library of Congress Cataloging-in-Publication Data

Names: Miskimmon, Alister, editor. | O'Loughlin, Ben, 1976– editor. | Roselle, Laura, editor.
Title: Forging the world : strategic narratives and international relations / edited by Alister Miskimmon, Ben O'Loughlin, and Laura Roselle.
Description: Ann Arbor : University of Michigan Press, [2017] | Includes bibliographical references and index.
Identifiers: LCCN 2016040292| ISBN 9780472130214 (hardcover : acid-free paper) | ISBN 9780472122509 (e-book)
Subjects: LCSH: International relations. | Communication in politics. | Persuasion (Psychology)
Classification: LCC JZ1242 .F68 2017 | DDC 327—dc23
LC record available at https://lccn.loc.gov/2016040292

Contents

Preface and Acknowledgments		vii
1 |	Introduction *Alister Miskimmon, Ben O'Loughlin, and Laura Roselle*	1
2 |	Strategic Narratives: Methods and Ethics *Ben O'Loughlin, with Alister Miskimmon and Laura Roselle*	23
3 |	Strategic Narratives and Great Power Identity *Laura Roselle*	56
4 |	Finding a Unified Voice? The European Union through a Strategic Narrative Lens *Alister Miskimmon*	85
5 |	The Power of Strategic Narratives: The Communicative Dynamics of Chinese Nationalism and Foreign Relations *Ning Liao*	110
6 |	Beyond Neoliberalism: Contested Narratives of International Development *J. P. Singh*	134
7 |	Public Diplomacy, Networks, and the Limits of Strategic Narratives *Robin Brown*	164
8 |	Strategic Narratives of the Arab Spring and After *Amelia Arsenault, Sun-ha Hong, and Monroe E. Price*	190

9 | Narrative Wars: Understanding Terrorism
in the Era of Global Interconnectedness 218
Cristina Archetti

10 | Filling the Narrative Vacuum in a Global Crisis:
Japan's Triple Disaster 246
Ben O'Loughlin

11 | Understanding International Order
and Power Transition: A Strategic Narrative Approach 276
Alister Miskimmon and Ben O'Loughlin

12 | Conclusions 311
Alister Miskimmon, Ben O'Loughlin, and Laura Roselle

Contributors 325

Index 329

Preface and Acknowledgments

This book has emerged out of a dialogue with colleagues working in the fields of International Relations and Political Communication to better understand how persuasion works in international affairs. It builds on our 2013 monograph, *Strategic Narratives*, which sought to conceptualize the impact of the new media ecology on how political actors seek to influence others. Communication is a vital, and much underexplored, aspect of the study of International Relations. We hope this collection of essays by leading scholars working at the intersection of International Relations and Political Communication will encourage greater discussion about the challenges and opportunities faced by those trying to influence world politics today. We also hope that the broad range of topics covered in the book's chapters will interest the policy-making community, by illustrating how narratives, strategically deployed, are a common feature of international affairs. We hope it will aid policymakers' understanding of political communication as they grapple with working within the constraints and opportunities of the new media ecology in their careers. We believe the concept of strategic narrative has great potential to explain why actors are sometimes able, or unable, to get third parties to do as they wish.

The value and significance of this volume is threefold. First, the chapters show the *durability* of the strategic narrative concept. They demonstrate how the stages of narrative formation, narrative projection, and narrative reception are intertwined and often lead to unexpected outcomes. We illustrate how policy narratives, narratives about the identity of political actors, and narratives about the international system itself operate together across a range of case studies. Second, the volume illustrates the *inclusivity* of the strategic narrative approach. Authors explore different points on a spectrum of approaches to persuasion, enriching our understanding of how influence works. Third, the volume shows the *potential* of the strategic narrative approach. All the contributing authors added ideas beyond what we the editors expected and developed aspects of our original framework in different ways.

Why narratives? Storytelling is something that unites all corners of the globe. It is central to how we understand our history and our future, and how we organize the complexity of our political, economic, and social relations in a comprehensible, manageable way. Strategic narratives are sense-making devices deployed by political actors, designed to capture the political center ground, to shape our understanding of policies and emerging events. Strategic narratives can forge shared meanings. Former Australian prime minister Kevin Rudd suggests that "a common strategic narrative between [China and the United States] could act as an organizing principle that reduces strategic drift, and encourages other more cooperative behaviors over time."

Understanding the narratives of political opponents can inform negotiation in areas where potential cooperation is achievable, and, indeed, areas of weakness can be exploited. The negotiations between the P5+1 and Iran over the past decade have demonstrated the material impact of narrative contestation between opposing actors. Diplomacy, both public and private and over many years, has allowed leaders to forge a collective narrative on Iran's nuclear technological capabilities. At the conclusion of negotiations in July 2015 President Barack Obama suggested that knowing and understanding Iran's narrative was an important aspect of finding an agreement with a hitherto sworn enemy. In a *New York Times* interview, President Obama stated:

> [E]ven with your enemies, even with your adversaries, I do think that you have to have the capacity to put yourself occasionally in their shoes, and if you look at Iranian history, the fact is that we had some involvement with overthrowing a democratically elected regime in Iran. We have had in the past supported Saddam Hussein when we know he used chemical weapons in the war between Iran and Iraq, and so, as a consequence, they have their own security concerns, their own narrative. It may not be one we agree with. It in no way rationalizes the kinds of sponsorship from terrorism or destabilizing activities that they engage in, but I think that when we are able to see their country and their culture in specific terms, his-

torical terms, as opposed to just applying a broad brush, that's when you have the possibility at least of some movement.[1]

The chapters in this volume demonstrate how the analysis of narratives is key to understanding many of the central issues in international affairs. We outline a research agenda that we hope students and scholars will run with as we seek to develop ever greater sophistication in how we analyze communication in International Relations.

We have many people to thank for helping make this book possible. First, Melody Herr at the University of Michigan Press has been enormously patient and encouraging as the project developed. Thanks also to Danielle Coty for her help with finalizing the manuscript.

We are grateful to a number of colleagues who have commented on ideas, drafts, or presentations of the chapters in this volume. They include Michelle Bentley, Janice Bially Mattern, Natalia Chaban, Fabrizio Coticchia, Clyde Ellis, Charlotte Epstein, Federica Ferrari, Karin Fierke, Alan Finlayson, Marie Gillespie, Ian Hall, Isabelle Hertner, Andrew Hoskins, Stephen Hutchings, Floor Keuleers, Dave Levine, Nicola Liscutin, Kimberly Marten, Allan McConnell, Ellen Mickiewicz, Helen Miskimmon, Sarah Oates, James Pamment, Chris Perkins, Anna Reading, Jens Ringsmose, Ken Rogerson, Phil Seib, David Smith, General Sir Rupert Smith, Devon Simons, Amy Skonieczny, Sharon Spray, Holly Steel, Rebecca Suter, Carolijn van Noort, Alban Webb, and Ayşe Zarakol.

Much of our work involves liaising with policymakers who themselves are trying to craft strategic narratives or evaluate their effectiveness. Critical to our thinking has been the U.K. Select Committee on Soft Power and U.K. Influence. Ben O'Loughlin was Specialist Advisor to this committee and had the opportunity to call upon the knowledge of a wonderful selection of experts and to engage with how foreign policy practitioners go about the business of influence on a daily basis. The committee consulted academics such as Professors Joseph Nye, Gary Rawnsley, Philip Seib, and Peter van Ham; those whose careers involved critical moments of strategic narrative projection, including Sir Jeremy Greenstock; former Prime Minister Sir John Major, former Foreign Secretary Jack Straw; Sir Antony Acland, former head of the U.K. diplomatic service and Ambassador to Washington; Lord Hannay of Chiswick, former U.K. permanent representative to the European Economic Community and the United Nations;

policymakers exercised with narratives at the time, including Justine Greening, Secretary of State at the Department for International Development: Mark Harper, then Minister for Immigration, Home Office: Maria Miller, Secretary of State for Culture, Media and Sport, Department for Culture, Media and Sport: Hugo Swire, Minister of State at the Foreign and Commonwealth Office; Dr. Andrew Murrison, Minister for International Security Strategy, Ministry of Defence: and Conrad Bird, Director of the GREAT Britain Campaign in the Prime Minister's Office; from the world of foreign policy and diplomacy, including Ambassadors Rudolf Adam (Germany), Keiichi Hayashi (Japan), Roberto Jaguaribe (Brazil), Kim Traavik (Norway), and Tara Sonenshine, former Under Secretary for Public Diplomacy and Public Affairs for the U.S. Department of State, (2012–13), and Director of Foreign Policy Planning for the National Security Council during the Clinton administration; leaders of organizations that form part of Britain's narrative identity in the world, including Martin Davidson CMG, Chief Executive of the British Council; Peter Horrocks, Director of the BBC World Service; Dr. Jonathan Williams, Deputy Director at the British Museum; and Richard Scudamore, Chief Executive of the Premier League; journalists charged with reporting strategic narratives, including the *Economist*'s John Micklethwait and the *Guardian*'s Richard Norton-Taylor; and experts in conceptualizing and measuring influence in international affairs, especially Indra Adnan, Simon Anholt, Jonathan McClory, and Emile Simpson. The committee was chaired with grace and ingenuity by Lord David Howell. We wish to thank Her Majesty's Government, which responded thoughtfully to the committee's suggestions, not least to their patient explanation of why HMG was not then inclined toward installing a Strategic Narrative Unit in No. 10 Downing Street.

We have enjoyed sparring in recent years with those charged with communicating narratives. At NATO we have had productive dialogues with Jaap de Hoof Scheffer, Mark Laity, and Jamie Shea. At the U.S. Department of State, Katherine Brown is always a source of insight and critical questions. Hugh Elliott at the U.K.'s Foreign and Commonwealth Office has offered us food for thought about the challenges of narrating across cultures and media formats, and Tom Fletcher provides continual examples of the nuances of influence. Dr. Joanna Kaminska has also provided valuable insights into the complexity of projecting a coherent European Union foreign policy narrative.

Alister Miskimmon and Ben O'Loughlin would like to thank Professor

Martin Holland and Professor Natalia Chaban and their colleagues at the Centre for Research on Europe, University of Christchurch, New Zealand, for organizing a fascinating symposium on Strategic Narratives of Identity: The EU, Europe and the World on February 27, 2015. We have benefited immensely from engaging with Martin and Natalia's extensive work on perception in International Relations in developing our understanding of strategic narrative. We would also like to thank Dr. James Headley at the University of Otago for hosting us for a seminar on February 24, 2015 on Weaponising Information: Putin, the West and Competing Narratives on Ukraine, which stimulated lots of interesting discussion.

Ben O'Loughlin benefited greatly from discussions with Akil Awan, Abbas Barzegar, and Shawn Powers about strategic narratives around the Syria crisis. This was made possible by funding from the British Council's Bridging Voices program, support from the Carter Center in Atlanta, Georgia, and the guidance of Tim Rivera Roberts.

Laura Roselle has gained insight from Elon's Technology and Information Working Group and especially from colleagues David Levine and Megan Squire of that group. She also benefited from participation in the American University Law School's Program on Information Justice and Intellectual Property. Roselle's early work on this project was supported by an Elon Senior Research Fellowship.

We are grateful to Laura Shepherd for convening a symposium on Strategic Narratives in *Critical Security Studies* and to the authors who engaged with our work and helped us refine our ideas—Lucian Ashworth, Monika Barthwal-Datta, Rhys Crilley, María Martín de Almagro, Jan Hanska, Cai Wilkinson, and Laura herself.

We also appreciated conversations with Monroe Price and colleagues at the University of Pennsylvania's Annenberg School in May 2014.

We also must acknowledge the International Communication Section of the International Studies Association. Our colleagues in this group have consistently supported our work on strategic narratives, and we have had many important discussions about the topic at ISA conferences.

The three of us are fortunate to be surrounded by excellent students carrying out research on communication and influence in international relations. In particular, Billur Aslan, Luuk Molthof, Mark Pope, Mary Rouse, and Greg Honan have all contributed to our thinking while this book was being written and it has been a pleasure to have them in our respective departments.

Of course, this volume would not have been possible without the chapters written by the contributing authors. We would like to thank them for their open engagement with the concept of strategic narrative. This openness has challenged us to refine our thinking, and outlined many avenues for future research.

Alister Miskimmon, Ben O'Loughlin, and Laura Roselle
Senate House, London
July 2015

NOTES

1. Thomas L. Friedman, "Obama Makes His Case on Iran Nuclear Deal," *New York Times*, July 14, 2015.

1 | Introduction

Alister Miskimmon, Ben O'Loughlin, and Laura Roselle

Communication and power are the touchstones for the study of strategic narrative. The concept of strategic narrative focuses our attention, as both International Relations scholars and analysts of foreign policy—and as students wishing to understand more about the world around us—on a world in which power and communication technologies are in the midst of a rapid transition. The aim of this volume is to highlight the explanatory power of the concept of strategic narrative. We do this by focusing on a set of empirical studies across a range of important issues in international affairs. These studies demonstrate how strategic narrative analysis can add to our understanding of a wide range of important themes in International Relations. We argue that in order to understand processes of influence in the world we need a fuller understanding of how communication and power align.

The title of this book was chosen to highlight the dynamism, energy, and agency implied by a focus on strategic narratives. "To forge" has two meanings. First, it means "to create (something) strong, enduring, or successful" (Ryan and Thomas 2003, x). Political actors attempt to create a shared understanding of the world, of other political actors, and of policy through the use of strategic narratives. The hope for these political actors is that strong narratives will triumph over counternarratives, that legitimacy will be strengthened, that power will be heightened. The second meaning of "to forge" is "to produce a fraudulent copy or imitation of (a document, signature, banknote, or work of art)" (ibid). This, too, captures part of what we think is important about understanding strategic narratives. Strategic narratives may be designed to elicit particular behavior by referring to historical stories as "forging and forgery are frequently engaged in a complicated sort of interplay and entanglement" (ibid). Neither kind of forging is guaranteed to deliver results or put an end to a political situation. We are, writes Arthur A. Frank, "cast into multiple scripts that are all unfinished" (2010, 7).

The concept of strategic narrative applied to International Relations emerged from Lawrence Freedman's 2006 study of how narrative could be deployed strategically to counter opponents in military conflict. Strategic narratives are viewed by Freedman as a tool to challenge the legitimacy of enemy forces. This raised interesting discussions around how we can understand persuasion and influence in international affairs more broadly, which we elaborated on in our 2013 book, *Strategic Narratives: Communication Power and the New World Order*. Our starting point is to argue that narrative has wider relevance to understanding a broad range of issues within the study of International Relations, not solely narrative contestation within military conflict, or indeed foreign policy analysis. In addition to this, our aim is to demonstrate how narratives are used to influence international politics.

Strategic narratives are not confined to the world of academic study. Strategic narratives are increasingly referenced in the policy world. We have seen policy debates in the United States around the use of narrative, sparked by the publication of a recent policy paper calling for greater focus on projecting an effective narrative of the United States in international affairs (Porter and Mykleby 2011). Branding and soft power are two additional concepts that appear in the academic and policy literature. They are seen as different from narrative, but as Cristina Archetti demonstrates in chapter 9 of this volume, a brand can also be understood as a story. What a political actor narrates about its place in the world is a key aspect of soft power, and is increasingly important in a period when the global rules of international order are being reshaped with the rise of new powers (Roselle, Miskimmon, and O'Loughlin 2014). As we have argued (Miskimmon, O'Loughlin, and Roselle 2013), strategic narratives come in three main forms: (1) strategic narratives about the international *system*, which articulate how a political actor conceives their understanding of international order; (2) narratives employed by political actors seeking to influence the development of *policies*, such as in international arms control negotiations, or in challenging opponents in armed conflict; and (3) arratives of *identity*, which are central to how political actors ject their identity in international affairs, as Laura Roselle outlines in chapter 2 of this volume. An actor able to align system, policy, and identity narratives has a greater chance of influence.

This book seeks to move away from predominantly state-centric approaches to strategic narrative to demonstrate how a wide array of political actors and institutions attempt to influence international affairs, and the challenges they face in doing so. We recognize the importance of material power, but in a shifting international order with growing numbers of voices wishing to exert influence on agendas and policies, communication and social power demand analysis (Howell 2013; Roselle, Miskimmon, and O'Loughlin 2014; van Ham 2010). Communication is viewed in the study of international affairs as both good and bad. On the one hand communication is the way we can bring about greater understanding of different positions of political actors. Discussing the evolution of how China and the United States view each other, former Australian prime minister Kevin Rudd argues:

> The basic reality is that as China's economy grows and supplants the US as the largest economy in the world, and as China gradually begins to narrow the military gap between the two over the decades ahead, there is a new imperative for a common strategic narrative for both Washington and Beijing. In the absence of such a common narrative (if in fact such narrative can be crafted), the truth is that the two nations are more likely to drift further apart, or at least drift more rapidly apart than might otherwise be the case. By contrast, a common strategic narrative between the two could act as an organizing principle that reduces strategic drift, and encourages other more cooperative behaviors over time. So long, of course, as such a narrative embraces the complex reality of the relationship, and avoids motherhood statements which provide negligible operational guidance for those who have day-to-day responsibility, for the practical management of the relationship. (Rudd 2015, 17)

For Rudd, strategic narrative is a means to forge better understanding and closer cooperation on the basis of shared understanding. Rudd's understanding of strategic narrative is in accord with the argument we put forward in our 2013 book.

On the other hand, communication is viewed in less benign terms as a means to achieve selfish objectives. The crisis in Ukraine and Crimea propelled the importance of communication in conflict onto the public agenda in Western countries. Vladimir Putin's hybrid war doctrine, using communication to dissemble and distract the attention of international audiences, was viewed as a highly effective strategy to influence domestic and international opinion (Miskimmon and O'Loughlin 2014). Yet International Relations as a field of study still struggles when trying to account for and analyze political communication. Some scholars underestimate the extent to which the new media ecology has dramatically altered the space in which political actors communicate. Others overemphasize the ability of one actor to change the behavior of third parties through strategic narrative.

Powerful political actors are seeking to channel the potential of communication strategy to reassert their voices and shape international debates. News headlines call attention to information warfare, propaganda, and the battle of the narratives. Can the West's soft power overcome the terrorist group's brand? Whatever the crisis, issue, or domain, we now find strategic narratives. Strategic narratives are often formalized in policy documents that outline future objectives. Political actors are placing increasing importance on crafting strategic narratives such as the European Security Strategy of the European Union from 2003 or NATO's strategic concept of 2010 (European Council 2003; NATO 2010). National debates reflecting on what strategic narrative to project internationally require an internal discussion on the identity of an actor (House of Lords 2014). Jack Snyder has argued that through analyzing strategic narratives we can see how political actors attempt to persuade others of their political vision (Snyder 2015). He argues that narratives make possible the "conceptual integration of facts and values (of 'is' and 'ought') in strategic persuasion and the political integration of diverse perspectives among partners in a strategic coalition" (171). Hayden White argues that despite the constant contestation around narrative accounts of history, narratives nonetheless are important in shaping our understanding of the past and present. Narrative interpretations make the past real to us (White 1984). David Campbell suggests this can depoliticize history in ways that suit a particular version of what has happened:

> [T]he very act of proclaiming the end of the cold war serves to write history in such a way that the cold war becomes an era the understanding of which is not problematic. In considering the issue of where we go from here there is a tendency to uncritically accept a

particular story of how we got to here. By constantly invoking a
new phase in world politics, analysts tend to accept one particular
reading of the period from which we are emerging, a rendering that
privileges the legitimacy of "the West." (Campbell 1992, 17)

We are not alone in taking narrative seriously. There has been a "narrative turn" in International Relations, and indeed in social science in general (Roberts 2006; see also Squire et al. 2015). Narrative analysis is increasingly important in the field of International Relations to scholars of a wide variety of perspectives. Narratives are seen as being vital in the construction of a political actor's identity and their understanding of their role in the world (Berenskoetter 2014; Porter and Mykleby 2011). Entrenched narratives of dominant groups often result in the marginalization of weaker members of societies (Kinnvall and Nesbitt-Larking 2010; Kinnvall and Nesbitt-Larking 2013). Conversely, as Steele (2010) argues, narrative can be used to challenge the powerful (see also Skonieczny 2010). The *Journal of Narrative Politics*, founded in 2014, "aims to imagine futures free from colonial, racial, gendered, and economic violences."[1] The use of narrative is also viewed as an effective means to organize the identity of political groups (Kinnvall and Svensson 2010) and international organizations (Kaldor et al. 2007; Ciuta 2007).

Narratives are seen by some as having force to coerce others to do the will of the powerful in international affairs, as the work of Janice Bially Mattern (2005) has demonstrated. Michelle Bentley's work demonstrates how actors seek to shape our understanding of threats in international affairs using narrative to align with political objectives (Bentley 2013, 2014). Narrative analysis also helps explain how political actors forge agreement and cope with the complexity of international negotiations (Epstein 2008; Hajer 1995). Public diplomacy scholars have highlighted the importance of narrative in the strategies of states to influence others (Brown 2005; Melissen 2005; Pamment 2014). We also see a focus on the role of narrative in military conflict (Betz 2015; Hoskins and O'Loughlin 2010; Miskimmon, O'Loughlin, and Roselle 2015) and how narratives projected by states shape responses to crises (Lang 2006; Miskimmon 2012). The work of Lene Hansen (2011) has been important in reinforcing that images are an important component of political communication, and there is a pressing need to research and understand how narratives are projected visually (Crilley 2015). Lastly, the work of Natalia Chaban and Martin Holland and their colleagues has made an important contribution to how we understand the reception of narratives in third countries through their studies of how the European Union (EU) is perceived in countries outside of Europe (see, for example, Holland and Chaban 2011). Their work also asks how particular dyads in international affairs such as relations between the United States and the European Union are viewed by outsiders (Chaban, Bain, and Stats 2007). A narrative about the EU or the United States is a narrative about how the EU and the United States relate to each other.

Where we aim to build on and contribute to existing forms of narrative analysis in International Relations is in our contention that only by understanding how narratives are formed, how they are projected, and, vitally, how they are received by third parties, can we more fully understand the complexity of persuasion in international politics.

Strategic Narratives: Definition and Framework

The contributors to this volume explore the concept of strategic narrative as central to understanding international relations. We begin with the definition of strategic narrative developed in our conceptual book *Strategic Narratives: Communication Power in a New World Order*. Strategic narratives are a means by which political actors attempt to construct a shared meaning of the past, present, and future of international politics to shape the behavior of domestic and international actors.

Narrative

There are a number of ways to understand political narratives. Shenhav (2006), in reviewing the literature, sets out two strategies for defining the concept of narrative that we find interesting. First, minimalist structural definitions emphasize "time sequence" (cf. Frank 2010). Second, Shenhav notes that many definitions of narrative add characteristics to the basic time sequence structure, including causality, inclusion of a past-present-future structure, some attempt at resolution, and a notion of nonrandomness (that events are connected in a nonrandom way). We recognize the importance of time sequence to the definition of narrative but build on this, incorporating Kenneth Burke's work. To a large degree we do this because Burke focuses on agency and narrative, and says people use language to act (1966). He describes a person as a "symbol-making, symbol-using, symbol-misusing animal." For us, narratives contain the following components:

- Character or actors (agent)
- Setting/environment/space (scene)
- Conflict or action (act)
- Tools/behavior (agency)
- Resolution/or suggested resolution/goal (purpose)

Focusing on this narrative structure allows us to identify actors and actions while recognizing the importance of temporality. This suggests that the past (history), the present, and the future (where are "we" going) are tied together through explication of the setting, action, and goal or purpose. In addition, as scholars such as Frank (2010) have noted, Burke was concerned with understanding the relationship between the component parts of a narrative in a dynamic way rather than in rote categorization of component parts—how the *misfit* of elements drove action. Thus, narratives have a structure that sets them apart conceptually from framing or branding—although both framing and branding can be seen to trigger or evoke narratives.

Narratives and Strategy

Narrative and strategy have often not been explicitly linked in academic studies. Policy literature has been more explicit in linking narrative and strategy, and often draws upon studies from the field of strategic communication. Strategy traditionally has been linked with the amassing of primarily economic and defense capabilities to achieve political objectives, often under the banner of a state's grand strategy (Gray 1999; Posen 1984; Simon 2013). Communication has not been considered central to this. Rather, the focus of much of the literature on grand strategy has been how ideas gain or lose prominence in political debates, without unpacking *how* the debating of narratives around a state's identity, its conception of order, and the policies it wishes to pursue shape which ideas become accepted. The current debate in the United States on its declining power should be understood in these terms.

Types of Strategic Narratives

We suggest that it is helpful to distinguish between three different types of strategic narratives: system, identity, and issue narratives.

First, international system narratives describe how the world is structured, who the players are, and how the system works. Examples would include narratives such as the Cold War, the War on Terror, and the rise of China. A Cold War system narrative, for example, sets out a fairly clearly defined bipolar system with characters that are familiar. This narrative could very well constrain Western thinking on reactions to Russian aggression, for example. Roselle makes the case in her chapter about U.S. and Russian narratives after the fall of the Soviet Union that domestic policies related to war in the Middle East and in Chechnya hurt the ability of international actors to construct a new post–Cold War international system narrative. These old Cold War narratives were quickly revitalized as conflict related to Ukraine heated up.

A second type of narrative is an identity narrative. These set out what the story of a political actor is, what values it has, and what goals it has (Holsti 1970; Thies 2012a and 2012b). In this volume, Ning Liao focuses on this type of strategic narrative in his analysis of Chinese narratives. He argues that Chinese political leaders use narrative related to history to shape understandings of Chinese values and China's role in the international system. Differences in these narratives can shape perceptions about what is appropriate behavior and the possible in terms of policy, and are shaped in an iterative process as elite and public views are considered.

Finally, there are policy narratives that set out why a policy is needed and (normatively) desirable, and how it will be successfully implemented or accomplished. Issue narratives set political actions in a context, with an explanation of who the important actors are, what the conflict or issue is, and how a particular course of action will resolve the underlying issue.

It is important to recognize that the strategic narratives at these different levels are inextricably linked. Contradictions between narratives at different levels can undermine the effectiveness of strategic narratives related to policy.

Strategic Narratives and the Communicative Process: Formation/Projection/Reception

We take seriously the nexus of international relations and communication, and thus our conception of strategic narratives focuses squarely on how strategic narratives are formed, projected, and received.

- **Formation**—addresses how narratives are formed. What is the role of political actors in constructing strategic narratives? Through what institutions and procedures are narratives agreed upon? Chapters in this book address how political elites and nonstate actors including terrorists, international organizations, domestic political interests, and public opinion influence the formation of strategic narratives or may be embedded in a strategic narrative formation process.
- **Projection**—addresses how narratives are projected (or narrated) and contested, particularly in a new media environment. Each contribution to this volume analyzes the difficulty of projecting strategic narratives today. Ben O'Loughlin's chapter on the Fukushima nuclear disaster in 2011 pays special attention to this dynamic, explaining how social media and international news organizations wrested control of the disaster narrative from the Japanese state. Many of the chapters note that the need to consider domestic publics affects the projection of elite-constructed strategic narratives.
- **Reception**—addresses how narratives are received. This means their reach or saturation as well as how individuals understand and process information. The number of clicks on a video or website, for example, may not be assumed to mean agreement with the content. Twitter hashtags can be co-opted. Reception happens in social contexts where narratives may be discussed socially as well as processed individually. Reception depends on the availability of specific mediums like radio or services like Facebook, and each medium offers different possibilities for communicating back.

Understanding formation, projection, and reception requires a multifaceted approach to the analysis of strategic narratives and this is covered in detail in the second chapter. The formation, projection, and reception of strategic narratives does not happen in a vacuum. They can only be understood by accounting for the media ecologies in which they circulate and have effects. Next we define media ecology and explain its development, and then outline a spectrum of different kinds of persuasion that can be traced through world politics.

Understanding Media Ecologies

> Media are not only devices of information; they are also agencies of order. They not only send messages about human doings and our relations with our ecological and economic systems; they are also, in the expanded sense of the media concept that I will argue for, constitutive parts of those systems. (Peters 2015; Loc 47 of 9689 Kindle edition)

By "media ecology" we refer to the simple idea that media technologies can be understood and studied like organic life-forms.[2] They exist in a complex set of relationships within a specific balanced environment. Rapid developments or a disruptive new technology can upset the existing balance. This affects the entire "ecology." Since this ecology is the condition that shapes how information flows and knowledge is spread through a society, a changing ecology affects the distribution and form of authority, legitimacy, and—ultimately—power.

In the last decade, media ecologies have enjoyed a major realignment. The meteorite known as digital media hit the media jungle around 2000, destabilizing previous patterns of interdependence between the big media beasts and us little audiences. Some big beasts died, some limp along still, but many adapted to the new ecological conditions and came to provide services that created an even broader audience than previously. It is helpful to think of three phases of media ecologies that provide the conditions for international relations today (Hoskins and O'Loughlin 2015). First, the broadcast era of media ecologies of the late twentieth century saw national and satellite television and the press enjoy a lock on what mass audiences witnessed. Governments could exercise relative control of journalists' access and reporting. By the turn of the millennium, mass Internet penetration and the post-9/11 War on Terror signaled a second phase (Hoskins and O'Loughlin 2010). Here, the embedding of digital content enabled more of international affairs and their consequences to be recorded, archived, searched, and shared. An unprecedented sense of chaos and flux beset both those conducting foreign policy and mainstream media organizations used to having a monopoly on its reporting. Content seemed to emerge from nowhere and uncertainty reigned. This was a Wild West moment in which much of the media ecology felt "out there," a continual source of risk to policymakers' reputation and credibility and to the legitimacy of policy itself.

We now witness a third phase of media ecology, one in which the chaos of the second phase has been tamed. Professional media and policy institutions have arrested the seemingly anarchic social media dynamics and more effectively harnessed them for their own ends. The U.S. State Department has long tried to intervene in online conversation about the United States in world affairs. Russia operates a "troll army" of cyber professionals paid to promote a Russian worldview on message boards and below-the-line spaces in different online spaces (Gallagher 2015). And for the news media, user-generated content may create a mass of images and content for journalists and editors to filter and verify, but when a crisis breaks, that content adds authenticity and often striking images to news organizations' coverage. The third, current phase of the media ecology involves a reassertion of the mainstream and power elites in government, the military, and the news media.

Complicating this ability to dominate communication, John Peters sees the scope of media shifting over time. In his book *The Marvelous Clouds*, he argues:

> Media are civilizational ordering devices. Getting this insight requires us to see just how exceptional media were in the last century. During much of it, "media" such as radio, television, film, newspapers, and magazines were seen as providing information for voters, enticement for consumers, entertainment for workers, and ideology for dupes. Media were largely conceived, in other words, as distributors of messages and meanings designed on a human scale. They were generally taken as influential, to be sure, but not as infrastructural—as figure, but not as ground. In the past half century, as the dominant technologized form of communication has shifted from broadcasting and telephony to the Internet, things have re-

verted back to the historical norm of a more chaotic media world. One-to-many communication on a mass scale is still around but is much less routine than in the age of "drama for a dramatized society" that filled the airwaves for a good part of the twentieth century. We are back to the age-old modes of some-to-some, one-to-few, and even one-to-none—to a communication environment in which media have become equipment for living in a more fundamental way. (Peters 2015, Loc99 of 9689 Kindle edition)

Certainly, we find variation in how quickly different kinds of institutions have adapted to these developments. Democratic governments, militaries, and finance ministries are still struggling through phase two, worrying about chaos and risk. Their institutional responsibilities mean they cannot experiment quite so playfully with communication strategies and embrace unpredictable social media dynamics in the way a news organization, terrorist group, or nongovernmental organization (NGO) can. Does this have a knock-on effect on the relative power of different kinds of organizations to communicate and to affect public debate about international issues?

Attention to media ecologies helps us identify change and continuity in the strategic narrative environment. We must consider how narratives travel across media ecologies too, for the Internet of China or Iran is different to that of Italy or Canada. We must also consider changes to who narrates:

We have to fundamentally change how we think of political units and order. Who communicates? Who has a voice in international affairs? These are crucial questions in the context of thirty billion devices connected to the internet by 2020 and increasing numbers of the world's eight billion population owning such devices or living in societies with at least some infrastructure depending on digital connectivity. Digital media have changed the way we use our social networks and allowed us to be political actors when we choose to be. The agency of individuals is being enhanced by the device networks of the internet of things. Increasingly, international relations will be about interpersonal relations and how devices talk to one another. (Howard 2015, 224–25)

When we wrote *Strategic Narratives* in 2013 we could see information infrastructures as increasingly important spaces of communication, agency, and power. Now this is coming more clearly into view, with a collision between different Internets based on different values and interests. We must also think about complex interdependencies between them: the various penetrations and alliances of technology firms and state regulators who together produce the ecologies within which narratives circulate and have effects.

In accounting for the ways media ecologies shape how information, knowledge, and narratives circulate, this gives us a much more precise grasp of how ideas matter in international relations. It is one thing to say an idea—or a narrative, for that matter—is "dominant" or "hegemonic." It is another thing altogether to explain how and why an idea dominates policy or public agendas. To answer this more important question, we must account for the way in which that idea or narrative is communicated and how different mediums condition how it is contested. Persuasion is not the simple replacement of one idea with another. The volume or presence of an idea in public space is no guide to whether people like or endorse that idea. Indeed, if communication in world politics is marked today by a proliferation of visual, viral content, it is not enough to make assumptions about what idea or narrative it conveys or what it means to policy elites or publics. Scholars trying to explain how political outcomes occur and political actors trying to create political outcomes need to know how the characteristics of a specific media ecology enable and constrain actors' communication: how, when, and why media ecologies make a difference.

How the Book Will Proceed

Our concept of strategic narrative helps broaden an understanding of international relations by advancing the literature on how states and other political actors seek influence. The chapters in this volume address the formation, projection, and reception of strategic narratives related to central issues associated with international relations. This volume presents contributions by scholars who address how strategic narratives affect central conceptual issues in international relations scholarship today:

- Great power behavior and international security concerns in a post–Cold War international order;

14 | Forging the World

- International organizations and integration;
- The global information economy;
- Social networks, public diplomacy, and the international community;
- Domestic determinants of international relations and foreign policy.

Contributors were asked to focus on substantive issues in international relations through a strategic narrative lens.

In chapter 2, Ben O'Loughlin, with Alister Miskimmon and Laura Roselle, outlines the central conceptual innovations of strategic narrative and details the methodological challenges of doing strategic narrative research. These include questions of theory, data, and evaluating the effect or impact of narratives, temporality, and level of analysis. The chapter reviews studies across a spectrum of approaches to persuasion, and argues that while some approaches might seem more "scientific," all can aspire to transparency and clarity. It surveys the parallel efforts of scholars and foreign policy practitioners: governments are trying to theorize and trace strategic narratives too. In light of this, the chapter introduces some of the ethical and practical difficulties scholars will face when relations with policymakers develop.

In chapter 3, Roselle examines the factors that affect the construction and use of great power strategic narratives. She asks, under what conditions do great power strategic narratives constrain or shape behavior, or both? Specifically, she analyses U.S. and Soviet/Russian strategic narratives in a post–Cold War environment and argues that they contain underlying assumptions about the characteristics and actions of great powers. Domestic and international interactions shape, and are shaped by, great power strategic narratives in patterned ways. In fact, the stickiness of strategic narratives used during the Cold War has significant consequences for American and Russian policy behavior today. In addition, a new communication environment has changed the way that these narratives are received and with what results. Hence, Roselle operationalizes both state and media ecology aspects of the strategic narrative approach.

In chapter 4, Ning Liao examines strategic narrative in the case of China as a rising power. He outlines the process of framing history and memory in China and its impact on Chinese foreign policy. He argues that selective myths of national history—constructed for the purpose of directing domestic social grievance and enhancing regime legitimacy—have emerged as a societal force that may internalize external historical conflicts. Collective memory of a traumatic national history can be constructed and manipulated by the regime in power, but cannot always be an on-demand resource to exploit, as it can in turn bound the rationality of foreign policy making. As the constructor and consumer of this communicative nationalism, the relationship between state and society cannot be simplistically dichotomized, as the two sides are mutually transforming.

Taking the example of the European Union, in chapter 5 Miskimmon questions how international organizations attempt to construct and deploy an effective strategic narrative in the face of a diverse membership. The European Union has relied on a strategic narrative from its inception to the present day. This narrative has been used to build support within Europe for deeper integration and to forge influence internationally. Over the years this narrative has shifted from a grand strategic vision of the people of Europe to a narrative of strategic calculation in the post–Cold War period. The formation, projection, and reception of the EU strategic narrative is complicated by the hybrid nature of the institution—reflecting both supranational and intergovernmental aspects, which complicates efforts to speak with a single European voice in international affairs. This chapter argues that the EU has in recent years lost a vision for a grand narrative of European integration as integration has encroached on ever more national-level policies. This has hampered the EU's strategic impact. In addition, he argues that the asymmetric impact of the global financial crisis, coupled with the persistent diversity of foreign policies of member states, remain impediments to the EU's ability to deploy an effective strategic narrative.

In chapter 6, J. P. Singh examines the global economy and development. As he writes, it is hard to underestimate the significance of narratives that have for half a century identified the majority of humanity as "developing" and built regimes and policies around this. Singh focuses on how strategic narratives are resolved or not resolved in international negotiations, with a particular focus on the Millennium Development Goals. Like Miskimmon's analysis of the European Union, Singh finds that interaction between different intergovernmental and transnational institutions, and between the member states, technocrats, NGOs, and others within them, bring about tensions, contestation, and plural competing narratives. Singh provides a comprehensive analysis of how strategic narratives operate within such organizational settings, focusing on state and nonstate actors. He shows that the task of finding an overarching narrative around the Millennium Development Goals did not allow for any firm consensus, but the process provided the communicative space within which different organizations, states, and peoples could connect. This process is of wider significance to international relations, when the ideal and the achievable often collide. And it is no exaggeration to say that, because these processes of narrative contestation decide the regimes and principles that will structure the global economy for generations, lives are at stake.

In chapter 7 Robin Brown argues that strategic narratives projected through public diplomacy programs succeed only insofar as these communications become interwoven with existing social networks and communities. Existing public diplomacy programs have failed because they have neither penetrated existing social networks nor generated new networks. He proposes that today this is feasible, methodologically, insofar as social networks are constituted through digital media. It remains a significant limit, undoubtedly, that much of the social life public diplomats would like to target is face-to-face or proceeding through nondigital media. Nevertheless, the spread of mobile telephony and the Internet in the developing world will afford opportunities to trace how states' strategic narratives are received, negotiated, and sustained or challenged in local contexts. Brown's chapter operationalizes the tracing of narratives and their effects through media ecologies.

Amelia Arsenault, Sun-ha Hong, and Monroe Price focus on strategic narratives during the Arab Spring in chapter 8. After Western states found a clear strategic narrative to justify intervention in Libya, they explore why this was not the case when confronted with a growing crisis in Syria. Their analysis illuminates the mechanisms by which narratives can be used as tools to enforce behavioral change in a target audience. Narratives can be used to suggest to dissenting leaders why they must change their behavior "or else." This draws attention to the coercive and intentional dimensions of language use in politics. They offer five measures of narrative success that will be of interest to scholars and policy practitioners alike. They analyze a large corpus of news reports in many countries, the statements of political leaders, and public opinion data. Their analysis also puts these relations of media, policymakers, and publics into historical context. They set out a number of lines of inquiry that should contribute to future agendas in strategic narrative research.

In chapter 9, Cristina Archetti's analysis of the narratives and counternarratives advanced by al Qaeda and by security agencies trying to counter it demonstrates how narrative content in itself is no predictor of narrative impact, and that the relation of narrative to action, or word to deed, remains critical for international audiences. Archetti explains why narratives are more than "scripted messages" and are instead complex socially and relationally constructed communications. By adopting this relational definition of narrative, Archetti is able to explain why narratives become attractive to those often described as "radicalized." This turns upside down how policymakers tasked with countering the narratives of al Qaeda or the Islamic State should operate day to day. The chapter also considers how branding can be considered alongside strategic narrative as an approach to communication; given that governments increasingly turn to branding and marketing consultants, these reflections are important for those in the policy world. Above all, Archetti's chapter makes a substantial contribution to understanding how nonstate actors use strategic narratives.

In chapter 10, O'Loughlin explores how the changing media ecology constitutes the condition for strategic narrative work by political actors. Today's information infrastructure makes possible the real-time circulation of scientific data, social media commentary, and international news reporting, an ecology of institutions and interdependencies through which the meaning of international events emerges. This study investigates the narratives told and meanings made in the aftermath of Japan's triple disaster of March 2011, when an undersea earthquake triggered a tsunami. Waves reached the Fukushima Daiichi nuclear power plant and caused a meltdown. The Japanese authorities failed to develop or project a strategic narrative to reassure domestic or international audiences despite relative control of domestic news media. This failure was made transparent "from the inside" and "from the outside"; Japanese citizens and international scientific, political, and media agencies filled this gap of meaning with their own narratives of crisis and response. The lack of direction provided by the Japanese authorities is explained by the difficulty of conceptualizing and preparing for contemporary global risks, and by a shifting social compact between state and society in which citizens are expected to act independently and responsibly rather than expect direction from the state. Such a compact breaks down in situations of uncertainty and risk, since citizens lack the knowledge upon which to evaluate what constitutes responsible action. The triple disaster thus saw a perfect storm of a catastrophic risk event and weak state communication. The significance of this chapter is to show how media ecologies matter to narrative projection, reception, and contestation; to show that it is difficult to project a confident strategic narrative amid uncertainty, but that states have no choice but to try; and, consequently, that states will continue to adapt and learn as crises and catastrophes continue to unfold.

In chapter 11, Miskimmon and O'Loughlin assess how strategic narratives play a vital role in defining international order and power transitions. They highlight the narrative work undertaken by hegemonic and emerging powers during periods of power transition. Previous power transitions have seen one hegemon replace another—the United Kingdom acquired primacy, then was challenged by Germany, which in turn was overtaken by the United States, and now there is a surge in speculation about a post-U.S. order. Power transition theory underpins conventionalist realist IR and therefore Western foreign policy. That theory suggests that when the challenger reaches parity in material power, a war to define the rules of the international system takes place before a new order is institutionalized (Organski 1958; Gilpin 1983). But the rise of China, the rise of "the rest," and the emergence of digital and network power all suggest we are entering a new *kind* of power transition. Even though the economic (GDP) power of China and the EU surpass that of the United States, neither is challenging the United States in a systemic war or seeking to assume hegemony. Instead, international order is increasingly based on competition for *recognition* in the context of plural narratives. This makes communication central to how international order is constituted. Every country and city has a soft power and branding strategy. Price (2002) writes of a "marketplace for loyalties." Each country that seeks recognition as a major power has an international broadcaster. In short, public and cultural diplomacy have become integral to the negotiation of identity and recognition in this new kind of power transition. The stakes again are high. Previous power transitions resulted in total war. Will a communication-based competition cultivate the conditions for a conflict-free power transition?

In the conclusion, chapter 12, we draw together the broader conclusions emerging from the chapters in this volume. We restate the importance of continued efforts to study how persuasion can be traced and understood in the study of International Relations. We also explain how the insights presented here might help policymakers navigate an increasingly challenging communication ecology. The chapters in this collection contribute greatly to understanding the wide applicability of strategic narrative. They detail a number of interesting future research directions where the concept can be applied. We conclude with a restatement of our contention that wrestling with the complexity of communication in today's world should be a central task of International Relations, in order to gain a fuller understanding of how influence works.

NOTES

1. See http://journalofnarrativepolitics.com/
2. A useful account of "media ecology" is provided by Merrin (2014), esp. 44–60. Cf. McLuhan 1964; Postman 1970; Fuller 2007.

REFERENCES

Bentley, Michelle. "War and/of Words: Constructing WMD in US Foreign Policy." *Security Studies* 22 (2013): 68–97.
Bentley, Michelle. "Strategic Taboos: Chemical Weapons and US Foreign Policy." *International Affairs* 90 (2014): 1033–48.
Berenskoetter, Felix. "Parameters of a National Biography." *European Journal of International Relations* 20 (2014): 262–88.
Betz, David. "Searching for El Dorado: The Legendary Golden Narrative of the Afghanistan War." In *Strategic Narratives, Public Opinion and War: Winning Domestic Support for the Afghan War*, edited by Beatrice De Graaf, George Dimitriu, and Jens Ringsmose, 37–56. London: Routledge, 2015.
Bially Mattern, Janice. *Ordering International Politics: Identity, Crisis, and Representational Force*. New York: Routledge, 2005.
Brown, Robin. "Information Technology and the Transformation of Diplomacy." *Knowledge, Technology and Policy* 18, no. 2 (2005): 14–29.
Burke, Kenneth. *Language as Symbolic Action: Essays on Life, Literature, and Method*. University of California Press, 1966.
Burke, Kenneth. *On Symbols and Society*. Chicago: University of Chicago Press, 1989.
Campbell, David. *Writing Security: United States Foreign Policy and the Politics of Identity*. University of Minnesota Press, 1992.
Chaban, Natalia, Jessica Bain, and Katrina Stats. "'Frenemies'? Images of the US-EU Relations in Asia-Pacific Media." *Critical Policy Analysis* 1 (2007): 62–96.
Ciută, Felix. "Narratives of Security: Strategy and Identity in the European Context." In *Discursive Constructions of Identity in European Politics*, edited by Richard Mole, 190–207. Basingstoke: Palgrave Macmillan, 2007.
Crilley, Rhys. "Seeing Strategic Narratives?" *Critical Studies on Security* 3, no. 3 (2015): 331–33. http://dx.doi.org/10.1080/21624887.2015.1103016
Epstein, Charlotte. *The Power of Words in International Relations: Birth of an Anti-Whaling Discourse*. Cambridge, MA: MIT Press, 2008.
European Council. *The European Security Strategy*. European Council, 2003.
Frank, Arthur W. *Letting Stories Breathe: A Socio-Narratology*. Chicago: University of Chicago Press, 2010.

Freedman, Lawrence. "Networks, Culture and Narratives." *Adelphi Papers Series* 45, no. 379 (2006): 11–26. Accessed July 1, 2015. http://dx.doi.org/10.1080/05679320600661640

Fuller, Linda K. *Community Media: International Perspectives*. Macmillan, 2007.

Fuller, Matthew. *Media Ecologies*. Cambridge, MA: MIT Press, 2005.

Gallagher, Paul. "Revealed: Putin's Army of Pro-Kremlin Bloggers." *Independent*, March 27, 2015. Accessed March 27, 2015. http://www.independent.co.uk/news/world/europe/revealed-putins-army-of-prokremlin-bloggers-10138893.html

Gilpin, Robert. *War and Change in World Politics*. Cambridge: Cambridge University Press, 1983.

Gray, Colin S. *Modern Strategy*. Oxford: Oxford University Press, 1999.

Hajer, Maarten A. *The Politics of Environmental Discourse: Ecological Modernization and the Policy Process*. Oxford: Clarendon Press, 1995.

Hansen, Lene. "Theorizing the Image for Security Studies: Visual Securitization and the Muhammad Cartoon Crisis." *European Journal of International Relations* 17 (2011): 51–74.

Hayden, Craig. *The Rhetoric of Soft Power: Public Diplomacy in Global Contexts*. Lanham, MD: Lexington Books, 2012.

Hertner, Isabelle, and Alister Miskimmon. "Germany's Strategic Narrative of the Eurozone Crisis." *German Politics and Society* 33 (2015): 42–57.

Hoffman, Frank G. "Grand Strategy: The Fundamental Considerations." *Orbis* 58 (2014): 472–85.

Holland, Martin, and Natalia Chaban. "The EU as an Agent for Democracy: Images of the EU in the Pacific Media 'Mirror.'" *Journal of European Integration* 33 (2011): 285–302.

Holsti, Kalevi J. "National Role Conceptions in the Study of Foreign Policy." *International Studies Quarterly* 14, no. 3 (1970): 233–309.

Hoskins, Andrew, and Ben O'Loughlin. *War and Media: The Emergence of Diffused War*. Cambridge: Polity, 2010.

Hoskins, Andrew, and Ben O'Loughlin. "Arrested War: The Third Phase of Mediatization." *Information, Communication & Society* 18 (2015): 1320–38.

House of Lords Select Committee on Soft Power and the UK's Influence. "Persuasion and Power in the Modern World." March 28, 2014. Accessed March 28, 2014. http://www.publications.parliament.uk/pa/ld201314/ldselect/ldsoftpower/150/150.pdf

Howard, Philip N. *Pax Technica: How the Internet of Things May Set Us Free or Lock Us Up*. New Haven: Yale University Press, 2015.

Howell, David. *Old Links and New Ties: Power and Persuasion in an Age of Networks*. London: I. B. Tauris, 2013.

Kaldor, Mary H., Mary E. Martin, and Sabine Selchow. "Human Security: A New Strategic Narrative for Europe." *International Affairs* 83 (2007): 273–88.

Kinnvall, Catarina, and Paul W. Nesbitt-Larking. "The Political Psychology of (De) Securitization: Place-Making Strategies in Denmark, Sweden, and Canada." *Environment and Planning D: Society and Space* 25 (2010): 1051–70.

Kinnvall, Catarina, and Paul W. Nesbitt-Larking. "Securitising Citizenship: (B)ordering Practices and Strategies of Resistance." *Global Society* 27 (2013): 337–59.

Kinnvall, Catarina, and Ted Svensson. "Hindu Nationalism, Diaspora Politics and Nation-Building in India." *Australian Journal of International Affairs* 64 (2010): 274–92.

Lang, Anthony F., Jr. "Punitive Justifications or Just Punishment? An Ethical Reading of Coercive Diplomacy." *Cambridge Review of International Affairs* 19 (2006): 389–403.

McLuhan, Marshall. *Understanding Media—The Extensions of Man*. London: Routledge and Kegan Paul, 1964.

Melissen, Jan. *The New Public Diplomacy*. Basingstoke: Palgrave Macmillan, 2005.

Merrin, William. *Media Studies 2.0*. London: Routledge, 2014.

Miskimmon, Alister. "German Foreign Policy and the Libya Crisis." *German Politics* 21 (2012): 392–410.

Miskimmon, Alister, and Ben O'Loughlin. "Weaponising Information: Putin, the West, and Competing Strategic Narratives on Ukraine." *European Geostrategy* 18 (December 2014). Accessed December 18, 2014. http://www.europeangeostrategy.org/2014/12/weaponising-information-putin-west-competing-strategic-narratives-ukraine/

Miskimmon, Alister, Ben O'Loughlin, and Laura Roselle. *Strategic Narratives: Communication Power and the New World Order*. London: Routledge, 2013.

Miskimmon, Alister, Ben O'Loughlin, and Laura Roselle. "Great Power Politics and Strategic Narratives of War." In *Strategic Narratives, Public Opinion and War: Winning Domestic Support for the Afghan War*, edited by Beatrice De Graaf, George Dimitriu, and Jens Ringsmose, 57–77. London: Routledge, 2015.

NATO. *Strategic Concept: Active Engagement, Modern Defence*. Brussels. November 19, 2010. Accessed November 19, 2010. http://www.nato.int/cps/en/natohq/topics_82705.htm

Organski, Abramo F. K. *World Politics*. New York: Knopf, 1958.

Pamment, James. "Strategic Narratives in US Public Diplomacy: A Critical Geopolitics." *Popular Communication* 2 (2014): 48–64.

Peters, John Durham. *The Marvelous Clouds: Toward a Philosophy of Elemental Media*. Chicago: University of Chicago Press, 2015.

Porter, Wayne, and Mike Mykleby. "A National Strategic Narrative." Presentation at Woodrow Wilson International Center for Scholars, Washington, DC, April 8, 2011. Accessed April 10, 2011. https://www.wilsoncenter.org/sites/default/files/A%20National%20Strategic%20Narrative.pdf

Posen, Barry R. *The Sources of Military Doctrine: France, Britain, and Germany between the World Wars*. Ithaca: Cornell University Press, 1984.

Postman, Neil. "The Reformed English Curriculum." In *The Shape of the Future in American Secondary Education*, edited by Alvin Christian Eurich, 160–68. New York: Pitman Publishing, 1970.

Price, Monroe E. *Media and Sovereignty: The Global Information Revolution and Its Challenge to State Power*. Cambridge: MIT Press, 2002.

Roberts, Geoffrey. "History, Theory and the Narrative Turn in IR." *Review of International Studies* 32 (2006): 703–14.

Roselle, Laura, Alister Miskimmon, and Ben O'Loughlin. "Strategic Narrative: A New Means to Understand Soft Power." *Media, War & Conflict* 7 (2014): 70–84.

Rudd, Kevin. "How Ancient Chinese Thought Applies Today." *New Perspectives Quarterly* 32 (2015): 8–23.

Ryan, Judith, and Alfred Thomas, eds. *Cultures of Forgery: Making Nations, Making Selves*. New York: Routledge, 2003.

Shenhav, Shaul. "Political Narratives and Political Reality." *International Political Science Review* 27 (2006): 245–62.

Simon, Luis. *Geopolitical Change, Grand Strategy and European Security: The EU-NATO Conundrum.* Basingstoke: Palgrave Macmillan, 2013.

Skonieczny, Amy. "Interrupting Inevitability: Globalization and Resistance." *Alternatives: Global, Local, Political* 35 (2010): 1–28.

Snyder, Jack. "Dueling Security Stories: Wilson and Lodge Talk Strategy." *Security Studies* 24, no. 1 (2015): 171–97.

Squire, Corinne, Mark Davis, Cigdem Esin, Molly Andrews, Barbara Harrison, Lars-Christer Hydén, and Margareta Hydén. *What Is Narrative Research?* London: Bloomsbury, 2015.

Steele, Brent J. *Defacing Power: The Aesthetics of Insecurity in Global Politics.* Ann Arbor: University of Michigan Press, 2010.

Thies, Cameron G. "International Socialization Processes vs. Israeli National Role Conceptions: Can Role Theory Integrate IR Theory and Foreign Policy Analysis?" *Foreign Policy Analysis* 8, no. 1 (2012a): 25–46.

Thies, Cameron G. "The Roles of Bipolarity: A Role Theoretic Understanding of the Effects of Ideas and Material Factors on the Cold War." *International Studies Perspectives* 14, no. 3 (2012b): 269–88.

Van Ham, Peter. *Social Power in International Politics.* London: Routledge, 2010.

White, Hayden. "The Question of Narrative in Contemporary Historical Theory." *History and Theory* 23, no. 1 (1984): 1–33.

Zarakol, Amy. *After Defeat: How the East Learned to Live with the West.* Cambridge: Cambridge University Press, 2010.

Zarakol, Amy. "What Made the Modern World Hang Together: Socialisation or Stigmatisation?" *International Theory* 6 (2014): 311–32.

2 | Strategic Narratives

Methods and Ethics

Ben O'Loughlin, with Alister Miskimmon and Laura Roselle

We are on the cusp of being able to better understand questions in International Relations hitherto considered unanswerable due to methodological limitations of the discipline. Methodology is vital to the enterprise of studying strategic narrative because the right methods allow us to explain how strategic narratives are formed, projected, received, and interpreted. Only then can we build explanations of the roles narratives play in persuasion, influence, identity-formation, alliance-building, order-shaping, and other major concerns of IR. There is a sense today among those practicing international relations that the rapid transformation of global political communication has opened up new opportunities to manage relations between countries and to manage change in the international system. The primary challenge for those researching the nexus of communication and international relations is explaining the effects of narratives on audiences at home and abroad—those to be persuaded, influenced, those who could be allies or could support your preferred global order. Do narratives cause confusion and offense, undermining any strategic aim behind their projection? Under what conditions might audiences find the narrative attractive and "buy in" to its representation of world politics? This chapter offers a guide to research, covering questions of theory, data, evaluation, temporality, and level of analysis. It reviews the theories and methods used by academics and policymakers.

This chapter sets out a framework to understand and explain the role and potential effects of strategic narratives. The framework is based on the idea that this is a spectrum of how persuasion is theorized in IR, from thin rationalist explanations right up to thick poststructural accounts. The choice of approach or position on this spectrum is usually a function of the question being asked and the tradition the researcher feels most comfortable within. The choice of approach also leads to methodological choices. Hence, different approaches to the study of strategic narratives will entail the use of different methods. Researchers will mix methods together in different ways, and we expect to see in the next decade a series of patchwork, adaptive, broader methodologies.

In parallel to academic research, foreign ministries and national media organizations are tasked with measuring the effects of their national strategic narratives—projections about the past, present, and future of the international system and their country's role in it. This chapter considers how these bureaucracies join theories and models of international communication with methods to identify and explain the effect of their narrative campaigns. This exploration of practical initiatives has direct relevance to IR scholars, many of whom are also trying to explain how persuasion has effects through processes such as norm diffusion and public diplomacy, and this chapter compares policy practitioner and scholarly research designs.

Digital technology and big data promise a step change in capacity for real-time multilingual monitoring of narrative effects on target population behavior and attitudes, such that digital methods may take on a life of their own in generating new connectivity and visibility in international relations. However, these methods' utility depends on their integration with "old" methods and the competence and remit of bureaucracy-embedded teams. We encourage researchers to think about how to assemble *methods* into a coherent *methodology*. By methodology we refer to "the definition of knowledge and the overall goal of . . . research" (Jackson 2011, 25). There must be an alignment between theory and data and recognition that some questions can only be answered by assembling some methods and not others.

In the coming decade there are some big questions to answer for IR scholars who are interested in explaining how strategic narratives work. Policymakers will continue to form and project strategic narratives not only because they fear losing out in the soft power "marketplace" (Price 2015) but because some genuinely believe that narratives can have "power." The idea still holds for some leaders that the West won the Cold War because its narrative offered a preferable future to repressed citizens and even leaders in the East (Hall and Smith 2013). Nevertheless, identifying and explaining the effect of narratives remains a problem. **First, perfect communication is impossible** (Peters 2012). Hearing is not the same as listening, and listening is not the same as understanding (Dreher 2009). Understanding is not agreeing. Interests clash. Thus, ensuring that target audiences are exposed to one's narrative and even ensuring they engage with it and discuss its pros and cons does not mean a meeting of minds, let alone a guarantee of agreement. **Second, establishing the clear causal impact of narratives is very difficult** and, as such, may require oversimplifying relationships in order to demonstrate "influence." In this chapter we look at a spectrum of approaches to persuasion and its evaluation, as introduced briefly in this book's introduction.

Third, narratives can create negative effects. It is not simply that strategic narratives may have no identifiable positive impact (Zhang 2013, 3). Rather, efforts to generate desired effects by projecting strategic narratives may create unintended and adverse consequences. China's record is hardly a success story for strategic narrative projection (as highlighted in Liao's chapter and Miskimmon and O'Loughlin's chapter on order). Narratives can make overseas publics aware of discrepancies between what a nation says about its role in the world and what it actually does—the "say-do gap" (Simpson 2012, 181). Finding out that one's country and its narrative score poorly on the various international indexes and polls could lead to bad feelings toward foreigners (Hall and Smith 2013, 12). **Fourth, political actors may have no strategy**. If strategic narrative is strategy in narrative form, as Emile Simpson (2012) suggests, what if there is an absence of clear goals? **Finally, political actors might not know what effects to aim for**. Even if there is a clear strategy, how should its ends be conceived? Should narratives contribute to measurable "outputs" like the number of hits on an embassy website, or should it bring about more diffuse outcomes such as attitudinal or behavioral change? What counts as the "value" of a narrative?

Scholarly study of strategic narrative does not happen in a vacuum. As scholars we are often in dialogue with policymakers. Academics in the 21st century are under pressure from governments to show "knowledge transfer" so that their research "affects" how those policymakers work, or how the wider public understands a particular issue. Academic researchers' methods are not independent of the world they research. This demands reflection about how scholarly research is situated in the politics of the current historical moment. This chapter investigates how research along different points of the spectrum of persuasion is situated and implicated in the world being studied. Digitization and the emergence and deployment of digital methods to map communication and influence in IR implicate IR and strategic narrative studies in contemporary political trends. We are in a moment in which open data, big data, and evidence-based policy have made methodology a matter of public concern, and IR must engage with this.

This chapter brings into dialogue issues of methodology, ethics, and politics in strategic narrative research. It tries to put on the table "the stakes involved" in what we are doing by researching strategic narratives (Savage 2013, 4). Who benefits from strategic narrative research? Being able to explain how to move people is useful knowledge to those charged with moving people. The study of language and power matters because it gets used. In their study of photographic icons in U.S. public culture, Hariman and Lucaites note the glib assumption that language or pictures are ephemeral to "real" power. Some assume that

> [t]hey are merely pictures, not laws or armies, votes or money, institutions or peoples. Representations rather than actions, they seem to justify the political scientist's disregard for the epiphenomena of language, symbolism and other *ornaments of material power*. (Hariman and Lucaites 2007, 3; italics added)

Images, icons, and narratives are not mere ornaments: they do things. There are four basic positions being taken in the field: (1) studying strategic narrative on your own as a purely academic exercise, for the joy of explaining how it works; (2) studying strategic narrative in order to critique how political leaders use narratives to manipulate publics and obfuscate an underlying reality; (3) studying strategic narrative in order to help policymakers use them more effectively; and (4) studying strategic narrative *with* policymakers in order to make those actors more reflexive about their practices and more informed by the ethical and political concerns academics bring to the table. All four positions are open to exploitation but also provide an opportunity to influence policymakers. As young scholars enter this field of study it is important that they understand how their research is used and that they think strategically about how to manage their relationship to policy and practice as it unfolds. We must take responsibility for how our research is used.

Explaining Persuasion along the Spectrum of Persuasion

Explanations of the role of communication in international relations range along a spectrum. At one end are those who take a system and set of actors as a given and study the interaction and persuasion between them. At the other end we find those who ask how that system and the identity and interests of actors form in the first place. How are the conditions for interaction and persuasion generated and who benefits from those conditions? In the study of strategic narratives this translates into a spectrum (cf. Steele 2011; see also Katzenstein 2009, on dispositional versus discursive analysis). At the first pole, scholars identify the narratives of a given set of actors who are negotiating a problem and ask whose narrative finally best informs the resulting decision or affects public opinion (e.g., de Graaf, Dimitriu, and Ringsmose 2015). At the other pole we find scholars who ask how historical narratives shape understandings of the international system or what it means to be a state, an NGO, or an activist, and how those meanings can be taken into account in political debates (e.g., de Almagro Iniesta 2013). We call this the spectrum of persuasion (Miskimmon, O'Loughlin, and Roselle 2013). There are four main positions on that spectrum.

Position 1: Rationalist Analysis

At one pole is *very thin* analysis. Such analysis is often referred to as rationalist. Observable outcomes can be explained through analysis of observable interactions between actors with given preferences within a given structure of anarchy. Persuasion is often secondary to material inducement through coercion or bargaining. Communication is conceptualized as a rhetorical skill that signals intentions: "cheap talk" used by one actor to manipulate the perceptions and preferences of others. Persuasion can involve trapping others into committing to action they otherwise would not take. Persuasion does not necessarily entail creating a shared worldview, simply compelling others into a specific action. The media ecology is taken as an arena within which actors transmit information. Some actors hold more power in media systems and can exert more control over who knows what and when. These studies usually seek correlations and, ideally, causal relations between discrete variables. Variables might include the clarity or content of narrative projection, public opinion on the relevant issue, and decisions ultimately taken by relevant actors toward addressing the issue or obstacle being narrativized. These variables can be conceptualized with a degree of precision to ensure the explanation is valid, analyzing exactly what it says it analyzes.

Krebs and Jackson (2007) analyze the extent to which language produces behavioral change in target audiences. They argue that we can only truly explain what we can observe. Therefore, we can only observe the way actors in international society frame an issue and then the decision eventually reached. We cannot say that an actor was persuaded by the others because we cannot get inside leaders' minds to know whether their minds were really changed and, if so, what produced that change. Krebs and Jackson assert that we do not need to know the intentions of actors to explain outcomes in world politics. We can only analyze the claims made in public and identify whose claims seem to win the day. If we look at any single contentious episode, they argue, we find that these claims have "real causal impact on political outcomes" by trapping dissenting states into supporting a plan by denying them any resources to make a successful counterclaim (42). Their analysis depends on a game-theoretic structure of discrete actors faced with two choices (accept or refute the other's claim).

Krebs and Jackson's account of communication and persuasion in international relations does not address wider aspects of communication and persuasion because they argue that claims about these cannot be empirically substantiated. Their soft rational approach sees limitations in how we can understand the construction of shared norms and beliefs. They do not "capture the long-term processes" by which the underlying discourses of international relations are formed, contested, and deployed (61n27). All that is possible is to analyze the frames actors use in public (44). This focus on individual decisions uncovers some interesting findings and has contributed to debates about persuasion. Yet much of the political communication literature takes a wider view. International affairs involves stable rituals of communication in which actors are not trying to coerce one another into voting for a certain decision. Think only of the spectacle of summit diplomacy, the phases of crisis communications around natural disasters and military conflicts, or the long-term narrative projections about future world order contained in foreign policy strategies. All of these contain stages of formation, projection, anticipation, circulation, interpretation, and contestation that can be analyzed empirically to build richer models of influence.

Another example of this approach is provided by a comparative set of studies led by de Graaf, Dimitriu, and Ringsmose (2015). They demonstrated that the projection of a clear, consistent narrative about a country's purpose can boost public support for overseas military intervention. They examined how political and military elites in North Atlantic Treaty Organization (NATO) countries tried to win public backing for operations in Afghanistan in the decade following the 9/11 attacks in the United States. Elites in Denmark and, after 2009, the United Kingdom found clear and consistent narratives and this translated into public support, but elites in Holland, France, Italy, and Germany were uncertain whether the purpose of intervention was war, peacekeeping, or counterinsurgency. This suggests elites can be agents who lead, not just windsocks being buffeted by public opinion. It also suggests that an international organization like NATO, which has 28 member states, will always face difficulty creating the same public response across all its members, even if they do share an identity loosely defined as "the West."

Very thin studies can also seek to identify the effect of who speaks the narrative, not just the effect of the narrative itself. Goldsmith and Horiuchi (2009) examine the effect of overseas visits by U.S. political leaders and diplomats on public opinion in 61 countries from 2001 through 2006, using survey data from 19 studies. They found that visits made attitudes toward the United States more *negative* once U.S. foreign policy became unpopular. The tipping point was 2004. That year, images were released taken in Abu Ghraib prison in Iraq showing abuse of Iraqis by U.S. soldiers. By then, the insurgency against the United States in Iraq had grown stronger and the Central Intelligence Agency (CIA) had rejected claims about the existence of weapons of mass destruction in Iraq, thereby discrediting a major motive of U.S. intervention in the first place. Publics outside the United States had become more aware of U.S. foreign policy, more critical of U.S. foreign policy, and more likely to view U.S. public diplomacy efforts as hypocritical. Hence, the very act of trying to project a positive narrative was damaging to the United States. Goldsmith and Horiuchi did not analyze what was said, just the relationship between the discrete actors (U.S. diplomats and publics) to identify causal effects over time.

Position 2: Study of Communicative Action

Next, what we describe as *thin* analysis is often referred to as the study of communicative action. These studies begin with rational actors seeking to persuade one another by making convincing claims. Attention is paid to the nature of the media ecology, conceptualized as a public sphere. The distribution of access and voice and the norms of civility, style, and genre shape how debates unfold within that sphere. Spheres may overlap. A national public sphere may entwine with transnational linguistic or cultural spheres. Media are not a neutral space. The process of debate weeds out weak and unconvincing claims. At this point, analysis goes beyond very thin. There is a focus on how participants become socialized into the norms of rational debate and can create a shared identity or at least respect and recognition among a community of participants. This remains thin analysis because at the start of analysis all players are still taken to be coherent, rational actors with relatively stable preferences and identities.

Compared to very thin accounts, thin accounts expand the field of analysis to include periods before and after negotiation. Informed by Jürgen Habermas's theory of communicative action, they distinguish two forms of persuasion in international relations. The first is strategic action, in which state A manipulates state B toward state A's goal, for instance by undermining its right to speak, by forming an alliance around state A's goal so state B has incentives to join up, or through sanctions or other coercive means. Communication is only a tool for state A to achieve its pregiven interests; this is the "cheap talk" of very thin accounts. The second form of persuasion is communicative action, in which states A and B treat each other as equals and try to come to a shared understanding and consensus for action. When states engage in communicative action, they set aside any single interest they had beforehand and open themselves up for persuasion by good arguments. Since much of international relations is the interaction of actors with divergent understandings and interests, reaching any kind of cooperation requires much communicative action, possibly for many years, before agreement is possible. Much of this is played out in public, as leaders make regular statements about national strategy and policy ambitions that are debated in domestic media, clear for all to see in other countries (Lynch 2002, 196–97).

Marc Lynch (2002) tries to show how U.S. attempts to integrate China into a liberal international order in the 1990s underwent various changes. He analyzes the speeches of U.S. foreign policy makers and academic accounts of the period, and infers from these the motives and strategies behind decisions made by U.S. and Chinese leaders. He argues that from 1992 U.S. president Bill Clinton used strategic action to try to force China to comply with U.S. policies, without success. China was hardly unaware of what the United States was attempting. Clinton used communicative action instead from 1996 onwards, building U.S.-China forums on many policy areas and gradually increasing the layers of dialogue between the two countries. This allowed China to integrate into the liberal order while allowing that order to be slightly modified. From a U.S. perspective this was a success. Dialogue continued, allowing U.S. officials to try to alter Chinese preferences through argument rather than risk threats and sanctions and allowing U.S. officials to stay reasonably informed about Chinese strategy. With the media and public scrutiny afforded such dialogues, any statements by either country would carry high credibility—neither country's leaders could risk saying one thing in negotiations then another to home audiences. Lynch is candid about proving causal effects of such communicative action over time. In line with Jeffrey Checkel's earlier studies (1999, 2001, 2002, 2003), he writes: "Persuasion entails the actor consciously agreeing to a new set of beliefs. Such direct preference change is both the most ambitious of the claims for communicative action, and the hardest to document empirically" (Lynch 2002, 214).

What such studies can offer are levels of *plausibility*. Lynch offers accounts of mechanisms through which U.S. and Chinese leaders interacted and perhaps socialized one another. After some time elapsed, changes in behavior were evident. For instance, China signed up to an arms control treaty it had previously opposed and joined the World Trade Organization (WTO). Lynch's accounts would be strengthened by closer scrutiny of the leaders' texts (actual phrases or discourse are not analyzed systematically) and of the responses by domestic audiences in the two countries. He treats the relationship as entirely bilateral, as if the relationship between the United States and China existed in isolation from world politics. However, it is a reasonably parsimonious analysis of a process of give-and-take and persuasion in which China was brought a step further into the U.S. multilateral order.

Thomas Risse (2000) has offered case studies that fall within the thin band of persuasion studies. In one he explains how Soviet president Mikhail Gorbachev accepted a U.S.-led offer at the end of the Cold War. The United States proposed that Germany would reunify and be a member of NATO. From Risse's readings of the negotiations between Gorbachev, his fellow Soviet diplomats, and their U.S. and European counterparts, it seemed the USSR lacked any firm preferences. The Soviets entered negotiations thinking about German reunification through the prism of national security. Surely a reunified Germany would become a threat to the USSR? Gorbachev did not "really want to see a replay of Versailles, where the Germans were able to arm themselves" (Gorbachev, cited in Risse 2000, 26). However, he reached agreement with the United States when he was convinced of the moral claim that the new Germany should decide its own security arrangements. "Note that self-determination had originally motivated the demands for Germany unity articulated by the peaceful protestors in East Germany," Risse writes, "from 'we are the people!' to 'we are one people!'" (28).

Risse analyzes the memoirs of those involved to explain their actions. The analysis focuses on interaction over time, but not as the exchange of discrete messages with identifiable effects. Rather, the process was one of argument and to-and-fro where context and sequence were important. Identities were strong but preferences could be altered. Risse writes, for example, that "actors can construct common lifeworlds (i.e., shared assumptions and ways of talking) through narratives during prenegotiations in order to establish mutual trust in their authenticity as speakers" (33). If very thin studies examine either the what (Krebs and Jackson) *or* who (Goldsmith and Horiuchi) of international communication, Risse tries to explain how the what *and* who interact. Certain content was more persuasive from certain actors under certain conditions and after a certain sequence of ritual diplomatic exchanges.

A third example of thin studies concerns efforts to get the "international community" to act, in this case to use military intervention. In 2011 France and the United States were successful in their efforts to have UN Security Council Resolution 1973 accepted for intervention in Libya, despite the abstention of a number of important Security Council members. The narrative projected by France and the United Kingdom was successful in influencing the United States to support their proposals despite the publicly stated reservations of President Barack Obama and Secretary of State Hillary Clinton. France and the United Kingdom swiftly projected a narrative that appealed to U.S. identity as the global leader and supporter of a stable international order. France and the United Kingdom were also able to carry domestic opinion, albeit by a slim majority that waxed and waned throughout the operation (Adler-Nissen and Pouliot 2014; Miskimmon, O'Loughlin, and Roselle 2013; Miskimmon 2012). Such analysis does not make strong inference about actors' motives or internal psychological states (Adler-Nissen and Pouliot 2014), but interpretation of language exchanges and routine practices does allow for claims about how the United States was persuaded.

Such studies also place value on data such as memoirs, research interviews, or private correspondence, which rationalist scholarship finds problematic. Interviews with policymakers in private settings or their private correspondence must be treated with the same caution as any primary data, and triangulated where possible. However, to write off Adler-Nissen's ethnography with diplomats or the memoirs Risse uses to make sense of the actions of an entire generation of Cold War warriors seems rash. No other branch of the social sciences or humanities dismisses research that engages the primary subjects in that field because they might all be compromised. Historians do not ignore letters. Sociologists do not avoid focus groups. Based on a suspicion that all talk is cheap talk, we run the risk of drawing an arbitrary line that would exclude much relevant data from our analysis of international relations.

Position 3: Complex, Reflexive Communication

Next we find *thick* analysis. Here, actors are taken to be highly reflexive. They are not simply seeking to maximize utility or realize given preferences. As they monitor each others' communications and actions they learn subtleties of interaction, including managing each others' emotional states. Anxieties about status or recognition beset actors at all levels and can be exploited. An actor's identity can be challenged and undermined to the extent that it seeks a new narrative about its place in the world and its history. Communication here is more than the exchange of rational claims and the media ecology is more than a given structure. It is an unpredictable, textured, and recursive set of overlapping ecologies in which history can be mobilized through visuals, symbols, and appeals to emotion. Much of this may be unintentional.

In his book on the growing role of India in international affairs, Tharoor (2012, 72) suggests: "The associations and attitudes conjured up in the global imagination by the mere mention of a country's name is often a more accurate gauge of its soft power than a dispassionate analysis of its foreign policies." How can we research the meaning of a country's name or the power of its invocation? How do these processes work? How do elites or publics reflect on identity, status, and prestige? Through what narratives is the meaning of countries or institutions made concrete? As we move to thick studies, we find more complex conceptualizations of actors, identities, and processes of communication, recognition, and influence.

For instance, language is treated as expressive, not just instrumental. This increased complexity necessarily reduces the parsimony of analysis. But it can still address the exercise of power.

Brent Steele (2011) argues that the insecurities of powerful states afford the opportunity for less powerful actors to tease and provoke and tempt the powerful into mistaken and violent policies. This resonates strongly with our idea of identity narratives. "Because state agents 'narrate' about the nation-state, they create potential Selves that that nation-state seeks to realize through its policies" (Steele 2011, 3). This self here is aesthetic. The state has a face and wants to feel good about how it is seen, not least when it acts. This leaves it vulnerable, anxious about the views of others and whether it is living up to its "best" face or "true" self. This means that states do not only act to increase their material interest. They act to be seen to be moving well—with strength, swiftness, even boldness. But David can tempt Goliath into a move that makes it look clumsy or thoughtless; al Qaeda could lure the United States into the quagmires of Afghanistan and Iraq after the 9/11 attacks. Methodologically, this entails evaluating an actor's sense of movement or stasis. A focus on narrative here—on how the actor depicts the scene, the obstacles they face, the action they decree necessary—can allow us to capture this sense analytically.

As the focus on interaction steps beyond what is communicated to what is felt or sensed, so the conception of communication becomes theoretically more complex. Above all, analysis must take into account how media ecologies amplify or contain these feelings and senses. Here there is scope for attention to communication as a ritual process, not a matter of the linear transmission of messages or a question of whose frame "dominates" in quantitative terms. Instead, scholars examine the role frames play on an hour-by-hour or day-by-day basis. How do terrorist groups ensure their videos are a continual presence in news broadcasts? How do public diplomacy practitioners go about "*getting into the cycle of news frames*" (Hayden 2011, 790, emphasis in original)?

It is here that an important move can be made. Scholars of communication have long since stopped conceptualizing media and political institutions *only* as discrete actors that "effect" each other. The most cursory examination of how news is made illuminates how political actors learn to navigate daily news cycles and learn how to manage interdependencies with journalists, public relations firms, citizens online, and so on. Media is part of politics and vice versa. In the early 2000s a move was made from studying the mediation of politics to the mediatization of politics. Stig Hjarvard writes:

> Mediatization is to be considered a double-sided process of high modernity in which the media on the one hand emerge as an independent institution with a logic of its own that other social institutions have to accommodate to. On the other hand, media simultaneously become an integrated part of other institutions like politics, work, family and religion as more and more of these institutional activities are performed through both interactive and mass media. (Hjarvard 2008, 105)

The logics of international relations, depending on one's theoretical perspective, are to act to enhance the national interest, to gain allies and minimize hostility, and to construct, institutionalize, and legitimize desirable norms. The logics of traditional broadcast and press media were the maximization of stories with "news value" (immediacy, visuality, celebrity, proximity to power) and the primacy of form over content (it doesn't matter much what politicians say, just that they say it in a way that allows for a conventional 30-second package). These logics give a certain rationality to the daily work of journalists, editors, and those seeking to work with media (Altheide and Snow 1979) and eventually become invisible or commonsensical to them. But just as political actors came to grips with the logics of mass media, social media arrived with their own logics. Facebook, Twitter, and Weibo have different temporal and network dynamics than traditional media. Van Dijck and Poell (2013, 5) define social media logic as "the processes, principles, and practices through which these platforms process information, news, and communication, and more generally, how they channel social traffic." One social media logic is popularity. Algorithms drive stories quickly, gaining attention to virality, and thus further attention. Connectivity is another. Platforms allow human contact, but this is also driven by automated recommendations of who and what to connect to. Since 2011 we have seen how protestors in different countries have tried to harness social media logics to gain attention and give political and emotional impetus to revolutionary action in countries where leaders who grew up with mass media logics still think making a television address is enough to pacify populations. This is illustrated in Arsenault and Price's chapter in this volume examining how

Egyptian president Hosni Mubarak hoped his televised addresses would prevent revolution.

In the broadcast era of late Cold War politics, Roselle (2006) showed how Soviet and U.S. leaders worked daily with the mass media logics of their media systems to project narratives legitimizing "failure"—their withdrawals from Afghanistan and Vietnam, respectively. In the context of long-standing U.S.-Iran information warfare, Price (2015, 135–36) examined Iran's "bureaucracy of defense: the shaping of cultural redoubts and the equivalent of sort fortresses and propaganda." In the postbroadcast era, Mor (2012) has explored how Israel tries not just to project a compelling narrative but attempts to perform credibility, to maintain the moral high ground in social and traditional media debates at home and abroad during military conflicts with its neighbors. These are thicker accounts of persuasion.

When we explain how ministries of foreign affairs produce strategic narratives, we cannot take their actions in isolation. Their actions and interactions are guided by the logics of mass and social media and cannot be explained without accounting for this. While their actions should be assumed to be guided primarily by the logics of international relations, how they put this into practice—their decisions, strategies, and tactics—will be guided also by media logics. Skillful political actors learn how to harness these logics; they grasp that power works *through* this.

Position 4: Poststructural Analysis

Finally, at the *very thick* pole we find analysis often labeled as poststructural. The political actor articulates a discourse that features subject positions that others fill, giving them a clear identity from which they then speak and act. Discourses are structured and the set of roles is structured. These discourses can be presented in various forms, whether material or representational, including narratives. Discursive structures are to some extent malleable (hence poststructural). There is a tension between these hard-to-shift structures and agents seeking political change, since the very identities and interests of those agents and their sense of agency are generated by and constituted by existing discourse. It makes little sense to say A has power over B since both are products of the same discourse. Media ecologies are one more system of discourse, with enduring rules and roles that result in stable forms of news and political information.

Poststructural accounts of international relations theorize that politics is made up of discourse—systems of power/knowledge made manifest in institutions, practices, and language. There is scientific discourse, legal discourse, religious discourse, news discourse—each has its own rules that determine what gets said, who is privileged to speak, and what counts as truth. Discourses emerge over long periods of time and are hard to shift. They produce populations with certain identities, norms, and common-sense ideas. Nevertheless, discourses provide the raw materials from which political leaders can craft strategic narratives.

If discourses are hard to transform, in what ways can an actor be strategic? Shepherd (2015) draws attention to a move we make in *Strategic Narratives* to address this question. We argue that even in studies of discourse that question the strategic actor, rationality can be found or, as we write, "rational action kicks back in" (Miskimmon, O'Loughlin, and Roselle 2013, 16). If actors were unable to reflect on the way their identity and politics more generally are constituted, then history would be the automatic unfolding of those given identities, rules, roles, and so on. If all politics is only the effect of discourse, there is no scope for craft and creativity; or, rather, craft and creativity are the effects of prevailing discourses and therefore already determined. For examine, in David Campbell's *Writing Security* (1992), a poststructural analysis of U.S. foreign policy, he finds strategic actors. These people may be constituted in and through discourses—traditions and anxieties particular to the U.S. historical experience and passed down through generations—but there is a moment when they must decide. Here we find intention and strategy. "This constant and deliberate re-writing of national purpose," Campbell argues (31), allowed figures such as George Kennan to craft a narrative about the dangers of an unstable Europe that became warped—against his best intentions—by other policymakers who claimed the real danger was the Soviet Union's intrinsically threatening character. These alarmist policymakers were "responsible" for "the making of the world in which they worked" (32). They created a Cold War and a bipolar order. Leaders today may be trying to make a multipolar or a unipolar or a postpolar order. It is this making of the world that fascinates us and drew us into writing *Strategic Narratives*. And for this reason, we find below that strategic action plays an important role at the thick end of analysis in International Relations.

Take the strategic use of ambiguity. Drawing on traditional discourse theory (e.g., Laclau and Mouffe 2001), scholars look for "empty signifiers"— terms that are so indeterminate that people can "read in" their preferred meaning and find a reason to offer support. President Obama's use of terms like "change," "hope," and "we" has been shown to resonate with domestic U.S. audiences (Kumar 2014), but it may have led to skepticism overseas among those who may see little change in U.S. foreign policy toward their country. European Union leaders might talk about being a "global power" or a "civilian power" facing up to the "challenges" of "globalization," but are these terms so loose as to mean whatever people want (Rogers 2009; Rosamond 1999)? Given that no state or company could argue against "climate protection," have initiatives in the name of protecting the climate become a smokescreen for politics as usual (Methmann 2010)? This close attention to language can be used to illuminate how the meaning of dates can be established and defended, and the role this can play in lending credibility to certain narratives. Dates such as 1938 ("appeasement"), 1989 ("end of an era," "new world order"), or 9/11 ("stand with us or against us") can be used to represent watersheds in historical time, to create heroes and villains, to legitimize a new course of action, and to justify ignoring previous concerns (cf. Vázquez-Arroyo 2013). The application of discourse analysis methods can bring to light how actors use the material and features of discourse to construct narratives for strategic purposes.

In environmental politics, for instance, Charlotte Epstein (2008) has demonstrated how the narrative work of activists persuaded the bulk of the world's states and citizens to shift from prowhaling to antiwhaling positions in the 1960s and 1970s. Epstein shows that while language structured actors' identity and understanding of political possibility, naturalizing a certain status quo in which whaling was a normal industrial practice, activists in the 1970s worked out how to exert agency within those conditions to shift those linguistic and conceptual parameters. By the 1980s, public opinion turned antiwhaling as people understood whales through a new narrative about saving the planet. This made it easy for policymakers to create an international ban on whaling.

Lilie Chouliaraki (2013) explores how narratives of suffering are constructed by NGOs and news journalists in order to create empathy from Western audiences. The strategic aim of these narratives is to generate attention that translates into behavioral outcomes. NGOs want public donations and public support. News journalists want high and sustained ratings for their reports. NGOs in particular have altered their narratives since the late twentieth century. Chouliaraki's analysis is useful because it shows how actors' use of narratives must work with the grain of social change. It is not a simple matter of inducement and manipulation, as in very thin accounts; it is a matter of what actions are attractive within cultures. As Western societies became more individualistic and web 2.0 enabled audience participation in international public conversations, it made sense for NGOs to produce narratives targeting individuals' propensity to express personal emotions. A general discourse of "connectivity" and empowerment via media participation had emerged by the mid-2000s. Chouliaraki points to an advertisement by the charity ActionAid: "Find Your Feeling: How Could ActionAid Make You Feel?" ActionAid provided a quiz asking you how you feel about certain images of suffering, to identify which groups you feel most empathy toward. The result is narratives about *you*, not about the structural causes of inequality, disaster, and suffering. Gone are the images of "starving babies" and solidarity with distant others; instead, you engage with the NGO's brand and website, with celebrities, or with citizen journalism; at no point is the voice of those suffering heard (Chouliaraki 2013, 19; see also Chouliaraki 2006). These humanitarian communication campaigns do not simply address audiences as individual citizens, but produce audiences as (caring) publics. In this way, narratives do more than transmit information; they are used to position and construct the audience and its identity so that a responsive disposition is cultivated.

The weakness of Chouliaraki's analysis is that she looks only at texts, not how audiences actually consume and interpret these communications or how producers construct them. She follows a "hermeneutics of suspicion" that seeks to show how texts produce power effects (Chouliaraki 2013, 21), but such suspicions are only confirmed by her interpretation. Whether ActionAid's advertisement actually engaged people in the way she infers from analyzing the advertisement itself would require empirical investigation of the responses of those who engaged with the advertisement. In other words, such poststructural analysis has yet to offer full accounts of narrative reception.

These examples show that even within the assumption that the actors and interactions of international relations are deeply embedded within, and structured by, discourse, actors can craft narratives from that discursive material to give a fresh sense to contemporary events. This strategic action can be used to project and, ideally, normalize preferred narratives of system, identity, or issue.

In summary, in studies across the spectrum there is an agent trying to achieve something. Each agent formulated a narrative and found a way to project it to their target audience through the relationships and forums they thought most appropriate. Some also harnessed news media to relay their narrative and reach their target audience. Finally, agents monitor how the target audience receives and interprets their narrative. In some cases the interpretation was sufficiently positive for the target to thereafter behave in the way the agent intended. Deals were sealed, decisions were supported, norms shifted. In this way it becomes clear that—whatever position on the spectrum the researcher takes—the study of strategic narratives involves tracing the formation, projection, and reception/interpretation of narratives that particular actors are using to try to influence others. How do actors themselves try to measure the effects of what they're doing?

Each approach has different standards of evidence and validity to support their argument. Do some approaches seem more scientific than others, and does this matter? In his discussion of the manner in which some International Relations scholars claim to be "scientific" and criticize others for not being sufficiently scientific themselves, Jackson (2010) notes the very narrow and often realistic notion of science being deployed. "Science" is taken to be the empirical testing of hypotheses, the gradual accumulation of accounts that have withstood falsification, and the separation of the scholar from the world they are seeking to explain. This leads to the privileging of quantitative methods because they appear to work with "objective" data that can be reduced to numbers, whereas qualitative data work with language and involve subjective interpretation. The problem is that actual scientists do not work like this (Kuhn 1962). Physicists, for instance, take many "facts" for granted in order to build models of a process; not everything is subject to falsification. Far better, Jackson argues, first to view science as "systematic enquiry designed to produce factual knowledge," and second, to recognize that this makes the purpose of science different from politics, which is the attempt to persuade others and get what one wants (2010, 24). It therefore does not matter what methods are used, as long as the research procedure is transparent and has some empirical or conceptual basis. Such research can by all means be motivated by political goals—for critical scholars, the point of producing knowledge is to expose insidious power structures or develop new ways of thinking and acting that would empower those currently marginalized. But as long as the actual production of knowledge is systematic, transparent, and able to be evaluated by others in the scholarly community, then it is no less "scientific" than any other piece of research. And given that scientists and philosophers of science cannot agree on what science means anyway, scholars of International Relations should not waste their time quibbling over this when they should be producing accounts of events in world politics.

Hence we treat the four approaches equally. Each aspires for transparency regarding its procedures of choosing a question, gathering evidence, analyzing it, and making inferences. Table 2.1 outlines how formation, projection, and reception are researched along the spectrum, the levels of analysis focused upon, and the methods and methodology usually employed.

Methodologies Used by Policymakers

Governments are increasingly turning to strategic narratives as a framework to organize their international communication. It is striking that they use methods similar to those of academics as they set out trying to analyze their own narratives' projection and reception. For instance, some use a mixture of qualitative focus group work, quantitative surveys, and big data analysis of social media comments in order to understand how overseas publics respond to their narratives (Vinter and Knox 2008; Matwiczak 2010). Consequently, governments face the same problems of establishing causality as scholars of international political communication. Policymakers use slightly different terminology, for example they try to measure "outputs" and "outcomes." Policymakers' use of theory is often implicit.

James Pamment (2012) notes that foreign ministries have become much more systematic in their approach to measuring their country's strategic communication. He points to the adoption of linear "logic models." These models require the foreign ministry to set strategic objectives, the tools to be used to meet those objectives, and the outcomes that would indicate the objectives have been met (table 2.2). Demonstrating the effects of the campaign—the outputs, outtakes, and outcomes—all require social science methods. Surveys, focus groups, policy analysis, and other methods would allow policymakers to show that attitudes, behavior, or decisions have been effected by the communication campaign.

Let us imagine that a Latin American country wishes to use the 2016 Olympics in Rio de Janeiro to launch a communication campaign about the attractiveness of the region in which to do business. This may incorporate a geopolitical narrative such as "the rise of the rest" or "emerging powers are the future." Those formulating the campaign's strategic priori-

TABLE 2.1. Methods Used across the Spectrum of Persuasion

Spectrum:	**Very Thin**	**Thin**	**Thick**	**Very Thick**
Approach:	Rationalism	Communicative Action	Reflexive	Poststructural
Ontology of IR	Interactions between actors with given preferences within a given structure of anarchy	Actors have given identities. They interact, leading to shared understandings of international affairs; preferences can be changed.	Actors whose identities are mutually implicated and whose identities and actions generate responses from others	Discourse (power-knowledge systems) are manifest in practices (linguistic and material)
Example studies	Krebs and Jackson (2007) on rhetorical coercion; Ringsmose and Borgensen on conflict; Goldsmith and Horiuchi (2009) on U.S. public diplomacy	Risse (2000) on the end of the Cold War; Lynch (2002) on U.S.-China relations; studies of the 2011 Libya intervention by Adler-Nissen and Pouliot (2014) and by Miskimmon (2012)	Steele (2011) on the aesthetics of insecurity; Price (2015) on U.S.-Iran soft war; Mor (2012) on Israel's impression management; Price/Arnesault, in this volume	Epstein (2008) on whaling; Hansen on security; Holland on U.S. foreign policy; Chouliaraki (2013) on humanitarian charity narratives
Formation	The strategic narrative expresses known interests and preferences	A state forms a strategic narrative based on their analysis of the world and what they think is normatively desirable	Narratives are part of actors' "biographies" and identities, and so form over long periods. Leaders can adapt those narratives tactically to give sense to new events.	IR is grounded in enduring discourses—legal, economic, historical. Leaders craft narratives from this discursive material to give sense to contemporary events.
Projection	Strategic. Signaling or "cheap talk" used to manipulate impressions. Identifiable "frames" move from policy elites to media to publics	States project truth claims about how the world is or how it ought to be	Strategic moments in which actors target the contradictions and anxieties in others' self-identities while upholding their own	Leaders articulate narratives through speeches and actions that "instantiate" that narrative

TABLE 2.1.—*Continued*

Approach:	Rationalism	Communicative Action	Reflexive	Poststructural
Reception	Actors perceive narratives as information. They then exhibit attitudes or sentiment toward the narrative and policy, pro- or anti-.	Others take those claims into account, consider the evidence, and formulate a strategy for give-and-take discussions	Are targets discomforted by attacks on identities?	Fundamental. Stable discourses define what counts as valid, normal talk and action. Actors enact that discourse. Responses therefore fairly predictable.
Interaction	Secondary to material inducement (coercion). But possible.	In multilateral forms: Give-and-take occurs between actors treated as equals, with the aim of creating a consensus. In international public sphere, INGOs and activists have asymmetric relation to states and international organizations	Getting others to change their behavior by publicizing their faults	All actors are born into and produced through discourse. But discourses are not static and some benefit more than others. Interstices form, allowing struggle and change.
Level of analysis	Either interstate or two-level game of elites and domestic forces (media, publics, parties)	Institutional forums where claims are made, or bilateral state-state interactions. Risse's public sphere brings in wider array of actors and more levels.	Elite-focused, but elites constantly in the public sphere accounting for their state's reputation. Journalists, NGOs, and filmmakers can be vital.	"Levels" is not a valid metaphor. All actors and practices exist in and through discourse.
Methods and methodology	Texts, surveys, and decisions. Content analysis of speeches and news reports, correlated with political decisions and shifts in public opinion survey data.	Inferences from positive data, sequences of interactions charted over time. Some inference beyond the data since actors' identities are deemed vital.	Analysis of state language and gestures. IR akin to theater, so visuality and emotion are important. Multimodal and cultural analysis needed, but not often done.	Trace through time how discourses produce relations, effects, identities. Identify how actors use any freedom. Primacy of language entails analysis of visual and verbal texts.

ties will identify the target audience and what they wish that audience to think and do as a result of the campaign. It may be that they target European business leaders who might invest in the region. Once funds and staff are deployed and the campaign put into practice, the team may use surveys of European business associations to evaluate which business leaders were reached and what parts of the campaign they were exposed to. Follow-up interviews with a sample of the business leaders might be used to identify what communication content might have made them think differently about investing in the region. Did certain events or images cause them to "buy in" to the emerging powers narrative, or did the authority of certain narrators have a persuasive effect? Government economic data can be used to measure how much extra investment occurred over the following 12 months. Network analysis could identify whether certain clusters of businesses or businesses in specific industrial sectors invested more or less. Finally, the foreign ministry would develop a new "post-Rio" strategy adapted to the new environment that would take into account lessons learned from the 2016 campaign.

This model neatly captures the pressures policymakers face to show linear cause-effect relations in order to justify budgets and prove that money was "well spent." It is simplistic, however (Pamment 2012, 39). In reality, audiences respond to the very formulation of the policy, since that formulation is reported in new media. Who is involved, who is consulted, does it respond to an agreed problem, is it the continuation of past failed policy? Formation *is* projection. The European business leaders might

TABLE 2.2. Pamment's Outline of a Logic Model

Component	Characteristic
Identification of priorities	Design an organization's strategic priorities as the baseline against which the campaign as a whole is to be evaluated
Inputs	Resources for meeting the objectives, such as staff and funds
Outputs	The reach and exposure generated by the campaign
Outtakes	The opinions and perceptions of those exposed to your campaign
Outcomes	Changes to the environment
Reassessment of priorities	Did outcomes meet the priorities? Should strategy be reoriented around different priorities?

have reacted negatively to the fact that they were being courted by a country piggy-backing on an event run by their Brazilian neighbor. They might have been similarly courted by other countries, or be fed up filling out surveys about their investment behavior. They might be aware that the country running the campaign has a reputation for economic instability and wonder why the campaign did not honestly address questions of reputation and credibility. Meaning lies with the audience, and audiences make meaning at all times and on their own terms, not just within the framework of a campaign.

How have foreign ministries put this into practice and responded to these difficulties? Pamment himself compared how three countries—the United States, the United Kingdom, and Sweden—each try to measure the impact of their public diplomacy practices, to understand how their efforts were received by their intended audiences overseas. U.S. policymakers had a very linear understanding of international communication. This is in part because the Smith-Mundt Act of 1948 legislates that U.S. policymakers can only project information to overseas publics, not to those in the United States. The result is that the United States formulates foreign policy, then decides how to narrate this to the outside world. Pamment found that audience research was rarely used within the State Department or gathered in a strategic way. This made it very unlikely that the United States would be able to evaluate its public diplomacy and know how or whether it was changing minds or behavior. Starting in 2006 the State Department did carry out annual surveys in seven or eight countries among those who had and had not engaged with U.S. public diplomacy campaigns. However, these were based on small sample sizes and did not isolate the effects of the campaigns vis-à-vis other factors. Further, the United States is a large and heterogeneous country; asking about attitudes "to the United States" would be meaningless. The most successful U.S. public diplomacy examples Pamment could find were spontaneous efforts by individual U.S. ambassadors who formed personal relationships with peers in other countries, which led to new business exchanges.

Sweden operated according to a different model of communication altogether. The strategic priority of Swedish public diplomats was to create a positive image of Sweden; being liked was more important than generating behavioral change in others. A positive image was to be achieved by creating Swedish spaces that overseas visitors could attend, for instance a House of Sweden in Washington, DC, where visitors would have the chance to *live* Sweden, to enact Swedish values by doing Swedish things, or doing things in a Swedish way. Alongside this, Swedish families were paired with U.S. families to encourage the latter to learn about living green, and a virtual Swedish embassy was built in Second Life, an online virtual world, were these relations could expand. The medium is the message: we Swedes are friendly, open, and technologically savvy. While Swedish policymakers lacked methods to evaluate the success of these initiatives, they were under less institutional pressure to do so than their U.S. and U.K. equivalents. One could imagine academics at the thick end of the spectrum of persuasion would be well placed to analyze how these discursive practices shaped the identities and interests of those encountering these Swedish spaces of influence.

Efforts by U.K. actors to project strategic narratives were built on assumptions midway between the U.S. transmission model and the Swedish cultural experience model. U.K. policymakers used a mix of methods to evaluate their success in influencing foreign targets, Pamment found. From 2006 the logic models of table 2.2 were in place, although it was unclear whether U.K. voices such as the Foreign and Commonwealth Office, the BBC World Service, and the British Council were supposed to formulate strategies for the national interest or for their institutional interests. Evaluation proved difficult, too: the cost of carrying out discourse analysis of media, opinion, and behavior research in multiple countries often outweighed the cost of the public diplomacy campaign itself. By 2009, however, staff across institutions had become acclimated to regular data collection and evaluation, including quantitative measures of social networks and public opinion and qualitative analysis of whether targets engaged with the U.K.'s narrative. For instance, the British Council employed a storyboarding method to represent the experience of those participating in their cultural diplomacy efforts. None of this could provide causal proof of influence, but the combination of a patchwork of mixed methods alongside measures of actual behavior allowed the British Council to present a plausible account of how its relationships and communications worked. In academic terms, U.K. institutions get beyond thin rationalist approaches; the mixed methods approaches used could be used to probe how persuasion and identity-formation work.

These efforts to manage strategic narratives must be understood in the political and economic context of the country being analyzed. In the United States and the United Kingdom, regimes of public accountability have shaped public diplomacy strategy and practice in the past decade— foreign ministries must show "value for money." The importance of national political context is evident from the way in which each country's politicians and civil servants conceptualize influence or the importance they put on national image (Sweden) or demonstrating outcomes like trade deals (the United Kingdom).

It is striking that these methods are not just tools; the implementation of these methods changes how international relations works. Methods have a "life" beyond the intention of those who created them. If methods allow policymakers to know how foreign publics think, then if these methods were adopted by every country the result would be a global communication space characterized by continual listening, engaging, and trying to influence each other. This could have political consequences. States could use these methods to take into account and be more sensitive to each other's wishes, creating a more benign and cooperative international system. Those who use audience research more effectively could be best placed to lead in addressing global problems because they would have the greatest understanding of which countries are likely to cooperate and why. However, national interests still dominate the thinking of foreign policy makers, and competition to develop the most effective methods could bring advantages to those at the cutting edge of social science. Would not the country with the highest quality audience research be best placed to manipulate overseas publics, not just understand them? And might we not expect leading states to learn how to simulate transparency while using these methods to manage their own domestic public opinion?

We conclude this section by noting a gap in practitioners' as well as scholars' approaches to strategic narrative research. Nobody analyzes the *narratives* through which audiences interpret international affairs. It is the elephant in the room in the world of international political communication. Across the spectrum of persuasion, no researchers try to identify the narratives people hold about world politics. Surveys of public opinion get at sentiment toward issues, while thicker studies might look at the representations users make online to get a slightly richer account of how people are thinking about world politics. There are well-publicized "indexes" of soft power and national brands, but these do not research narratives. Their surveys are designed to measure what countries or cities people find attractive. This is not the same as identifying the plot, characters, obstacles, and endings that people think about when they are talking about history, wars, disasters, or the world economy.

Strategic narrative analysis faces a twofold challenge, then: to find methods to identify people's narratives, and then integrate this into a broader account or model of the circulation, role, and effect of strategic narratives.[1]

Methods Alive! Managing the Effects of Strategic Narrative Research

The way we analyze international relations can affect how people think about and act in international relations. A great example is Samuel Huntington's idea of the clash of civilizations. Peter Katzenstein writes:

> Huntington was very explicit in wishing to give his readers a compelling paradigm for a better understanding of world politics. He may have been wrong . . . in asserting that civilizations are tightly coupled and coherent actors. But the very success of his writing created a primordial category that naturalized the world and made it intelligible to many of his readers. (Katzenstein 2009, 13)[2]

We take issue with positivist approaches to social science that assume methods can represent an independent world, and with constructivist approaches that assume methods can explore how those representations create experiences of an independent world. Our interest is in drawing attention to the ways in which methods constitute the world (Law, Ruppert, and Savage 2011; Savage 2013). Methods produce classifications that people act upon to produce the world in that way. Huntington constructed a historical methodology that suggested the world was divided into enduring, separate regions or civilizations that were bound to compete and eventually conflict. In domestic politics, surveys produce social categorizations that underpin policies that then reproduce and enact those categorizations. Hence, it is impossible to separate methods, knowledge, and reality.

Ironically, the methods we use are part of the political world we study. Policymakers and practitioners use opinion polls and elite interviews. Methods are both subject and object. And thanks to digital media, methods have entered a period of flux when new techniques and forms of data pose enormous theoretical and practical questions. Take, for instance, a researcher conducting a comparative study seeking to explain how narratives circulate through different national media systems. William Merrin (2010) writes that the "media researcher's year-long project looking in detail at one carefully isolated aspect of the media world is increasingly like studying a cup of water to understand the sea." He neatly sums up the methodological problem:

> What makes this especially important is the interconnected nature of the changes: digital intercommunication between devices increases our capacities and accelerates these processes, continually breaking down the fixity of the broadcast era. Today, therefore, the idea of fixed, separate media forms becomes problematic. After a period of experimentation the broadcast era refined and was dominated by a small number of broadly standardised, fixed and separate commercial forms, whose slow evolution did not challenge their essential form and rarely changed the user-experience (exceptions such as FM radio, colour TV and commercial VCRs are memorable precisely because they were rare). In contrast the post-broadcast era is marked by a permanent process of invention and innovation in which media forms are continually re-made, reconfigured, obsolesced and revolutionised. This is the era of the permanent "beta" in which all digital forms are tested in the market and continually improved and upgraded. The result is a new, almost-unchartable, fluid, hybrid ecology, in which even the identification of particular forms collapses as they are re-made and cross-breed as vehicles of digital content. (Merrin 2009, 23)

Andrew Chadwick (2013, 15) claims that the emergence of hybrid media systems creates a new ontological situation, one in which the social is constituted by "simultaneous integration and fragmentation." Stable old units of analysis in political communication such as television and the audience are being reconstituted; it is not that they disappear but that digitization and new participatory cultures reconfigure how these "units" operate. This makes "systematic study" almost an oxymoron. Chadwick bases his new holistic study of what he calls the "hybrid media system" on a series of small-scale scoping studies. Chadwick decided what media practices to follow as events break, rather than follow a predetermined set. David Karpf (2012) argues that since media technology and its effects are constantly changing, systematic longitudinal studies of media and society no longer have validity. Studying the effects of "the Internet" or the role of "blogging" makes no sense because what each of those phenomena are changes continually. Karpf calls for a methodological ethos he describes as "kludgy": "the use of hacks or workarounds that allow for messy-but-productive solutions where more elegant choices would prove unworkable" (2012, 642). For example, since social media firms keep changing the accessibility of data on their sites, researchers will have to work with what software is available at that time to access as much data as they can afford. No comprehensive dataset is possible; the goal of comprehensiveness stops making sense. Far better to have partial but transparent use of methods.

But is transparency enough? The idea that research is not independent of society forces us to attend to the political forces that determine what research and knowledge is generated:

> [M]ethods are of the social. . . . research methods embody the concerns of advocates and subsist in particular contexts or environments. [This] illustrates the importance of thinking about method, about what it is that methods are doing, and the status of the data that they're making. (Law, Ruppert, and Savage 2011, 7, underline in the original)

This leads to a set of reinforcing relationships or dependencies: there is research, its methods, representations, and findings; there is knowledge and the realities these constitute beyond the researchers, in public; and there are advocates and institutions that ensure this kind of research, knowledge, and reality are maintained. Law and his colleagues conclude:

> The implication is that there's a kind of triple lock at work here. And this, if it's right, makes it very, very difficult to know differently, to shape new realities, or to imagine different . . . modes of knowing. For all of these have to be shifted together. (Law, Ruppert, and Savage 2011, 13)

What relationships does the study of strategic narrative fit within? How are these acts of communication situated in discrete professional practices, for instance at the U.S. Department of State or U.K. Foreign and Commonwealth Office, and within broader political-historical contexts such as the postglobal financial crisis drive for accountability and "value"?

Our approach is to try to understand and explain how actors use strategic narratives to achieve their goals. Those narratives might be foolish, duplicitous, imperialist, colonialist, or whatever political position you wish to critique. But in the study of strategic narratives we can treat deception or obfuscation as one more type of action alongside others; it is another way to justify action to others to influence their behavior. We can treat narratives of imperialism or colonialism as content the same as any narrative of nationalism, cosmopolitanism, or liberalism. We see political claims and criticisms around narrative contestation not only as ideologies to be critiqued but as instruments utilized by actors trying to accomplish immediate goals and longer strategies. While we could criticize strategic narratives on empirical, normative, or conceptual grounds, our task is to analyze and theorize how narratives are used, how existing narratives constrain what is thinkable and considered possible, and how citizens and leaders criticize each other or justify their actions through the projection and contestation of such claims. What matters is not whether a narrative is more true or more false, but what effects the narratives has.

Conclusion

A changing media ecology creates new opportunities for mobilization, socialization, norm diffusion, persuasion, legitimation, and contestation in international relations. In this chapter we have offered a concept (strategic narrative) and framework (spectrum of persuasion) that scholars can use to explain the scope, mechanisms, and limits of these processes. We have set out a range of methods and approaches to methodology that can be used to generate the data to underpin such explanations.

There is a risk that explanations of the effectiveness or ineffectiveness of strategic narratives cannot but be brought under the leash of state interests. At the end of Pamment's (2012) book-length analysis of efforts made by the U.S., U.K., and Swedish state departments to measure the effect of their public diplomacy, he concludes that whatever methods they use, public diplomacy is still just a tool to realize "the national interest," and what that means is rarely if ever questioned by policymakers. In the context of Pamment's lament, what can scholars do if their analysis is useful for policymakers thinking only in those terms?

One can remain independent. Explaining how power and persuasion operate is a useful function in democratic societies. However, for those interested in the strategic dimension of strategic narratives it is then more difficult to make claims about the intention of policymakers, journalists, and others involved. Critical claims about malevolent intent or supportive claims about goodwill both appear weak without actual firsthand contact with them as they formulate strategy. Scholars must instead think imaginatively about constructing extremely systematic analysis of those actors' statements, actions, and reactions and about how inferences about strategic intention can be validated.

Alternatively, one can work with policymakers and practitioners, talking to and observing them as they formulate strategy or respond to events. It may take some years to build up the trust required for access. However, there are lots of examples of this happening. This opens up opportunities to try to use scholarly analysis and the kind of critical questions academics can ask to change how policymakers and practitioners think and act. Some scholars may want to help their states improve their existing strategic narrative operations. Others may want to help states work according to different ethical requirements, think about interests in a different way, or be more inclusive in their policy making. And others still will wish to work with nonstate actors to help them craft compelling narratives to advance their causes and interests. Our concept of actor is open to those beyond the state (Miskimmon et al. 2013, 30–59) and avoids valorizing any particular actor: the concern with who narrates and who is perceived to be narrating and what difference this makes to processes of power and influence in international relations. Public diplomacy functions can be performed by citizens, NGOs, companies, and international organizations, alone or through collaboration.

In discussing the application of strategic narrative analysis to different research areas and questions, we have tried in this chapter to explore multiple methods for analyzing strategic narratives. But while elegant theorizing and precise conceptualization are valid goals, we hope in this chapter to have made clear that strategic narrative research is just as much a matter of politics and ethics.

NOTES

1. Laura Roselle has led efforts to investigate public narratives using Q methodology, an experimental design in which participants are given a set of statements that reflect the narratives projected by political elites about foreign affairs, and then organize them to reflect their own narratives of how events are unfolding. "This is a qualitative research method that allows individuals to construct personal opinion maps through the organization of authentic narrative statements or other stimuli that either closely or not so closely match individuals' values, beliefs and understandings of a particular issue area" (Spray and Roselle 2012, 4). For more information, see the conclusion of this volume.

2. David Calleo (2011) makes a similar point when discussing the work of Philip Cerny and G. John Ikenberry. Calleo argues, "If there is a fair criticism . . . it is that they remain too narrowly tied to their own professional camp and view of the world. Each presents an influential view of the present and a provocative view of the future. But each would have been more interesting had it ventured into the insights of the other. Accomplished writers like Cerny and Ikenberry are guardians of their nation's political imagination. They have a special obligation to keep enlarging our views of reality" (Calleo 2011, 168).

REFERENCES

Adler-Nissen, Rebecca, and Vincent Pouliot. "Power in Practice: Negotiating the International Intervention in Libya." *European Journal of International Relations* 20 (2014): 4889–4911.

Altheide, David L., and Robert P. Snow. *Media Logic*. Beverly Hills, CA: Sage, 1979.

Calleo, David P. "Visions of Order and Disorder." *Survival: Global Politics and Strategy* 53, no. 5 (2011): 157–68. http://dx.doi.org/10.1080/00396338.2011.621643

Campbell, David. *Writing Security: United States Foreign Policy and the Politics of Identity*. Minneapolis: University of Minnesota Press, 1992.

Chadwick, Andrew. *The Hybrid Media System: Politics and Power*. New York: Oxford University Press, 2013.

Checkel, Jeffrey T. "Social Construction and Integration." *Journal of European Public Policy* 6 (1999): 545–60.

Checkel, Jeffrey T. "Why Comply? Social Learning and European Identity Change." *International Organization* 55 (2001): 553–88.

Checkel, Jeffrey T. "Persuasion in International Institutions." ARENA Working Paper WP 02/14. Universität Oslo: ARENA, 2002.

Checkel, Jeffrey T. "'Going Native' in Europe? Theorizing Social Interaction in European Institutions." *Comparative Political Studies* 36, nos. 1–2 (2003): 209–31.

Chouliaraki, Lilie. *The Ironic Spectator: Solidarity in the Age of Post-Humanitarianism*. Cambridge: Polity, 2013.

de Almagro Iniesta, María Martín. *EU Engagement with Local Civil Society in the Great Lakes Region*. Rome: Istituto Affari Internazionali, 2013.

De Graaf, Beatrice, George Dimitriu, and Jens Ringsmose, eds. *Strategic Narratives, Public Opinion and War: Winning Domestic Support for the Afghan War*. London: Routledge, 2015.

Dreher, Tanja. "Listening across Difference: Media and Multiculturalism beyond the Politics of Voice." *Continuum: Journal of Media & Cultural Studies* 23, no. 4 (2009): 445–58.

Epstein, Charlotte. *The Power of Words in International Relations: Birth of an Anti-Whaling Discourse*. Cambridge, MA: MIT Press, 2008.

Goldsmith, Benjamin E., and Yusaku Horiuchi. "Spinning the Globe? US Public Diplomacy and Foreign Public Opinion." *Journal of Politics* 71, no. 3 (2009): 863–75.

Hall, Ian, and Frank Smith. "The Struggle for Soft Power in Asia: Public Diplomacy and Regional Competition." *Asian Security* 9, no. 1 (2013): 1–18.

Hariman, Robert, and John Louis Lucaites. *No Caption Needed: Iconic Photographs, Public Culture, and Liberal Democracy*. Chicago: University of Chicago Press, 2007.

Hayden, Craig. "'Beyond the 'Obama Effect': Refining the Instruments of Engagement through US Public Diplomacy." *American Behavioral Scientist* 55, no. 6 (2011): 784–802.

Hjarvard, Stig. "The Mediatization of Society." *Nordicom Review* 29, no. 2 (2008): 105–34.

Jackson, Patrick T. *The Conduct of Inquiry in International Relations: Philosophy of Science and Its Implications for the Study of World Politics*. London: Routledge, 2011.

Karpf, David. "Social Science Research Methods in Internet Time." *Information, Communication & Society* 15, no. 5 (2012): 639–61.

Katzenstein, Peter J. "A World of Plural and Pluralist Civilizations: Multiple Actors, Traditions and Practices." In *Civilizations in World Politics: Plural and Pluralist Perspectives*, edited by Peter J. Katzenstein. New York: Routledge, 2009.

Krebs, Ronald R., and Patrick Thaddeus Jackson. "Twisting Tongues and Twisting Arms: The Power of Political Rhetoric." *European Journal of International Relations* 13, no.1 (2007): 35–66.

Kuhn, Thomas. S. *The Structure of Scientific Revolutions*. Chicago: University of Chicago Press, 1962.

Kumar, Anup. "Looking Back at Obama's Campaign in 2008: 'True Blue Populist' and Social Production of Empty Signifiers in Political Reporting." *Journal of Communication Inquiry* 38, no. 1 (2014): 5–24.

Laclau, Ernesto, and Chantal Mouffe. *Hegemony and Socialist Strategy: Towards a Radical Democratic Politics*. London: Verso, 2001.

Law, John, Evelyn Ruppert, and Mike Savage. "The Double Social Life of Methods." CRESC Working Paper Series, Working Paper No. 95. Milton Keynes: CRESC, Open University. Accessed January 20, 2016. http://research.gold.ac.uk/7987/1/The%20Double%20Social%20Life%20of%20Methods%20CRESC%20Working%20Paper%2095.pdf

Lynch, Marc. "Why Engage? China and the Logic of Communicative Engagement." *European Journal of International Relations* 8, no. 2 (2002): 187–230.

Matwiczak, Kenneth. "Public Diplomacy Model for the Assessment of Performance." Lyndon B. Johnson School of Public Affairs, Policy Research Project Report Number 170, September 2010. Accessed July 1, 2015. http://www.state.gov/documents/organization/149966.pdf

Merrin, William. "Media Studies 2.0: Upgrading and Open-Sourcing the Discipline." *Interactions: Studies in Communication & Culture* 1, no. 1 (2009): 17–34.

Merrin, William. "Studying Me-dia: The Problem of Method in a Post-Broadcast Age." *Media Studies 2.0 Blog*, March 9, 2010. Accessed July 7, 2015. http://mediastudies2point0.blogspot.co.uk/2010/03/studying-me-dia-problem-of-method-in.html

Methmann, Chris Paul. "'Climate Protection' as Empty Signifier: A Discourse Theoretical Perspective on Climate Mainstreaming in World Politics." *Millennium–Journal of International Studies* 39, no. 2 (2010): 345–72.

Miskimmon, Alister. "German Foreign Policy and the Libya Crisis." *German Politics* 21, no. 4 (2012): 392–410.

Miskimmon, Alister, Ben O'Loughlin, and Laura Roselle. *Strategic Narratives: Communication Power and the New World Order*. New York: Routledge, 2013.

Miskimmon, Alister, Ben O'Loughlin, and Laura Roselle. "*Strategic Narratives*: A Response to the *Critical Security Studies* Symposium." *Critical Security Studies* 3, no. 3 (2015).

Mor, Ben D. "Credibility Talk in Public Diplomacy." *Review of International Studies* 38, no. 2 (2012): 393–422.

Pamment, James. *New Public Diplomacy in the 21st Century*. London: Routledge, 2012.

Peters, John Durham. *Speaking into the Air: A History of the Idea of Communication*. Chicago: University of Chicago Press, 2012.

Price, Monroe. *Free Expression, Globalism, and the New Strategic Communication*. Cambridge: Cambridge University Press, 2015.

Risse, Thomas. "'Let's Argue!': Communicative Action in World Politics." *International Organization* 54, no. 1 (2000): 1–39.

Rogers, James. "From 'Civilian Power' to 'Global Power': Explicating the European Union's 'Grand Strategy' through the Articulation of Discourse Theory." *JCMS: Journal of Common Market Studies* 47, no. 4 (2009): 831–62.

Rosamond, Ben. "Discourses of Globalization and the Social Construction of European Identities." *Journal of European Public Policy* 6, no. 4 (1999): 652–68.

Roselle, Laura. *Media and the Politics of Failure: Great Powers, Communication Strategies, and Military Defeats*. Basingstoke: Palgrave Macmillan, 2006.

Savage, Mike. "The 'Social Life of Methods': A Critical Introduction." *Theory, Culture & Society* 30, no. 3 (2013): 3–21.

Shepherd, Laura J. "Ideas/Matter: Conceptualising Foreign Policy Practice." *Critical Security Studies* 3, no. 3 (2015).

Simpson, Emile. *War from the Ground Up: Twenty-First-Century Combat as Politics*. London: Hurst, 2012.

Spray, Sharon, and Laura Roselle. "Understanding Communication about the Environment: Narratives of Climate Change and Foreign Policy." Paper prepared for the Annual Convention of the International Studies Association, San Diego, April 1–4, 2012.

Steele, Brent J. *Defacing Power: The Aesthetics of Insecurity in Global Politics*. Ann Arbor: University of Michigan Press, 2011.

Tharoor, Shashi. *Pax Indica: India and the World in the 21st Century*. New Delhi and New York: Allen Lane, 2012.

Van Dijck, José, and Thomas Poell. "Understanding Social Media Logic." *Media and Communication* 1, no. 1 (2013): 2–14.

Vázquez-Arroyo, Antonio Y. "How Not to Learn from Catastrophe: Habermas, Critical Theory and the 'Catastrophization' of Political Life." *Political Theory* 41, no. 5 (2013): 738–65.

Vinter, Louise, and David Knox. "Measuring the Impact of Public Diplomacy: Can It Be Done?" In *Engagement, Public Diplomacy in a Globalised World*, edited by Jolyon Welsh and Daniel Fearn. London: Foreign and Commonwealth Office, 2008. Accessed June 1, 2015. http://ics.leeds.ac.uk/papers/pmt/exhibits/3055/pd-engagement-jul-08.pdf

Zhang, Juyan. "A Strategic Issue Management (SIM) Approach to Social Media Use in Public Diplomacy." *American Behavioral Scientist* 57, no. 9 (2013): 1312–31. http://dx.doi.org/10.1177/0002764213487734

3 | Strategic Narratives
and Great Power Identity

Laura Roselle

After the dissolution of the Soviet Union, there was a moment for possible post–Cold War narrative alignment as some leaders on each side sought a new world order; a moment to move beyond the Cold War narrative of East versus West. George H. W. Bush set out a system narrative of international cooperation that important leaders in the former USSR shared. But in the years that immediately followed, short-term tactical conflicts on each side meant that this moment for alignment was squandered—visions of order reverted back to Cold War narrations—with the United States seeking to be leader of the free world again by upholding order in the 1991 Gulf War and spreading democracy in the 2003 Iraq War and Russia trying to assert itself as a strong and independent power by attacking Chechnya in two wars. For those who wonder why the Crimea 2014 crisis is explained by so many through a Cold War narrative, with two leading characters of differing moral qualities struggling against one another—this time via a proxy conflict in Ukraine—this chapter explains why that Cold War narrative endured. This examination of U.S. and Russian conflicts in the 1990s and 2000s and the narratives each country projected through these decades shows how narratives of particular conflicts can reinforce much broader strategic narratives about global order and power transition.

Questions about U.S. and Russian strategic narratives derive from questions about the residual effects of decades of confrontation during the Cold War and the (re)construction of great power narratives. For much of the 20th century the United States and the Soviet Union were locked in a competition marked by ideological, political, and economic differences.

Building competing alliance structures, claiming superiority, and encouraging their citizens to see their own state as superior to the other, the United States and the Soviet Union claimed great power status in a bipolar world. This narrative of the world is recognized by Miskimmon, O'Loughlin, and Roselle (2013) as a great power narrative.

This chapter traces changes in U.S. and Russian strategic narratives as the Cold War ended in the early 1990s and then into the new millennium. The demise of the Soviet Union demanded a new system narrative and political leaders in both countries sought to describe a new international order. War, however, challenged new narratives, and in both cases great power narratives were reasserted as perceived security threats (in Iraq and Chechnya) increased over time. This chapter focuses on how war affected the system, identity, and issue strategic narratives of the United States and the Russian Federation during this period. In the United States this includes 1990–91 and 2003–4 and a focus on the Iraq wars. In the Russian case this includes 1994–96 and 1999–2004 and a focus on Chechnya. The narratives that supported these wars helped to foster the reassertion of a Cold War system narrative as Russia annexed Crimea in 2014. In both countries, great power narratives helped political leaders secure domestic political support for the use of force and enhanced their power. The formation, projection, and reception of narratives can be understood through careful study of leadership narratives found in speeches, analysis of media structure and content, and through an assessment of public opinion polling results and focus group audience narratives. The final section of the chapter discusses how the complex media environment of the 2010s challenges the formation, projection, and reception of new and nuanced strategic narratives while supporting older, more familiar Cold War narratives that constrain behavior in world politics today.

Constructing Narratives

The introduction to this work on strategic narratives makes the important distinction among system, identity, and issue narratives. System narratives describe the structure of the international system itself, including who the actors are, how the system works, and which actors pose a challenge to the system. Glasnost and perestroika in the Soviet Union, the fall of the Berlin Wall, and the eventual dissolution of the Soviet Union in 1991 fell outside of the bipolar Cold War narrative of good and evil that had described the international system since the late 1940s. The 1990s presented an opportunity for a new strategic narrative about the international system itself. But political leaders that attempt to craft a new system narrative will not necessarily be successful. Identity narratives, for example, may undermine the resonance of new system narratives. Identity narratives "are about the identities of actors in international affairs that are in a process of constant negotiation and contestation" (Miskimmon, O'Loughlin, and Roselle 2013, 7). One would expect that political leaders would have to make very clear how existing identity narratives are in accord with new system narratives, and this can be very difficult—as the cases below clearly show. Finally, issue or policy narratives that are strategically developed may support or undermine new system narratives. Building a broadly based coalition for war supports a very different narrative about the international system than does a unilateral and preemptive use of force, for example.

One of the challenges of studying strategic narratives is that the process of communication is not linear in nature or limited in scope. Narratives may be strategically (re)constructed by political actors, but there is a recursive nature to this process. Still, for analytical reasons I will focus on the processes of formation, projection, and reception of strategic narratives in the post–Cold War international system (Miskimmon, O'Loughlin, and Roselle 2013, 8–12). One way to do this is through careful case studies that are theoretically informed. During periods of transition leaders may be willing to adopt new system narratives, but they can be constrained by domestic political concerns, events on the ground, and competing narratives projected in a rapidly transforming and much more complex communication ecology.

The case studies of the United States and the Russian Federation below focus on strategic narrative formation by analyzing the speeches and communication strategies of leaders in both countries. The speeches analyzed for each case are found in table 3.1.

Media coverage of the wars was analyzed in various ways to assess the dissemination of strategic narratives. There have been numerous studies that have analyzed media coverage of the wars discussed here (*on Iraq:* Aday, Livingston, and Hebert 2005; Entman, Livingston, and Kim 2009; Paletz 1994; Entman 2003; Luther and Miller 2005; Hoskins and O'Loughlin 2010; *on Chechnya:* Mickiewicz 1999; Koltsova 2000; Belin 2000; Oates and Roselle 2000; Mickiewicz 2008). In addition to relying on these secondary sources, additional analysis was done for the U.S. case on a sample of NBC coverage from January 17 to February 28, 1991, and during a sample of dates in 2003–4. In the case of the First Chechen War, the focus is on Russian television coverage on ORT and NTV—the two most far-reaching television channels in the Russian Federation—directly after the war starts in December 1994, during the 1995 Duma election campaign (November 15–December 16), and during the 1996 presidential election campaign (first round, May 13–June 15 and second round, June 17–July 3). For the Second Chechen War, the focus was on ORT and NTV particularly during the presidential campaign in 2000 (March 3–24) and during the 2003 Duma campaign.[1] The coverage in all cases was examined to identify system, identity, and policy (war) narratives. In addition, in each case the media's structure and access to information are examined.

Audience reactions were assessed in the cases of the second war for each county through focus group data. This analysis seeks to assess the reception of strategic narratives. Polling data give a broad overview while

TABLE 3.1. Speeches Analyzed

Conflict	Leader	Date	Communication Type/Audience
Iraq 1	GHW Bush	1/16/1991	Address to the nation on the invasion of Iraq
Iraq 1	GHW Bush	3/6/1991	"New world order" speech
Iraq 2	GW Bush	3/20/2003	War message
Iraq 2	GW Bush	5/1/2003	End of major combat in Iraq
Iraq 2	GW Bush	9/7/2003	Update on the war on terror
Iraq 2	GW Bush	5/24/2004	Outline for the future of Iraq (Army War College, Carlisle, PA)
Chechnya 1	B Yeltsin	12/27/1994	Speech to the nation
Chechnya 2	V Putin	1/15/2000	ORT interview
Chechnya 2	V Putin	11/20/2000	Speech to top commanders of the Russian Armed Forces
Chechnya 2	V Putin	12/25/2000	ORT interview
Chechnya 2	V Putin	9/24/2001	Major television address
Chechnya 2	V Putin	2/27/2002	Chechnya: Speech by Russian President at a Security Council meeting, the Kremlin, Moscow
Chechnya 2	V Putin	11/10/2002	Speech by Russian president Vladimir Putin at meeting with representatives of Chechen public
Chechnya 2	V Putin	3/16/2003	President Vladimir Putin addressed the residents of the Chechen Republic
Chechnya 2	V Putin	5/16/2003	Putin's annual message to the Federal Assembly of the Russian Federation

focus groups allow the researcher to understand more about how strategic narratives are (re)constructed by individual audience members. Focus groups were conducted in Russia and the United States during December 2004 and allow a more detailed look at the discourse surrounding the Iraq and Chechen Wars, respectively.[2] Since I am interested in strategic narratives, it is important to look at how citizens describe the wars in conversation with others. While focus group analysis is not generalizable, it allows us to identify how people conceptualize and describe wars, the context they put each war in or the precedents they invoke, how they evaluate leaders' statements or media coverage, and how they account for their own views and uphold and justify when exchanging views with other focus group members.

The case studies are guided by the following questions:

- What are the leaders' dominant identity and policy narratives during the wars?
- To what degree do identity and policy narratives resonate with system narratives in transition?
- What narratives are disseminated via mass media?
- How are narratives received by audience members?

In the 1990s changes in the international system opened space for the articulation of new strategic narratives about the international system itself. The case studies show that the wars in Iraq and Chechnya undermined (and continue to undermine) the ability of political leaders in the United States and the Russian Federation to set out a new system narrative in a post–Cold War era. The implications of this may be constrained thinking about the possible future of international relations.

The United States

Formation

U.S. president George H. W. Bush was inaugurated as president in 1989 at a time marked by substantial changes in the Soviet Union and the "end" of the Cold War. Bush emphasized the interdependent nature of the international system and stressed the ability of states to cooperate against overt aggression, suggesting that the Soviet Union was no longer a powerful threat to the United States. In fact, both Soviet president Gorbachev and President Bush used the phrase "new world order" to describe a fundamental change in international relations emphasizing cooperation and interdependence. Still, Bush stressed American leadership in the world, especially in creating the coalition against Iraqi aggression against Kuwait, for example in his speech to a joint session of Congress on September 11, 1990.

President Bush spent considerable diplomatic energy constructing an alliance to take part in military actions in Kuwait and Iraq in late 1990 and early 1991. Because of this identification with others in a coalition of forces, sanctioned by the United Nations, one would not expect a narrative that emphasized American great power status and patriotic images, but rather one that emphasized a global reaction to Iraqi aggression. As expected, at least before and into the early stages of combat, Bush's speeches on the Persian Gulf War clearly stressed an international consensus. Four times within his January 16, 1991, speech announcing the attack on Iraq Bush used the phrase "while the world waited," and once "while the world prayed," suggesting the world was joined together in opposition to Saddam Hussein. Bush suggested that Saddam Hussein tried to make this conflict about the United States:

> [H]e tried to make this a dispute between Iraq and the United States of America. Well, he failed. Tonight 28 nations—countries from five continents, Europe and Asia, Africa and the Arab League—have forces in the Gulf area standing shoulder-to-shoulder against Saddam Hussein. These countries had hoped the use of force could be avoided. Regrettably, we now believe that only force will make him leave. (Bush 1991)

The narrative then described the countries of the world standing against Saddam Hussein.

Bush's narrative also referred to the United Nations as having a central role in peacekeeping. For example, in his speech Bush highlighted the Iraqi violation of United Nations resolutions and said that through this war a new world order would be established:

> This is an historic moment. We have in this past year made great progress in ending the long era of conflict and cold war. We have

before us the opportunity to forge for ourselves and for future generations a new world order—a world where the rule of law, not the law of the jungle, governs the conduct of nations. When we are successful—and we will be—we have a real chance at this new world order, an order in which a credible United Nations can use its peacekeeping role to fulfill the promise and vision of the U.N.'s founders. (Bush in Barnett 2005, 26)

The narrative in this case does not appeal to great power status of the United States, focusing instead on the power of the coalition in cooperatively defending a new order within the system.

The First Iraq War (the Gulf War) began in January 1991 as the United States led a coalition force of 34 countries to remove Iraq's army from occupied Kuwait.[3] The coalition force first launched an air war and then quickly moved ground troops through Kuwait and into Iraq. President George Bush declared Kuwait liberated on February 27. Later Bush and former national security advisor Brent Scowcroft explained why they had not moved to overthrow Saddam Hussein: it would have severely divided the coalition and the political and human costs would have been too high (Bush and Scowcroft 1998). Domestically, the American public and political elites supported the coalition actions in Iraq (Kohut and Toth 1994). In this case, the war had limited and clearly defined objectives, and coalition ground troops were withdrawn when these were accomplished.

On March 6, 1991, in his address to Congress, President Bush discussed the future after the conclusion of the war on February 28. Here his narrative did allude to the leadership of the United States in the world:

To all the challenges that confront this region of the world, there is no single solution, no solely American answer. But we can make a difference. America will work tirelessly as a catalyst for positive change.

But we cannot lead a new world abroad if, at home, it's politics as usual on American defense and diplomacy. (Bush 1991)

Bush's rhetoric suggests that the United States came out of the Persian Gulf War as a reinvigorated leader in the world. Still, he suggested that a new world order could be achieved even with the "uncommon coalition" that was created to address the Iraqi invasion of Kuwait.

Projection and Reception

While the narrative at times may have emphasized the coalition and a new world order, analyses of the content of media coverage of the first Persian Gulf War show that television "coverage was nationalistic (if not jingoistic) and overwhelmingly relayed the Bush administration and Pentagon perspectives, relied on US sources, adopted the military's sanitized lexicon of war, and transmitted US military disinformation" (Paletz 1994, 282). Scholars suggest that this was due, in part, to the focus on the war itself and restrictive media policies, designed in light of perceived "lessons" associated with the American experience with the media during the Vietnam War (Hoskins 2004). The belief was that there had been too much latitude for journalists in that war. Press pools were established during the Iraq War, for example, and reporters were not allowed wide access. In addition, the military supplied a significant amount of the information to the press, hoping to curtail independent reporting. Compelling video footage of missiles hitting their targets supplied a high-tech, and some would say video-game, aura to the combat coverage that was immensely popular with audiences. One significant difference with Vietnam was the growing level of technological sophistication in the media and the emergence of other information outlets. Satellite technology, for example, allowed televised pictures of air strikes in Baghdad. Even though some journalists balked at the new Pentagon press rules, the conflict's short time frame did not allow for a prolonged discussion about the war or its coverage. Troops came home and the media turned to other stories. Even the continuing air strikes were not covered extensively.

However, a sample of NBC *Nightly News* coverage in January and February 1991 shows patriotic stories that go well beyond coverage of Bush administration statements and high-tech video supplied by the military. These include one story on January 17—broadcast a day after Bush's war announcement—that plays "Proud to Be an American" by Lee Greenwood in the background and covers "war fever" in the country. Supporters with flags, people praying, and a military recruitment center receiving new recruits are shown. Another story on January 23 covers "patriotism as a hot ticket" and reports that "the flag is everywhere." The owner of a company that makes flags says he has "never seen so many American flags." In addition, the story reports that the "windfall of patriotism" is coming through the sale of American flag hats and pins, Army fatigues, target posters of

Saddam Hussein, and *Gulf Strike* video games. And even though President Bush may have stressed the importance of the coalition, the media coverage of the military operation does not. The focus is squarely on American forces, American power, and American pride.

The coverage of the First Iraq War, then, is marked by patriotic television coverage emphasizing a great power narrative even as the leadership claims that a new world order is marked by international cooperation. This shows a tension between the two narratives. The degree to which patriotic images are evident, however, is dwarfed when compared to what was to come under President George W. Bush in the year 2003.

Second Iraq War: A Focus on 2003–2004

Formation

More than a decade later, in March 2003, the United States military forces returned to Iraq under the direction of President George W. Bush.[4] The United States led a "coalition of the willing" after the United Nations refused to support a military intervention in Iraq, and Bush declared major combat over or "mission accomplished" on May 1, 2003. Violence continued, however, with a growing armed insurgency against the American-led occupation and reconstruction of Iraq. The limited objectives of the First Iraq War had been replaced by the much broader objective of democratizing Iraq. In June 2004 the United States announced the transfer of sovereignty to the Iraqi government, but approximately 150,000 American troops were on the ground in Iraq in early 2009, more than four years later. This war was marked by a great power narrative that struck a chord with many U.S. citizens.

The Second Iraq War began with air strikes on March 20, 2003. In 2003 the Bush administration had not been successful at building a coalition for the use of military forces. The United Nations Security Council did not support the American actions, and the social cohesion evident in the First Gulf War had disappeared. In some ways this is not surprising because President George W. Bush's administration had a very different perspective on the role of the United States in the international system. In many ways this is related to the worldview of this President Bush and the administration's reaction to September 11, 2001. After 9/11 President Bush, in a September 20, 2001, speech, set out a choice for other states in the world: either you are with the United States (and civilization and good) or you are against the United States (and with barbarians and evil) (see Hoskins and O'Loughlin 2010; Tumber and Palmer 2004; Secunda and Moran 2007; Altheide 2006). As Michael Hirsh describes it:

> In the year since Bush first gave voice to his doctrine, it has become the animating concept of American foreign policy, transforming the entire focus of his administration. The Bush doctrine has been used to justify a new assertiveness abroad unprecedented since the early days of the Cold War—amounting nearly to the declaration of American hegemony—and it has redefined U.S. relationships around the world. (Hirsh 2002, 19)

The Bush doctrine is not only justification, however. It represents a great power narrative that shaped policy choices as well and fit much more squarely with the use of force, even unilaterally.

Alliances, interdependence, and cooperation were not at the heart of the Bush administration's perception of the post–Cold War world. The United States was prepared to and did "go it alone" in a number of different substantive areas including the environment and security. When the United Nations refused to condone military action against Iraq in 2003, the Bush administration proceeded without approval. There were small contributions of troops or supplies from 35 different countries, but this was hardly the coalition of the First Gulf War. And in his March 20 speech announcing the commencement of military operations, President Bush mentioned this coalition but focused on American forces: "To all the men and women of the United States armed forces now in the Middle East, the peace of a troubled world and the hopes of an oppressed people now depend on you."

In the beginning of the military effort, Bush's narrative consistently tied the war to the threat of terrorism directed against the United States. When announcing the end to major combat in Iraq on the flight deck of the USS *Lincoln* under a sign with the words "Mission Accomplished" superimposed over an American flag, Bush said that "the battle of Iraq is one victory in a war on terror that began on September 11th, 2001." In this speech Bush also emphasized the hard power of the United States, telling military personnel, "You have shown the world the skill and the might of the American armed forces." Yet, despite the end of major combat activities, after May 1, 2003, violence continued and American ground forces met determined resistance and suffered escalating numbers of U.S. casualties over time.[5] Bush emphasized success, even as violence continued. Events were to contradict Bush's strategic narrative, raising doubts about its credibility (Miskimmon, O'Loughlin, and Roselle 2013, 47). In September 2003 Bush reiterated that Iraq possessed weapons of mass destruction and had sponsored terrorism. In addition he stressed the rebuilding of Iraq. In the next year Bush highlighted democratic processes, and in May 2004 he discussed the June 2004 handing over of "sovereignty" to the Coalition Provisional Authority. Thus, the narrative described movement toward a stable, democratic Iraq as a happy ending.

Projection

As in the case of the First Gulf War, we know from multiple content analyses of U.S. media coverage of the Second Gulf War that administration themes and positive views of the war were covered extensively. In the American media, combat was sanitized and dissent minimized (Aday, Livingston, and Hebert 2005), reporters deferred to White House officials (Entman, Livingston, and Kim 2009), and military actions were emphasized (Kolmer and Semetko 2009). To a significant degree the Bush administration's narrative was dominant, at least at first, in part because of the calls to patriotism-supportive media coverage.

In part the focus on military actions is understandable in light of the government's communication strategy of embedding journalists with military units in Iraq (Katovsky and Carlson 2003). The Pentagon's new plan set out the rationale for embedding as follows:

> Ultimate strategic success in bringing peace and security to this region will come in our long-term commitment to supporting our democratic ideals. We need to tell the factual story—good or bad—before others seed the media with disinformation and distortions, as they most certainly will continue to do. Our people in the field need to tell our story. (quoted in Tumber and Palmer 2004, 16)

Approximately 600 reporters (mostly American and British) covered the war from positions with the troops.[6] Many journalists appreciated the access afforded through embedding, especially those from smaller media outlets that might not have had access otherwise (Katovsky and Carlson 2003). Some did suggest that their stories were shaped by the camaraderie they developed with soldiers in the field. Overall, the use of embedded journalists focused coverage on the everyday experiences of soldiers. Critics of embedding argued that journalists lost objectivity and could not focus on the forest for the trees.

A sample of NBC news coverage supports these other analyses, and again shows that the coverage goes beyond what political officials say to focus on patriotic images and society—at least in the sample covered here from 2003 and 2004.[7] For example, on March 21, 2003, one day after President Bush's speech on the commencement of the war, one set of stories focused on the military campaign (relying on official sources), one story dealt with the first military casualties and showed their families at home, and one story focused on the home front. This story began with the statement that all in the United States were unified by concern for U.S. troops involved and then said that "American patriotism is on display." In almost every town, the reporter says, there are flags and yellow ribbons. Antiwar protesters are mentioned, but the story says that they are "drowned out by drumbeats of support" and "patriotism has become a for-us or against-us debate." There is even coverage of the canceling of the red carpet entrances at the Academy Awards because there is fear that actors will speak against the war. This highlights the fact that there was contestation over the narratives of war, and there were attempts to curtail the ability of opponents to project their narratives.

Reception

If we turn to the audience, we see that a substantial majority of the American public and political elites supported intervention in Iraq in 2003. In October 2002, the House of Representatives and the Senate approved resolutions that gave the president authority to use means that he deemed appropriate. Pew Center polls showed that around 70 percent of those polled supported the military intervention.[8] In 2003, 69 percent of respondents in a Pew Research Center poll of the United States said that they displayed the flag at their home, office, or on their car. Support continued into 2005 when public support eroded and congressional critics grew more outspoken. The success promised by the administration was contradicted by continued violence.[9]

Focus group data collected after the 2004 presidential election show the degree to which a great power narrative shaped many Americans' discussion of international relations. The focus group data suggest that great power narratives resonated with many people, and surprisingly this was true even of those that identified great power narratives as problematic and those that were opposed to the Iraq War or President Bush, or both.

Among focus group members, there was clearly an understanding of the issues associated with media coverage of the war. Many participants recognized that the media were America-centric and often relied on government officials for information and news. Some even bemoaned the fact that international perspectives were difficult to find in the American media and said that they turned to the BBC or other outlets for a broader perspective. Participants also suggested that they understood that they received a particular view of the Iraq War and that if they relied on non-American media, they would get a different view.

Still, participants quite frequently spoke using terms to describe the United States that suggested that great power status was accepted: "our wonderful country," "the best in the world," "the richest," "the strongest," "proud of our strength," "we're the biggest country in the world," among others. As one woman says, "So much of the world, I think, hates the U.S. because we are so powerful and wealthy and have everything." Or another man:

> I think that as long as we're the international superpower if we want to . . . we always have to have the most power to feel safe and as long as we do that we're going to be making enemies because it's human nature to want to be the best.

Here we see a paradox in the description of insecurity in the United States after 9/11 even as the country is depicted as the most powerful in the world. In addition the speaker feels part of the nation, using "we" to describe the actions of the country.

And U.S. leadership is often lauded by those in the focus groups, even by those who did not support President Bush's reelection bid. Many referred to the president as the leader of the free world and suggested that Americans would not abide being "pushed around." One man said, "I think the United States is different as a nation-state. I think the United States entrenches when you start trying to do something like that to us [threaten us]."

Some of the participants even directly addressed the issue of patriotism in the United States. After looking at campaign ads from President Bush and Democratic presidential candidate John Kerry, for example, participants agreed with one man who said this is what he noticed: "I think the use of the flag, nationalism, stoking the fires of nationalism, you know wave the flag, 'hey everybody rally around old glory.' . . . I mean they all did it." Another woman replied to a question about the media and the showing of flag-draped coffins with this response:

> When you look at rows and rows and rows of it [flag-draped coffins] at airport auditoriums and Arlington [military cemetery], it's a reverence. It makes it real that each is a body. Some mother and father . . . each one is an individual heartache. But it gives an allegiance when you feel the country is looking at them and makes awareness of the sacrifice. I'm a flag lady. I think it's reverence [flag-draped coffins].

The focus groups, then, suggest that Americans recognize that media coverage has a perspective shaped by the political leadership, but most do not realize how much U.S. great power narratives pervade their own view of the world.

Taken together, one can see not a linear relationship from political leadership to media to audience, but an overlapping of beliefs about the appropriate role of the state in the international system. These pieces fit together and are often mutually reinforcing. Add to this a heightened level of fear in the society at large and a great power narrative can serve as a comfort to many individuals.[10] Thus, President George W. Bush's system narrative resonated with great power narratives associated with identity narratives and seemed to fit with war policy narratives in a way that the system narrative of his father did not. The war, in fact, reinforced and helped (re)construct great power narratives and a system narrative that stressed unilateral action. Even when, eventually (2005–6), the majority of the public turned against the Second Iraq War, the great power narrative survived. Turning to the Russia case, a similar pattern is evident.

Russia

The demise of the Soviet Union in December 1991 brought on a complex and difficult economic and political reconstruction, but most important for the world, and arguably most interesting, is that it was also relatively peaceful. Chechnya was one of a few notable exceptions. It is important to acknowledge at the outset that Chechnya is a different case from Iraq for many reasons, not the least of which is that Chechnya is found within the boundaries of the Russian Federation. This war then is not interstate, but technically intrastate, in nature. This raises an additional set of issues and suggests that one might expect a strong narrative aimed at the territorial integrity of the Russian state. However, the dissolution of the Soviet Union also created a context in which state symbols were being negotiated or were relatively new.

The First Chechen War

Formation

In the early 1990s Chechen separatists demanded an independent state and the Russian Federation resisted. In November 1994 the Russian military offensive that became known as the First Chechen War began. In spite of President Boris Yeltsin's prediction that the war would end quickly, the Russian military did not regain control of Chechnya, and a peace agreement was not signed until August 31, 1996. In the following few years, various factions, including Islamic fundamentalist groups, fought for influence and power, and made continued demands for independence from Russia. Levels of violence increased and in October 1999 the Russian military took action again, and began what is called the Second Chechen War.

At the beginning of the First Chechen War, President Yeltsin presided over the newly formed Russian Federation. Not only had its precursor, the Soviet Union, ceased to exist (on December 25, 1991), but the constituent republics of the USSR had become independent states in their own right. The Russian Federation was engaged in a process of state-building and a contestation over system and identity narratives (English 2000; Mankoff 2009, 21). Bennett (1999), for example, argues that competing groups held competing perspectives on identity in Russia. Liberals focused their narratives on Russia as a part of Europe and the West, and did not favor the use of force in the near abroad (i.e., the countries of the former Soviet Union). Pragmatists wanted good relations with Europe but also were willing to use force as a last resort. Nationalists asserted a narrative of Russian dominance in the region and stressed cultural issues as central (Bennett, 306–9). Thus there were competing system narratives that emphasized different roles for the Russian Federation in the international system. Narrative contestation took place within the context of and was affected by Chechnya.

Yeltsin ruled out force in Chechnya as late as October 1994 (Bennett 1999, 331), but there was a shift in the following months. While moving closer to a nationalist position and narrative, Yeltsin can be seen more accurately as a pragmatist. When he did defend the invasion in February 1995, Yeltsin focused on the effect of lawlessness on Russia, not Russian nationalism:

> Such blisters like the Medellin cartel in Colombia, the Golden Triangle in southeast Asia and the criminal dictatorship in Chechnya do not disappear by themselves. . . . To preserve its sovereignty and integrity the state can and must use the force of power.[11]

Yeltsin internationalized events in Chechnya, and invited consideration of what kind of order could allow these equivalent problems to be addressed. Here an order of cooperation is implied. In addition, Yeltsin's narrative stressed the fact that it was the criminal behavior in Chechnya that made the situation unacceptable for Russia, and that the Constitution and the state had to be protected. This emphasis on the rule of law and the Constitution can be found in a number of Yeltsin's speeches, and fits squarely with Yeltsin's "state of the federation" speech in February with its narrative that emphasized the cooperation of Russia and the West.

Many scholars note that in the early 1990s, important political elites "led by Boris Yeltsin, Yegor Gaidar, and Andrei Kozyrev resoundingly embraced a Western and liberal internationalist self-image [narrative] of Russia" (Clunan 2009, 54). This narrative was heavily contested. For example, Clunan notes that the public regretted the collapse of the Soviet Union more than political elites did (54–55). This suggests that narratives that emphasize cooperation with the West might not resonate with the public if this cooperation is perceived as weakness. Over time this is what happened.

Projection

A leader's projection of narratives is affected by the structure of media within a country as well as the content of the narratives themselves. After the fall of the Soviet Union, Russian media were restructured in the midst of economic and political transformation. At first new publications, and radio and television channels, proliferated. By early 1993, however, no longer supported by state subsidies, it was increasingly difficult for media outlets, particularly newspapers, to compete for readers. Some television channels remained state-owned or controlled, as was the first channel, Ostankino, or then renamed ORT, for Russian Public Television (in 1994). Others were privately owned, including NTV (founded in 1993). The range of programming on these channels increased greatly as Western television programming was introduced alongside Russian programs. In the early 1990s many journalists and scholars looked forward to the development of the media as a fourth estate, able to serve as a watchdog for democratic development. Yet, even as journalists debated and explored their role in the new system, the power of television was not lost on political and economic elites (oligarchs), and the coverage of important events was followed closely by leaders (Mickiewicz 1999). During the early 1990s, political leaders could certainly guide coverage, but some channels and some journalists were able to present stories and views that did not conform to the government's narrative.

Even so, one must look not only at structure, but at the content of coverage as well to see how successful the political leadership was in projecting its narrative. Mickiewicz notes that coverage on Channel One's *Vremya* news program emphasized the importance of a unified Russia and the dangers of separatism (Mickiewicz 1999, 252–54). A content analysis of Ostankino television coverage of the Russian use of military force in Chechnya during the first week found the following arguments for military force covered: to settle political issues (6 occurrences); to save constitutional processes (13); to eradicate criminal activity (9); to help/save Chechen citizens (10); to prepare for democratic elections (7); to preserve Russian strength (2); the will of Russia (1) (Zhurnalistika i Voina 1995, 45, table 40). For the most part Russian actions were legitimized as important to the development of constitutional processes and to quell crime in the region. It was not presented as a means to preserve Russian strength or as a nationalist war against non-Russians. This closely mirrors the descriptions made by political leaders.

Still, the political leaders were not satisfied with the coverage of the Chechen War and the primary reason was the coverage of the conflict on NTV—independent television. When the conflict began, Yeltsin and his government attempted to limit information about the conflict, claiming that the military was engaged only in "pinpoint" bombing and emphasizing the cruelty of Chechen rebels. Moreover, the government's narrative included the story that rebels were destabilizing a part of the Russian Federation. The government narrative stressed battlefield successes even as the troops became bogged down. The government did have a significant amount of control over Channel One (Ostankino), and its coverage reflected the government's description of the battles (Mickiewicz 1999). But Ostankino was only one channel.

On the first day of the war, NTV had four crews on the ground in Chechnya (Mereu and Saradzhyan 2005). NTV's coverage of the war went beyond the limited governmental statements, as reporters covered battlefield atrocities, death, and destruction, and proved that "pinpoint" bombing claims were false (Mickiewicz 1999; Malinkina and McLeod 2002). One strategy that certainly failed was the Russian leadership's attempt to curtail coverage by denying journalists access to Russian soldiers. Journalists at NTV turned to Chechen fighters for news and information about the war. In addition, Russian politicians and the military viewed journalists as enemies, hardly helping to facilitate favorable coverage. NTV's president, Igor Malashenko, recognizing the new prerogatives of the media, "reminded the government that Chechnya was not Afghanistan" (Mickiewicz 1999, 10). His implication was that the government could no longer control the narrative about the conflict, and reflected the belief held by many journalists working in commercial television that glasnost or openness in coverage should be the new professional norm for journalists. So while the media certainly covered the political leader's narrative about the conflict, NTV showed that what the government claimed to be true about the execution of the war was often simply not true.

Reception

Russian political leaders miscalculated the time it would take to stabilize the situation in Chechnya, and public opinion was consistently hostile to the war effort, with between 58 and 63 percent of poll respondents opposed to the war (Mickiewicz 1999, 256–57). One reason was that television showed the inconsistencies in Russian reports about the war, and showed the destruction and bloodshed.[12] Government credibility was questioned as television exposed divisions in elite and public opinion. In a public opinion survey taken in January 1995, respondents were asked, "What do you think? How should a real patriot of Russia regard the operation in Chechnya?" Fifty-two percent said a real patriot should speak out against the operation, while only 19 percent said a real patriot should support the operation (Mickiewicz 1999, 255).

This illustrates a much more fundamental point about narratives during transition. During this time, the Russian identity narrative was in a state of flux. It may be true that the political leadership was concerned about Russian international prestige and influence as support for negotiations in Chechnya shifted to support for the use of force (Bennett 1999, 295–347); but there was also a faction within the political elite and a large percentage of the general public whose narratives emphasized that Russia was now a "normal" country in Europe, and focused on negotiations and the process of building democracy. For example, in 1996 only 29 percent of polled respondents said that Russia should have a great and powerful army by any means possible (Petrova 2000). Some of the strongest criticism of intervention in Chechnya came from within the Russian military, and especially from veterans of the Afghan conflict (Bennett 1999, 339), although this would change in later years. In 1996 a settlement was reached that would end the active conflict until it reignited in 1999 under Yeltsin and his successor, Vladimir Putin. Under Putin the narrative emphasizing Russia as a "normal" country in Europe would shift to focus on the great power status of the Russian Federation.

The Second Chechen War

Formation

The Second Chechen War began in the later months of 1999, just before Vladimir Putin was appointed by Yeltsin as president. Putin would be elected to that post in March 2000. Yeltsin's narrative of the conflict in November 1999 was similar to that which he had used during the first war. For example, in a speech to the summit of the Organization for Security and Co-operation in Europe in Istanbul, Yeltsin said:

> You have no right to criticise Russia over Chechnya.
> A total of 1,580 people, the civilian population, suffered as a result of the bloody wave of terrorist acts that swept over Moscow and other towns and villages of our country.
> The pain of this tragedy was felt by thousands of families in all corners of Russia. In the past three years, terrorists kidnapped 935 hostages—not just Russians, but Britons, Americans, Frenchmen.
> Some 200 captives are still being held by bandits, and they are

being subjected to terrible torture—one simply cannot remain indifferent.

A sense of proportion and humanitarian action are not issues for terrorists.

Their aim is that of killing and destroying.[13]

Again, Yeltsin is legitimizing military action by arguing that terrorist activity compels Russia to action, depicting the country as pursuing legal means to deter aggression within the international system as the United States did in the First Iraq War in light of Saddam Hussein's violation of Kuwaiti sovereignty.

Putin would develop a different emphasis in his narrative about Chechnya. Putin's narrative about the place of the Russian Federation increasingly emphasized the great power status of the Russian Federation. Anna Politkovskaya, a journalist who covered the Chechen War extensively, and was murdered in Moscow, wrote: "Chechnya provides the yeast for the growth of the great-power mentality, the basis of Putin's state morality" (2001a). Andrei Tsygankov said that Putin saw Russia as a normal great power.[14] This phrase is especially appropriate because it underscores the connection of those two narratives, which are often portrayed as mutually exclusive or competitive in nature. To be a "normal" state in the Russian language and context has a weight that is not adequately translated into English. It implies that Russia will be a part of the community of nations, breaking with the Soviet ideology of two separate systems. It also implies that Russia will take its "proper" role or place in the system as a great power.

For example, in Putin's November 2000 speech to top commanders of the Russian armed forces, Putin said that "everyone must know that no one will be allowed to resolve issues with Russia from a position of strength."[15] In addition, however, Putin also disputed that notion that Russia was lapsing into "imperial policies," saying, "What matters is that this territory must never be used by anyone as a bridgehead for attacking the Russian Federation." Putin, on a number of occasions, suggested that the First Chechen War had been handled poorly, at the cost of national humiliation. His rationale for conducting the second war included the need to protect the Russian Federation from attacks emanating from Chechnya.

By 2002, Putin's narrative emphasized the normalization of the situation in Chechnya (Kramer 2005). In February 2002, for example, he suggested that there was a "serious stabilization" in Chechnya (Putin 2002a). Still, he stressed the importance of maintaining the Russian state: "We are referring not only to the fight against separatism or to a local conflict in a region of the Russian Federation. The fight against extremism and terrorism is today a fight for the preservation of the Russian state. This is what is at stake" (Putin 2002b). Putin also noted that he was referring to all nationalities within the Russian Federation when he called for support and suggested that terrorists wanted to foment anti-Chechen sentiment in Russia to destabilize the country.

Projection

Putin was highly critical of NTV's coverage of the First Chechen War. This led, in part, to a reassertion of governmental control over the media system. Thomas argues that changes occurred because the Russians had analyzed "their public relations disaster of the first war," studied NATO's press handling in Kosovo, and appointed experienced people to supervise press operations (Thomas, n.d.). More important was the government's challenge to television ownership and threats to journalists if they did not cover the government's story (Politkovskaya 2001b). The leadership's television strategy was to control information, press their description of their opponents as terrorists, and emphasize military success. Rebel bombings (in Moscow, for example) and hostage-taking supported government narratives about terrorism. The government claimed that security would be restored and law and order reasserted.

The inability of the political leaders to control the situation in Chechnya led to calls for restoring order within the destabilized area. The Russian words used here are important. Many Russian citizens will use the terms *narod* (people) or *rodina* (homeland). Sarah Oates suggests that *rodina* implies a positive force, almost maternal in nature, rather than a Western concept of nationalism.[16] This sense of patriotism harkens back to Soviet times, if not to the Soviet system. It was a call to the Motherland that rallied citizens during World War II, for example.

Access to the battlefield during the Second Chechen War was extremely restricted, and journalists had to obtain special credentials and stay in certain regions. The military refused to take NTV journalists to the front, but did allow correspondents from other media outlets to go. "Censorship is now the rule of the game in Chechnya," said Oleg Panfilov, head of the Center for Journalism in Extreme Situations. "The republic is an isolated territory. We do not get any information from there. Comparing our press now to what it was during the first war would be like comparing the European press to the North Korean press" (Mereu and Saradzhyan 2005). Government spokesmen had specific rules on how to present the war, including calling the opposition "terrorists" and citing the bravery of the great Russian army and its solders. These specific directives are certainly reminiscent of Soviet ways.

The content of the coverage highlights the state narrative about terrorism. Stories about Chechnya during this period refer to "terrorist" bombings that occurred in 1999 and especially apartment bombings in Moscow. By 2001, the Russian media depicted "Chechnya as 'returning to normal,' and the ongoing military campaign as having no alternative" (Weir 2004). According to governmental guidelines, media were to avoid mentioning Chechnya and "setbacks should continue to be referred to as events 'in the context of international terrorism'" (cited in Kramer 2005, 5–6n11). Thus, the introduction by the United States of "the War on Terror" was picked up in the Russian narrative as well.

Oates's analysis of television coverage during the 2003 parliamentary elections notes the significant differences across the state-run Channel One with its nightly newscast Vremya and the commercial station NTV with the newscast *Sevodnya*.[17] The state-run channel focused attention on "the efficacy of President Putin; the prominence of top leaders of the pro-government United Russia party and their close political relationship with the president; how the central government fixes problems in the region; and Russia's role in the international sphere" (Oates 2006c). NTV had more stories about Chechnya, but they were more in accord with the official narrative (Belin 2002).

Reception

By 2000 there was a change in the mood of the Russian people about Chechnya and Russian identity.[18] In January 2000, a Russia-wide poll showed that 67 percent of respondents approved of military actions by Russian forces in Chechnya (Petrova 2001). Between 1996 and 2000, those who supported having a great and powerful army by any means increased from 29 percent to 49 percent ("We Are Peace-Lovers" 2002). In addition, the percentage of respondents who felt that there was an enemy "out there" rose from 44 percent in August 1997 to 73 percent in April 1999 (Petrova 2000). The indecisive outcome in Chechnya in 1996, combined with almost a decade of economic and political upheaval, increased the public's desire for stability and order. Many Russian felt a resonance with the great power identity of the past.

Focus group data from March and April 2004 allow an analysis of how great power narratives resonated with groups of Russian.[19] First, it is interesting to look at the responses to questions about which media people preferred. In many cases it was the state-owned channel that was preferred. Some of the participants said that this was because people understood it to represent the government position clearly. In regard to coverage of Chechnya on television, some participants in the focus group felt that there was not much coverage of it anymore on television. Others said that the coverage was only about progress.

Using strength to combat chaos was emphasized by many of the participants in the focus groups. Some harkened back to Soviet days: "we had a powerful government when the Soviet Union existed." Some suggested that under Soviet leadership there were not problems with terrorism such as that emanating from Chechnya. One woman said that under Soviet rule, when she was in school, all sat together and all were friends: "Who was Tartar, who was who. We didn't know. But now we always know." Others stressed the need for Russia to reassert its power, especially in Chechnya. And some even referred to the actions of the United States and the need for the Russian Federation to react: "We have a weak government. If you talk about politics, about the war on terrorism for the last 4 years . . . [t]he Americans went into Central Asia, the Americans went into Afghanistan, in the countries of the Baltics next to us they fly F-16s. . . . the mass media on this are very superficial. They need to shout about that."

Overall, then, in the Russian case of Chechnya, leaders and the public use narratives about the place of Russia in the world and the need to reestablish a great power position to justify the use of force in Chechnya. Leaders took the lesson of the First Chechen War to be that a freer press was dangerous, and they moved to constrain journalists and control information more concretely in the second war. The public, meanwhile, showed considerable support for what they perceived to be the security and order associated with strong leadership. This has resonated with a new Russian great power narrative that emphasizes security and strength. In addition, the Russian public has been quite cynical about an "independent" media, and journalists' professionalism is in serious jeopardy (Oates 2006a).

Conclusions

This chapter shows that the use of force by the United States and Russia contributed significantly to the development of renewed great power narratives. In the early 1990s President H. W. Bush set out a system narrative that described a new world order characterized by greater international cooperation and shared interests. The Second Iraq War (2003–11) is marked by a significant increase in the use of great power narratives used to legitimize a preemptive and unilateral use of force. This narrative was made more resonant by 9/11. In the Russian case of the First Chechen War, leaders, the political elite, and the public perceived their own state as joining the "normal" states of Europe. This social identification as a state within a European community provided the context for messages about the first war. This narrative shifted, however, in the mid-1990s as the Russian leadership began to question the willingness of Europe, and especially of the United States, to include Russia in a substantive and meaningful way in a European community. A great power narrative also played into enhancing the domestic political power of Vladimir Putin. This shift can be seen in the narratives surrounding the Second Chechen War that emphasized the great power status of Russia and its ability to act unilaterally in Chechnya. In both cases fear of terrorism is used as well as patriotic themes.[20]

One important result of the reemergence of great power identity narratives during the second wars in Iraq and Chechnya is the undermining of new system narratives that emphasize international cooperation and shared interests. This sets the stage for heightened tensions surrounding international issues and attempts by both sides to gain the upper hand as we see in the late 2000s and early 2010s with Iran, the Arab Spring, Syria, and Ukraine. This narrative also continues to play into domestic politics within each country as leaders try not to "look weak." In addition, this may play into the view that Cold War narratives are appropriate for understanding Russian actions in Ukraine, constraining the range of options for foreign policy maneuvers by both sides.

NOTES

Some of this chapter can be found in Laura Roselle, *Media and the Politics of Failure* (New York: Palgrave, 2011), reproduced with permission of Palgrave Macmillan.

1. Much of the analysis of the 1994 and 1995 comes from Khlebnikov (1995). I am deeply appreciative to Sarah Oates at the University of Maryland for working with me

over the years on the analysis of Russian television coverage, including on analysis of 1993 and 1996. I rely extensively on the work of Oates for the 2000 and 2003 data.

2. Focus groups were conducted in the United States in St. Petersburg, Florida; Washington, DC; Columbia, Missouri; and Gainesville, Florida. Focus groups were conducted in Russia in Ulyanovsk and Moscow. British Economic and Social Research Council/New Security Challenges Programme Grant R223250028, *The Framing of Terrorist Threat in U.S. and Russian Elections*, October 2003–October 2005, £44,000. Sarah Oates, principal investigator.

3. On January 12, 1991, Congress had authorized the use of the military to force Iraq out of Kuwait.

4. After the 1991 war a no-strike zone was set up.

5. Casualties passed 1,000 in September 2004, and on October 25, 2005, stood at 2,000.

6. http://www.pbs.org/newshour/bb/media/jan-june03/embeds_04-01.html

7. The sample was restricted to this period to correspond with what themes the focus groups—conducted in November and December 2004—might be aware of.

8. http://www.pbs.org/newshour/bb/middle_east/jan-june03/opinion_3-30.html, accessed October 21, 2005.

9. Although this paper focuses on 2003–4, a growing opposition movement in the United States took to the Internet and the streets, especially after 2004. Questions about the veracity of the governmental rationale for the war, including issues associated with intelligence reports about weapons of mass destruction and the rising casualty rates among American forces, began to undermine the leaders' legitimation strategy.

10. In almost all focus groups one of the most cited political ads of the campaign was a Bush ad about a wolf at the door and being prepared to defend against that wolf. One participant likened this to Reagan's bear ad that implicitly referenced the Cold War.

11. *New York Times*, February 17, 1995.

12. This does not mean that television *caused* the lack of support for the war. As Mickiewicz (1999, 258) writes, "The bloody events of the Chechen war had pushed their moods into greater disorientation."

13. BBC online, http://212.58.226.17:8080/1/hi/world/monitoring/526343.stm

14. Putin's vision of "Russia as a normal great power" is discussed by Andrei P. Tsygankov, "Vladimir Putin's Vision of Russia as a Normal Great Power," *Post-Soviet Affairs* 21, no. 2 (April–June 2005): 132–58.

15. President of Russia, official web portal, www.kremlin.ru

16. Personal correspondence with author, February 2007.

17. Oates analyzed coverage on *Vremya* (9 p.m. weekday edition) and *Sevodnya* (7 p.m. weekday edition) from November 7 through December 5, 2003.

18. The tie between strict controls over media and Russian opinions on the war in Chechnya are discussed in Theodore P. Gerber and Sarah E. Mendelson. "Russian Public Opinion on Human Rights and the War in Chechnya," *Post-Soviet Affairs* 18, no. 4 (2004): 298–99.

19. This is part of the project cited above for the American case.

20. It is important to note that this is not the case in the United Kingdom, for example (Oates 2006b).

REFERENCES

Aday, Sean, Steven Livingston, and Maeve Hebert. "Embedding the Truth: A Cross-Cultural Analysis of Objectivity and Television Coverage of the Iraq War." *Harvard International Journal of Press/Politics* 10, no. 1 (2005): 3–21.

Altheide, David L. *Terrorism and the Politics of Fear*. Lanham, MD: Rowman and Littlefield, 2006.

Belin, Laura. "Russian Media Policy in the First and Second Chechen Campaigns." *Journal of Slavic Military Studies* 13, no. 4 (2000): 57–83.

Belin, Laura. "Russian Media Policy in the First and Second Chechen Campaigns." Paper prepared for presentation at the Political Studies Association, Aberdeen, Scotland, April 5–8, 2002.

Bennett, Andrew. *Condemned to Repetition? The Rise, Fall, and Reprise of Soviet-Russian Military Interventionism, 1973–1996*. Cambridge, MA: MIT Press, 1999.

Bush, George H. W. "Address to the Nation Announcing Allied Military Action in the Persian Gulf." January 16, 1991. http://www.presidency.ucsb.edu/ws/index.php?pid=19222&st=&st1=

Bush, George H. W. "George Bush: Address to the American People." In *The Iraq Wars and the War on Terror and Index*, edited by Brooke Barnett, 26. Greenwood Library of American War Reporting, vol. 8. Westport, CT: Greenwood, 2005.

Bush, George H. W., and Brent Scowcroft. *A World Transformed*. New York: Alfred A. Knopf, 1998.

Clunan, Anne L. *The Social Construction of Russia's Resurgence: Aspirations, Identity, and Security Interests*. Baltimore: Johns Hopkins University Press, 2009.

English, Robert D. *Russia and the Idea of the West*. New York: Columbia University Press, 2000.

Entman, Robert M. "Cascading Activation: Contesting the White House's Frame after 9/11." *Political Communication* 20, no. 4 (2003): 415–32.

Entman, Robert. *Projections of Power: Framing News, Public Opinion, and U.S. Foreign Policy*. Chicago: University of Chicago Press, 2004.

Entman, Robert M., Steven Livingston, and Jennie Kim. "Doomed to Repeat: Iraq News, 2002–2007." *American Behavioral Scientist* 52, no. 5 (2009): 689–708.

George, Alexander. "Domestic Constraints on Regime Change in U.S. Foreign Policy: The Need for Policy Legitimacy." In *American Foreign Policy: Theoretical Essays*, edited by G. John Ikenberry, 583–608. Glenview, IL: Scott, Foresman.

Groeling, Tim, and Matthew Baum. "Resetting the Index: Media Bias and Elite Foreign Policy Evaluations 1979–2003." Paper presented at the Annual Meeting of the American Political Science Association, Washington, DC, August 31–September 3, 2005.

Hirsh, Michael. "Bush and the World." *Foreign Affairs* 81 (2002): 17–43.

Hoskins, Andrew. *Televising War: From Vietnam to Iraq*. London: A&C Black, 2004.

Hoskins, Andrew, and Ben O'Loughlin. *War and Media*. Cambridge: Polity, 2010.

Katovsky, Bill, and Timothy Carlson. *Embedded: The Media at War in Iraq*. Guilford, CT: Lyons Press, 2003.

Kemmelmeier, Markus, and David G. Winter. "Sowing Patriotism, But Reaping Nationalism? Consequences of Exposure to the American Flag." *Political Psychology* 29, no. 6 (2008): 859–79.

Khlebnikov, Petr. "Zhurnalistika i voĭna: Osveshchenie rossiĭskimi SMI voennykh deĭstviĭ v Chechne." Redaktor A.G. Rikhter. Moscow: Issledovatel'skaiâ gruppa Rossiĭsko-Amerikanskogo Informatŝionnogo Press-Center, 1995. See http://classic.iucat.iu.edu/uhtbin/cgisirsi/?ps=FYr1LpPKHB/B-WELLS/326992108/5/0

Kohut, Andrew, and Robert C. Toth. "Arms and the People." *Foreign Affairs* 73, no. 6 (November/December 1994): 47–61.

Kolmer, Christian, and Holli A. Semetko. "Framing the Iraq War: Perspectives from American, U.K., Czech, German, South African, and Al-Jazeera News." *American Behavioral Scientist* 52, no. 5 (2009): 643–56.

Koltsova, Elena. "Change in the Coverage of the Chechen Wars: Reasons and Consequences." *Javnost–the Public* 7, no. 3 (2000): 39–54.

Kramer, Mark. "The Domestic Political Context of Russia's War in Chechnya." Paper presented at the Conference on Post-Soviet In/Securities: Theory and Practice, Mershon Center, Ohio State University, October 7, 2005.

Luther, Catherine A., and M. Mark Miller. "Framing of the 2003 US-Iraq War Demonstrations: An Analysis of News and Partisan Texts." *Journalism & Mass Communication Quarterly* 82, no. 1 (2005): 78–96.

Malinkina, Olga V., and Douglas M. McLeod. "The Russian Media Role in the Conflicts in Afghanistan and Chechnya: A Case Study of Media Coverage by Izvestia." In *Media and Conflict: Framing Issues and Making Policy Shaping Opinions*, ed. Eytan Gilboa, 213–36. Ardsley, NY: Transnational Publishers, 2002.

Mankoff, Jeffrey. *Russian Foreign Policy: The Return of Great Power Politics*. Lanham, MD: Rowman and Littlefield, 2009.

Mereu, Francesca, and Simon Saradzhyan. "Smokescreen Around Chechnya." *Moscow Times*, March 18, 2005. Accessed June 20, 2016, via http://faculty.maxwell.syr.edu/rdenever/PPA-730-27/Mereu%20and%20Saradzhyan.pdf

Mickiewicz, Ellen Propper. *Changing Channels: Television and the Struggle for Power in Russia*. Durham, NC: Duke University Press, 1999.

Mickiewicz, Ellen. *Television, Power, and the Public in Russia*. Cambridge: Cambridge University Press, 2008.

Miskimmon, Alister, Ben O'Loughlin, and Laura Roselle. *Strategic Narratives: Communication Power and the New World Order*. London: Routledge, 2013.

Oates, Sarah. *Television, Democracy and Elections in Russia*. London: Routledge, 2006a.

Oates, Sarah. "Comparing the Politics of Fear: The Role of Terrorism News in Election Campaigns in Russia, the United States and Britain." *International Relations* 20, no. 4 (2006b): 425–37.

Oates, Sarah. "Through a Lens Darkly? Russian Television and Terrorism Coverage in Comparative Perspective." Paper prepared for The Mass Media in Post-Soviet Russia International Conference, University of Surrey, 2006c.

Oates, Sarah, and Monica Postelnicu. "Citizen or Comrade? Terrorist Threat in Election Campaigns in Russia and the US." Paper prepared for presentation at the Annual Meeting of the American Political Science Association, Washington, DC, August 31–September 3, 2005.

Oates, Sarah, and Laura Roselle. "Russian Television's Mixed Messages: Parties, Candidates and Control on Vremya, 1995–1996." Paper presented at the Annual Meeting of the American Political Science Association, Washington, DC, 1997.

Oates, Sarah, and Laura Roselle. "Russian Elections and TV News: Comparison of Campaign News on State-Controlled and Commercial Television Channels." *Harvard International Journal of Press/Politics* 5, no. 2 (Spring (2000): 30–51.

Paletz, David L. "Just Desserts?" In *Taken by Storm: The Media, Public Opinion, and U.S. Foreign Policy in the Gulf War*, edited by W. Lance Bennett and David L. Paletz, 277–92. Chicago: University of Chicago Press, 1994.

Pan, Zhongdang, and Gerald Kosicki. "Framing as a Strategic Action in Public Deliberation." In *Framing Public Life: Perspectives on Media and Our Understanding of the Social World*, edited by Stephen D. Reese, Oscar H. Gandy Jr., and August E. Grant, 35–65. Mahwah, NJ: Lawrence Erlbaum, 2001.

Petrova, A. "A Great and Powerful Army—by Any Means Necessary." *Public Opinion Foundation Database*, August 24, 2000. http://bd.english.fom.ru/report/cat/societas/rus_im/Great_Power/eof003401

Petrova, A. "Attitudes towards Military Actions in Chechnya Are Changing." *The Public Opinion Foundation, Russia-wide Poll of Urban and Rural Populations. January 15 and July 8, 2000; January 27 and June 9, 2001*, June 14, 2001. Accessed July 1, 2002. http://bd.english.fom.ru/report/cat/societas/Chechnya/truck_war/eof012102

Politkovskaya, Anna. *A Dirty War: A Russian Reporter in Chechnya*. London: Harvill Press, 2001a.

Politkovskaya, Anna. "Remember Chechnya." *Washington Post*, November 14, 2001. *Johnson's Russia List*, 2001b. Accessed November 15, 2001. http://www.cdi.org/russia/johnson/5545-6.cfm

Putin, Vladimir. "Introductory Remarks at a Security Council Meeting on the Situation in Chechen Republic." February 27, 2002a. www.kremlin.ru

Putin, Vladimir. "Opening Remarks at a Meeting with Representatives of the Chechen Republic." November 10, 2002b. www.kremlin.ru

Roselle, Laura. *Media and the Politics of Failure: Great Powers, Communication Strategies, and Military Defeats*. New York: Palgrave Macmillan, 2006.

Schatz, Robert T., and Howard Lavine. "Waving the Flag: National Symbolism, Social Identity, and Political Engagement." *Political Psychology* 28, no. 3 (2007): 329–55.

Secunda, Eugene, and Terence P. Moran. *Selling War to America from the Spanish American War to the Global War on Terror*. Westport, CT: Praeger Security International, 2007.

Shlapentokh, Dmitry. "The Illusions and Realities of Russian Nationalism." *Washington Quarterly* 23, no. 1 (1999): 173–86.

Skitka, Linda A. "Patriotism or Nationalism? Understanding Post-September 11, 2001, Flag-Display Behavior." *Journal of Applied Social Psychology* 35, no. 10 (2005): 1995–2011.

Thomas, Timothy L. "Manipulating the Mass Consciousness: Russian and Chechen 'Information War' Tactics in the 2nd Chechen-Russian Conflict." *Foreign Military Studies Office Publications*. N.d. http://fmso.leavenworth.army.mil/documents/chechiw.htm

Tumber, Howard, and Jerry Palmer. *Media at War: The Iraq Crisis*. London: Sage, 2004.
Ware, Robert Bruce. "Will Southern Russian Studies Go the Way of Sovietology?" *Journal of Slavic Military Studies* 16, no. 4 (2003). http://www.siue.edu/~rware/Chech_Review_A4.pdf
"We Are Peace-Lovers and They Want a War." *Public Opinion Foundation Database*. September 2002. http://bd.english.fom.ru/report/cat/societas/rus_im/Great_Power/ed021832
Weir, Fred. "Quietly, Tide of Opinion Turns on Chechen War." *Christian Science Monitor*, November 17, 2004. http://www.csmonitor.com/2004/1117/p04s01-woeu.html

4 | Finding a Unified Voice?

The European Union through a Strategic Narrative Lens

Alister Miskimmon

> In telling the story of our becoming, as an individual, a nation, a people, we establish who we are. Narratives may be employed strategically to strengthen a collective identity but they also may precede and make possible the development of a coherent community, nation, or collective actor.
> —Francesca Polletta

This volume argues that analyzing strategic narratives in international affairs is central to our understanding of the forces that shape the world today. This chapter assesses how international organizations construct and deploy an effective strategic narrative—in this case, the European Union. The EU has relied on a strategic narrative from its inception to the present day. The EU has tried to use this narrative to build support within Europe for deeper integration and sought to forge influence internationally. Over the years this narrative has shifted from a grand strategic vision of the people of Europe—working together across national boundaries for the collective interest to avoid war—to a narrative of strategic calculation in the post–Cold War period, culminating in the debates surrounding the Eurozone crisis. The formation, projection, and reception of the EU strategic narrative is complicated by the hybrid nature of the institution—reflecting both supranational and intergovernmental aspects, which frustrates efforts to speak with a single European voice in international affairs. This chapter argues that despite significant integrative steps since the end of the Cold War, the EU still struggles to offer a coherent narrative—both internally and externally, thus potentially hampering the EU's strategic impact. In addition, we argue that the asymmetric impacts of the global financial crisis, coupled with the persistent diversity of domestic and foreign policies of member states, remain impediments to the EU's ability to deploy an effective strategic narrative. This chapter argues that the EU struggles to project an effective strategic narrative because it struggles to communicate in areas where existing narratives have already taken hold.

The EU is inextricably linked with a strategic narrative, primarily aimed at bringing European states together in a cooperative project and to project a collective voice. Studying the EU as an international actor comes up against a number of persistent questions: What kind of actor is the EU? Is the EU a state in the making or a sui generis phenomenon? What is the EU's role in the world—is it an emerging power that should assume the traditional traits of great powers? What are the main aspects of the EU's external relations and how does the development of the EU's foreign and security policy relate to its constituent parts—that is, the 28 member states? The European Union faces significant challenges in projecting a strategic narrative due to the continued centrality of member states as the main foreign policy actors. This is reinforced by a limited Europeanization of foreign policy,[1] an area in which cooperation is largely voluntary, rather than legally enforceable, as in the communitarized aspects of the EU.

The EU's structure and inner workings have often made it very difficult to maintain and deploy a consistent narrative, which has been laid bare with the Eurozone crisis. There have been a number of ways in which scholars have sought to conceptualize the EU as an international actor. These conceptions have often been intimately linked with normative claims about what type of actor the European Union is. François Duchene's conception of the European Community's civilian power status suggested that in the highly charged atmosphere of the Cold War, that the European Community's lack of military capability offered it a chance to be a new type of international player (Duchene 1972, 1973).[2] This tradition of asserting the EU's distinctiveness in how it exercises power and influence in the world has been continued in the work of Ian Manners in his conception of the EU as a normative power (Manners 2002, 2006; see also Diez 2005). Manners appreciates that this conception of the EU is mired is myth and lore:

> [T]he normative power myth functions as a narrative about the EU's puny size and capabilities at the end of the cold war, and how

> these were gradually enlarged and strengthened throughout the 1990s.... the normative power myth performs an important role in the make-up of the EU as a global actor seeking to transform itself in anticipation of the more complex, increasingly globalized, 21st century. (Manners 2010, 77)

These attempts to selectively narrate both Europe's past and its current status are at the heart of the EU's efforts to position itself in international affairs. However, the difficulty of normative power as a concept is in charting its effects. Further contributions to debates concerning Europe's narrative include Aggestam (2008) who argues that the EU is an ethical power. Kaldor, Martin, and Selchow (2007) have called for an EU foreign policy founded on a strategic narrative of human security as a means to gain international influence and reinforce domestic support for EU external affairs. These narratives of the EU's international role rest on a conception of the EU as being a force for good (Nicolaidis and Howse 2002). There is, however, an emerging literature that is more skeptical of these claims and a growing application of realism to understanding EU external action (Rynning 2010; Youngs 2004; Zielonka 2008). Despite this there is still considerable interest in what has been defined as the EU's transformative power—its ability to diffuse norms and practices internationally (Youngs 2005; see also Boerzel and Risse; van Ham 2010).[3] All of these approaches are predicated on the idea that the EU offers a distinct vision of international affairs that is both progressive and inclusive.

Zakaria (2008, xxiv) argues that "Global Power is, above all, dominance over ideas, agendas and models." This is complicated by that fact that emerging powers in the international community are dissecting the narratives, arguments, and assumptions of the West and countering them with a different view of the world (35). The EU's interests and values are likely to be challenged, particularly in light of the crisis in the Eurozone, the poor image that the protracted treaty revision negotiations of the 2000s displayed, and the EU's inability to position itself as a key player in shaping global order (Walker 2010). In 2008 the EU's Council of Ministers declared, "To ensure our security and meet the expectation of our citizens, we must be ready to shape events. That means becoming more strategic in our thinking and more effective and visible around the world" (Council of Ministers 2008). The EU has accepted the necessity to present a more unified and strategic vision of foreign policy, but the implementation of this has yet to be fundamentally addressed.

The EU has sought to narrate its own emergence as an international actor along a number of lines. First, that the EU is a "force for good" in the world, having learned the lesson of a bloody European past. According to this narrative, this bloody past, overcome by the integration of states around a common set of goals, sets it apart as a different type of actor. The overcoming of its internal divisions prepares it well for diverse challenges at the international level. Second, the EU's success has made it inherently attractive to others. Ian Manners's idea of normative power Europe suggests an actor possessing enormous soft power, securing influence through the power of attraction. Peter van Ham's stress on social power fits neatly with the narrative of the EU as an emerging actor on the world stage. The work of Natalia Chaban, Ole Elgström, and Martin Holland suggests that such narratives of European integration and the EU as an international actor are perceived in many different ways by actors outside of Europe—and not as always intended by EU members (Chaban et al. 2013; Chaban and Elström 2014; Chaban and Holland 2008; Chaban and Magdalina 2014). The EU faces a dilemma around how it can communicate its identity, its role in the world, how it understands the emerging international order, and how it narrates emerging policy challenges both within the EU and further afield. Inevitably, the EU's attempts to narrate its identity, how it views the international order, and how it addresses policy developments comes up against entrenched narratives, emanating primarily from the EU's member states. The EU's narrative of an emerging cosmopolitan supranationalism fits uneasily with views of citizenship based on the nation-state. Likewise, the EU's efforts to play a leading role in the shifting international order face counternarratives of the role of existing and emerging great powers shaping the rules of the game. The EU's desire to be considered a new type of international actor comes under pressure to demonstrate influence in the face of powerful nation-states.

Challenges to an EU Strategic Narrative

We define strategic narratives as a means by which political actors attempt to construct a shared meaning of international politics to shape the behavior of domestic and international actors (Miskimmon, O'Loughlin, and Roselle 2013, 2). This is reflected in van Ham's conception of social power, which he argues is the ability to establish norms and rules that other actors can converge around (van Ham 2010). Strategic narratives are, therefore, employed and deployed by actors to pursue their preferences and shape the expectations of third parties.

The European Union recognizes the challenges it faces in forging a strategic narrative. The European External Action Service's (EEAS) 2015 Strategic Review states:

> The very nature of our Union—a construct of intertwined polities—gives us a unique advantage to steer the way in a more complex, but connected, but also more contested world. (EEAS 2015, 1)

This review is a precursor to agreement on a new European Security Strategy in 2016. The first European Security Strategy of 2003 came at a time of deep discord over the decision to invade Iraq, and sought to stake out a set of principles that would guide the emerging Common Security and Defence Policy of the European Union. Its creation forced EU member states not only to more explicitly address its external environment but also to look within, to project a narrative of the EU to the rest of the world. In 2015 the EU faces considerable challenges, necessitating a renewed assessment of its aims and capabilities. The crisis in Ukraine and in relations with Russia, continued instability in the neighborhood, the response to the Eurocrisis, and the concomitant demotion of foreign policy on the agenda of the EU necessitates a rethinking of the EU's foreign and security policy strategy.

In the conclusion of the 2015 Strategic Review the EU makes a bold call for action:

> In a more connected, contested and complex world, we need a clear sense of direction. We need to agree on our priorities, our goals and the means required to achieve them. We must refine the art of orchestration of the polyphony of voices around the table and the panoply of instruments at our disposal. We need a common, comprehensive and consistent EU global strategy. (EEAS 2015, 20)

The theme of polyphony is picked up in Jan Zielonka's 2014 book *Is the EU Doomed?* This musical metaphor is central to Zielonka's argument of how to better organize European integration. He sees increasing danger in a state-centric monophonic approach to integration, which has caused chaos and cacophony, and argues for a polyphonic system of integration founded on "interaction, respect, differentiation and improvisation" as providing a solution to the current impasse (Zielonka 2014, 98). Herein is the nub of the debate—should the EU press on toward ever closer union to overcome what the 2015 strategic review calls the "[v]ertical and horizontal silos [that] hamper the EU's potential global role" (EEAS 2015, 20)? Or should it follow a strategy or embracing coordinated diversity without pressing for a single strategic narrative? Placed in the context of the EU's current challenges, defining the very nature of the problems, let alone the solution and the potential outcome of EU decisions, remain deeply contested. The EU's hybridity throws up competing conceptions of crisis management, reflecting and reinforcing polyphony rather than a clear unified European voice.[4]

Narrative Analysis of EU Policy Making

Narrative analysis of the EU has the potential to uncover how policies emerge and to illustrate the process of contestation surrounding policy making within and outside the EU. There are a number of different ways in which narrative broadly defined has been used in the study of the EU. In addition to the use of narrative in understanding the external affairs of the EU as outlined above, Vivien Schmidt's (2001, 2002a, 2002b, 2002c) work on discursive institutionalism is very useful in understanding institutional change within the EU. Schmidt makes important claims that "factors such as timing, political salience, policy viability, and fit in terms of national values, tradition, and culture" (Schmidt 2011, 62) are important in determining which ideas matter and when. However, Schmidt's analysis largely focuses inside institutions and does not focus on a wider understanding of how narrative conditions responses as well as how narrative can be used strategically to achieve policy goals. Strategic narrative builds upon Schmidt's work as it factors in greater complexity of communication—especially in light of the Eurozone crisis in which internal and external narratives collide. Successful narratives need to both evoke existing ideas and to suggest a compelling way to address a current challenge facing policymakers (Schmidt and Radaelli 2004, 201).

Narratives are often aimed at overcoming complexity in policy making. This links to Maarten Hajer's work on environmental politics. Hajer stresses the importance of storylines in understanding the complex web of actors and issues being negotiated:

[s]torylines are narratives on social reality through which elements from many different domains are combined and that provide actors with a set of symbolic references that suggest common understanding. (Hajer 1995, 62)

But, in contrast to storylines, narratives have a greater fixity of meaning and are less malleable to achieve policy outcomes. In member states narratives overwhelmingly reinforce the national, with the EU often being conceived as a power maximizer or secondary institution to pursue national interests, rather than suggesting the emergence of shared European interests (Lacroix and Nicolaidis 2010). In general, narrative analysis in public policy focuses on processes of identifying the nature of the problem at stake, outlining a solution to that problem, and indicating what the outcome will be (Fischer 2003).[5]

Formation, Projection, and Reception of the EU's Strategic Narrative

The EU has often been slow or reluctant to explicitly set out a strategic narrative. The reluctance to outline a clearer sense of purpose has been criticized by Biscop (2009), among others. This restraint has largely been due to the interplay between the community institutions and the member states on issues relating to foreign policy. There have, however, been some attempts at developing a more coherent approach, notably by Margot Wallström who sought to raise the importance of EU public diplomacy. In a speech to Georgetown University, Wallström was at pains to stress that raising the profile of public diplomacy was a response to international trends:

> This is not an exercise in "'national branding'"; it is not "'propaganda,'" because we know that this does not work. It is the recognition of a fundamental shift, and especially so in relatively open societies, of how power, influence and decision-making has spread, and how complex it has become. (Wallström 2008)

The Lisbon Treaty provisions for a permanent president of the European Council and the creation of the post of high representative of the Union for foreign affairs and security policy have not overcome the tension between collective and national policy making (Carta and Wodak 2015). Rather than seeing these new officeholders becoming important agents in forming and projecting the EU's strategic narrative, member states have continued to dominate, ensuring no common, unifying narrative has emerged on the Eurozone or crisis management (Hertner and Miskimmon 2015). Nicolaidis and Howse (2002, 789) suggest that the EU's focus on a "narrative of projection" to the outside world is a means to paper over the internal challenges that the EU faces.

Strategic narrative features in a number of ways for the EU, both internally and externally. There are four main ways in which narrative plays a central role. First, the changing international order represents an important theme, raising pressures of relative decline and power transition. These have primarily taken the form of future-oriented strategic narratives about how the EU perceives itself in an emerging order (European External Action Service 2015). Second, the EU's narrative is a narrative about itself and the process of transition as an enlarged membership. Third, we have witnessed narratives of uncertainty reflected in the financial crisis and the EU's growing international responsibilities in crisis management. Finally, narratives of contestation between and among EU member states have become more prevalent as a result of the Eurozone crisis.

The European Union presents a considerable paradox in international affairs. On the one hand it is considered to lack power but it is influential. The EU's apparent weakness in material terms has been considered part of its attraction and a direct influence on its approach to engaging with international partners. Brent Steele argues that material power comes at a cost:

> More capably "powerful" states are somewhat imprisoned by their ability to influence more outcomes in international politics, and in this sense these capabilities, rather than allowing these states more freedom to act (as their acquisition is intended to accomplish) [instead] compromise this sense of freedom. (Steele 2008, 69)

As the EU's presence in the international system has grown and the scope of the Common Foreign and Security Policy has widened, pressure for a more coordinated projection of EU diplomacy has grown (Whitman 2005).[6]

The EU's growing role has largely been explained by scholars focusing on the impact of institutionalized cooperation within and outside of the EU. Vivien Schmidt has highlighted the role of coordinative discourse within the EU (Schmidt 2000, 2000b), as well as the notion of communicative discourse used to persuade those outside the coordinated EU network. Howorth (2004) has taken up this idea as he seeks to explain how European security went from a Cold War narrative of division and competition to coordinative discourse stressing the need for a collective EU response to the challenges facing European states. In this regard the European Security Strategy of 2003 can be viewed as a high-profile means to forge a coordinated strategic narrative in broad terms. This has coincided with the emergence of a more self-confident EU foreign policy, particularly since the turn of the century. There is no longer much value in "constructive ambiguity" (Heisbourg 2000) now that the EU has openly declared its intentions to be a more active player in international affairs. Active shaping of perceptions of the EU's global role among EU citizens and the wider world is potentially useful—which is where strategic narratives come in. Under the mantle of the Common Foreign and Security Policy more states have felt able to become more "extrovert" in their foreign affairs due to the collective weight that the EU offers even the smallest of EU member states (6).

Reception and projection of the EU's strategic narrative is complicated by an opaque institutional structure and organization that even EU citizens, much less non-Europeans, fail to grasp (Tonra 2011). This often leads to criticism due to a lack of coordinated action (Lowrey and Ewing 2012). There are those that contest that the EU still retains a compelling influence on other actors (Nicolaidis and Howse 2002, 771).

For Mark Leonard, the EU has been so successful that the rest of the world has sought to imitate the EU, resulting in what he calls a "regional domino effect" (2005, 7). However, the impact of the EU's narrative has come under increasing pressure due to a developing opinion that the EU's success story has been compromised by what is perceived as bad economic management. Breslin (2009) argues that this is contributing to great competition over the ideas that shape global politics where non-Western states are increasingly influential. European Commission president José Manuel Barroso's angry response to criticism of the European Union at the G20 meeting in Mexico in June 2012 suggested tensions over the EU's normative legitimacy as an effective economic and democratic actor.[7] The necessity to engage in strategic narrative competition is enhanced by the criticism that the EU currently faces and is heightened by the EU's leading position in the global economy; it forewarns the EU of the potential limitations of its influence with the growth of the BRICS (Brazil, Russia, India,

China, South Africa) as outlined in chapter 11 of this volume (see also Maull 2005).

Temporality is also a major factor in understanding strategic narratives in general, but this has particular challenges for the EU due to the heterogeneity of its membership and its formal coordination mechanisms, which in the fast-paced media environment struggles to project a timely message. Coordinating discourse as indicated by Schmidt comes under significant pressure in crisis management. The recent examples of the 2011 military intervention in Libya and the Eurozone crisis have highlighted a return to a lead group around either France and Germany or France and the United Kingdom that seizes leadership opportunities. In security and defense policy small-group leadership and influence over the formation and projection of an EU strategic narrative becomes even more pronounced given the permanent membership on the UN Security Council of France and the United Kingdom (Miskimmon 2012). This proves problematic for Ben Tonra who argues that "the Union remains reliant upon an unstable intersection of national foreign policy narratives and the weak instantiation of an elite European narrative based on exceptionalism" (2011, 1190).[8] The reception of the EU's narrative highlights the complexity of forging a strategic narrative that resonates both domestically and internationally (Harpaz and Shamis 2010; see also Tocci 2005).

The problematic reception of the EU's strategic narrative is recognized by EU policymakers. In a study of the future of the EU undertaken by the foreign ministers of Austria, Belgium, Denmark, Italy, Germany, Luxemburg, the Netherlands, Poland, Portugal, and Spain, the interim report of June 15, 2012, stated:

> Europe is sometimes seen as part of the problem rather than part of the solution. What is more, the existing "narrative" of the European Union as an instrument for banishing war in Europe is no longer sufficient for today's "Erasmus generation." The fruits of integration, for example freedom of movement in the Schengen area, are advantages all too often taken for granted. The cost associated with the European project often receives more attention than the value it creates for our citizens.[9]

This underlines the challenge of strategic narrative projection: how an actor wishes to be understood often differs from the perception of third parties. Without a clear sense of what the EU's narrative is, it makes it very difficult to project. This demonstrates the need to analyze formation, projection, and reception of narratives as a cycle of communication. Zaki Laïdi understands the EU's biggest post–Cold War challenge as one of finding meaning:

> [A] Europe of meaning will end naturally in a Europe of power. But a Europe of power will never see the light of day if it does not first manage to offer meaning to its inhabitants and the rest of the world. . . . This strong dialectic between meaning and power is a source of extreme vulnerability, since the loss of meaning is regarded as a weakening of power. Meaning thus magnifies the representation of power, positively when a meaning is proposed and negatively when it seems to be slipping out of reach. (Laïdi 2012, 144)

Laïdi's linkage of meaning and power within and without the EU fits with our understanding of strategic narratives. Steele contends, however, that this can be fraught with danger: "By seeking out aesthetic integrity, power facilitates its own vulnerability" (2012, 21). The EU's narrative is received and recontextualized in different national contexts (Kutter 2015), making it very challenging to offer meaning in international affairs (Carta and Morin 2014).

Competing Strategic Narratives and the Euro Crisis

The Eurozone crisis has demonstrated the challenges of projecting a coherent strategic narrative in the European Union. There are a number of limiting factors working against the emergence of a cohesive strategic narrative of the euro. Kenneth Dyson argues that over the course of the first ten years of the euro,

> domestic political elites shied away from the discursive challenge of crafting a positive and persuasive narrative about the euro. Their incentive was reduced by problems of communication with suspicious publics. Public opinion had been made brittle by widespread experience and perception of the euro's introduction as inflationary and then anxious by painful adjustment challenges from an appreciating euro, low growth, and high unemployment. Political elites were anxious to keep the euro off the agenda of domestic reform. In

consequence, and in contrast to euro accession, the cutting edge of the euro as an external discipline was blunted. (Dyson 2009, 4)

Even before the beginnings of the euro crisis in 2009, Dyson suggests that there was not a sustained attempt within Eurozone countries to create a narrative that forged domestic support for the currency. For instance, no sooner had Germany introduced the euro in January 2002 that Germans began calling the new currency the "Teuro," merging *teuer* (expensive) and euro to suggest that prices had increased since its introduction. This contrasts with the pronouncements of European Central Bank president Jean-Claude Trichet that sought to highlight the euro's success in the formative years of the single currency (Marsh 2011). This disconnect between the domestic and EU-level narratives has conditioned the response of national policymakers driven by electoral pressures. National politicians have found it increasingly difficult to craft a narrative that seeks to support the euro internationally and responds to domestic skepticism about the euro's benefits. The euro crisis has not seen a shared narrative emerge. Rather, it has often been characterized by narratives based on binaries such as austerity versus growth, discipline versus recklessness, and winners versus losers.

Who Narrates?

The question of who narrates the narrative of the euro crisis strikes at the heart of the problem the EU faces. The hybrid nature of the European Union, which displays both supranational and intergovernmental policymaking dynamics, complicates who narrates policy within the organization. Central scripting of the EU's euro crisis narrative is therefore very challenging. Representatives of supranational institutions in Brussels invariably present a positive narrative of the euro's success and capacity to respond to the financial crisis, such as in Barosso's Los Cabos G20 statement blaming the United States and not the EU for the euro crisis. Domestic political actors within the EU, many of whom have been high-profile casualties at the ballot box, such as French president Nicholas Sarkozy in 2012 and Italian prime minister Mario Monti in 2013, have struggled to present a narrative in which domestic and European economic interests remain compatible. Supporting the euro in the face of domestic austerity drives has not been a successful electoral tactic within the

Eurozone. Looking at some of the main actors in the crisis demonstrates that we can outline how distinct narratives correspond to divergent policy options, and therefore contribute to the ongoing inability to address some of the underlying issues of the Eurozone. Throughout 2012, Eurozone leaders' debates focused on a number of central issues. First, what level of domestic reform was necessary to stabilize the currency area? Second, what level of intervention was needed to stabilize the Euro and help member states recover? This chapter will now focus on two central players in the Eurozone—Mario Draghi, president of the European Central Bank, and Angela Merkel, the German chancellor. We will analyze how Draghi and Merkel sought to project a persuasive strategic narrative of the euro crisis throughout 2012, highlighting the degree and nature of narrative alignment and nonalignment. Draghi's communication strategy was heavily focused on Germany during this period, which makes for an interesting comparison with Merkel's narrative.

Mario Draghi—A Narrative of Collective Action

President of the European Central Bank Mario Draghi has sought to project a strategic narrative that demands domestic economic reform within the Eurozone while simultaneously seeking to reassure citizens within the Eurozone of the success of the single currency. Draghi's 2012 speeches, reproduced on the ECB website, seek to strike a balance between charting a necessary reform process with an onus on domestic economic reforms and narrating the wider importance of European integration within the EU. This is illustrated by Draghi's remarks to the European Parliament of April 25, 2012:

> The economic policies of euro area countries are, ultimately, domestic policies for the euro area. Precisely because of spill-over effects, they must be subject to mutual surveillance, and corrected if required in the collective interest of the euro area as a whole. This should apply both to fiscal and macroeconomic policies.
> . . . European integration has brought peace and prosperity. While I hesitate to sketch out the long-term end point of the integration process, I am convinced that we need to actively step up our reflections about the longer term vision for Europe as we have done in the past at other defining moments in the history of our union. (Draghi 2012b)

Draghi's narrative sought to avoid some of the more controversial discourse of the crisis. For instance, in an interview with the *Wall Street Journal* (2012), he talks of consolidation rather than austerity. As the euro's main institutional supporter Draghi's narrative sought to counter the mostly negative comments elsewhere. In a speech in Berlin on March 26, 2012, Draghi argued that "the doomsday predictions were always exaggerated" and that progress has been made since 2009 when the crisis hit: "The Eurosystem, the EU institutions and national authorities have all played a role in constructing a comprehensive and coherent response to the economic, financial and fiscal challenges that we face" (Draghi 2012a).

Draghi is associated with perhaps the most significant statement on the euro during 2012. In a speech in London on July 26, 2012, Draghi declared, "Within our mandate, the ECB is ready to do whatever it takes to preserve the euro. And believe me, it will be enough" (Draghi 2012c). This calculated communication was used to overcome the skepticism of the Bundesbank, which fiercely opposed the ECB entering the bond market to prop up ailing Eurozone economies (*Wall Street Journal* 2012b). Bundesbank president Jens Weidmann's response was to criticize Draghi by characterizing him as Mephisto, drawing on Goethe's *Faust* where the devil suggests that the emperor solve his financial problems by printing paper money on the promise of future unearthing of gold (Munchau 2012; Weidmann 2012).[10] Weidmann's underlying fear of the ECB as an undisciplined printer of money, going against traditional Bundesbank norms, drove the allusion in his speech. Draghi's intervention was decisive, demonstrated in the European Council's decision of July 2012 to support the ECB's moves to ease Eurozone states' debt burdens. Draghi's move demonstrated the status of the ECB as a strategic player in the euro crisis, "intruding" in debates in an attempt to structure proceedings. Francisco Torres argues that such "intrusions" "are driven by a sense of mission of an institution that perceives itself as an anchor of stability and confidence within a highly fragmented political system" (2013, 294).

Draghi's strategic narrative addresses one of the euro's underlying issues—that of whether the euro had been faulty from the beginning by pursuing economic union before political union (Draghi 2012b). The "coronation theory" favored by former Bundesbank head Hans Tietmeyer had been rejected by German chancellor Helmut Kohl, who favored a neo-functionalist "spillover" from economic to political union (Dyson and Featherstone 1999). Draghi's narrative of "economics first" is skilful in that it supports politicians within the Eurozone, chastened by the difficult passage of the Lisbon Treaty in 2009, who have sought to focus on economic reforms, despite the necessity of agreeing on new and more robust governance structures to formalize Eurozone reform. A lot of Draghi's communication is directed at Germany. Asked in an interview what he needed to do to address growing concerns within Germany concerning Berlin's increasing commitments to supporting fellow Eurozone members, he stated, "We need to explain what we do better in Germany, what our intentions are and what precautions we are taking" (Draghi 2012f). Draghi's strategic narrative stresses the need for member states to implement reforms both individually and collectively to ensure the survival of the euro. This narrative of individual responsibility allied with collective action is a means of persuading Eurozone member states of the continued viability of the single currency. In this way he projects a narrative of a two-level process of mutual adjustment. As Draghi states, "We have to make clear that EMU [European Monetary Union] is a union based on stability at national and aggregate levels" (2012d). Draghi is faced with braking a disintegrative dynamic caused by the Eurozone crisis, which increasingly witnesses greater discursive differences between member states in a growing series of policy areas (Schmidt 2012).

German Chancellor Angela Merkel—Defender of the Eurozone?

Angela Merkel's narrative of the Eurocrisis is both constrained and reinforced by a powerful metanarrative of Germany's role in the European integration process (Hertner and Miskimmon 2015). The centrality of the European Union to West Germany's rehabilitation after World War II is discernible in the deep influence that the EU has had within German political, economic, and cultural institutions. Despite the Europeanization of Germany, the issue of the single currency has been problematic from its inception. For many Germans the success of the deutsche mark symbolized Germany's recovery after World War II and was the bedrock of Germany economic success, which was built on strong exports supported by a strong and stable currency. Helmut Kohl's decision to create the euro, while demonstrating the united Germany's continued commitment to European integration after the end of the Cold War, removed a potent symbol of German national identity, even though the Bundesbank and German monetary policy provided the blueprint for the single currency. Merkel's difficulty has been to influence the principles governing how the euro is managed while at the same time not appearing to question its future nor the commitment of other Eurozone member states to its success. Merkel has not succeeded in projecting a strategic narrative that manages to balance reform and a pro-EU stance. This has led leading public intellectuals in Germany and beyond, such as Ulrich Beck, Jürgen Habermas, and Timothy Garton Ash, to question her commitment to the euro and to European integration in general (Beck 2013; Jarausch 2010; Garton Ash 2013).

The risk inherent in Merkel's euro narrative is that her disillusionment with the single currency and her Eurozone partners manifests itself in greater skepticism in Germany toward the euro and the EU itself. Merkel's slowness to resolve the crisis is seen by some as suggestive that Germany is seeking not to end the crisis prematurely (Bergsten 2012) as a means to Germanize the Eurozone (Joffe 2012). Taking this view, Merkel views the Eurocrisis as a policy window to resolve some of the euro's underlying weaknesses. Dudley (2013) suggests that there is a temporal aspect to policy windows that narratives play a role in. A successful narrative, according to Dudley, is demonstrated in the conversion of a policymaker's narrative into an institutional form that outlasts its initial inception. Paradoxically, despite many studies suggesting that Germany's power in Europe is growing as a result of the Eurocrisis, Merkel's ability to narrate the crisis and unilaterally determine the EU's policy response is constrained.

Merkel has faced limited opposition to her response to the Eurocrisis within the Bundestag. Only the Left Party has consistently called into question her approach. More significant has been the role of the Bundesbank under the leadership of Jens Weidmann, her former economics adviser. Weidmann has been in many ways a useful barometer of domestic support for Merkel, as to the extent to which Merkel can agree to Eurozone policies. Although the Bundesbank does not wield the same influence as it did before the introduction of the euro, Weidmann has been a critic of measures that threaten to destabilize the euro and run counter to traditional Bundesbank norms. Weidmann (2012a) understands the tough austerity process as that of "rebalancing"—a clear signal that Greece and other Eurozone states have run imbalanced economies. German domestic fiscal tightening in the form of the *Schuldenbremse*, which constitutionally limits the creation of new national debt, is demonstrated in Merkel and Weidmann's expectation of other states within the Eurozone to do likewise.

Merkel's strategic narrative has been driven by the need to maintain domestic political support and to influence reform of the Eurozone without exposing Germany to excessive financial commitments to shore up the single currency (Hertner and Miskimmon 2015). Merkel has sought to stress that Germany's involvement in supporting other Eurozone countries through the establishment of the European Stability Mechanism is part of Germany's wider commitment to European integration:

> Germany, the strongest economic nation in Europe, has a special responsibility in this situation, and Germany takes this responsibility. The happy history of Germany after the Second World War, the development into a free, unified and strong country, cannot be separated from European history, not even in thought. . . . Germany lives in the European Union in a union of destiny. We owe it decades of peace, prosperity, and friendship with our neighbours. (Merkel 2010)

Such a narrative references Germany's metanarrative of German integration within Europe. Yet, as the extent to which Germany has needed to support the euro has grown, Merkel's narrative has fluctuated between solidaristic expectations and domestic political and economic realities. German domestic debates on the Eurozone crisis have focused on whether Germany benefits from its membership. As the extent of the crisis became known, Germany's status as a "winner" since the introduction of the single currency has become contested within Germany (Ferguson 2013).[11] Merkel's narrative vacillates between saving the euro and limiting German exposure to excessive bailouts. In a barbed statement in 2011, she suggested that "member states face many years of work to atone for past sins" (Merkel quoted in Hall 2012, 368). Merkel's emotive narrative contrasts with the technocratic language of functional alignment between units and levels that Draghi projects. In a less confrontational tone, speaking to the Bundestag later in 2011, Merkel stated:

> We have always said: those who take responsibility can count on the solidarity of the European partners. Solidarity is the second pillar of the new stability and fiscal union. (Merkel 2011b)

Merkel's commitment to the euro was reinforced when she contended that "[w]hen the Euro fails, Europe fails" (2011a). Yet Merkel's narrative stresses responsibility as the flip side to solidarity in her calls for more reforms within the Eurozone to meet German expectations (Hertner and Miskimmon 2015).

Conclusion

The EU faces particular challenges in articulating a strategic narrative. The EU's hybrid institutional structure, which is composed of supranational and intergovernmental components, differentiates it from state actors with more conventional decision-making structures. This hybridity has particular effects when it comes to the formation and projection of a strategic narrative. An identifiable EU narrative is often difficult to discern. EU and member state actors working in external relations often claim to speak for Europe, which amplifies the EU's diplomatic cacophony. Despite these challenges, the EU has sought to develop a more discernible narrative of its role in international affairs based around broad principles contained in formal texts such as the European Security Strategy of 2003. These principles have become reflected in the national security strategies of EU member states.[12]

However, crises represent major hurdles for the EU as it is in high-pressure, high-stakes events that latent competing narratives, which in the day-to-day politics of the EU are often finessed, become visible. Returning to our definition of strategic narrative as *a means to construct a shared meaning of international politics to shape the behavior of domestic and international actors*, the EU has a paradoxical track record in developing a shared meaning of international politics. On the one hand, the EU often descends into conflicting narratives in crisis situations and appears ill-prepared to respond as one. Changes in decision-making structures to include more qualified majority voting rather than unanimity among all member-states, and greater flexibility for core groups of interested members to pursue greater integration, has had only a modest impact on how nimble the EU is in international affairs. This is largely due to the continued singularity of national strategic narratives as witnessed in the case of the Eurozone crisis. Taking a longer time frame, however, brings contradictory evidence to bear. Mark Leonard's contention that the EU will run the 21st century might now appear illusory.

NOTES

1. Despite indicators that EU member states were converging in foreign and security policy, there still remain considerable obstacles to closer cooperation. Paul Cornish and Geoffrey Edwards, "Beyond the EU/NATO Dichotomy: The Beginning of a European Strategic Culture," *International Affairs* 77, no. 3 (2001): 587–603; Paul Cornish and

Geoffrey Edwards, "The Strategic Culture of the European Union: A Progress Report," *International Affairs* 81, no. 4 (2005): 801–20; Anand Menon, "European Defence Policy from Lisbon to Libya," *Survival* 53, no. 3 (2011): 75–90.

2. François Duchene, "The European Community and the Uncertainties of Interdependence," in *Nation Writ Large: Foreign Policy Problems before the European Communities,* edited by Max Kolistamm and Wolfgang Hager (London: Macmillan, 1973). See also François Duchene, "Europe's Role in World Peace," in *Europe Tomorrow: Sixteen Europeans Look Ahead,* edited by Richard Mayne (London: Fontana, 1972). Hedley Bull famously challenged this conception, calling for Europe to take on more responsibility for its defense. Hedley Bull, "Civilian Power Europe: A Contradiction in Terms?," *Journal of Common Market Studies* 21, no. 2 (1982): 149–70.

3. Richard Youngs, ed., *Global Europe 02: New Terms of Engagement* (London: Foreign Policy Centre, 2005). See also Tanja Boerzel and Thomas Risse's research project on transformative Europe, http://www.polsoz.fu-berlin.de/en/v/transformeurope/. Peter van Ham argues persuasively that the EU's preference for projecting social power is grounded in two reasons. First, the prioritizing of social power is a reflection of the EU's political identity. Second, the EU perceives itself as having a comparative advantage in social power over more materially powerful actors (van Ham 2010, 34–35).

4. Catarina Carta and Ruth Wodak's work on EU discourses clearly demonstrates how different actors within the EU pursue different discursive strategies, thus highlighting competing policy preferences among the EU's institutions. Caterina Carta and Ruth Wodak, "Discourse Analysis, Policy Analysis, and the Borders of EU Identity," *Journal of Language and Politics* 14, no. 1 (2015): 1–17. See also Caterina Carta, "The Swinging 'We': Framing the European Union's International Discourse," *Journal of Language and Politics* 14, no. 1 (2015): 65–86.

5. See Frank Fischer, *Reframing Public Policy* (Oxford: Oxford University Press, 2003). Narratives are often conceived as means to bridge uncertainty in times of change. See, for instance, Jelena Subotić, "Narrative, Ontological Security, and Foreign Policy Change," *Foreign Policy Analysis* (online first), http://dx.doi.org/10.1111/fpa.12089

6. Richard Whitman argues: "The EU needs to become more muscular in its approach towards public diplomacy and focusing upon value transplants and value interpreters operating in third countries is crucial. If the ends of EU diplomacy are to be appropriately understood in third countries there is the need to be more aggressive in ensuring that there is an audience sympathetic to the EU's aspirations. This does require an instrumental form of engagement which is itself intended to facilitate the greater exercise of European power. It will not be an approach that will yield quick results but is an essential component to smoothing the path of the EU as its goes global" (2005, 30).

7. Barroso repeated the claim that it was North America, and not the EU, that was the source of the financial crisis. Accessed June 21, 2012. http://www.telegraph.co.uk/finance/financevideo/9342988/EC-President-Jose-Manuel-Barroso-blames-North-America-for-economic-crisis.html

8. Ben Tonra, "Democratic Foundations of EU Foreign Policy: Narratives and the Myth of EU Exceptionalism," *Journal of European Public Policy* 18, no. 8 (December 2011): 1190–1207. The narrative of exceptionalism in a state's foreign policy is often anything but exceptional. See, for instance, Kal Holsti, "Exceptionalism in American

Foreign Policy: Is It Exceptional?" *European Journal of International Relations* 17, no. 3 (2010): 381–404.

9. Foreign Ministers' Group on the Future of Europe, Chairman's Statement for an Interim Report, "The Time for a Debate on the Future of Europe Is Now," June 15, 2012. Accessed June 22, 2012. http://euobserver.com/media/src/3f1d57b5e556a953646816f85eec29ab.pdf

10. Wolfgang Munchau, "Draghi Is Devil in Weidmann's Euro Drama," *Financial Times*, September 23, 2012; Jens Weidmann, "Speech 'Traf Goethe ein Kernproblem der Geldpolitik,'" Frankfurt am Main, September 18, 2012, https://www.bundesbank.de/Redaktion/DE/Reden/2012/2012_09_18_weidmann_begruessungsrede.html. The same allusion is drawn in Tommaso Padoa-Schioppa's book on the euro from 2004. Tommaso Padoa-Schioppa, *The Euro and Its Central Bank: Getting United after the Union* (Cambridge, MA: MIT Press, 2004), 16.

11. Niall Ferguson, "Merkel's 'Deutsche Michel' Ploy Is Bad Economics," *Financial Times*, July 11, 2013; Hans-Werner Sinn, "It's Wrong to Portray Germany as the Euro Winner," *Financial Times*, July 22, 2013; Bertelsmann Stiftung, "How Germany Benefits from the Euro in Economic Terms," Policy Brief 2013/1: http://www.bertelsmann-stiftung.de/cps/rde/xbcr/SID-113A7614-39120542/bst_engl/xcms_bst_dms_37730_37731_2.pdf

12. See, for example, Office of Prime Minister of Finland (2004), *Finnish Security and Defence Policy 2004*, Government Report 6/2004 (Helsinki: Prime Minister's Office: Publications, 18/2004), http://www.defmin.fi/files/311/2574_2160_English_White_paper_2004_1_.pdf (accessed June 6, 2013); Republic of Estonia (2004), *National Security Concept*, https://www.files.ethz.ch/isn/156841/Estonia-2004.pdf (accessed June 6, 2013); French Republic (2008), *The French White Paper on Defence and National Security* (Paris: Odile Jacob, 2008); Irish Department of Defence (2007), *White Paper on Defence: Review of Implementation* (Dublin), http://www.military.ie/fileadmin/user_upload/images/Info_Centre/Docs2/White_Paper_Review2007.pdf (accessed June 6, 2013); Republic of Poland (2007), *National Security Strategy*, https://www.files.ethz.ch/isn/156796/Poland-2007-eng.pdf (accessed June 6, 2013).

REFERENCES

Aggestam, Lisbeth. "Introduction: Ethical Power Europe?" *International Affairs* 84, no. 1 (2008): 1–11.

Beck, Ulrich. *German Europe*. Cambridge: Polity, 2013.

Bergsten, C. Fred. "Why the Euro Will Survive: Completing the Continent's Half-Built House." *Foreign Affairs* 91 (2012).

Bertelsmann Stiftung. "How Germany Benefits from the Euro in Economic Terms." Policy Brief 2013/1, 2013. Accessed February 2, 2014. http://www.bertelsmann-stiftung.de/cps/rde/xbcr/SID-113A7614-39120542/bst_engl/xcms_bst_dms_37730_37731_2.pdf

Biscop, Sven, ed. "The Value of Power: The Power of Values: A Call for an EU Grand Strategy." Egmont Papers 33. Brussels: EGMONT, The Royal Institute for International Affairs, 2009.

Boerzel, Tanja, and Thomas Risse. "Research Project Website on Transformative Europe." http://www.polsoz.fu-berlin.de/en/v/transformeurope/
Breslin, Shawn. "Understanding China's Regional Rise: Interpretations, Identities, and Implications." *International Affairs* 85, no. 4 (2009): 817–35.
Bull, Hedley. "Civilian Power Europe: A Contradiction in Terms?" *Journal of Common Market Studies* 21, no. 2 (1982): 149–70.
Carta, Caterina, and Jean-Frédéric Morin. "Struggling over Meanings: Discourses on the EU's International Presence." *Cooperation and Conflict* 49, no. 3 (2014): 295–314.
Carta, Caterina, and Ruth Wodak. "Discourse Analysis, Policy Analysis, and the Borders of EU Identity." *Journal of Language and Politics* 14, no. 1 (2015): 1–17.
Chaban, Natalia, and Martin Holland, eds. *The European Union and the Asia-Pacific: Media, Public and Elite Perceptions of the EU*. London: Routledge, 2008.
Chaban, Natalia, and Ana-Maria Magdalina. "External Perceptions of the EU during the Eurozone Sovereign Debt Crisis." *European Foreign Affairs Review* 19, no. 2 (2014): 195–220.
Chaban, Natalia, and Ole Elgström. "The Role of the EU in an Emerging New World Order in the Eyes of the Chinese, Indian and Russian Press." *Journal of European Integration* 36, no. 2 (2014): 170–88.
Chaban, Natalia, Ole Elgström, Serena Kelly, and Lai Suet Yi. "Images of the EU beyond Its Borders: Issue-Specific and Regional Perceptions of European Union Power and Leadership." *JCMS: Journal of Common Market Studies* 51, no. 3 (2013): 433–51.
Council of Ministers. *Report on the Implementation of the European Security Strategy—Providing Security in a Changing World*. Brussels, December 11, 2008. S407/08. Accessed July 1, 2015. http://www.consilium.europa.eu/ueDocs/cms_Data/docs/pressdata/EN/reports/104630.pdf
Daily Telegraph. "EC President Jose Manuel Barroso Blames North America for Economic Crisis." June 19, 2012. Accessed June 21, 2012. http://www.telegraph.co.uk/finance/financevideo/9342988/EC-President-Jose-Manuel-Barroso-blames-North-America-for-economic-crisis.html
Diez, Thomas. "Constructing the Self and Changing Others: Reconsidering 'Normative Power Europe.'" *Millennium* 33, no. 3 (2005): 613–36.
Draghi, Mario. "Remarks at the Annual Reception of the Association of German Banks." Berlin, March 26, 2012a. Accessed March 27, 2012. https://www.ecb.europa.eu/press/key/date/2012/html/sp120326_1.en.html
Draghi, Mario. "Introductory Remarks: Hearing at the Committee on Economic and Monetary Affairs of the European Parliament." Brussels, April 25, 2012b. https://www.ecb.europa.eu/press/key/date/2012/html/sp120425.en.html
Draghi, Mario. "Speech by Mario Draghi, President of the European Central Bank at the Global Investment Conference in London." July 26, 2012c. Accessed July 30, 2012. https://www.ecb.europa.eu/press/key/date/2012/html/sp120726.en.html
Draghi, Mario. "Draghi Statement to Economic and Monetary Affairs Committee of EP." July 9, 2012d. Accessed July 21, 2012. https://www.ecb.europa.eu/press/key/date/2012/html/sp120709.en.html
Draghi, Mario. "Interview." *Die Zeit*, August 29, 2012e.
Draghi, Mario. "Interview." *Sueddeutsche Zeitung*, September 14, 2012f.

Duchene, François. "Europe's Role in World Peace." In *Europe Tomorrow: Sixteen Europeans Look Ahead*, edited by Richard J. Mayne. London: Fontana, 1972.

Duchene, François. "The European Community and the Uncertainties of Interdependence." In *Nation Writ Large: Foreign Policy Problems before the European Communities*, edited by Max Kolistamm and Wolfgang Hager. London: Macmillan, 1973.

Dudley, Geoff. "Why Do Ideas Succeed and Fail over Time? The Role of Narratives in Policy Windows and the Case of the London Congestion Charge." *Journal of European Public Policy*, 20, no. 8 (2013): 1139–56.

Dyson, Kenneth. *The Euro at 10*. Oxford: Oxford University Press, 2009.

Dyson, Kenneth, and Kevin Featherstone. *The Road to Maastricht*. Oxford: Oxford University Press, 1999.

European Council. *A Secure Europe in a Better World: European Security Strategy*. Brussels, December 12, 2003.

European External Action Service. "The European Union in a Changing External Environment: A More Connected, Contested and Complex World." EU Strategic Review 2015. Accessed July 1, 2015. http://eeas.europa.eu/docs/strategic_review/eu-strategic-review_strategic_review_en.pdf

Ferguson, Niall. "Merkel's 'Deutsche Michel' Ploy Is Bad Economics." *Financial Times*, July 11, 2013. Accessed July 12, 2013. http://www.ft.com/cms/s/0/37460eb4-e983-11e2-9f11-00144feabdc0.html#axzz3fQOpVuGB

Finnemore, Martha. "Legitimacy, Hypocrisy, and Social Structure of Unipolarity: Why Being a Unipole Isn't All It's Cracked Up to Be." *World Politics* 61, no. 1 (2009): 58–85.

Fischer, Frank. *Reframing Public Policy*. Oxford: Oxford University Press, 2003.

Foreign Ministers' Group on the Future of Europe. "Chairman's Statement for an Interim Report, 'The Time for a Debate on the Future of Europe Is Now.'" June 15, 2012. Accessed June 22, 2012. http://euobserver.com/media/src/3f1d57b5e556a953646816f85eec29ab.pdf

Garton Ash, Timothy. "The New German Question." *New York Review of Books online*. August 15, 2013. Accessed August 8, 2013. http://www.nybooks.com/articles/archives/2013/aug/15/new-german-question/?pagination=false

Habermas, Jürgen. "Germany and the Euro-Crisis." *Nation*, June 28, 2010. Accessed August 8, 2013. http://www.thenation.com/article/germany-and-euro-crisis#

Hajer, Maarten A. *The Politics of Environmental Discourse: Ecological Modernization and the Policy Process*. Oxford: Oxford University Press, 1995.

Hajer, Maarten A., and David Laws. "Ordering through Discourse." In *The Oxford Handbook of Public Policy*, edited by Robert E. Goodwin, Michael Moran, and Martin Rein, 251–68. Oxford: Oxford University Press, 2008.

Hall, Peter A. "The Economics and Politics of the Euro Crisis." *German Politics* 21, no. 4 (2012): 355–71.

Harpaz, Guy, and Asaf Shamis. "Normative Power Europe and the State of Israel: An Illegitimate EUtopia?" *Journal of Common Market Studies* 48, no. 3 (2010): 579–616.

Heisbourg, François. "Europe's Strategic Ambitions: The Limits of Ambiguity." *Survival* 42, no. 2 (2000): 5–15.

Hertner, Isabelle, and Alister Miskimmon. "Germany's Strategic Narrative of the Eurozone Crisis." *German Politics & Society* 33, no. 1–2 (2015): 42–57.

Holsti, Kal. "Exceptionalism in American Foreign Policy: Is It Exceptional?" *European Journal of International Relations* 17, no. 3 (2010): 381–404.

Howorth, Jolyon. "Discourse, Ideas and Epistemic Communities in European Security and Defence Policy." *West European Politics* 27, no. 2 (2004): 211–34.

Jarausch, Konrad H. "Beyond the National Narrative: Implications of Reunification for Recent German History." *German History* 28, no. 4 (2010): 498–514.

Joffe, Josef. "I Come to Praise Ms Merkel Not to Bury Her." *Financial Times*, June 19, 2012. Accessed June 19, 2012. http://www.ft.com/cms/s/0/a438a8a6-b8ab-11e1-a2d6-00144feabdc0.html#axzz3fQOpVuGB

Kaldor, Mary, Mary Martin, and Sabine Selchow. "Human Security: A New Strategic Narrative for Europe." *International Affairs* 83, no. 2 (2007): 273–88.

Kutter, Amelie. "A Model to the World?" *Journal of Language and Politics* 14, no. 1 (2015): 41–64.

Lacroix, Justine, and Kalypso Nicolaidis. *European Stories: Intellectual Debates on Europe in National Context*. Oxford: Oxford University Press, 2010.

Laïdi, Zaki. *A World without Meaning: A Crisis of Meaning in International Politics*. London: Routledge, 2012.

Leonard, Mark. *Why Europe Will Run the 21st Century*. New York: Public Affairs, 2005.

Lowrey, Annie, and Jack Ewing. "A Tarnished Standing for Europe." *New York Times*, April 19, 2012. Accessed April 19, 2012. http://www.nytimes.com/2012/04/20/business/global/for-europe-scrutiny-and-diminishing-influence.html?_r=1

Manners, Ian. "Normative Power Europe: A Contradiction in Terms?" *Journal of Common Market Studies* 40, no. 2 (2002): 235–58.

Manners, Ian. "Normative Power Europe Reconsidered: Beyond the Crossroads." *Journal of European Public Policy* 13, no. 2 (2006): 182–99.

Manners, Ian. "Global Europe: Mythology of the European Union in Global Politics." *Journal of Common Market Studies* 48, no. 1 (2010): 67–87.

Marsh, David. *The Euro: The Battle for the New Global Currency*. New Haven: Yale University Press, 2011.

Maull, Hanns W. "Europe and the New Balance of Global Order." *International Affairs* 81, no. 4 (2005): 775–99.

Merkel, Angela. "Regierungserklärung zu den Hilfen für Griechenland." May 5, 2010. Accessed May 6, 2010. http://www.bundeskanzlerin.de/Content/DE/Regierungserklaerung/2010/2010-05-05-merkel-erklaerung-griechenland.html

Merkel, Angela. "Regierungserklärung zum Europäischen Rat und zum Eurogipfel." October 26, 2011a. Accessed October 27, 2011. http://www.bundeskanzlerin.de/Content/DE/Regierungserklaerung/2011/2011-10-27-merkel-eu-gipfel.html

Merkel, Angela. "Regierungserklärung zu den Ergebnissen des Europäischen Rates." December 14, 2011b. Accessed December 15, 2011. http://www.bundeskanzlerin.de/Content/DE/Regierungserklaerung/2011/2011-12-14-merkel-ergebnisse-eu-rat.html

Miskimmon, Alister. "German Foreign Policy and the Libya Crisis." *German Politics* 21, no. 4 (2012): 392–410.

Munchau, Wolfgang. "Draghi Is Devil in Weidmann's Euro Drama." *Financial Times*, September 23, 2012. Accessed September 23, 2012. https://next.ft.com/content/9095a970-03dd-11e2-9322-00144feabdc0

Nicolaidis, Kalypso, and Robert Howse. "'This Is My EUtopia . . .': Narrative as Power." *Journal of Common Market Studies* 40, no. 4 (2002): 767–92.

Padoa-Schioppa, Tommaso. *The Euro and Its Central Bank: Getting United after the Union*. Cambridge MA: MIT Press, 2004.

Polletta, Francesca. "Contending Stories: Narrative in Social Movements." *Qualitative Sociology* 21, no. 4 (1998): 419–46.
Rynning, Sten. "Realism and the Common Security and Defence Policy." *Journal of Common Market Studies* 49, no. 1 (2011): 23–42.
Schmidt, Vivien A. "Democracy and Discourse in an Integrating Europe and a Globalising World." *European Law Journal* 6, no. 3 (2000a): 277–300.
Schmidt, Vivien A. "Values and Discourse in the Politics of Welfare-State Adjustment." In *Welfare and Work in the Open Economy*, vol. 1, *From Vulnerability to Competitiveness*, edited by Fritz W. Scharpf and Vivien A. Schmidt, 229–309. Oxford: Oxford University Press, 2000b.
Schmidt, Vivien A. "The Politics of Adjustment in France and Britain: When Does Discourse Matter?" *Journal of European Public Policy* 8 (2001): 247–64.
Schmidt, Vivien A. "Does Discourse Matter in the Politics of Welfare State Adjustment?" *Comparative Political Studies* 35, no. 2 (2002a): 168–93.
Schmidt, Vivien A. *The Futures of European Capitalism*. Oxford: Oxford University Press, 2002b.
Schmidt, Vivien A. "Europeanization and the Mechanics of Economic Policy Adjustment." *Journal of European Public Policy* 9, no. 6 (2002c): 894–912.
Schmidt, Vivien A. "Reconciling Ideas and Interests through Discursive Institutionalism." In *Ideas and Politics in Social Science Research*, edited by Daniel Béland and Robert Henry Cox, 47–64. Oxford: Oxford University Press, 2011.
Schmidt, Vivien A. "European Member State Elites' Diverging Visions of the European Union: Diverging Differently since the Economic Crisis and the Libyan Intervention." *Journal of European Integration* 34, no. 2 (2012): 169–90.
Schmidt, Vivien A., and Claudio Radaelli. "Change and Discourse in Europe: Conceptual and Methodological Issues." *West European Politics* 27, no. 2 (2004): 183–210.
Slaughter, Anne-Marie. "Foreword." In *A National Strategic Narrative*, by Mr. Y. Woodrow Wilson Center. Accessed July 1, 2011. http://www.wilsoncenter.org
Sinn, Hans-Werner. "It's Wrong to Portray Germany as the Euro Winner." *Financial Times*, July 22, 2013. Accessed July 22, 2013. https://www.ft.com/content/bbb2176a-ed70-11e2-8d7c-00144feabdc0
Snyder, Jack. "Dueling Security Stories: Wilson and Lodge Talk Strategy." *Security Studies* 24, no. 1 (2015): 171–97.
Steele, Brent J. *Ontological Security in International Relations: Self-identity and the IR State*. London: Routledge, 2008.
Steele, Brent J. *Defacing Power: The Aesthetics of Insecurity in Global Politics*. Ann Arbor: University of Michigan Press, 2012.
Subotić, Jelena. "Narrative, Ontological Security, and Foreign Policy Change." *Foreign Policy Analysis* (online first). 2015. http://dx.doi.org/10.1111/fpa.12089
Tocci, Nathalie. "The Widening Gap between Rhetoric and Reality in EU Policy towards the Israeli–Palestinian Conflict." Centre for European Policy Studies Working Paper No. 217, 2005.
Tonra, Ben. "Democratic Foundations of EU Foreign Policy: Narratives and the Myth of EU Exceptionalism." *Journal of European Public Policy* 18, no. 8 (2011): 1190–1207.
Torres, Francisco. "The EMU's Legitimacy and the ECB as a Strategic Political Player in the Crisis Context." *Journal of European Integration* 35, no. 3 (2013): 287–300.

van Ham, Peter. *Social Power in International Politics*. London: Routledge, 2010.
Walker, Markus. "Europe Sees Dream of Global Power Wane as 'G-2' Rises." *Wall Street Journal*, January 26, 2010. Accessed January 26, 2010. http://online.wsj.com/article/SB10001424052748704905604575027094159815012.html
Wall Street Journal. "Q&A: ECB President Mario Draghi." February 23, 2012. Accessed February 23, 2012a. http://blogs.wsj.com/eurocrisis/2012/02/23/qa-ecb-president-mario-draghi/
Wall Street Journal. "How ECB Chief Outflanked German in Fight for Euro." October 2, 2012b. Accessed October 2, 2012. http://online.wsj.com/article/SB10000872396390443507204578020323544183926.html
Wallstrom, Margot. "Public Diplomacy and Its Role in EU External Relations." Speech to Georgetown University, October 2, 2008. Accessed August 1, 2012. http://europa.eu/rapid/pressReleasesAction.do?reference=SPEECH/08/494&guiLanguage=en
Weidmann, Jens. "Rebalancing Europe." March 28, 2012a. Chatham House, London. Accessed March 28, 2012. http://www.bundesbank.de/Redaktion/EN/Reden/2012/2012_03_28_weidmann_rebalancing_europe.html?nn=2094
Weidmann, Jens. "Speech 'Traf Goethe ein Kernproblem der Geldpolitik.'" Frankfurt am Main, September 18, 2012b. Accessed September 30, 2012. www.bundesbank.de
Whitman, Richard. "Winning Hearts and Minds for Europe." In *Global Europe 02: New Terms of Engagement*, edited by Richard Youngs, 30–37. London: Foreign Policy Centre, 2005.
Youngs, Richard. "Normative Dynamics and Strategic Interests in the EU's External Identity." *Journal of Common Market Studies* 42, no. 2 (2004): 415–35.
Youngs, Richard, ed. *Global Europe 02: New Terms of Engagement*. London: Foreign Policy Centre, 2005.
Zakaria, Fareed. *The Post-American World*. New York: W. W. Norton, 2008.
Zielonka, Jan. "Europe as a Global Actor: Empire by Example?" *International Affairs* 84, no. 3 (2008): 471–84.
Zielonka, Jan. *Is the EU Doomed?* Cambridge: Polity, 2014.

5 | The Power of Strategic Narratives

The Communicative Dynamics of Chinese Nationalism and Foreign Relations

Ning Liao

The symbolic representation of collective identity—an essential communicative element of nationalism—invariably involves the strategic deployment of narratives. An archetypical example in this regard is the creation and transmission of master commemorative narratives. In the nexus of Chinese domestic politics and foreign relations, such historical accounts are central to the internal and external legitimation of the nondemocratic state. By bestowing determined meanings upon the past, which is causally related to the present and future of the Chinese nation-state, this sort of strategic narrative defines the identity role of the Chinese Communist Party (CCP) in China's sociopolitical development and projects varied self-images of the People's Republic of China (PRC) in diverging semantic contexts. While structuring the expectation and behavior of the actors involved, nationalist discourse is not only a sense-making tool maneuvered by the CCP in its domestic rule and the pursuit of its diplomatic aims, but an effective communicative device as well for both domestic and international audiences in contesting and transforming the state-projected narratives.

In order to highlight the intended meanings of nationalist discourse for the purpose of policy advocacy and legitimation, master commemorative accounts often select and call attention to some facets of national history. By making a connection between particular identities and pertinent social values sustained in the indigenous political culture, the characters of political actors are evaluated in accordance with certain normative expectations (Miskimmon, O'Loughlin, and Roselle 2013). Such framing, motivated by the actor's political objectives, aptly integrates the interests and goals of the nation-state by lending narrativity to the experiential elements of its historical development that are discerned as constituting parts of the national identity. In organizing the historiographical "storyline" within the selected frames, communicators can "emplot" those seemingly disconnected events and actions that are unified into a coherent whole under a proposed theme (ÓTuathail 2002, 627; Polkinghorne 1991, 141; also see Ricoeur 1984). As the communicative frames are endowed with temporality and causality, the rhetorical potency of nationalist discourse is manifested in the cognitive and normative operation of narrative structuring (Antoniades, Miskimmon, and O'Loughlin 2010, 5), which increases the probability that the audience's interpretation of, and response to, domestic and international affairs are primed in those frames preferred by the communicator.

Along with its key role in structuring storylines, strategic narratives are operationalized in a discursive terrain where the agencies of elites and masses are mutually constitutive. This is evidenced in the rhetorical transaction of Chinese nationalist discourse. While conducive to the CCP's regime legitimacy, such a discursive element of Chinese domestic and foreign policy interaction shapes the behavior of the state in its interaction with domestic societal groups and international society. Given that nationalist sentiment and opinion have constituted a significant audience cost of the CCP's foreign policy making, counternarratives, which are appropriated from the state-imposed category of political communication and transmitted through the commercialized media, undermine Beijing's effort to mediate those emotionally charged interstate conflicts. Viewed in this light, the communicative dynamics of Chinese nationalism can be better captured in the discursive arena where the authoritarian state and societal forces are mutually empowering in the marketized media ecology.

With such an intellectual orientation, this chapter attempts to systematically investigate the formation, projection, and reception of Chinese nationalist discourse, which is implicated in the construction and consumption of collective memory. Starting with the social pragmatics of political communication, the first section examines the way that the symbolic representation of Chinese historiography via the state's mythmaking is structured in the historical narratives in Mao Zedong's China and the post-Tiananmen era. In order to shed light on the discursive texture of the "linkage politics" (Rosenau 1969) of Chinese foreign relations, the second section maps the domestic and international reception of the victimhood discourse—a thematic thesis of the patriotic education staged by the CCP from the 1980s onward—and the reconfiguration of Beijing's diplomatic discourse in reworking the PRC's public image in the international arena. As illustrated in tumultuous Sino-Japanese relations, the strategic narratives crafted to enhance regime legitimacy have backed the CCP into a quandary, due to the conflict between its rational calculation in conducting a pragmatic diplomacy and the mandate of social norms with which the mythologized national history is enmeshed. The empirical examination of how the projection of official nationalist narrative is disrupted in China's media ecology, as explored in the third section, is an informative step to understand the precise way the authoritarian state and the commercialized media are mutually co-opted and exploited in the marketplace of foreign affairs coverage.

Remembering or Forgetting: The Selective Paradigms of Narrated Memory

As a pragmatic function of narratives, the structuring of historical storylines entails selective remembering and forgetting of certain parts of the past to fit the ontological reflection of the contemporary world. Given its malleability, the construction of collective memory tends to be collapsed into the enactment and legitimation of "myth" in forming master historical accounts, which often reduces the complex and multifaceted historical process to a single-dimensional picture. It is this genre of narrative—"a shorthand for a particular interpretation of a historical experience . . . invoked in the present to justify certain policies" (Heuser and Buffet 1998, ix) that is often institutionalized as official discourse when the state is engaged in mythologizing national history.

In the historical mythmaking, symbolic elements extracted from communication events are "emplotted" within particular framing paradigms, which provide the epistemic resource to ratify those collective identities that embody the moral judgment of the masses. Such narrative framing includes two semiological dimensions involving the communicative constituents of political symbolism. The first is the semantic relationship between "the symbol and the political reality . . . it refers to" (Dittmer 1977, 571). Since the selection of symbols is contingent upon the semantic context that conditions the state's mythmaking, the framing of historical events is subject to the elites' structural imperatives under shifting domestic and international circumstances. Second, the chosen symbols bear socially binding connotations and hence register specific signs in public memory, whose relationship reflects the syntactic dimension of historical accounts (571). With the mediation of the meanings connoted from the selected symbols, the syntax of master historical narratives structures the feelings of the audience regarding how domestic politics and international affairs work and their comprehension of the distinct signs associated with the mythic symbols (568).

These semiological elements of political symbolism are applied to the distinctive narrative paradigms prevalent in Chinese state-led history education. Within the dominant narrative structures, two paradoxical symbols have been formed in projecting modern Chinese historiography: the triumph of the Chinese people in the Communist revolution led by the CCP and the national humiliation wrought by imperialist intrusion and aggression (see, e.g., Gries 2004, 69–85; Wang 2008; 2012, 95–117). The projection of these symbolic polarities are shaped by the agenda-setting of narrative framing, which underscores "particular causal interpretation, moral evaluation, and/or treatment recommendation" (Entman 1993, 52) concerning the structural constraints of the party-state in diverging situations. The chosen symbols selected for framing have signified antithetical national identities into the narrated memory. In this communicative process, the syntax of master commemorative accounts enables the CCP to "filter identity discourse" (Checkel 2004, 234) that is instrumental in justifying its domestic and foreign policy.

In Mao's era, since China was headed by a charismatic leader who was obsessed with the purported "grand enterprise of continuous revolution" (Chen 2001), the definition of the major challenges confronting the party-state was structured within the frame of class struggle. Predicated by such agenda setting, those actors in an ideological camp considered as heresy to a revolutionary state were identified as the primary culprits conspiring to overthrow the regime. In the face of the imminent threats from these archenemies, the state was in need of a heroic image communicated through the mobilizing "identity discourse" to substantiate its capability of enduring the adverse diplomatic environment and mustering broad-based popular support for the "continuous revolution." Within such a semantic context, the Communist victory in the warfare of national independence and liberation—including the Chinese resistance against the

Japanese invasion and the civil war between the CCP and the nationalist Kuomintang (KMT)—became a salient symbolic resource for framing modern Chinese history.

As a framing technique in fostering popular identification with the Communist elites, the determined meaning connoted from the mythic symbol of Communist triumph was accentuated through the juxtaposition of two protagonists of the same historical period. In the narration of the war of resistance against Japanese aggression, the competence of the CCP-led army and underground forces, which were given full credit for national independence, affirmed the "victor" identity of the nation-state. This was in sharp distinction to the impotence of the KMT troops, whose corruption and yielding to the Japanese aggressors were diagnosed as a primary cause for the agony of the Chinese nation under nationalist rule. In a syntactic sense, the social categorization textually implied in such "self-glorifying" and "other-maligning" (He 2006, 70) conveyed the normative evaluation of the historical narrative frame, which effectively promoted the moralism of the Communist state.

The signification of the dichotomized identities attributed to the patriotic CCP and the traitorous KMT in the "structures of attention" logically means that some aspects of the same historical event that were incompatible with the dominant frame must be simultaneously consigned to "structures of inattention" (Bal 1988). During much of the Cold War period, the nationalist forces led by Chiang Kai-shek was "almost a codeword for any political dissident tendency" in Chinese political discourse (Mitter 2000, 283). The internal conflict between the two actors representing diametrically opposed classes overshadowed the international fissure between China and Japan in the CCP's political legitimation. Since the trauma inflicted upon the Chinese people in the Sino-Japanese War was not an appropriate symbol, by which the narrative audience would remember and interpret a historical issue in the way that a revolutionary state wished, this symbolic element was stylized as a peripheral issue in the narrated memory of modern Chinese history (e.g., Reilly 2006, 192). As a manipulative technique of mythmaking, such intended amnesia directed nationalist hatred toward the reactionary actors and Beijing's ideological opponents rather than an external entity whose conflict with China was in discord with the class-struggle frame of the master historical account.

On the foreign relations front, Japan's strategic position in the balance-of-power configuration of the Asia Pacific region pushed Beijing to engage Tokyo in an attempt to hedge against Western containment of the fledging regime. In step with this calculation, a distinction was made between the Japanese people at large and the coterie of Japanese militarists whose brutality, as asserted in the official historical account, was the real cause of Chinese war misery (He 2006, 73–74). In accordance with this "separation" thesis, historical feuds, considered as secondary to the normalization of bilateral relations that was more profitable in geopolitical terms, were largely slighted. Instead of being singled out for special commemoration, Japanese intrusion was pinned down as one of the objects of the Communist victory in countering foreign imperialism and domestic reactionary forces.

In the post-Mao reforming era, the profound transformation of China's domestic social structure and the external contextual constraints has led the state to revamp the framing package of historical accounts. The narratives celebrating revolutionary heroism could not ameliorate the rampant complaints made by a large part of the populace that was adversely affected by the socioeconomic reform. Given the volatile domestic and international environment in the aftermath of the Tiananmen crackdown, the pressing task of the CCP's narrative framing was to mitigate the glaring fissure between the authoritarian state and the disgruntled society. As the endpoint dictating the narrative frame has shifted from justifying the radical initiatives of class struggle to energizing a populace disillusioned by the waning appeal of the orthodox ideology on which the CCP could claim its legitimacy, a new mythic symbol that can distract the Chinese public from the cauldron of socioeconomic problems must be conjured in the transformative reproduction of the impoverished official discourse.

With the overhaul of agenda setting, the endemic memory of China's victimization in the "century of humiliation," lasting from the Opium War through the founding of the PRC, stood out from the "symbolic reserve" (Liu and Atsumi 2008, 330) for the state's mythmaking. At the critical moment when its moral standing fell to an all-time low, the CCP inaugurated an extensive propaganda campaign of patriotic education, centering on the national trauma foisted on the country by foreign colonial powers. In the so-called education on national conditions (*guoqing jiaoyu*), the categorization of the *self* and *other* actors, which connotes how the woeful memory is related to the chief perils of contemporary Chinese politics, is less premised upon the Communist-Nationalist rivalry than on the ethnic conflicts between the Chinese nation and foreign invaders (Wang 2008, 791). The framing of the Anti-Japanese War has thus departed from emphasizing Chiang's nonresistance policy to eulogizing the KMT's contribution in the anti-Japanese war, which gives ground to the common interest and joint efforts of the antagonist actors in opposing foreign intrusion (He 2006, 80). This adjusted "emplotment" dissociates the demonization of a former negative sign from the syntactic context of historical account and ushers in those external entities that are identified as the "causal agent" (Entman 1993, 52) in the formation of the Chinese "victim" identity.

With regard to the "connotative property" (Dittmer 1977, 568) of the traumatic symbol, no other foreign encroachment can better stoke Chinese "victim" identity than Japanese incursion. In the reformulated narrative paradigm, Japanese war crimes deemphasized in the Maoist historiography are brought into the center of the "structures of attention." The tragic tale of the ferocious ravaging of the Chinese victims by Japanese militarists has been revived as one of the showpieces in the "new remembering of the World War II" (Waldron 1996). With the reinvigoration of the external sign, the causal interpretation and normative evaluation carried with the mythic symbol—that the former intruders and aggressors, the most egregious one being Japan, are the worst villains in modern Chinese history—tend to activate a particular "state emotion" when the ingroup is infuriated by the out-group's provocations (Liao 2013). In such cases where the threats imposed by the contemporary "victimizers" hearken back to their past savage act, the Chinese populace, whose intersubjective understandings of foreign affairs are framed in the historical narrative paradigm, coheres as a "victim" group. The normative orientation created by the master historical account thus distracts the general populace from mounting internal tensions in the painful domestic transition.

Despite the dominant position of the victimization discourse in the discursive package of patriotic education, the state's mythmaking strikes a balance between the marked focus on the magnitude of foreign subjugation and the concurrent portraying of Chinese fortitude displayed in their indomitable resistance (e.g., Gries 2004, 43–53). Such a nuanced narrative arrangement suggests a social action—national rejuvenation—in remedying China's past victimization and orienting the audience to the future of the traumatized community. In the nationwide discussion initiated by the newly installed CCP leadership over "the Chinese dream" (*zhongguo meng*), the meaning of this catchphrase is syntactically borne out by a connotation of the master historical account, that is, "China's goal for the great national rejuvenation relies on the solidarity of the people and the strong leadership of the [CCP]" (Xinhua 2011). As epitomized in this nationalist call made by the *People's Daily* (*Renmin ribao*)—the mouthpiece of the party-state—in an editorial commemorating the 80th anniversary of the Japanese invasion, a structuring logic in the "symbolic enhancement" of the CCP's regime legitimacy is to project the "indissoluble linkage" (Dittmer 1977, 572, 574) between the party-state and the Chinese nation as a collectivity. Following this fundamental plot line, causal linkage is established between the source of national humiliation and the foundation of a positive "causal agent," whose decisive role in national independence and liberation certifies its capability in realizing the achievable goal of the nation-state.

Aggrieved or Accommodationist: Reception of the Victimization Discourse

In terms of the rhetorical transaction between elites and masses, how well the state-driven historical narratives are received by the general populace, according to Michael Schudson's exploration of the power of cultural symbols, depends on the extent to which the narrated memory comports with "the cultural tradition of the society the audience is a part of" (1989, 169). On the part of the domestic audience, the reception of the victimization discourse is a social product of the interaction between "memory makers" and "memory consumers" (Kansteiner 2002, 180) in the particular social milieu of Chinese political culture. Due to the calamitous memory of extraterritoriality and concession as a result of colonial predation and imperialist incursion, the absolutist notions of national independence and state sovereignty have been encoded in the Chinese collective memory as distinctive social norms. The narrative framing of the CCP's regime legitimacy—revolving around the historical agency of the Communist regime in unifying the nation and restoring its dignity—nicely fits the normative environment of a postcolonial society. The mainstay narrative structure of the CCP-staged patriotic education can be seen as a "culturally congruent" paradigm, to the extent that it "conveys an unambiguous and emotionally compelling frame to the public" (Entman 2003a, 416; 2003b), whose felt need of cleansing national humiliation can be vigorously fulfilled by the alleged defender of Chinese territoriality and sovereignty.

In the realm of identity politics, the narrative framing of the CCP's patriotic education appeals to both the normative and purposive elements of the national identity. As exemplified in the resurgence of the trendy word "Chinese dream," the notion of rejuvenating China in international society makes socially intelligible the tenacious struggle of generations of Chinese political elites in the "causal transformation" (Antoniades, Miskimmon, and O'Loughlin 2010, 4; Todorov 1977, 45) of reconstructing a strengthening state that used to be the "sick man of East Asia." Viewed in this light, the narration of the CCP's historical agency is typically a process of "frame alignment" (Snow et al. 1986). As the unique representativeness of the "memory maker" in the historical transformation meshes with the ongoing action of the Chinese nation, the state-driven narratives are compatible with the "existing schemata in [the] belief systems" (Entman 1993, 53) of the "memory consumers," who are exhorted to rally around the collectivity of the nation-state.

In conjunction with the domestic consideration of enhancing regime legitimacy, historical narrative is also a discursive venue for Beijing to justify its persistent quest for power status on the world stage. Notwithstanding its current power base and growing influence in international affairs, China's social rank in the status hierarchy of contemporary international society is perceived by the in-group members as incommensurate with its grandiose national history. Just as the "symbolic enhancement" of its domestic legitimacy needs an opposite sign, the enactment of Beijing's external legitimacy is premised upon the "relational comparison" (see Abdelal et al. 2006, 699) of China's moral identity with those of out-group entities that are incorporated into the PRC's identity narrative. The sign of the "victimizing" other is employed here to exhibit China's undeserved treatment in a Western-founded institutional context. Along with the poignant reminder entreating the domestic audience "not to forget national humiliation" (*wuwang guochi*), Beijing often claims that the Chinese nation, given "the moral authority of [its] past suffering" (Gries 2004, 50), has a thorough understanding of the value of peace and the price of inequality in the Westphalian international system. Along this line of reasoning, the victimization discourse is instrumental in presenting an "ethical argument" (Narlikar 2007, 986) attesting to China's possession of the normative credentials for membership in the social category of legitimate great powers.

Nevertheless, this "ethical argument" is more persuasive to the Chinese audience than to its Western counterpart. According to Vamik Volkan's conceptualization of "chosen trauma," what the narrators of national humiliation really "choose" is "to mythologize and psychologize the mental representation" of the traumatic symbol (1997, 36–69; 2004). Since the symbolic representation of the traumatic symbol dovetails with the collective psyche of the Chinese nation, the victimization discourse has infused the empathy among the "memory consumers." Once the "connotative property" of the "chosen trauma" is animated in response to foreign discrimination or mistreatment, the perceived provocations of the out-group tend to fortify the cognitive consistency of the Chinese populace in processing information about foreign affairs that is germane to historical grievance. Take the ongoing Sino-Japanese controversy over the Senkaku (Diaoyu) archipelago as an example. In the in-group members' evaluation, Japan's audacious move of nationalizing the islands is inevitably associated with its annexation of Chinese territory—a symbol signifying the onset of Japanese imperialist invasion—and its current reluctance to express real remorse for its wartime transgression. In the eye of a resentful actor that is instinctively hardwired to detect the illegitimate motives of its past invader, the latter's action affirms preexisting beliefs concerning its war-prone character and military ambition.

Viewed through the prism of social psychology, the propensity of threat perception is largely reactive vis-à-vis the out-group references, which are perceived as jeopardizing the in-group's crusade for national renaissance and infringing its identity-constitutive norms. Due to the conventional role prescribed to an illiberal political regime, however, the reigning Western powers often take the CCP to task for fanning domestic nationalist fervor in an attempt to keep its grip on power. For those taken aback by Beijing's muscular position when it is embroiled in emotionally charged diplomatic skirmishes, the reiteration of China's moral superiority, which rests on its modern humiliating history, does not grant it the accreditation of a full-fledged power, but rather paints China as an insecure and defensive actor. The cathartic venting of its populace in antagonistic intergroup interactions verifies their inference that the aggrieved strain of Chinese nationalism has developed into the aggressive display of a dissatisfied and bellicose power. Ironically, the PRC's "ethical argument" has brought upon itself an assertive and expansionist reputation that it regularly denounces. The threat perception constitutive in the Chinese "mental representation" of national trauma has been reciprocated with a negative image assigned by the foreign "other." It is on the basis of the intention stereotypically assigned to an out-group that the progenitors of the "China threat" thesis judge the PRC's international character and gauge the motivation of its diplomatic behavior.

The rising tide of acrimonious exchange between China and Japan provides a compelling annotation to the international reception of the victimization discourse. While frequently chastising Japan for being insufficiently repentant over the grave harms it brought to the Chinese nation, Beijing is perceived by Tokyo as a strategic rival competing for the stewardship of regional affairs. Insofar as anti-Japanese animus can be easily tapped by the CCP as a kind of leverage for its political ends, such as discrediting Japan's moral qualifications as an international actor, the excessive and disturbing hostility of the Chinese populace toward the erstwhile colonial overlord has led to the repugnance of the Japanese people. The everlasting xenophobic sentiments against Japan have reinforced Beijing's outlier status, to which it has been assigned by Tokyo, hardening the latter's diplomatic and defense posture in response to the former's burgeoning influence across Asia. In the vicious spiral of pernicious social categorization, the threat imputation to the "other" is concomitant with the magnification of the superior "self." Some Japanese members of the far right, while decrying the apologetic view of their country's military past, have openly glorified Japan's war aggression by counterframing the Pacific War as a "sacred struggle for Asian liberation" (Cui 2012, 215–16; also see Goto 2003, 290). As evidenced in the Chinese nationalist upsurge in 2005 protesting the approval of Japanese history textbooks that were claimed to distort the history of Japan's colonial imperialism, the adversarial nationalism on Japan's side has added fuel to the flare-up of mutual hostility.

The undercurrents of mutual antipathy have made the CCP reflect upon the weighty costs of the victimization discourse in its external legitimation. In actuality, the overreliance on the "othering" sign to represent China's moral identity has engendered its political estrangement from major powers and neighboring states. The derived denigration of China's international reputation has necessitated substantial adjustment in the rhetorical package of Beijing's diplomacy. In combating the discriminatory response from the concoctor of the "China threat" thesis, some strategic thinkers in Beijing's foreign policy establishment proposed the notion of "peaceful rise" (*heping jueqi*), a key watchword of the PRC's diplomacy that was revised later by the top leaders as "peaceful development" (*heping fazhan*)—out of the profound concern that the term "rise" would convey a disturbing connotation of China's global activism to an alarmed external audience (see, e.g., Glaser and Medeiros 2007).

The ascension and swift modification of the "peaceful" thesis is by no means the CCP's political expediency. To effectively dilute its intransigence displayed in the raucous frays with the foreign "other"—the target audience of the "peaceful" narrative—a gentler moral identity other than a victim state seeking historical redress is sorely needed in rebuilding China's public image. The "symbolic reserve" that the CCP capitalizes on for this end is the cultural repertoire of Confucianism. In the selective interpretation of this indigenous discourse, some of its core values with contemporary relevance to Chinese foreign relations are framed in a rehabilitated narrative paradigm, which orients the reconfiguration of identity narrative so as to reshape China's external image. To provide a cultural underpinning of Beijing's peaceful diplomacy, Confucian China's benign history is articulated as a metonym, bestowing credible meanings upon a fresh international identity for the PRC that is in tandem with its moderate approach to defusing long-standing tensions and thorny conflicts.

In Confucian social philosophy, two interrelated notions centering on the concept of harmony (*he*), among others, are held up as an exemplar of China's culturalist image. One is "harmony is most precious" (*he wei gui*), a dictum historicizing Beijing's conduct of foreign relations in the time-honored tradition of "Confucian pacifism" (Cao 2007, 437). Unlike the victimization discourse, which entails a negative and reactive image of a recalcitrant state, the harmony-centered Confucian discourse visualizes an amiable China with a peace-loving heritage. The international system it envisages is encapsulated in another Confucian adage, "harmony but without uniformity" (*he er bu tong*). This notion places a premium on the feasibility of peace that is achieved in a diverse and pluralistic global community (Cao 2007, 438). Given Beijing's ultrasensitivity to the specter of the negative identification of China's dispositional traits, the projection of an ideal vision of a world order based on the Confucian virtuous relationship is expected to cast its formulator as a humanitarian actor and thus to assuage apprehension about and distrust of China's rise.

In terms of normative evaluation, an intertextual allusion suggested in the harmony-based diplomatic rhetoric is the contrast between China's moral high ground and the hegemonic and democracy-exporting Westphalian international system. However, while the neo-Sino-centrism signified in the diplomatic syntax has to a large extent abated the external clamor of the "China threat" argument, the alignment of strategic narratives with recaptured Confucian values is not a panacea for Beijing's diplomatic impasse. In the cases where historical grievances come to the fore, the CCP often finds itself in a bind. On the one hand it needs to pursue a pragmatic diplomacy directed at an external audience suspicious of its power aspirations, while on the other hand it has to appease strident domestic public opinion. Such a scenario unveils the autonomy of text receivers in selecting a "culturally congruent" narrative that can structure the diplomatic behavior of its projector.

According to Daniel Bar-Tal (2000), the collective belief in victimization perpetrated by the out-group's atrocities and dedication to the in-group are important sources of an "ethos." Under the animosity-building circumstances where the Chinese collective memory of dismemberment and subjugation is readily retrieved from the victimization discourse, such an "ethos" entails the social action of preserving a cohesive nation, safeguarding state sovereignty, and upholding the national honor at all cost. Since such behavior is heavily supported by the "chosen trauma" frame instead of the discursive paradigm of the "peaceful" narrative, domestic text receivers' interpretation of the diplomatic situations reflecting the unwieldy character of historical grudges may well transcend the framing intention of the narrator. This explains the failed attempt of some liberal intellectuals to bring "new thinking" to China's Japan policy. In 2002, having witnessed the swelling of virulent popular nationalism, *People's Daily* journalist Ma Licheng (2002) lamented in an influential journal the misleading effect of Chinese media on parochial public opinion toward Japan, which he viewed as an obstacle to improved relations between China and its neighboring states. Echoing Ma's advocacy, Shi Yinhong (2003), a realpolitik scholar, suggested Beijing's rapprochement with Tokyo through shelving historical issues and seeking a comprehensive partnership with Japan to counter U.S. hegemony in East Asia. Almost predictably, the "new thinking" ignited a flurry of nationalist backlash, wherein both Ma and Shi came under vitriolic attack. Branded as a "traitor" to China, Ma even received death threats, prompting his move to Hong Kong (Gries 2005a). As Japan-bashers got the upper hand in the ensuing heated debate, those sharing a similar view on "cool diplomacy" toward Japan had to keep a low profile. Just as one scholar flatly explained, "We'll be regarded as traitors if we say anything positive about Japan. We may even be blacklisted" (*Strait Times* 2004).

The social resistance encountered by the short-lived "new thinking" exemplifies how a narrative recommending a cure to deteriorating Sino-Japanese relations is considered heresy to the "ethos" of memory-encoded norms. Whether or not Ma and Shi were nudged by the decision-making circle to express their viewpoints, the fact that their provocative articles were published shortly after the fourth generation of the CCP leadership came into office could be seen as a credible signal of Beijing's desire to navigate away from confrontation with Japan. Nevertheless, once the outgroup's provocations, which are perceived as a blatant offense to Chinese sensibilities, come under the spotlight, the Chinese "ethos" reified as sovereignty, territoriality, and national dignity are socially recognized as the "dominant national ideas" about "what the nation *should* do" (Legro 2007, 522, 523), which resembles the "scripts" that the state actor must follow on the diplomatic stage (see, e.g., Alexander 2006, 58–64; ÓTuathail 2002, 619–20). As the attention of domestic audience is decidedly bounded by a memory-based "ethos" rather than the judicious calculation of presenting China's benevolent image, the state's accommodationist stance does not squarely fit the normative paradigm that has figured prominently in the popular imaginary and is thus rendered unwarranted. Considering the narrated role of the CCP as indefatigable defender of the nation, the policy action rationalized by the pacific discourse carries a strong risk of abrading the regime's mnemonic legitimacy. Thus, not only does the victimization discourse shape the public expectation of the state's diplomatic behavior, it also creates an ideational structure capable of arresting Beijing's dexterity in handling crisis situations.

State-Centric or Society-Driven: Interactivity in the Contested Arena of Media Ecology

Nowhere is the CCP's dilemma in its diplomatic decision making, most notably its Japan policy, better illustrated than in China's media ecology, in which the formation and projection of strategic narratives can be seen as an ever-negotiated product of the interaction between the propaganda state and the Chinese public. As a primary trader of the information pertinent to foreign affairs, mass media are an intervening variable indispensable to the rhetorical transaction between elites and masses. Understanding how this discrete actor facilitates the disruption of state-driven strategic narratives and the mediation of counternarratives at the popular level is the key to unlocking the discursive dimension of Beijing's foreign policy making.

In prereform China, the projection of strategic narratives on the foreign relations front was undoubtedly a top-down process. The distribution of foreign-policy information, as part of the CCP's discursive colonization, was predominantly controlled by political elites whose conduct of diplomacy was unfettered by domestic audience cost. The role of Chinese media in the circulation of information as the "throat and tongue" (*houshe*) of the government was comparable to what some Western scholars view as an accommodating linkage in the political communication system, simply transmitting elite rhetoric to the passive recipients (see, e.g., Bloch-Elkon and Lehman-Wilzig 2002; Brody 1991) who were unable to wield significant influence on foreign policy making.

Due to the structural changes in China's media sector, mass media are now engaged in a tug-of-war between the supply and demand sides of commodified information. Just as Baum and Potter (2008) illustrate, media as a critical middleman in the information flow between the leadership and the public has its agency in shifting the foreign policy marketplace equilibrium, favoring either the elites or the masses. Despite the social engineering of the party-state in molding a uniform public thinking, the low discursive power of the Chinese public vis-à-vis the leadership does not mean a lack of demand for information. Assuming that the state-crafted narratives are inevitably slanted, the domestic audience is actively seeking additional sources for unframed and objective reportage. On the part of the information provider, the CCP is desperate for a professional and empathetic media to enhance the persuasive power of official discourse. In the challenging transformation to the market economy, various media outlets, including subsidiaries of the propaganda press, have evolved from being solely the mouthpiece of the party-state to economic entities operating on a competitive basis (see, e.g., Huang 2007; Shirk 2007). The growing, albeit partial, deregulated market forces have become a catalyst accelerator for the media to meet the popular demand for quality coverage of China's foreign affairs.

Lifting the strict restrictions on the informational flow is crucial for the state's engagement with an increasingly pluralistic and incompliant public. Such "liberalized authoritarianism," as noted by O'Donnell and Schmitter (1986, 9), is expected to "relieve various pressures and obtain needed information and support [for the authoritarian state] *without* altering the structure of authority." Given the CCP's regime legitimacy instituted in the state-driven history education, the discursive sphere of Chinese nationalism under the mantle of patriotism is opened up for the interest articulation and political claim-making of the general populace, which are closely monitored by the authoritarian state. While the agenda of official nationalism remains chiefly in the custody of the regime and its ideologues, nongovernmental actors, particularly commercialized media, have joined the state in whipping up the subject of patriotism. In Chinese foreign affairs, external affronts evincing Japan's attitude toward its imperial colonialism are prone to be perceived as violating the Chinese memory-encoded norm, thus providing market-driven media with the meat and potatoes to win a large readership. In the cutthroat competition, radicalizing the focal issues in bilateral relationships is most likely to catalyze the historical analogy function of the "chosen trauma" symbol, and has thus become a common market strategy for the commercialized media to make their discursive products distinguishable.

The media ecology featuring "liberalized authoritarianism" does not rule out the state's continued grip on managing public opinion. Given the intention of decision-making elites to ease constraints on their policy making, foreign-policy information flowing from official sources "usually comes prepackaged in a frame that leaders would prefer that the media retain" (Baum and Potter 2008, 50). As a discursive element operating in the CCP's diplomatic decision-making environment, anti-Japanese enmity always requires elite framing in official media coverage. Since the Sino-Japanese relationship sank to a historical nadir in 2005, state propaganda has been seeking a turnaround in the representation of Japan (Reilly 2011, 14–23). In October 2006, after a five-year hiatus in formal summits, Japan's prime minister, Abe Shinzo, selected China as the destination of his first state visit when he came to power. Without obtaining Abe's promise to quit his pilgrimages to the Yasukuni shrine to soldiers who died in Japan's wars, including World War II—a sensitive issue where the harsh stance of his predecessor, Junichiro Koizumi, had soured bilateral relations—Beijing still treated this "ice-breaking trip" as a real treasure to restore the festered relations with Tokyo. In reporting Abe's inaugural speech to the Diet, while highlighting his stated goodwill in rebuilding a "forward-looking" relationship with China and South Korea, the official Xinhua News Agency glossed over his pledge to propel Japan's bid for permanent membership on the United Nations Security Council and the disputed call for more "patriotism" in Japan's history education (Hughes 2008, 259). Considering the critical position that Beijing normally had taken toward Japanese conservatives, the anodyne coverage of the right-wing prime minister was conceivably the CCP's discursive strategy designed to reciprocate the olive branch extended by the new Japanese government.

Having said this, the positive spin on Japan has its limit. Once the high-profile events involving "hot" history issues come to the fore, the sanitized reportage of Japan woven in the elite-preferred frame tends to disconfirm the preexisting beliefs of the Chinese audience concerning the out-group culprit as illustrated in the master historical narrative. Such cognitive discord indicates that the state-driven narratives have overstretched what Baum and Potter (2008, 56–57) term the "elasticity of reality," thereby prompting the public demand for a "*realpolitik* account" (Cao 2007, 443) that is congruent with the "schemata" of the audience. In the aggressive exploitation of a commercial goldmine, market-oriented media may not be a proregime ally, but a discursive actor threatening to disrupt the narrative maneuvering of the elites in inculcating a "prepackaged" version of foreign affairs. Harnessed by the economic logic of profit maximization, commercialized media have an incentive to run prominent stories in a narrative frame contrary to the one retained in the official reportage. For instance, in a controversial remark made in March 2007, Abe cast doubt on the coercion of the sexual service provided by Asian "comfort women" during War World II. In response to Abe's comment on this contentious history issue, the restrained approach adopted by the mainstream media, wary of presenting an overly negative out-group image, was in stark contrast to the flood of indignation from Chinese tabloids (Reilly 2011, 24–25). The contestation between the propaganda-oriented media and their commercialized counterpart has offered the Chinese public competing frames on foreign affairs. The autonomy of the domestic audience in processing foreign-policy information has dramatically increased with the expansion of its informational capacity.

A significant force contributing to the shift in the equilibrium of the foreign policy marketplace in a direction favoring the Chinese populace is the new information and communication technologies (ICTs). The increased reach of ICTs has brought growing transnational information flows onto the scene. In situations where the party-controlled press has spun foreign affairs beyond the "elasticity of reality," alternative news sources empower the public's capacity for political advocacy. In spring 2005, at the initial stage of the popular protests against Japan's quest for a permanent seat on the UN Security Council, although Chinese media were not allowed to run incendiary reports, news coverage prohibited in domestic public sources and traditional media were available from transnational sources. After comparing Xinhua's reporting on Japan's bid with those of foreign media, some Chinese netizens participating in the discussion on the China-Japan forum—an online bulletin board under the Strong Nation Forum (*qiangguo luntan*) affiliated with *People's Daily*—

expressed their resentment by questioning "why the Chinese media still pretended to be deaf and dumb" (Liu 2006, 146). In such discursive contestation in the online community, the multiplication of news suppliers enabled by ICTs, which makes a total control of information flow increasingly difficult on the part of the authoritarian state, has engendered what Steven Livingston calls the "imposed transparency" (2002, 257) on the cyberspace platform, where the networked crowd can vigorously exchange news items obtained from external sources, thereby forcing the government to respond to and account for the queries and debates aroused in the virtual public sphere.

Since the discursive power of the CCP leadership is gradually evened out in the restructured pattern of information distribution, Beijing's foreign policy makers often find themselves unable to keep contentious issues off the public agenda. As the transmission of dramatic events has been enormously broadened by the boom of ICTs, under the conditions where public opinions are highly mobilized around an emotionally charged issue, traditional location-based nationalist protests can be replaced by transnational modes of digital contention. In the protest against Japan's bid for UN Security Council membership, the online petition initiated by a U.S.-based overseas Chinese civilian group in March 2005 was immediately followed by similar actions on domestic popular news portals such as sina.com, urging Beijing to block Japan's attempt (Zhang 2007, 24–25). Insofar as the Internet-based mass mobilization has sped up cross-national coalition building, transnational information flows also bring in "systematic transparency" (Livingston 2002, 257) by publicizing flashpoint diplomatic issues and coordinating collective actions on a large populace base. In spring 2005, the "common knowledge" generated in the real-time mediation of the signature campaign swiftly formed a "shared symbolic system" in the cyberspace (see Chwe 2013, 7–8). As individuals in this virtual community were aware that their peers had all received the mobilizing message, the information transparency unleashed by the internationalized news flow reinforced the collective identity of the Chinese in-group and thus brought its members into action.

To be sure, the Chinese foreign policy marketplace, as a breeding ground for the production and circulation of nationalist discourse, has become a contested site where state-driven narratives that are supposed to structure public opinion can in turn be exploited as a tool of popular agency. In China's political communication system, the instructed motto of patriotic education that the love of the nation is indistinguishable from allegiance to the state has given rise to an "agency (state/regime)-principal (nation) relationship [in] popular political consciousness" (Seo 2005, 142). The Chinese public, in claiming its right to the "principal," is entitled to articulate its own viewpoints about the nation. Under the situations where the diplomatic performance of the "agency" fails to live up to the normative principles habitually favored by domestic convention, the accusing finger that the Chinese populace points to the nation's putative enemy can be turned inward. In the age of multimedia communication, the proliferation of ICTs has provided an effective platform where the antiforeign nationalist fervor can forcefully mutate into discontent with the official narratives justifying the government's actions. In April 2005, when anti-Japanese demonstrations rocked dozens of Chinese cities, *Liberation Daily* (*Jiefang ribao*), a propaganda-focused newspaper run by the Shanghai municipal government, editorialized a formal warning that the large-scale protests were part of a conspiracy designed to sabotage the state government. Along with the postings calling for a hard-line approach to Japan, online activists, in a thinly veiled critique of *Liberation Daily*, launched a bitter diatribe against the government's blackout of media coverage and its deliberate attempt to rein in mass protests (Liu 2006, 147–48). In the discursive battleground where the negotiation and contestation of the propaganda state and societal forces unfold, the moral precept that "patriotism is sacred" (*aiguo wuzui*), which has intensely resonated with public consciousness as a social consensus, is something that the leviathan regime has to accommodate rather than stifle. Thus, nationalist counternarratives are framed as a bulwark, wherein patriotic discourse was employed as an "evocative transcript" (Humphrey 1994, 23)—a text intended to evoke popular invective about the government's lack of commitment to the foreign policy "scripts." Such discursive action operating in full view of hegemonic authorities has become a coded way of directing popular dissent to the state while effectively weeding out the official narratives that are deemed as unconvincing by the domestic audience.

Conclusion

As a discursive product of the CCP's regime legitimacy enhancement in the post-Tiananmen era, the victimhood discourse highlighting the "chosen trauma" in modern Chinese history has been essentialized as official "truth" in state-centric patriotic education. Such a master commemorative account can be construed as a hegemonic construct that is inextricably linked to Beijing's foreign policy environment. Rather than a fixed state of domination, hegemony always involves social resistance (Williams 1977, 112). While appealing to the patriotic consensus, the hegemonic nationalist discourse has animated a politically and morally engaged "critical community" (Rochon 1998, 22–53), in which the memory-encoded social norms are employed by the domestic audience as codified "scripts" in their assessment of the state's diplomatic behavior. Once the CCP's nationalist credentials, narrated as the paramount patriotic force, fail to ring true in diplomatic crisis situations, the projection of counternarratives dressed in a patriotic cloak is a convenient way of voicing heterodox social discourse.

In the realm of domestic-foreign policy interactions, the CCP is often stuck between a rock and a hard place. One the one hand, it needs the consensual notion of patriotism to validate its "indissoluble linkage" with the nation in an attempt to solidify social cohesion, while, on the other hand, nationalist discourse has lain in wait to internalize the external conflicts. Facing an external audience suspicious of China's rise, Beijing has made strenuous efforts to water down the aggressive implications of the aggrieved image projected through the victimhood discourse, in order to signal the pacific nature of its emergence on the international scene. However, with the leeway of conducting pragmatic diplomacy heavily constrained by the emotional needs of the Chinese public, anything less than a forceful move on the part of the victimhood state, most notably in the turbulent Sino-Japanese relationship, renders the CCP's leadership liable to domestic castigation. The raging criticism over the government's diplomatic performance can further morph into disgruntlement with domestic sociopolitical pains. As manifested in Internet-based discursive resistance, the state's monolithic control of nationalist discourse is undermined by the society-driven media ecology. In reconfiguring the way that foreign-policy information is formed, collected, and circulated, mass media have constituted a discursive arena for social resistance, which, as Peter Gries (2005b, 256) vividly describes, has significantly "[weakened] the hyphen that holds the Chinese Party-nation together."

REFERENCES

Abdelal, Rawi, Yoshiko M. Herrera, Alistair Iain Johnston, and Rose McDermott. "Identity as a Variable." *Perspectives on Politics* 4, no. 4 (2006): 695–711.

Alexander, Jeffrey C. "Cultural Pragmatics: Social Performance between Ritual and Strategy." In *Social Performance: Symbolic Action, Cultural Pragmatics, and Ritual*, edited by Jeffrey C. Alexander, Bernhard Giesen, and Jason L. Mast, 29–90. Cambridge: Cambridge University Press, 2006.

Antoniades Andreas, Alister Miskimmon, and Ben O'Loughlin. *Great Power Politics and Strategic Narratives*. Center for Global Political Economy, University of Sussex, 2010.

Bal, Mieke. *Death and Dissymmetry: The Politics of Coherence in the Book of Judges*. Chicago: University of Chicago Press, 1988.

Bar-Tal, Daniel. *Shared Beliefs in a Society: Social Psychological Analysis*. London: Sage, 2000.

Baum, Matthew A., and Philip B. K. Potter. "The Relationship between Mass Media, Public Opinion, and Foreign Policy: Toward a Theoretical Synthesis." *Annual Review of Political Science* 11 (2008): 39–65.

Bloch-Elkon, Yaeli, and Sam Lehman-Wilzig. "An Exploratory Model of Media-Government Relations." In *Media and Conflict: Framing Issues, Making Policy, Shaping Opinions*, edited by Eytan Gilboa, 53–169. New York: Transnational, 2002.

Brody, Richard A. *Assessing the President: The Media, Elite Opinion, and Public Support*. Stanford: Stanford University Press, 1991.

Cao, Qing. "Confucian Vision of a New World Order? Culturalist Discourse, Foreign Policy and the Press in Contemporary China." *International Communication Gazette* 69, no. 5 (2007): 431–50.

Checkel, Jeffrey T. "Social Constructivisms in Global and European Politics: A Review Essay." *Review of International Studies* 30, no. 2 (2004): 229–44.

Chen, Jian. *Mao's China and the Cold War*. Chapel Hill: University of North Carolina Press, 2001.

Chwe, Michael Suk-Young. *Rational Ritual: Culture, Coordination, and Common Knowledge*. Princeton: Princeton University Press, 2013.

Cui, Shunji. "Problems of Nationalism and Historical Memory in China's Relations with Japan." *Journal of Historical Sociology* 25, no. 2 (2012): 199–222.

Dittmer, Lowell. "Political Culture and Political Symbolism: Toward a Theoretical Synthesis." *World Politics* 29, no. 4 (1977): 552–83.

Entman, Robert M. "Framing: Toward Clarification of a Fractured Paradigm." *Journal of Communication* 43, no. 4 (1993): 51–58.

Entman, Robert M. "Cascading Activation: Contesting the White House's Frame after 9/11." *Political Communication* 20, no. 4 (2003a): 415–32.

Entman, Robert M. *Projection of Power: Framing News, Public Opinion, and U.S. Foreign Policy*. Chicago: University of Chicago Press, 2003b.

Glaser, Bonnie S., and Evan S. Medeiros. "The Changing Ecology of Foreign Policy-Making in China: The Ascension and Demise of the Theory of 'Peaceful Rise.'" *China Quarterly* 190 (2007): 291–310.

Goto, Kenichi. *Tensions of Empire: Japan and Southeast Asia in the Colonial and Postcolonial World*. Athens: Ohio University Press, 2003.

Gries, Peter Hays. *China's New Nationalism: Pride, Politics, and Diplomacy*. Berkeley: University of California Press, 2004.

Gries, Peter Hays. "China's 'New Thinking' on Japan." *China Quarterly* 184 (2005a): 835–50.

Gries, Peter Hays. "Chinese Nationalism: Challenging the State?" *Current History* 104 (2005b): 251–56.
He, Yinan. "National Mythmaking and the Problems of History in Sino-Japanese Relations." In *Japan's Relations with China: Facing a Rising Power*, edited by Peng Er Lam, 69–91. London: Routledge, 2006.
Heuser, Beatrice, and Cyril Buffet. "Introduction: Of Myths and Men." In *Haunted by Memory: Myths in International Relations*, edited by Cyril Buffet and Beatrice Heuser, vii–x. Oxford: Oxford University Press, 1998.
Huang, Chengju. "Trace the Stones in Crossing the River: Media Structural Changes in Post-WTO China." *International Communication Gazette* 69, no. 5 (2007): 413–30.
Hughes, Christopher W. *Japan's Remilitarisation*. Oxford: Routledge for International Institute for Strategic Studies, 2008.
Humphrey, Caroline. "Remembering an 'Enemy': The Bogd Khaan in Twentieth-Century Mongolia." In *Memory, History, and Opposition under State Socialism*, edited by Rubie S. Watson, 21–44. Santa Fe, NM: School of American Research Press, 1994.
Kansteiner, Wulf. "Finding Meaning in Memory: A Methodological Critique of Collective Memory Studies." *History and Theory* 41, no. 2 (2002): 179–97.
Legro, Jeffrey W. "What China Will Want: The Future Intentions of a Rising Power." *Perspectives on Politics* 5, no. 3 (2007): 515–34.
Liao, Ning. "Dualistic Identity, Memory-Encoded Norms, and State Emotion: A Social Constructivist Account of Chinese Foreign Relations." *East Asia: An International Quarterly* 30, no. 2 (2013): 139–60.
Liu, James H., and Tomohide Atsumi. "Historical Conflict and Resolution between Japan and China: Developing and Applying a Narrative Theory of History and Identity." In *Meaning in Action: Constructions, Narratives, and Representations*, edited by Toshio Sugiman, Kenneth J. Gergen, Wolfgang Wagner, and Yoko Yamada, 327–44. Tokyo: Springer, 2008.
Liu, Shih-Ding. "China's Popular Nationalism on the Internet: Report on the 2005 Anti-Japan Network Struggles." *Inter-Asia Cultural Studies* 7, no. 1 (2006): 144–55.
Livingston, Steven. "Transparency and the News Media." In *Power and Conflict in the Age of Transparency*, edited by Bernard I. Finel and Kristin M. Lord, 257–85. New York: Palgrave, 2002.
Ma, Licheng. "Duiri guanxi xin siwei: Zhongri minjian zhiyu" [New thinking on Sino-Japanese relations: Worries of peoples]. *Strategy and Management* [Zhanlue uy guanli] 6 (2002): 41–47.
Miskimmon, Alister, Ben O'Loughlin, and Laura Roselle. *Strategic Narratives: Communication Power and the New World Order*. New York: Routledge, 2013.
Mitter, Rana. "Behind the Scenes at the Museum: Nationalism, History and Memory in the Beijing War of Resistance Museum, 1987–1997." *China Quarterly* 161 (2000): 279–93.
Narlikar, Amrita. "All That Glitters Is Not Gold: India's Rise to Power." *Third World Quarterly* 28, no. 5 (2007): 983–96.
O'Donnell, Guillermo, and Philippe C. Schmitter. "Part IV: Tentative Conclusions about Uncertain Democracies." In *Transitions from Authoritarian Rule: Prospects for De-*

mocracy, edited by Guillermo O'Donnell, Philippe C. Schmitter, and Laurence Whitehead. Baltimore: John Hopkins University Press, 1986.

ÓTuathail, Gearóid. "Theorizing Practical Geopolitical Reasoning: The Case of the United States' Response to the War in Bosnia." *Political Geography* 21, no. 5 (2002): 601–28.

Polkinghorne, Donald E. "Narrative and Self-Concept." *Journal of Narrative and Life History* 1, nos. 2–3: (1991): 135–53.

Reilly, James. "China's History Activism and Sino-Japanese Relations." *China: An International Journal* 4, no. 2 (2006): 189–216.

Reilly, James. "Remember History, Not Hatred: Collective Remembrance of China's War of Resistance to Japan." *Modern Asian Studies* 45, no. 2 (2011): 463–90.

Ricoeur, Paul. *Time and Narrative* (Volume 1). Translated by Kathleen McLaughlin and David Pellauer. Chicago: University of Chicago Press, 1984.

Rochon, Thomas. *Culture Moves: Ideas, Activism and Changing Values*. Princeton: Princeton University Press, 1998.

Rosenau, James N. *Linkage Politics: Essays on the Convergence of National and International Systems*. New York: Free Press, 1969.

Schudson, Michael. "How Culture Works: Perspectives from Media Studies on the Efficacy of Symbols." *Theory and Society* 18, no. 2 (1989): 153–80.

Seo, Jungmin. "Nationalism and the Problem of Political Legitimacy in China." In *Legitimacy: Ambiguities of Political Success or Failure in East and Southeast Asia*, edited by Lynn White, 141–82. Hackensack, NJ: World Scientific, 2005.

Shi, Yinhong. "Zhongri jiejin yu 'waijiao geming'" [Sino-Japanese rapprochement and 'diplomatic revolution']. *Strategy and Management* [Zhanlue yu guanli] 2 (2003): 71–75.

Shirk, Susan L. "Changing Media, Changing Foreign Policy in China." *Japanese Journal of Political Science* 8, no. 1 (2007): 43–70.

Snow, David A., E. Burke Rochford, Steven K. Worden, and Robert D. Benford. "Frame Alignment Processes: Micromobilization and Movement Participation." *American Sociological Review* 51, no. 4 (1986): 461–81.

Strait Times. "China: Beijing Tightens Controls on Domestic Reporting on Japan." October 4, 2004.

Todorov, Tzvetan. *The Poetics of Prose*. Translated by Richard Howard. Ithaca: Cornell University Press, 1977.

Volkan, Vamık D. *Bloodlines: From Ethnic Pride to Ethnic Terrorism*. New York: Farrar, Straus and Giroux, 1997.

Volkan, Vamık D. *Chosen Trauma, the Political Ideology of Entitlement and Violence*. 2004. Accessed July 1, 2015. http://www.vamikvolkan.com/Chosen-Trauma,-the-Political-Ideology-of-Entitlement-and-Violence.php

Waldron, Arthur. "China's New Remembering of World War II: The Case of Zhang Zizhong." *Modern Asian Studies* 30, no. 4 (1996): 869–99.

Wang, Zheng. "National Humiliation, History Education, and the Politics of Historical Memory: Patriotic Education Campaign in China." *International Studies Quarterly* 52, no. 4 (2008): 783–806.

Wang, Zheng. *Never Forget National Humiliation: Historical Memory in Chinese Politics and Foreign Relations*. New York: Columbia University Press, 2012.

Williams, Raymond. *Marxism and Literature*. Oxford: Oxford University Press, 1977.
Xinhua. "People's Daily Urges Chinese 'Never Forget National Humiliation.'" September 18, 2011. Accessed September 12, 2012. http://news.xinhuanet.com/english2010/indepth/2011-09/18/c_131145289.htm
Zhang, Jian. "The Influence of Chinese Nationalism on Sino-Japanese Relations." In *China-Japan Relations in the Twenty-First Century: Creating a Future Past?*, edited by Michael Heazle and Nick Knight, 15–34. Cheltenham, UK: Edward Elgar, 2007.

6 | Beyond Neoliberalism

Contested Narratives of International Development

J. P. Singh

Efforts in international organization to improve human well-being and uplift millions of people from poverty constitute one of the greatest stories begun in the last century. The *idea of international development* can be traced back to the evolution of political economy as an academic discipline, but its instrumentalization as a set of strategic narratives to be pushed on to states and societies, initially from the imaginations of technocrats in international organizations charged with a development mandate, matured after World War II. The narrative continues to evolve as nearly one billion people in the world still live below the poverty line. At the same time, Africa now leapfrogs with mobile phone technology, while some countries join the ranks of the prosperous and others coalesce in people's imaginations as BRICs, an abbreviation Goldman Sachs economist Jim O'Neill coined in 2001 for the fast growing economies of Brazil, Russia, India, China, and South Africa (O'Neill 2001).

Stories change as do the agents narrating them. The narrative of international development, affecting as it did nearly two-thirds of global humanity living in what until recently was called the "Third World," could not be limited to the imaginations of technocrats and experts. Often the development imaginary is presented in scholarship as monolithic around a core set of beliefs that do not seem to change. However, even when the development imaginary was created to replicate the success stories of industrialization in the West, considerable critiques from the grassroots and within international organizations informed the narrative.

This essay details the way that the strategic narrative of international development has evolved, been contested, and become institutionalized in various ways within different international organizations. The term narrative in the singular refers to the efforts of directing development from international organizations such as the World Bank or the United Nations Educational, Scientific, and Cultural Organization (UNESCO). Within this grand narrative are micronarratives about specific development strategies rooted in the collective understandings of organizations. But in the singular, these international organizations share Enlightenment and liberal beliefs toward eradicating poverty (Jones 2004). These beliefs are now institutionalized in historically formed developmental ideals imagined at global agencies to provide a better future for humankind. International political economy concentrates on spaces of wealth production to locate the structural dimensions of global power. A focus on development narratives returns us to the imaginaries or narratives shaping the well-being of a majority of the world's population. It would be hard to describe the experience of development without attending to these narratives, which literally "identified" more than half the world as "developing" while its peoples responded by internalizing this identity in their aspirations.

Most extant accounts of international development tend to focus on the rise of the Washington Consensus or market-based solutions to alleviating global poverty since the late 1980s. This essay first provides the prehistory and the context that accounted for the rise of the Washington Consensus. This essay concurs with scholars that the Washington Consensus was a departure from the earlier narrative about state-led development, but it was not a major departure: it continued the *idea* of development from above and built upon many micro extant approaches. Within the consensus there were variations. The essay presents the state of international development practices at global governance institutions to present multiple mininarratives that arose starting in the late 1980s: rights-based approaches, human development approaches, and participatory and deliberative approaches. Empirically, the paper compares the approaches within and across the World Bank, the World Trade Organization, the United Nations Development Program, and UNESCO. The chapter shows how the contestation and tensions among these multiple narratives are resolved or not resolved in the Millennium Development Goals that came into being in 2000, and the way that they were understood in various global agencies.

This essay tells a messy story, but with a denouement whereby the tensions and synergies among various narratives are resolved through the idea of Millennium Development Goals framed by the United Nations in 2000. The idea of international development is a story, to employ the words of this volume's introduction, with no fixed content. But it does allow various organizations, states, and peoples to connect. In this sense, the idea of international development "constitutes the total imagination experience" for improving human conditions in the developing world (Miskimmon et al., introduction, this volume). In doing so, the strategic narratives of development undergo the same stages of narrativity as the other narratives explained in this volume. This includes the formation of the development narrative among elite actors, projection onto states and societies via a variety of communication mechanisms internationally, and the reception or acceptance or contestation of this narrative by global humanity or the audience affected by the narratives.

Staging Growth

The development imaginary of the postwar era was deeply situated in strategies to alleviate poverty in what came to be known as the modernization approach based on the European and U.S. industrialization experiences. The strategic narrative for development or eradication of poverty in the immediate postwar era, fashioned mostly by economists, reflected the dominant understandings regarding the industrialization experiences in Western Europe and the United States. Although the development narrative in these states had been market driven, there were significant variations in the varieties of capitalism and the instruments for their realization. States had also experimented with socialist industrialization strategies. Therefore, economists in international development agencies reflected both the consensus to forge a strategic narrative from above and the need to center this narrative on "magic bullets" such as industrialization. By the time the market-driven Washington Consensus took root in the 1980s, the development narrative had already been through an entire cycle of market-based and state-led industrialization practices and concurrent critiques. This section, therefore, disputes the idea that neoliberalism arrived in the 1980s. The next section will debate whether this neoliberalism was monolithic.

The idea narrative of international development is inextricably linked to the ideals informing global governance and the formation of the United

Nations (system narratives). The Enlightenment belief in progress and a budding international liberalism resulted in the creation of the United Nations. One of the great ideas to come from the UN and its agencies was "development strategies" (Jolly, Emeril, and Weiss 2009, chap. 7). The development narrative, crafted in the gilded halls of the United Nations and soon accepted among the state bureaucrats and policymakers in the developing world, was thus a top-down exercise. In doing so, the postcolonial world inherited its dominant meaning about its material well-being from a Western experience.

The evolution of the development agenda in international organizations was also not straightforward. The premier agency charged with economic development, the International Bank for Reconstruction and Development (World Bank), viewed its mandate chiefly in terms of the reconstruction of Europe in the early years. However, many factors were converging to make development economics a dominant narrative in the international agencies (Hirschman 1981). The postcolonial states were ready to proceed with what they perceived to be autonomous (noncolonial) development, and a mixture of market-based, Keynesian, central planning, and other experiences rooted in Western European economic history provided the narrative.

Walt Rostow's (1960) narrative about the "stages of growth" perhaps best captures the industrial development strategy that came to be known as modernization. With the European industrialization experience in mind, Rostow argued that there were five stages of growth from a "traditional society" to the "age of high mass consumption." The important stages for modernization were the "pre-take-off" and the "take-off" stages, which generated surpluses in agriculture that were channeled toward industrialization. This mimicked English industrialization (Landes 1969). Growth through capital became "the Holy Grail" of development strategies, in the words of Shahid Yusuf and Angus Deaton (2009, 7). In turn, the elite in the postcolonial worlds accepted that progress, industrialization, and material well-being were correlated. India adopted an ambitious state-led Industrial Policy Resolution in 1956, with Prime Minister Jawaharlal Nehru declaring: "Now India we are bound to be industrialized, we are trying to be industrialized, we must be industrialized" (quoted in Byres 1982, 135).

Development economics fashioned a narrative from a specific European experience, and both its assumptions and its transferability were eventually called into question by anthropologists and sociologists. Arturo Escobar (1995), in evaluating the modernization narrative, writes that representations are constitutive of reality. The modernization narrative assumed that there were "backward societies" and "underdevelopment" and that populations, imagined as docile and obedient in the narrative, were in need of the strategies advocated from technocrats housed in international institutions who propagated the narrative to the "native" governments (Hill 1986; Ferguson 1990; Escobar 1995). Such reasoning was part of the "authoritarian high modernism" that vested great authorities in states to direct the human condition (Scott 1998). Most of these projects failed or, as Scott puts it, "'fiasco' is too lighthearted a work for the disasters I have in mind" (3). Industries did not take off, agricultural yields did not improve, and social conditions remained static. Those questioning the modernization narrative tend to critique the way the developing world was imagined: like the thesis of Edward Said's *Orientalism* (1978), they were seen as inferior and in need of assistance from international organizations and Western governments.

There was another important element to the modernization narrative that did not reflect Western European industrialization history but borrowed from the centralized planning exercises that had been taken up in the Soviet Union and, later, China. State planning agencies in the developing world drew up planning goals, usually for five years, which shaped development agendas at all governance levels. The industrialization strategy was known as import substitution industrialization (ISI); instead of expensive imports, states would manufacture or license cheaper substitutes at home. China would manufacture bicycles instead of automobiles, India would ration resources into core sectors the state identified. Thus, the postwar narrative was not entirely Western.

> Rapid growth through industrialization that was planned and partially—or wholly—executed by government agencies and buffered by import and exchange controls was the model of development that the new nations adapted from the industrial West and from the then-resurgent communist bloc. (Yusuf and Deaton 2009, 6)

ISI was also not entirely state-driven. Although the size and share of public enterprises grew, most states also set up complicated licensing and regulatory regimes to jump-start private industry. The set of protections to both private and public industry was rooted in the infant industry argument that shielded them from competition while they nurtured their capital deployment. In particular, while states tended to control heavy industry (in resource extraction and metals, transportation and utilities), private business was encouraged in small- and medium-scale industries. Textiles and garments, often posited as the entry-level industry for industrialization, were also generally private sector driven (Vernon 1966). Similarly, private markets for exchanging goods and tertiary services also developed alongside public and private industry, though there were state controls in pricing and rationing. Behind all these mechanisms was an "omniscient state" that seldom appeared in the economic models disseminated from international organizations: as a black box, most economists believed the state would selflessly implement required policies in an efficient fashion. In practice, states garnered extraordinary power; with few checks on accountability or transparency, they supervised vast oversight regimes, best captured in the Indian postcolonial phrase "license-quote-permit-Raj" that replaced British rule.

ISI was a disaster. It delivered neither the growth rates nor industrialization, but led to bloated state apparatuses that became increasingly corrupt and debt-ridden. In India's case, the neglect of the rural agricultural basis of three-fourths of Indian society in the dominant industrialization narrative was costly. It led to almost a reversal to emphasize agriculture within a decade, and then increasing degrees of populism in politics. Import substitution was also import intensive. To start any type of industrialization meant galvanizing scarce resources, importing capital, and providing an infrastructure, including electricity and transportation. Initially, such capital came from development agencies such as the World Bank, but starting in the late 1960s world liquidity markets became flush with petrodollars. Governments, especially those in Latin America that were in relatively good health, began to borrow from international banks. On August 15, 1982, the Mexican finance minister announced that Mexico could no longer honor its debt-service payments. This snowballed to other Latin American economies, and a few in Africa and Asia, producing one of the biggest liquidity crises of the twentieth century. At the beginning of the crisis, the total debt burden of the developing world was $785 billion, which with nonpayments and rising interest rates in the 1980s, became $1.5 trillion in 1993 (Cupples 2005, 132).

Most economists acknowledge that there were improvements in indicators such as literacy and education, and the overall growth rate did improve from the colonial to the postcolonial era (table 6.1). However, these growth rates are often weighed against the counterfactual of countries that had opted for export-oriented and market-driven strategies, especially in what came to be known as the newly industrializing countries in East Asia. Such a picture also becomes apparent when comparing the growth rates of the ISI era in the 1970s and that of the 1980s and 1990s, which were marked with liberalization (table 6.2). While in theory state enterprises might have promoted growth and development, in practice most of the resources were diverted toward rescuing financially troubled enterprises. Belassa (1989, 176) notes that "the absence of clear-cut objectives for managers and state intervention in firm decision-making" accounted for gross inefficiency in the public sector.

The international development agencies furthered the ISI narrative, but alternative micronarratives also existed. One of these was the "basic needs" approach, which developed during Robert McNamara's presidency of the World Bank (1968–81) and also owed its origins to President Lyndon Johnson's War on Poverty. The basic needs approach shifted the bank focus from heavy industrialization toward provision of food, health, housing, and education. Again, though, the narrative worked from above, from the minds of technocrats and economists, and sought to recruit the same state officials and bureaucracies that had been so unsuccessful with the entire development enterprise in general. The black box of the state was a major lacuna in the development narrative.

TABLE 6.1. GDP Annual Growth Rates before and after 1950

	1913–50	1950–60	1950–68
Argentina	3.0	3.1	3.0
Brazil	4.6	5.8	5.3
Egypt	1.6	5.4	5.2
India	1.2	3.7	3.8
Mexico	2.6	6.1	6.2
Philippines	2.2	4.8	5.2
Taiwan	2.7	7.7	8.7

Source: Adapted from Bruton (1998), 915.

TABLE 6.2. GDP Annual Growth Rate after 1970 (Select Years)

Income Aggregates (countries)	1970	1980	1990	2000	2010
Low income	4.5	2.3	2.8	3.5	6.1
Lower middle income	6.7	9.7	3.8	4.0	7.3
Middle income	7.2	5.2	1.9	5.4	7.7

Source: World Bank Development Indicators. Accessed January 5, 2013. http://databank.worldbank.org

The way that development was conceived also reflected the history of poverty initiatives and community participation in contexts such as the United States. Most of these initiatives were top-down. Philip Selznick's (1984 [1949]) early study of the Tennessee Valley Authority showed that its grassroots approach was a narrative manufactured to recruit participants, and those opposed to this ideology were termed selfish by TVA. Similarly, Moynihan (1969) examines the Community Action Programs that came out of 1964 Economic Opportunity Act (President Johnson's War on Poverty) as representing the "misunderstandings" of liberal "activist social scientists" from New York rather than meaningful grassroots inputs. This ideology carried over into the paternalistic P.L. 480 food distribution and the green revolution initiatives from the U.S. Agency for International Development and the Rockefeller Foundation (Cullather 2010). As such, they informed Johnson appointee Robert McNamara's basic needs agenda as World Bank president from 1968 to 1981.

The stage was set in the 1980s for revisiting the dominant (top-down) and the micronarratives (central planning, ISI, basic needs). This came in the form of the turn toward markets. State controls had not worked, ISI had failed, and state enterprises reeked of corruption and inefficiency. There was thus a "bottom-up" push for deregulation and decentralization of state controls. This began to happen in Brazil after the fall of the military dictatorship in 1985, with the entry of Rajiv Gandhi into Indian politics in 1984, and in many other states. Regimes changed as their economies worsened. No doubt, the Washington Consensus, as it came to be known in 1989 after economist John Williamson coined the term, brought together the World Bank, the International Monetary Fund, and the U.S. Treasury Department together into pushing for markets, deregulation, and liberalization. However, it is a narrative stretch to argue that "neoliberalism," as it is sometimes pejoratively labeled, arose only from Washington. It reflected as much the grassroots consequences of the high-modernist ideology of ISI as it did the strategy rethink in Washington.

Neoliberalism and Its Contents

The narrative of international development did become increasingly market-driven from the late 1980s in the so-called triumph of neoliberalism. It represented moves toward deregulation, privatization, and the liberalization of enterprises and markets. It also reflected the failure of state-led import substitution strategies. Even as the new narrative unfolded, it showcased considerable variations in the particular neoliberal ideas that were adopted by various international development agencies. These ideas can be traced back equally to prominent actors in the Ronald Reagan administration in the United States or Margaret Thatcher's United Kingdom, and to growing frustrations with the ISI strategy among policymakers and bureaucrats in the developing world.

The role of ideas in pushing forward a narrative during windows of opportunity is well known. In this case, the international development organizations rejuvenated and reinforced ideas from neoclassical economics that already enjoyed some sustenance within their ranks. Even when the World Bank encouraged state-led growth, its rhetoric accommodated and pushed some forms of market incentives, and the entire focus on economic growth as the mantra of development was derived from neoclassical economics. The International Monetary Fund, the World Bank's neighbor across the street in Washington, DC, had always championed market measures, especially through its structural adjustment policies, which generally asked for severe devaluations and budgetary controls in return for loans to offset fiscal crises.

The following two quotations help us to understand the ideational dimensions of neoliberal institutionalization, but are careful in not overstating the departure from previous eras.

> The internationalization of economic training, through the Bretton Woods institutions and the graduate departments of American and European universities, has clearly increased the viability of orthodoxy by creating a cadre of economists in many developing countries who can understand its outlines and are attracted (in part) to its coherence. (Kahler 1990, 59)

> Ideas may have an independent explanatory role by way of a number of different transmission mechanisms. First, there may be general contagion effects and policy emulation. . . . Second, there may be a "trickle-up" process where ideas gain initial acceptance among academic economists, who subsequently press their policy advice on the political leadership. (Biersteker 1995, 185)

The neoliberal policies adopted at the World Bank and the International Monetary Fund are certainly consistent with these views. Nevertheless, the independent role of ideas in understanding the development narrative, without first placing them in material conditions, provides an incomplete picture, even though the material conditions may themselves be understood as resulting from previous ideas. Biersteker (1995, 185) acknowledges that while neoclassical ideas had been around for a long time, it "took a particular system-wide shock to prompt a major reversal in thought." Central planning had failed in the developing world, and the breakdown of communism in the Soviet Union and Eastern Europe further strengthened the case for market-driven policies.

At the broadest level, the turn to neoliberalism meant less faith in state-led development efforts. The dominant experience of the development narrative, nevertheless, remained unchanged even with the "new" liberal ideas: this experience still meant that there were magic bullets that would induce development. The neoliberal actors were also the same except in a new guise: the World Bank became strident about market-led strategies. A new generation of leaders in the developing world, from Rajiv Gandhi in India to Carlos Salinas in Mexico, began to dismantle state enterprises and allow private foreign and domestic investment.

The breakdown of the central planning model did not mean that states completely abandoned these exercises. Most countries that formulated these central plans earlier continue to do so. The breakdown of the central planning model did mean liberalization of the state's control over the economy. Private sector investment was to be favored and the existing public sector enterprises were corporatized and liberalized. Capital formation was slow during the ISI phase and labor productivity was low. The new narrative sought to hasten capital formation through private and foreign investment and competition, which would also raise labor productivity. The East Asian Miracle was often cited as an example of the success of an outward-oriented strategy (World Bank 1993).

Evolutionary narratives often reveal the influence of new agents and ideas. The rise of neoliberalism since the 1980s is often confused with old ideas and institutions. Harvey (2007, 19), for example, notes that the rise of neoliberalism in the 1980s was in large part a response "to restore the power of economic elites." The rest of this subsection argues otherwise. The neoliberal narrative, since the 1980s, was shaped within the broad context of old as well as emergent ideas in political economy and global governance, and was not as monolithic as critics of neoliberalism sometimes assume. It included many subvariants that were often not compatible with each other within and across various international organizations. A few of these are now explained including a focus on institutions, poverty and human development, and participatory development.

Institutions and Property Rights

The rationale for state intervention for development in the ISI era was located in the idea of market failure, apart from the belief to some extent in socialism or the social welfare state. A turn to neoliberalism with any kind of overwhelming faith in the developing world's markets that until then had been assumed not to exist, at least in a well-functioning way, would have been naïve. Thus the neoliberal turn as a problem-solving strategic narrative also sought to create markets rather than to assuming their existence. A few economists believed that neoliberal ideas could be introduced with one fell swoop, including Jeffrey Sachs, who changed his mind toward a gradualist approach in the 1990s. Most advocated a gradualist approach in creating market institutions. Both approaches were, however, ignorant of the fact that forms of transactional exchange that could be understood as markets already existed in most societies (Guyer 2004; Hill 1986), or that developing countries, in an exploitative sense, had been integrated into global labor and commodity chains since colonial days (Amin 1977; Cardoso and Faletto 1979; Ferguson 1990). Thus, the focus on creating markets, while cognizant of markets as being institutions, was again a top-down instrumental narrative instead of a bottom-up strategy that would seek to integrate existing markets into intended outcomes.

A narrative regarding the development of markets had evolved in the postwar era and generally became associated with institutional economics. This narrative put forth a case for organizing economic incentives through markets. Ronald Coase (1937), in his theory of the firm, had shown that firms did not trust markets to make all the decisions and internalized some decisions, even on prices. These were the beginnings of the literature on transaction costs, costs over and above those of factors of production including materials and labor to make a product. The implication was that well-functioning markets reduced transaction costs. As transactions occur in uncertainty, risk, and differential information, there are always opportunities for some actors to gain at the expense of others. Based on such analysis, North and Thomas (1973) elaborated their theory of property rights—formal or informal rules and incentives governing markets. Empirically, their argument drew mostly upon European economic history. If property rights confer privileges upon few, usually through their access to government, then the resulting growth would be stilted. Olson (1965, 1982) took a similar position, in fact to argue that collective action is easier for small groups who can then divert state resources and rules in their favor. In his Nobel Laureate address, Douglass North (1994, 361) argued the following: "It is exceptional to find economic markets that approximate the conditions necessary for efficiency. It is impossible to find political markets that do." North, therefore, urged a study of human learning and organizations in complex institutional environments.

The task of market creation was, therefore, deemed difficult in institutional economics because the economic elite had both the benefits of collective action and access to governments to capture all the benefits in their favor. When public sectors were liberalized, political elites in several countries became de facto oligarchs and owners of capital. Such instances also represented highly personalized forms of exchange rather than the arms-length impersonal exchanges that liberal economists argued led to market creation in Western Europe (Greif 2006).

Institutional economics concentrated on mechanisms that would thwart special interests and provide incentives for large sections of the population. This would include creating governance institutions that would limit the power of the elite. One popular idea was to create independent regulatory agencies that would be somewhat shielded from direct political pressures. Especially as the policy elite in developing countries liberalized markets, the incumbent public sector or newly privatized monopolies possessed enormous resources to block competition. Independent regulation and dispute settlement would ensure that latecomers were not penalized. Thus, the era of liberalization also led to the creation of regulatory agencies in the developing world, especially in the provision of investment licenses and in service sectors such as communication, transportation and freight, and energy supplies. Price evolution was another subject. Many prices under ISI were fixed by the state, making it hard to determine cost-based market prices. Institutional economists adopted several mechanisms that would either mimic market prices or reward enterprises for moving toward them.

As developing country elites began to move toward outward-oriented or export-led strategies, trade and exchange rate institutions also became important for them. However, monetary economists, who are less sympathetic toward the task of gradually creating market institutions, dominate institutions such as the IMF. The structural adjustment policies were often derogatorily called "sappy" policies; the devaluations caused prices to rise and produced social unrest and riots in many countries from the 1960s to the 1990s, while the IMF argued in favor of hard medicine that needed to be swallowed. Even in the late 1990s, though, while the IMF argued for central bank independence and diminishing of capital controls, the East Asian financial crisis in 1997 legitimized the opposite with states such as Malaysia and South Korea, which reinstated the role of the state and capital controls. After the Asian financial crisis, even the IMF tacitly accepted that its devaluation or structural adjustment policies had wreaked havoc in the past.

The World Trade Organization is mostly a negotiation forum to create markets. In policy terms, its approach is gradualist as states negotiate market liberalizing concessions with each other. In practice, trade economists inform WTO's dominant narrative rooted in the doctrine of comparative advantage, which notes that countries differ in their factor endowments and are advantaged to export those products that come from the abundant, and therefore relatively cheaper, factor in any economy. Developing countries have often been marginalized economically through this narrative: if the abundant factor was land or unskilled labor, they would be stuck in what economist Jagdish Bhagwati called "immiserizing growth," or one where they produced low-cost highly price sensitive products, while the developed world produced high-tech "price inelastic" items. Therefore, in trade institutions such as the WTO, developing countries demanded special and differential treatment, to protect their agricultural products from diminishing demands, or provide them breathing room to create or join markets. But special and differential treatment was not forthcoming in practice. One of the sticking points in the currently stalled Doha Round of trade talks, which began in November 2001, is the slow rollout of special and differential treatment. Trade ministers reached a mini WTO deal in Bali in December 2013 to encourage "trade facilitation," or making the rules and regulations governing markets affecting trade (including customs procedures) less onerous and more transparent.

In summary, institutional economics, especially the narrative practiced at the World Bank, remained top down and instrumental, even if it was gradualist in its approach. Economists would design strategies that would lead to market creation, even as some provisions were negotiated through the WTO, or protested on the streets as with IMF policies following the Asian financial crisis. As in the previous era, the efficacy of the institutions to be designed and the strategies to be followed were derived mostly from Western economic history. Nevertheless, the charge that neoliberal institutional economics only forwarded the interests of the economic elite is misplaced unless economists or the competitive enterprises they sought to create are understood only in elite terms. In their own terms, the economists were creating institutions whose benefits would accrue to large sections of societal populations. Institutional economics, which represents the training of perhaps a majority of economists at the World Bank, also parts company with neoclassical economics in many ways, especially in not keeping tastes, technology, and institutions as constant or ceteris paribus. Neoclassical economics is centered on prices, while other variables remain ceteris paribus. The neoliberal and neoclassical agendas can be conflated for the IMF and the WTO. However, the WTO has responded to the needs and agendas of the developing world. Another reason that the Doha Round is stalled is because the developed countries have been unable to prevail over or bully the developing world—especially coalitions featuring Brazil, China, India, and South Africa—not only on issues of importance to the developing world but even on issues of the high-tech new economies (Singh 2008). Here, rather than caving in to a neoclassical agenda, developing countries have sought to fashion it in their favor, albeit with mixed results.

Human Development

International development narratives are projected through international institutions, which further shape or adapt them. Just as the World Bank's approach to development moved from ISI to institutional neoliberalism, the critique among social scientists and policymakers that it was narrowly measured with economic growth or per capita incomes grew louder. The approach that countered the World Bank's claim has come to be known as human development and arose in practice from the United Nations Development Programme.

The human development approach is associated closely with the work of economists Amartya Sen and Mahbub ul Haq. Amartya Sen's work (1983, 1999) on entitlements and development as freedom sought to go beyond earning and growth to ask what sort of life people are entitled to in various societies. For example, high per capita incomes in various countries may not instruct us on the roles and freedoms that women might avail in strongly patriarchal societies. The human development theory is embedded in liberal political theory, and thus can be termed neoliberal both for its content and for the neoliberal development agency that houses the narrative.

The UNDP was created in 1965 through a synthesis of several development agencies. Unlike the World Bank, it does not offer loans but technical assistance. The UNDP and the World Bank are now often compared as offering different visions of development. Just as human development challenged the approach rooted in economic growth, the UNDP also countered the World Bank's flagship annual publication, the World Development Report, published since 1978, with an annual Human Development Report (HDR) that started to be published in 1990. The data listed in the World Development Report were about indicators such as growth rates in incomes, industrialization, and agricultural productivity. Instead, the HDR began publishing a Human Development Index, formulated by Mahbub ul Haq, which took into account income growth and social entitlements such as education and life expectancy.

The human development narrative was flexible enough to bring in concerns about governance and justice that impact people's entitlements and capabilities. The intellectual creativity had brought in academics and policymakers who do not converge on economics. The administrator for UNDP today is Helen Clark, the former prime minister of New Zealand and a sociology professor. Craig Murphy provides the following assessment of UNDP's work:

> One reason for the ever-expanding network at the core of the global HDRs is that most reports focus on one or another new dimension, a new side of the wealth of relationships and current policy choices that determine the degree to which every human being can enjoy a full life—for example, income inequality, poor governance, restrictive gender relations, and over- and under-consumption. . . . Each of the new dimensions explored have, in turn, helped to maintain the vitality of the larger human development research programme and of the concept itself. (Murphy 2006, 247)

The human development approach—or, broadly, development with a human face as it came to be known as at the United Nations Children Fund (UNICEF)—has paralleled or spawned other narratives that speak to similar concerns. To be sure, the focus on human beings themselves, rather than as part of some output ratio, had precedents. Economics Nobel Prize laureate Gunnar Myrdal famously derided the economists' capital-output ratios as violin-music ratios, which forgot the violinist. The United Nations Development Program (UNDP) thus succeeded in making these narratives institutional concerns during a period when international development narratives were settling into a dominant framework that came from the World Bank. In fact, UNDP helped to encourage similar initiatives within the Bank including participatory development (see below). The two agencies have also collaborated on various projects together.

Human development, or development with a human face, must also acknowledge its limitations. First, UNDP is as inaccessible as the World Bank to grassroots development practitioners, including NGOs, and even human development appears as a set of "technical assistance" programs designed in New York. While UNDP briefly turned toward community-led initiatives in the late 1990s, its connections to the epistemic communities in academia are stronger than knowledge generated at the community level (Murphy 2006, 347–49).

Second, in moving beyond UNDP, there are human initiatives that are well meaning and even institutionalized. But they are broadly philosophical, and neither the communities from below nor elite bureaucrats or policymakers know how to engage with them. One such approach is the characterization of poverty as a human rights violation. This approach, advocated by political theorist Thomas Pogge (2007), was briefly deliberated at UNESCO. Pogge argued that just as racism and slavery revealed societal prejudices, so does the continuation of poverty. Calling forth another analogy, Pogge (2007, 20) notes: "if torture is so horrible that one must not engage in it even when a great deal is at stake, then it is hard to deny that one ought to save a person from torture when one can do at small cost. If this inference is indeed undeniable, then the human right entails the moral duty." Poverty elimination was posited as a human rights issue in the sense of humankind's moral duty to prevent oppressive practices. Pogge's formulation narrative attracted the attention of Pierre Sané, former head of Amnesty International, head of UNESCO's Social and Human Sciences sector. The human rights approach was adopted by UNESCO in 2001 and is related to UNESCO's mandate to remove the structural causes of violence (Singh 2011). Nevertheless, within five years the initiative had died because of resistance from member states and the inability to spell out its feasibility (McNeill and St. Clair 2009, 125–28).

Participatory Development and Culture

Narratives are not only contested but they also respond to each other. The persistent counternarrative to ideas shaped and implemented from international organizations was that they were not in touch with grassroots contexts and participation. The instrumental imaginary of postwar international development is often characterized as monologic, while dialogic communication informs participatory development. Participatory narratives are, therefore, presented as inherently emancipatory in allowing populations voice and in bringing out the centrality of communication in the shaping of development narratives.

The concept of dialogic communication, as a pedagogy of development, dates back to the Brazilian educator and activist Paulo Freire, who locates its origins in consciousness awakening—a form of learning and knowing in which the subjects understand their historical circumstances and are able to name the world and themselves within it, thus finding a cultural voice. This is the necessary condition for the oppressed to see their circumstances "as a limiting situation they can transform" (Freire 2000 [1970], 49). The next step is dialogic communication, the sufficient condition, which entails problem-solving informed by multiple or dialectical perspectives. The latter allow the actors to examine their life situation from multiple perspectives and indulge in problem-solving. "In this theory of action one cannot speak of *an actor*, nor simply of *actors*, but rather of *actors in communication*" (Freire 2000, 129).

Latin American writers responded first to Freire, in the tradition of development praxis that came to be known as participatory action research (PAR), and it provided not just a critique of modernization theory but, more recently, of neoliberalism ideology in general. Broadly conceived, there is an element of participation at the local level in most development interventions these days. However, participation does not necessarily lead to consciousness awakening unless subjects are able to name their world, challenge or question existing power relations, and then articulate action (the A in PAR) aimed toward transformation. PAR scholarship seldom meets all these criteria. At the risk of sounding simplistic, most PAR scholarship so far has either critiqued models of development as being too driven by existing power holders or it articulates the hopelessness of being able to effect genuine participatory action. Huesca's (2003) essay analyzing the evolution of PAR records a 1978 seminar on participatory communication at the Center for Advanced Studies and Research for Latin America where scholars "concluded that uses of mass media in development imposed the interests of dominant classes" (211). He notes that in subsequent years the participatory paradigm may have been misused and hijacked by development agencies such as the World Bank where no genuine participation took place and power holders were unwilling to yield anything to the marginalized. He notes a few instances where alternative and participatory media might be utilized effectively, but in general this essay is pessimistic about the prospects for PAR. He concludes by noting that researchers should push the PAR agenda "by aligning themselves with new social movements that have recently emerged worldwide" (221). Similarly, Escobar's (1995) critique of modernization imaginary narratives, frequently cited by PAR scholars, remains a critique of modernization ideas rather than a constructive step toward laying out the feasibility of an alternative pedagogy as Freire had done. Huesca's call regarding social movements is misplaced; without genuine participation in grassroots development work, joining social movements, while a good expression of solidarity with the oppressed, can devolve into empty sloganeering. Freire's praxis was rooted in grassroots work with peasants in Latin America and Africa, which he understood as a call for cultural action (see Freire 2000 [1970], chap. 4). Therefore, engaging in grassroots development work rather than joining social movements may be a better avenue for PAR praxis (Singh and Hart 2004).

On the other hand, it must be acknowledged that central elements of dialogic communication are often missing from development projects that claim to be participatory. At a macro level, this includes the Poverty Reduction Strategy Papers (PRSPs) that the World Bank and the International Monetary Fund introduced in 1999 as a precondition for debt relief. Each country had to prepare these PRSPs, which entailed broad participation from communities, stakeholders, and policymakers. In practice, however, PRSPs yielded mixed results; not only is such broad participation very difficult to implement, but it also ignores existing power relations (Mansuri and Rao 2013; Gaynor 2010). Ghazala Mansuri and Vijayendra Rao (2013), World Bank economists themselves, are also skeptical of types of participation that are "induced" from states or power holders, rather than as outcomes of "organic" civil society or social movement processes. In a prior era, while exploring the precarious links between democratic participation and modernization in the developing world, Huntington and Nelson (1976) had distinguished between mobilized and autonomous participation. A widely used manual at the

World Bank on participatory methods (Rietbergen-McCracken and Narayan 1998) presents experts who engage people at the grassroots utilizing various participatory techniques. However, in most of these methods the emphasis is on engagement, rather than questioning the ways in which the experts acquired the codes and representations with which they wish to foster engagement.

Another way to foster participation is to engage, ideationally or in practice, with the broader context of culture of everyday life in an anthropological sense. Institutional economics, with its focus on evolutionary rules governing human behavior, hints at culture but does not engage explicitly. North (1994, 364) writes: "It is culture that provides the key to path dependence—a term used to describe the powerful influence of the past on the present and future." Nevertheless, the language of culture, like that of poverty as a human rights violation, is difficult to construct. An important publication from the World Bank (Rao and Walton 2004), reflecting the buildup of initiatives in other UN agencies described below, brought together interdisciplinary practitioners to conceptualize a development agenda rooted in cultural practices. The volume speaks to understanding preferences, incentives, and behaviors as rooted in cultural practices. However, the broader reaches of the World Bank have not responded to including cultural variables. President Obama's appointment of the anthropologist Jim Yong Kim as president of the World Bank could, however, move this issue forward.

Historically, UNESCO with its World Heritage program had begun to explicitly promote the idea of cultural policies but the links to development, in the form of alleviation of poverty and deprivation, had not been made. The 1982 World Conference on Cultural Policies, or Mondiacult, held in Mexico City tried to forge this link through an anthropological focus on culture. In 1987, UN secretary-general Javier Peréz de Cuéllar responded to pressures from the Group of 77 (G-77) developing countries to declare 1988–97 as the Decade for Culture and Development. The idea of a World Commission on Culture and Development originated from this decade.

In 1993, UN secretary-general Boutros Boutros-Ghali and UNESCO director-general Federico Mayor created the World Commission on Culture and Development. Peréz de Cuéllar, the former secretary-general of the UN, was appointed its president. The Commission presented its report, *Our Creative Diversity*, to both the UN General Assembly and the UNESCO General Conference in 1995. The central lesson of the report is aptly summarized in the oft-quoted first sentence of the report's executive summary: "Development divorced from its human or cultural context is growth without a soul" (Peréz de Cuéllar 1995, 15).

The World Commission on Culture and Development was responding to various historical and ideational narrative developments in its report (Arizpe 2004). As these ideas progressed through the UN and UNESCO, they also reflected the link between culture and development explicitly addressed in colonialist and postcolonial literatures that questioned the oppressive imposition of "White" cultures in the colonial worlds. Writers such as Aimé Cesaire, Amilcar Cabral, Frantz Fanon, Léopold Senghor, Steve Biko, and Paulo Freire highlighted the oppression of the cultural factors of colonialism that assigned people an inferior status: only through a consciousness awakening and a cultural voice from within would the developing world free itself of such oppression. "Poverty, national oppression, and cultural repression are one and the same," wrote Frantz Fanon (2004 [1963], 172). In 1978, Edward Said's powerful treatise *Orientalism* re-created in meticulous detail the genealogy of historical ideas in Europe that assigned inferiority to the Orient—its generalizability to all colonized and oppressed peoples was not difficult among intellectual communities. Like Fanon and Freire, Said (1978, 40) argued that the Occident created its superiority precisely by "othering" the Orient: "The Oriental is irrational, depraved (fallen), childlike, 'different'; thus the European is rational, virtuous, mature, 'normal.'"

Our Creative Diversity reflects the dual impetus to bring culture into debates on economic development, while being starkly aware that culture must be understood in a liberating sense of an ethic that allows for diversity, pluralism, and freedom. The report argued that "development embraces not only access to goods and services but also the opportunity to choose a fully satisfying, valuable, and valued way of life" (Peréz de Cuéllar 1995, 14). It also took into account Samuel Huntington's (1993) provocative thesis on the clash of civilizations, which posited that the differences between the Judeo-Christian and Islamic-Confucian civilization were irreconcilable and thus an endemic source of conflict. *Our Creative Diversity*, instead, argued that cultural diversity should lead and not thwart endeavors of peaceful coexistence in recognizing that diversity is the basis of interaction and cultural syntheses.

Our Creative Diversity adopted ideas from UNDP's Human Development Reports, and argued for development as entitlement to a dignified way of life. Interestingly, the report pushed for competitive markets to assure provision of communication media services to people around the world. It also called for increasing the participation of women and young people, and public and private organizations at all levels of governance, to mobilize people for culture and development. The 1998 Stockholm Intergovernmental Conference on Cultural Policies for Sustainable Development marked the end of the World Decade for Cultural Development and followed the work of the World Commission on Culture and Development. The Stockholm conference sought to prioritize culture in development strategies and expand efforts to galvanize financial and human resources in support of such efforts. A direct result of the *Our Creative Diversity* report was the publication of World Culture Reports (1998 and 2000) by UNESCO. In conclusion, though, the agenda for culture and development did not move forward much even as UNESCO has continued to produce reports that highlight its importance (UNESCO 2009). A mix of resource constraints, lack of clear incentives, and the dominance of other cultural issues within UNESCO are the likely causes. The culture and development narrative was, for example, overshadowed by the debates on cultural diversity, mostly about entertainment/cultural industries, at UNESCO (Singh 2011).

A Brief Assessment

From a distance, the overwhelming narrative of international development appears to be monolithic and unchanging. While the broad narrative for international development may be described as neoliberal, created chiefly by economists, and shaped and projected through the agenda of the international organizations, there are significant micro variations within the broad narratives and interesting points of convergence and contrast among these international organizations. Table 6.3 summarizes the micronarratives for four of the international organizations described above. It is also important to note that narratives respond to each other and to their critiques. This accounts for their evolution. In particular, all the narratives have responded to the communication and reception of development strategies in the developing world. Most global organizations accord some attention to participatory development. Strategic themes of human rights and human development also reflect bottom-up societal and policy concerns, although the specific articulation of these concerns has depended upon academics and international bureaucrats.

Millennium Development Goals

A traditional hallmark of storytelling is a denouement, where often the strings and the loose ends are brought together. The launch of the Millennium Development Goals (MDG) project in 2000 at the United Nations seems to follow this logic. It is an ambitious project bringing together almost the entire United Nations and the international development community to agree to implement eight important goals by 2015 to which national governments would be held accountable. These eight goals are poverty reduction, universal education, gender equality, child health, maternal health, ending HIV/AIDS and other diseases, environmental sustainability, and global partnerships. The last goal was unique and followed UN secretary-general Kofi Annan's (1997–2006) moves toward a Global

TABLE 6.3. Development Organizations and Narratives

	World Trade Organization	World Bank	UNDP	UNESCO
Main objective	Trade liberalization	Development loans	Technical assistance	Culture of Peace
Main narrative	Trade causes growth	Institutions and markets cause growth	Human development	Cultural and human rights approaches
Theoretical exemplars	Neoclassical trade theory	Institutional political economy, randomization	Amartya Sen; Mahbub ul Haq; Martha Nussbaum	UN Commission on Culture and Development; Thomas Pogge
Subsidiary narrative	Special and differential treatment; capacity building	Community development; participatory development	Markets and technology: instruments of change	Think tank of the world
Practices	Negotiating and enforcing rules	Ideas bank; development project implementation	Ideas bank; development project implementation	Norm-making
Main practitioners	Economists; government ministries	Economists, a few social scientists, government ministries, NGOs	Economists, development scholars, UN bureaucrats, government officials, a few NGOs	Intellectuals, UN bureaucrats, government agencies, a few NGOs

Compact to bring businesses and civil society into the UN's governance processes along with member states in addressing crucial areas of human rights, labor practices, and the environment.

The momentum toward MDGs came from many quarters. First, the unraveling of the Washington Consensus, which focused on industry liberalization and reform of public finance, had led to calls in the international development community for a return to human aspects of development. In fact, the efforts at the UNDP and UNESCO to broaden the context and definition of development reflected such thinking. Leaders such as President Bill Clinton in the United States and Prime Minister Tony Blair in the United Kingdom were particularly open to such initiatives. The G8 Okinawa Summit in July 2000 raised issues of development in the shadow of the Asian financial crisis, which was largely a result of loose capital controls and subsequently controlled through state interventions. Second, and relatedly, a host of UN summits had prepared the groundwork for the MDGs. Fukuda-Parr and Hulme (2011) underscore the importance of UN summits such as the 1990 World Summit for Children and the Copenhagen Declaration at the World Social Summit in 1995 for both preparing the groundwork and mobilizing a set of policy entrepreneurs that would push this agenda narrative. They place MDGs in Finnemore and Sikkink's (1998) framework of norm formation for which norm champions are necessary for them to be recognized before they get adopted in organizations and countries. International NGOs such as the International Women's Health Coalition and the Third World Network played an important role as did well-placed individuals within the UN such as Jim Grant, executive director of UNICEF, and Nafis Sadik, a Pakistani physician at the UN Population Fund. After the Millennial declaration, Mark Malloch Brown at UNDP vigorously championed the agenda because it fit in to UNDP's mandate and also provided an opportunity for resources.

Nearly 200 heads of state met at the UN in September 2000 to issue the Millennium Declaration that led to the formulation of the MDGs. The Monterrey Consensus followed in March 2002 from the International Conference on Financing for Development, exhorting donor countries to commit resources and recipient countries to do more toward being accountable through measures such as reducing corruption (Fukuda-Parr 2004, 398). The Millennial Project was launched in 2002 to outline concrete measures for accountability. The measures taken later were based on recommendations presented from a task force headed by economist Jeffrey Sachs (UN Millennium Project 2005). To galvanize donors and communities to participate, the Millennial Campaign was also launched in 2002.

The MDGs brought together various strands of the international development narrative. Hulme (2010, 120) notes that the MDGs were a compromise between the neoliberal and human development approaches. Certainly, the focus on reducing poverty and hunger, gender empowerment, health, and education went beyond narrowly defined approaches. Goal eight on partnerships spoke to neoliberal aspects of development. But the MDGs also exclude priorities, mostly at the urging of member states. The UN agencies, note Fukuda-Parr and Hulme (2011, 27), "were sensitive to the demands of political expediency: to come up with a list that would be accepted by nearly 200 governments." They note five issues that were excluded: reproductive health, governance of human rights issues such as through democracy, gender issues addressing particular inequalities, youth employment, and quantitative targets for goal eight.

The synthetic approach to development is apparent in the agencies that have been brought in from the UN system, including the UN specialized agencies, to help implement the goals. (A list is available at http://www.un.org/millenniumgoals/.) A few agencies, such as UNDP, UNICEF, and the United Nations Fund for Population Activities, were at the forefront and pushed the MDG agenda as it coincided with their own efforts. Others, such as UNESCO and the International Telecommunication Union, saw opportunities, in education for the former and global partnerships for the latter, that would help the organizations attract resources. Institutions like the World Bank, however, were pushed in these debates through their sheer competence, including in matters of education that are part of UNESCO's mandate. Finally, institutions like the WTO had to be asked to participate in the MDGs, because the buy-in for them was not obvious, even though the currently under way Doha trade round is also known as the development round. The WTO linked goal seven, environmental sustainability, to trade practices.

The MDG narrative is both synthetic and grand. It is synthetic for the reasons described above: it pulls together various strands of development thinking and tries to galvanize the entire international development community toward implementing its goals. For these reasons, it also appears to be a grand narrative. It is grand in the Jean-François Lyotard (1984) sense of promoting a metanarrative of change, including solutions that would affect almost all global actors engaged in development. Despite the impetus, however, the MDGs lacked resource commitments, and even where the UN agencies tried earnestly, their instruments still remained top down as before. After the global financial crisis in 2007–8, the MDG agenda struggled hard to survive, though miraculously it did. In September 2015, the UN adopted a set of 'Sustainable Development Goals' that are to be implemented by 2030. The process of formulating SDGs invited greater input and participation from the global development communities.

Not surprisingly, the results from the MDGs have been mixed. The first goal's agenda of halving the number of people living in extreme poverty was achieved by 2008, eight years ahead of schedule. Similarly, the goal of halving the number of people without access to clean drinking water was achieved by 2010, five years ahead of time. But most of these percentage reductions are due to reductions in large absolute numbers in China and India. The *Millennium Development Goals Report* (United Nations 2012) shows details that have not been achieved, regions such as Sub-Saharan Africa that remain challenging, and promises from donors and recipients that have not been kept.

The MDGs reflect a synthesizing of development practitioners from various organizations and that of a variety of development narratives. The implementation record is an important indicator of the MDGs impact. However, the deepest impact of the MDGs lies in encapsulating the global development experience and moving development practitioners worldwide toward this common experience. The experience is inclusive in the sense just mentioned but also exclusionary in leaving out politically sensitive goals and in being yet another iteration of development strategies advocated from above. Poku and Whitman (2011, 6) provide the following assessment: "The MDGs have proved to have considerably more than rhetorical force, but less than might have been expected from the combined moral weight of the goals themselves and the unanimity of the international community behind them."

Conclusion

Narratives thrive with rituals and symbolism that allow people to imagine themselves in the story and participate in it. Strategic narratives of international development provide solutions to the endemic problems of poverty and marginalization. In doing so, they literally "identify" not just the set of actors that propose the formation and projection of these narratives but also the human beings who are affected by them. Given the variety of actors involved, strategic narratives are inclusive; strategically, they have to be inclusive to allow actors to identify with them. In practice, they are exclusive as well; issues can be excluded, as noted above in the case of the MDGs, to address controversies or sensitivities, or they can be exclusive in the way strategy is formulated. The strategic narratives of international development, until recently, were top-down and projected from elite officials in the Global North to those in the Global South.

The idea of international development at global institutions is grand in its symbolic dimensions. It is also dynamic. A few elements in this narrative have remained constant, even as those shaping the narrative accommodate other counternarratives. There remains a belief that development can be induced, and despite participatory efforts from the ground up, from global agencies. The latest iteration is the Millennium Development Goals, which even with some partial input from civil society is really a "UN show." While the goalposts that the MDGS have set have been only partially met, and probably not due to UN efforts in large part, these goals serve well to define the international development landscape in the 21st century in deepening one of the greatest enterprises of the last century—poverty elimination through global governance.

The biggest strength of the international development narrative is its accommodation of contrary and micronarratives within the limits of its top-down worldview in general. Underlying the ideology of neoliberalism, with which this narrative is often charged, are narratives about institutions, power, participation, voice, markets, class, gender, and race, to name just a few. From UNESCO's racism studies in the 1950s to ILO's push against child labor, there's hardly a micronorm that has not been accommodated in the narrative. Nevertheless, narratives are projected not just through the people whose experience they enfold but also through institutional strengths and priorities, and there are narratives that have not resonated with people and institutions. One such instance mentioned in this essay is that of the elimination of poverty as a human rights problem.

In terms of future direction a few trends stand out. First, the evolution of the international development narrative will continue to accommodate multiple actors because they now have a voice. Kofi Annan's Global Compact reflected this trend. But the new voices also come from the World Social Forum, which brings together the voices of the marginalized to counter those of the privileged in places such as the World Economic Forum. Second, the idea of development, while continuing to be grand, will lead to the design and implementation of projects that are piecemeal. The entire thrust of the randomization movement from political economy—to conduct random and micro trials before implementing any initiative—certainly points in this direction (Banerjee and Duflo 2011). Randomization, more than the MDGs, is the mantra within global organizations such as the World Bank.

REFERENCES

Amin, Samir. *Unequal Development: An Essay on the Social Formation of Peripheral Capitalism*. New York: Monthly Review Press, 1977.

Arizpe, Lourdes. "The Intellectual History of Culture and Development Institutions." In *Culture and Public Action*, edited by Vijayendra Rao and Michael Walton, 162–84. Stanford: Stanford University Press, 2004.

Banerjee, Abhijit V., and Esther Duflo. *Poor Economics: A Radical Rethinking of the Way to Fight Global Poverty*. New York: Public Affairs, 2011.

Belassa, Bela A. *New Directions in the World Economy*. New York: New York University Press, 1989.

Bhagwati, Jagdish. "Immiserizing Growth: A Geometrical Note." *Review of Economic Studies* 25, no. 3 (1958): 201–5.

Biersteker, Thomas. "The Triumph of Liberal Economic Ideas in the Developing World." In *Global Change, Regional Response: The New International Context for Development*, edited by Barbara Stallings. Cambridge: Cambridge University Press, 1995.

Bruton, Henry J. "A Reconsideration of Import Substitution." *Journal of Economic Literature* 36 (1998): 901–36.

Byres, Terence J. "India: Capitalist Industrialization or Structural Stasis?" In *The Struggle for Development: National Strategies in an International Context*, edited by Manfred Bienefeld and Martin Godfrey. New York: John Wiley and Sons, 1982.

Cardoso, Fernando Henrique, and Enzo Faletto. *Dependency and Development in Latin America*. Berkeley: University of California Press, 1979.

Coase, Ronald Harry. "The Nature of the Firm." *Economica* 4, no. 16 (1937): 386–405.

Coase, Ronald Harry. "The Problem of Social Cost." *Journal of Law and Economics* 3, no. 1 (1960): 1–44.

Cullather, Nick. *Hungry World: America's Cold War Battle against Poverty in Asia*. Cambridge: Harvard University Press, 2010.

Cupples, Julie. "Debt Crisis." In *Encyclopedia of International Development*, edited by Tim Forsyth, 131–33. London: Routledge, 2005.

Escobar, Arturo. *Encountering Development: The Making and Unmaking of the Third World*. Princeton: Princeton University Press, 1995.

Ferguson, James. *The Anti-Politics Machine: 'Development', Depoliticization, and Bureaucratic Power in Lesotho*. Cambridge: Cambridge University Press, 1990.

Finnemore, Martha, and Kathryn Sikkink. "International Norms Dynamics and Political Change." *International Organization* 52, no. 4 (1998): 887–917.

Freire, Paulo. *Pedagogy of the Oppressed*. New York: Continuum, 2000 [1970].
Fukuda-Parr, Sakiko. "Millennium Development Goals: Why They Matter." *Global Governance* 10 (2004): 395–402.
Fukuda-Parr, Sakiko, and David Hulme. "International Norm Dynamics and the 'End of Poverty': Understanding the Millennium Development Goals." *Global Governance* 17 (2011): 17–36.
Gaynor, Niamh. *Transforming Participation? The Politics of Development in Malawi and Ireland*. Basingstoke: Palgrave Macmillan, 2010.
Greif, Avner. *Institutions and the Path to the Modern Economy: Lessons from Medieval Trade*. Cambridge: Cambridge University Press, 2006.
Guyer, Jane. *Marginal Gains: Monetary Transactions in Atlantic Africa*. Chicago: University of Chicago Press, 2004.
Harvey, David. *A Brief History of Neoliberalism*. Oxford: Oxford University Press, 2007.
Hill, Polly. *Development Economics on Trial: The Anthropological Case for a Prosecution*. Cambridge: Cambridge University Press, 1986.
Hirschman, Albert O. "The Rise and Decline of Development Economics." In *Essays in Trespassing: Economics to Politics and Beyond*, edited by Albert O. Hirschman. Cambridge: Cambridge University Press, 1981.
Huesca, Robert. "Participatory Approaches to Communication for Development." In *International and Development Communication: A 21st Century Perspective*, edited by Bella Mody. Thousand Oaks, CA: Sage, 2003.
Hulme, David. *Global Poverty: How Global Governance Is Failing the Poor*. London: Routledge, 2010.
Huntington, Samuel. P. "The Clash of Civilization?" *Foreign Affairs* 72, no. 3 (1993).
Huntington, Samuel P., and Joan M. Nelson. *No Easy Choice: Political Participation in Developing Countries*. Vol. 3. Cambridge: Harvard University Press, 1976.
Jolly Richard, Louis Emeril, and Thomas G. Weiss. *UN Ideas That Changed the World*. Bloomington: Indiana University Press, 2009.
Jones, Gareth Steadman. *An End to Poverty? A Historical Debate*. New York: Columbia University Press, 2004.
Kahler, Miles. "Orthodoxy and Its Alternatives: Explaining Approaches to Stabilization and Adjustment." In *Economic Crises and Policy Choice: The Politics of Adjustment in the Third World*, edited by Joan M. Nelson, 33–62. Princeton: Princeton University Press, 1990.
Landes, David. *The Unbound Prometheus: Technological Change and Industrial Development in Western Europe from 1750 to the Present*. Cambridge: Cambridge University Press, 1969.
Lyotard, Jean-François. *The Post-Modern Condition: A Report on Knowledge*. Minneapolis: University of Minnesota Press, 1984.
Mansuri, Ghazala, and Vijayendra Rao. *Localizing Development: Does Participation Work?* Washington, DC: World Bank, 2013.
McNeill, Desmond, and Asunción Lira St. Clair. *Global Poverty, Ethics and Human Rights: The Role of Multilateral Organizations*. London: Routledge, 2009.
Moynihan, Daniel P. *Maximum Feasible Misunderstanding: Community Action in the War on Poverty*. New York: Arkville Press, 1969.

Murphy, Craig N. *The United Nations Development Programme: A Better Way?* Cambridge: Cambridge University Press, 2006.
North, Douglass C. "Economic Performance through Time." *American Economic Review* 84, no. 3 (1994): 359–68.
North, Douglass C., and Robert P. Thomas. *The Rise of the Western World: A New Economic History*. Cambridge: Cambridge University Press, 1973.
O'Neill, Jim. *Building Better Global Economic BRICs*. Global Economic Paper No. 66. London: Goldman Sachs Economic Research Group, 2001.
Olson, Mancur. *The Logic of Collective Action: Public Goods and the Theory of Groups*. Cambridge, MA: Harvard University Press, 1965.
Olson, Mancur. *The Rise and Decline of Nations: Economic Growth, Stagflation, and Social Rigidities*. New Haven: Yale University Press, 1982.
Olson, Mancur. "Dictatorship, Democracy, and Development." *American Political Science Review* 87, no. 3 (1993): 567–76.
Peréz de Cuéllar, Javier. *Our Creative Diversity: Report of the World Commission on Culture and Development*. Paris: UNESCO, 1995. Accessed July 1, 2015. www.unesdoc.UNESCO.org/images/0010/001055/105586e.pdf
Pogge, Thomas, ed. *Freedom from Poverty as a Human Right: Who Owes What to the Poor*. Paris: UNESCO, 2007.
Poku, Nana, and Jim Whitman. "The Millennium Development Goals: Challenges, Prospects and Opportunities." *Third World Quarterly* 32, no. 1 (2011): 3–8.
Rao, Vijayendra, and Michael Walton, eds. *Culture and Public Action*. Stanford: Stanford University Press, 2004.
Rietbergen-McCracken, Jennifer, and Deepa Narayan. *Participation and Social Assessment: Tools and Techniques*. Washington, DC: World Bank, 1998.
Rostow, Walt W. *The Stages of Economic Growth: An Anti-Communist Manifesto*. Cambridge: Cambridge University Press, 1960.
Said, Edward. *Orientalism*. New York: Vintage Books, 1978.
Scott, James C. *Seeing Like a State: How Certain Schemes to Improve the Human Condition Have Failed*. New Haven: Yale University Press, 1998.
Selznick, Philip. *TVA and the Grassroots: A Study of Politics and Organization*. Berkeley: University of California Press, 1984.
Sen, Amartya. "Development: Which Way Now?" *Economic Journal* 93, no. 372 (1983): 745–62.
Sen, Amartya. *Development as Freedom*. New York: Alfred A. Knopf, 1999.
Singh, J. P. *Negotiation and the Global Information Economy*. Cambridge: Cambridge University Press, 2008.
Singh, J. P. *United Nations Educational Scientific and Cultural Organization: Creating Norms for a Complex World*. London: Routledge, 2011.
Singh, J. P., and Shilpa A. Hart. "Development as Cross-Cultural Communication: Anatomy of a Development Project in North India." *Journal of International Communication* 9, no. 2 (2004): 50–75.
United Nations. *Millennium Development Goals Report*. New York: UN, 2012.
UN Millennium Project. *Investing in Development: A Practical Plan to Achieve the Millennium Development Goals*. New York: UN, 2005.

UNESCO. *World Culture Report 1998: Culture, Creativity and Markets*. Paris: UNESCO, 1998.
UNESCO. *World Culture Report 2000: Cultural Diversity, Conflict and Pluralism*. Paris: UNESCO, 2000.
UNESCO. *World Report: Investing in Cultural Diversity and Intercultural Dialogue*. Paris: UNESCO, 2009.
Vernon, Raymond. "International Investment and International Trade in the Product Cycle." *Quarterly Journal of Economics* 80 (1966): 190–207.
World Bank. *The East Asian Miracle*. New York: Oxford University Press, 1993.
Yusuf, Shahid, and Angus Deaton. *Development Economics through the Decades: A Critical Look at 30 Years of the World Development Report*. Washington, DC: World Bank, 2009.

7 | Public Diplomacy, Networks, and the Limits of Strategic Narratives

Robin Brown

The debate over strategic narrative revolves around three claims. The first claim is that some narratives are *strategically* significant, for instance the BRICS narrative of the "rise of the rest" or the Taliban's account of the role of NATO forces in Afghanistan. These accounts of the world influence how people and organizations understand the world and act within it (Miskimmon, O'Loughlin, and Roselle 2013). The second claim is that an actor can successfully promote their own narrative to *strategically* advance their position in the world. A strategic narrative provides a simple and persuasive account of a strategy that helps to bind an army or a country or a coalition together and perhaps even goes further and explains to neutrals or even opponents why they should support or at least not oppose that narrative (Miskimmon, O'Loughlin, and Roselle 2013, chap. 5). Essentially a strategic narrative in this second sense can become a strategically significant narrative in the first sense through its impact on the world. The third claim is that strategic narratives are becoming more influential in the world through changes in the media environment; that is, the rise of a hypermedia ecology is reducing the influence of states and promoting that of nonstate actors (1).

This chapter seeks to investigate these claims, particularly the second and third, using cases from the practice of public diplomacy. Public diplomacy is understood here as the effort to conduct foreign policy through the influencing foreign publics (Cull 2008).

The chapter begins by outlining the scope of public diplomacy and the problem for International Relations of incorporating public diplomacy into its theoretical frameworks. The following section suggests a way forward in the intersection of narratives and networks offered by relational sociology. The second part of the chapter applies this perspective to a historical case: the attempt to influence American policy during the period of U.S. neutrality during the First World War and to two contemporary cases: the efforts of Russia to promote its position during the Ukraine crisis and the activities of the Islamic State. An examination through the lens of historical relational sociology suggests that narratives need be examined in conjunction with the networks that carry them, that successful narrative projection is potentially difficult to achieve, and that the impact of innovations in communications technologies is unlikely to change this. The chapter concludes that in contentious cases narrative mobilize supporters but the impact on outcomes is uncertain and depends on the influence of sympathizer networks rather than the properties of the narrative itself.

Public Diplomacy and Narratives

Why do strategic narratives become influential? Part of the answer may be that states have developed organizations to "tell their story to the world," that is, through public diplomacy. Although the term public diplomacy is relatively new, dating from the 1960s, most of the practices that it designates date back to the end of the 19th and the beginning of the 20th century. This provides a rich field of cases with which to explore the life cycle of narrative and the sources of narrative impact.

In American usage public diplomacy covers three sets of foreign policy activities aimed at foreign publics: the supply of information, whether directly or via media organizations; educational and cultural activities, for instance, teaching English or conducting exchanges; and international broadcasting. The extent to which these are part of the same enterprise is hotly contested (and has been since the 1940s), but the implied scope provides a useful focus for the chapter.[1] Despite using this American term, it is important to note that the United States came late to these activities; by the 1880s France and Germany were already developing concepts and institutions that exist down to the present (Burrows 1986; Chaubet 2006; Roche and Pigniau 1995; Paschalidis 2009; Trommler 2013). Indeed, the persistence of distinct national debates and approaches is a striking feature of this entire area. Many countries followed the models offered by France and Germany and placed the idea of "culture" at the center of their activity; in contrast, Britain and the United

States emphasized "information" and "broadcasting." Despite these conceptual differences there has been much overlap in practices. While the activities of France, Germany, the United States, and Britain are the most extensively documented cases, almost all other countries, large and small, have also engaged in these activities.

The development of public diplomacy activities reflects some of the key dynamics of change in world politics from the 19th century. The growing influence of publics on foreign policy suggested that there may be benefits from cultivating favorable views of your country. The growth of transportation and communications technologies created more interdependencies between different areas of the world and new opportunities for exerting influence. States were expanding the range of functions that they carried out, which tended to create a greater sense of nationality and often nationalism among their populations. This meant that many of the early enthusiasts for engaging with foreign publics came from civil society, although their initiatives soon came to draw support from states (Rosenberg 2012; Mann 1993; Mattelart 1994).

The linked processes of nationalization and globalization provided the overall context in which public diplomacies emerged, but for individual countries the timing and form of the new practices reflected specific national situations. France saw language and culture as a way of offsetting the material advantages of Germany and Britain (Roche and Pigniau 1995). Germany, like Italy, wanted to ensure that compatriots outside the borders of the national state were not assimilated into an alien culture (Conrad 2010). Britain remained largely aloof until the First World War when it sought to leverage its domination of the international telegraph system and maritime trade to ensure the dissemination of its version of the war (Sanders and Taylor 1982; Read 1992). Although it was the old European states that provided models, states beyond Europe and the countries that emerged at the end of the First World War also embraced informational and cultural tools (see, for instance, Paikert 1952; Orzoff 2011; Volz 2011).

Countries have developed public diplomacy programs in response to interstate competition and conflict. At the same time the creation of new states both leads to more national programs and more countries that can be engaged by them (Szondi 2009). The classic repertoire of techniques—visits, scholarships, book promotion, exhibitions, language teaching, translations, information centers, cultural institutes, and press relations—is supplemented by each new media innovation, from radio to Twitter (Paschalidis 2009; Hauser 2011; Jansen 2004; Archetti 2012; Denscheilmann 2013).

It is important to note that not all of these are concerned with the direct projection of narratives. An important strand of thinking about public diplomacy identifies relationships as the key concern of the activity and critiques an excessive concern with "messaging" or narrative in public diplomacy practice. In fact, as we will see later in this chapter, relationships provide the conduit through which narratives can be projected (Zaharna 2010).

Public Diplomacy as a Theoretical Problem

Although in *The Twenty Years Crisis* E. H. Carr identified influence over public opinion as one of the three sources of power in world politics, public diplomacy has attracted little theoretical attention (Carr 1946). One source of this difficulty is a long-running mismatch between the practice of international politics and the way it has been theorized. Even before the First World War, policy debate in Germany was strongly influenced by what was seen as the way in which, driven by civil society, France, Britain, and the United States were pursuing their cultural mission in the world. For instance, German scholars anxiously estimated the number of Chinese children being taught by missionaries of different nationalities and argued that the Reich needed to catch up (Düwell 1976; Conrad 2010). The assumption in this writing and in the practice of most public diplomacy is a view that business, scholars, news, artists, and education have a nationality and by projecting them abroad a country strengthens its relations with the world and its influence in it. The irony is that even as they joined societies dedicated to the promotion of Germany's foreign relations, successive generations of historians and theorists insisted on the autonomy of foreign policy from "the social" sphere; an insistence that was carried over into American International Relations theory (Scheuerman 2007; Iggers 1983). The result has been that the dominant theoretical narratives in International Relations have tended to oppose a view of the world that is made up of states subject to unchanging geopolitical logic, constantly being undermined by a world of transnational civil society activism (Keck and Sikkink 1998; Kahler

2009). Public diplomacy practice suggests a world in which states routinely conduct their own transnational activities and where civil society is happy to be deployed as part of the national capacity.

To the extent that public diplomacy has been subject to theoretical analysis it has normally been treated as an issue of communications. The difficulty with this approach is that examination of historical public diplomacy cases tends to suggest that the effects and outcomes of public diplomacies are strongly influenced by factors outside the scope of communications analysis. For instance, historical analysis suggests that reception of American messages in the Middle East is strongly influenced by the relationship between the United States and Israel regardless of the type of communications strategies used (Vaughan 2005; Rugh 2005). This suggests the need for a theoretical approach that can provide a context for public diplomacy activity both at a local and an international level.

As a result this chapter draws on the type of network relational approach advocated by Daniel Nexon among others (Nexon 2009; Jackson and Nexon 2013). Social network theorizing was classically concerned with networks as structures, but over the past two decades it has become increasingly concerned with the role of stories, narratives, and rhetorics in the constitution of networks. Figures associated with what has been termed the "New York School of relational sociology" have sought to integrate the view of society as a network of networks with a concern with how these relations present themselves in phenomenological terms (Mische 2011; Pachucki and Breiger 2010; Mutzel 2009).

The core claim of this school of thought is that social formations were constituted as nested and overlapping sets of relationships that had both structural and narrative properties. These structures created, in the traditional sense of network analysis, a position in a network that had consequences for the opportunities and constraints for an individual or organization. Narratives were important in the sense that stories about relationships give meaning to those relationships but also that organizations and fields of action have their own narratives and rhetorics that define them and constitute appropriate modes of action (White 2008). Within this framework, identity is constituted by membership in multiple networks. Switching between networks is marked by changes in the mode of speech or other communication (Mische and White 1998). Publics are understood as spaces between networks where participants are not subject to the disciplines of particular organizations or realms (Ikegami 2000). There is an interdependent relationship between relationships and narratives. Narrative can be a mode of stabilization or a mode of change depending on the circumstances. Because actors operate within multiple networks it cannot be assumed that a change in the narrative within one network has any particular effect on actions although, depending on the circumstances, it might do so. The social fabric is constituted by a dense overlapping set of relationships associated with particular configurations of stories and ideas.

Given this ontological foundation, how then should we think of the international, the transnational, and the national? Most relationships are relatively local and focused on families, neighbors, and coworkers located in villages, towns, and cities. These spatial clusters are connected across longer distances by sparser sets of relationships of different types. Some of the local and long-distance relationships are promoted by governing organizations that in the modern period have used their networks to create narratives and network forms of statehood (and frequently nationhood). The extent to which this has happened varies between countries, across them, and across time. The nation is an imagined community, as Anderson (1983) argued, but the extent to which that imaginary is shared has much to do with organizations that can produce integration across local communities. For instance, as Weber (1976) argued in the case of French railways, national education and military service were important aspects of the institutional bases of the nation. Processes of nationalization are always incomplete and partial. For instance, in many countries weak states face strong societies where narratives and networks of, for instance, family or localism stand against those of the state (Migdal 1988). Having said that, the state and nation are powerful ensembles of narrative and network. Once the nation-state is understood in this way, the transnational is simply the set of relationships that cross state borders, but these network relationships are simply linking other clusters of relationships. State organizations are also networks that engage with other networks both inside and outside the territory of the state, including through the activities of public diplomacy.

Public Diplomacy as Network Construction

Public diplomacies involve one country attempting to influence people in another through using existing relationships or constructing new ones. Not all public diplomacy is primarily concerned with narrative, but all public diplomacy requires some sort of relationship and some sort of story about that relationship. Even the simplest case of a broadcast message requires some sort of relationship between the audience and broadcasters. Most public diplomacy requires a more complex set of relationships. Achieving influence requires the construction of a set of relationships and the deployment of narratives in the context of other relationships and narratives that may obstruct, sidetrack, or block such efforts (White 2008).

What can be termed "influence chains" run through the organizational networks of states and frequently through formally independent organizations that implement programs of work on behalf of the foreign ministry. Much public diplomacy seeks to work through locally organized groups in foreign countries—for instance, diaspora organizations or business groups—but also through the social (and narrative) infrastructures of the host country, especially the media and education systems.

The most effective public diplomacy is that which encourages or facilitates interest, sympathy, or interaction under private or commercial auspices without the need for continuing support. Indeed, the irony is that really successful public diplomacy would create a situation where it would seem implausible that any government-funded program had ever been necessary to support the relationship between two countries, yet even among allies such as France and Germany or Britain and the United States such programs of work remain in place (Krotz 2007; Scott-Smith 2006). The corollary is that public diplomacy becomes most visible (and has the greatest expectations placed upon it) precisely when this situation does not occur, when the relationship between the two countries or with third parties becomes contentious. The upsurge of interest in public diplomacy in the United States after the 9/11 attacks illustrate this point (Epstein and Mages 2005; Fitzpatrick 2010).

The micropolitics of public diplomacy networks also need to be taken into account. Although some public diplomacy work is carried out by diplomats, it also involves employees who are part of the host nation, artists or teachers from the sending country, and also people from the receiving country who choose to become involved with the public diplomacy work whether out of attachment to the country or because of perceived benefits, opportunities, or ideological sympathy. In some cases this network may be that all that is required, but frequently the hope is that this network of sympathizers will create a public that will allow the country's narrative to diffuse more broadly. Particularly where perceptions of a foreign country are negative, public diplomacies often find it difficult to reach beyond the "usual suspects"—for example, for the Soviet Union to reach beyond Communist Party members in 1950s America, or for 21st century Denmark to reach father than liberal NGOs in the contemporary Middle East (Magnusdottir 2010; Danish Ministry of Foreign Affairs 2013).

It is important to recognize that these networks do not exist in isolation from other networks, both those that constitute the target country and competing public diplomacies. Someone who is involved with a foreign country's public diplomacy network is also part of other social networks, such as family, employment, and cultural interest networks. A public diplomacy network does not exist in isolation; neither is it purely a matter of representations or ideas. Contextualized in this way, we are better placed to understand the life cycle of public diplomacy networks. Assessing the influence of networks and publics also depends on the features of the network: its size, capacity for mobilization, and position in relation to the other social actors given its network position.

Public Diplomacies in Practice:
Some Evidence from History

The second part of this chapter explores the relationship between networks and narratives in practice. The chapter draws on three cases. The first are efforts to influence American policy prior to the U.S. entry into the First World War. The second and third are contemporary: the campaign by Russia to influence Western policy during the 2013–14 Ukraine Crisis and the information activities of the Islamic State organization in 2014.

The First World War case is particularly rich because it allows us to make comparisons between the efforts of Germany, France, and the United Kingdom. It also takes place relatively early in the development of public diplomacy and in a media environment that lacked not only digital technologies but also broadcasting technology. The Russia example provides a contemporary state-centric case while that of the Islamic State of Iraq and Syria (ISIS) offers some insight into nonstate practice. In terms of the range of public diplomacy cases these are relatively unusual in that they are extremely conflictual. However, much of the discussion of strategic narrative has focused on conflicts and thus the impact in such cases is a central concern. The conclusion takes up the question of how nonconflictual cases may differ.

Within the relational-network approach outlined in the previous section the discussion of the cases focuses on the effects of the effort to promote narratives strategically. The analysis examines six specific questions that emerge from the basic network and narrative theoretical framework:

1. How does the strategic narrative interact with the network and vice versa?
2. How does the choice of network affect political outcomes?
3. How does the choice of narrative affect the public impact of the public diplomacy effort?
4. What is the interaction between external events and the narrative network?
5. How do others seek to counter the strategic narrative?
6. What sort of outcomes can result from the deployment of strategic narratives in public diplomacy?

The Battle for America: Competing Belligerent Narratives, 1914–1917

From the summer of 1914 to the spring of 1917 the United States pursued a policy of neutrality toward the conflict raging across the Atlantic. For nearly three years the European powers worked to influence the U.S. interpretation of neutrality and its attitude toward intervention. The attempts at influence were conducted via diplomatic channels but in parallel campaigns were directed at American publics in an attempt to influence their narrative of the conflict.

What were the assets the belligerents had at their disposal, and how did this affect the narratives they sought to promote? Before the First World War both Germany and France had taken steps to promote their own culture in the United States. The key difference between the two countries was that there was a sizeable German minority in the United States and German organizations had worked to maintain the identification of the diaspora with the homeland. In contrast, France lacked a "usable diaspora." Its prewar organization had been centered on the formation of committees of the Alliance Française, a voluntary organization dedicated to the promotion and defense of French language and culture (Trommler 1993; Young 2004; Dubosclard 2000; Haglund 2012). The organizing principle of these networks was Germany ethnicity, on the one hand, and cultural sympathy for France, on the other. To maintain the adherence of individuals and organizations to the networks certain types of narrative expectations had to be maintained. In the United States this was more of problem for Germany since the German narrative tended to prioritize the consolidation of the German nation over influence on foreign audiences. The outbreak of war had masked the political conflicts within Germany between the monarchical regime and the rising support for socialism, and the strategy of the German narrative was to cement this unity (Chickering 1998; Welch 2005; Trommler 2013). The German narrative could flow through sizeable network of German-American organizations and newspapers. In contrast the French (and British) activity operated through networks of sympathizers whose support could not be taken for granted. Thus, Allied narratives tended to focus on the values and interests that were shared across the Atlantic and the way that these were threatened by German militarism.

This leads us to the second point. Pro-Allied feeling was strongest on the East Coast of the United State among relatively wealthy and well-educated elites. On the other hand, German Americans were largely concentrated in the Midwest (Young 2004; Dubosclard 2000). Leading newspapers, including the *New York Times*, supported the Allies, but the reach into the much more neutrally oriented Midwest was limited. The sympathy of many owners, editors, and journalists was reinforced by the fact that at the outbreak of war the Royal Navy had cut all the telegraph cables linking Germany with the outside world. As a result, even newspapers unsympathetic to the Allied cause were strongly exposed to their version of the war with German dispatches or newspapers often taking weeks to reach the United States (Peterson 1968). Sympathizers with Germany tried to broaden their network by mobilizing the support of other groups, such as Irish Americans, that were antagonistic toward the Allies. Germany also sought to improve the communication of its case by covertly buying newspapers, notably the *New York Evening Mail* (Doerries 1993, 150–51; Doenecke 2011, 17). Yet in a confrontation with the resources controlled by the pro-Allied elites, Germany's supporters were at definite disadvantage.

In his discussion of public diplomacy Robert Entman argues that one of the key elements in the success of a public diplomacy activity is its "cultural congruence." A framing of a message is more likely to be accepted if it is consistent with the existing framings within a country. This claim is probably correct, but it gives little guidance as to how to establish congruence or what factors influence it (Entman 2008). In the neutral United States, German Americans and protagonists of Britain and France accepted European narratives of the war and emplotted America's role as sympathizer, intervener, or neutral accordingly. The majority of Americans showed little interest in the conflict (May 1959, 35–37; Doenecke 2011, 20–21).

Although there was no unified Franco-British narrative their focus was on the aggressive and expansionist nature of German foreign policy and its rejection of the established rules of war, both of which were expressions of its authoritarian and militaristic political system. Here we see the alignment of policy narratives, system narratives, and identity narratives (see this volume's introduction). America needed to stand with Britain and France to defend the international legal order and civilization in general. The Allied narrative sought to identify the United States, along with France and Britain, as part of the community of *civilized* states—an appeal that had a strong resonance among educated Americans. In this narrative civilization was opposed to German *kultur*, which was portrayed as the expression of Germany's innate barbarity (Young 2004, 49; Sanders and Taylor 1982, chap. 4; Peterson 1968, chap. 3).

The opposition between "civilization" and "*kultur*" was one that German narrators were happy to embrace. In Germany *kultur* was taken to represent a true expression of their identity as against the empty sophistication and glitter of French *civilisation*, an opposition that dated back to the initial expression of German nationalism (Elias 2000, 5–9). Hence, rather than reject the "othering" of *kultur* favored by the Entente (the alliance of Russia, France, and Great Britain), the German narrative embraced it. Soon after the outbreak of war Allied intellectuals sought to communicate that this was not a war against the German people but against German militarism. The response was the famous open letter *An Die Kulturwelt* ("To the Culture World") signed by 93 leading German intellectuals that proclaimed the unity of the German culture, people, and army, hence that a war against German militarism was a war against all of Germany (Lepenies 2006, 17).

More broadly the core of the German narrative was the encirclement of the country by an unholy alliance that included the uncivilized Russian Empire (discrediting the claims to civilization of Britain and France), and thus the country had no alternative but to defend itself. The German narrative effort had to cope with the fact that the Allied narratives were more congruent with dominant American narratives. It was easy to portray Germany as a land of autocratic militarism because that was how it often portrayed itself. In the context of America's political culture the liberal powers had an advantage (Doenecke 2011, 26–27; Doerries 1993, 142; Peterson 1968, 142–43).

The two narratives did not just have to contest with each other; they had to cope with the flow of events. The unfolding of events influenced the extent to which narratives were accepted cognitively and the extent to which they could mobilize people to act. Hence another difficulty faced by the Germans was that events outside the narrative seemed consistent with the Entente narrative; after all, it was the German army that was occupying Belgium and part of France and it was a German submarine that sank the *Lusitania*. Whatever the legalities of the blockade, American deaths at sea were bound to echo with the American public as were numerous acts of sabotage carried out by German agents against munitions manufactured for the Entente (Peterson 1968, 147–51; MacDonnell 2004, 13–17). Of course the impact of events was not one way; the Irish Rebellion of 1916 and its suppression provided much ammunition for critics of the British (Doenecke 2011, 174–75).

The narrative conflict was not only played out at the level of rhetoric. The British sought to counter the German narrative by discrediting the network that produced it. First, they worked to publicize the activities of German agents by supplying documents stolen from the Germans to the American authorities and media. Second, they tried to marginalize those that made the case for Germany by exploiting the already existing fear of "hyphenated Americans" (Peterson 1968, 147–51; MacDonnell 2004, 17–21; Finkelman 1993, 182–83).

Did the decision of the United States to enter the war indicate the success of the Anglo-French strategic narrative? The dominant American public narratives of the war were couched in terms of American interests, especially the right of U.S. shipping to use the seas. There were popular movements that urged "national preparedness," which explicitly or implicitly pushed for a more assertive U.S. role in world politics. At the same time, other groups demanded a new system of international relations that would prevent the recurrence of the conflict (Doenecke 2011).

The major points of tension between the United States, Germany, and Britain were around the issue of trade. Because Britain could prevent German use of the seas while it could trade with the United States, Germany tried to counter the advantage by using submarine warfare. The German submarines led to an escalating series of crises where attacks on shipping were followed by U.S. protests and German promises of restraint. Finally, at the beginning of 1917 the German government decided to take the gamble that an unlimited submarine campaign would end the war before any significant U.S. intervention could occur. For Woodrow Wilson it was the consequent sinking of American ships that led to the decision for war. As he put it in his request to Congress for a declaration of war, "There is one choice we cannot make, we are incapable of making: we will not choose the path of submission and suffer the most sacred rights of our Nation and our people to be ignored or violated" (Wilson 1917). The narrative was of a defense of American rights but also of a broader defense of international law.

The narrative efforts of both sides created a degree of political mobilization in support of their causes. The Allied effort had more resonance with uncommitted publics, but the degree of support was mediated through American concerns and events. Whatever the success of the Allies in promoting their narrative of the war, it did not directly produce the decision to intervene. It fed into how the conflict was understood and created sympathy for the Allied side and hostility toward Germany. Despite the efforts of some postwar commentators to attribute U.S. entry into the war to the effects of Allied propaganda activities, the analysis of this case suggests that the promotion of a strategic narrative was one element within a more complex political configuration (Sproule 2005; Gary 1999).

If it is not possible to attribute the U.S. entry into the First World War to the impact of the Allied narrative, once the decision had been made elements of that narrative immediately appeared in the work of the Committee on Public Information, the de facto ministry of information that Wilson created. The Committee on Public Information immediately began to recycle Anglo-French tropes that assigned responsibility for the war to Germany and its authoritarian political system. Backed up by a regime of censorship and the political repression of German American networks and antiwar groups, the narrative of German militarism formed an important part of the new U.S. account of the war. The Allied narrative effort may not have produced a direct effect, but it was strategically pressed into service (Mock and Larson 1939; Finkelman 1993).

Strategic Narratives in the 21st Century

In this section of the chapter we take up two cases of 21st century narrative projection, the first Russian strategic narratives in the 2013–14 Ukraine

Crisis and secondly that of the Islamic State of Iraq and Syria. To what extent is it possible to assess the claim that strategic narratives are becoming more important? In both cases claims have been made for the power of narrative in advance of what are seen as malevolent forces by Western observers and policymakers.

The crisis over Ukraine that emerged in the autumn of 2013 and escalated during the first half of 2014 focused attention to the divergence of Russian and Western narratives around the Ukrainian situation in particular and the broader issues of Russia's role in the international system. The first observation is the plural nature of the narrative activity. There were three clusters of Russian narrative activity: first, a narrative of Russia; second, an account of the United States and the European Union and their role in the situation; and, third, a more specific policy narrative of the situation in Ukraine.

Russia's own narrative portrayed itself as a great power sitting in the context of a Eurasian economic space and a "Russian World," the space constituted by the Russian diasporas created by the demise of the Soviet Union and a broader community of Russian speakers (Sherr 2013, 58–59). This Russian space, with its unique identity and culture, was under threat by the combined forces of Western liberalism represented by the United States, NATO, and the EU. The United States was presented as a lawless and violent superpower that had broken promises not to expand NATO up to the borders of Russia (NATO 2014, 24). The EU partnered the United States in promoting popular uprisings in countries that resisted incorporation into the Western bloc and rejected its liberal values. It was in this context that the events in Ukraine were portrayed as part of a Western political offensive where a coup by Nazi-sympathizing Ukrainian nationalists had taken place and, as a result, citizens groups and their armed supporters took power in Crimea and eastern Ukraine (NATO 2014, 22–23; Reisinger and Golts 2014, 6). Western states responded with waves of sanctions on Russian entities.

Russian public diplomacy operated through multiple channels. Over a considerable period the Russian government has been exercising greater control over the content of domestic media to ensure that it conformed to the general approach of the government. Russian television is widely watched throughout the post-Soviet space because it has access to better programming than the television services of less populous neighboring states. For instance, it is reported that Russian television channels in Lithuania have deals for some Western programs that prevent them being shown in languages other than Russian (Satter 2014; Grigas 2012). The reach of Russian media is supplemented by the activities of Russian World organizations, including the Russian Orthodox Church (Sherr 2013, 87–91; Kudors 2010, 2–4). Russia has pursued a liberal policy of "passportization," of granting citizenship to residents of other post-Soviet countries, which in turn creates diasporas that can be granted Russian state support (Reisinger and Golts 2014, 3).

The broader context is that despite the two decades since the breakup of the USSR the post-Soviet space is marked by relationships that reflect that history: business, political, social, and religious relations, as well as physical networks like natural gas pipelines (Grigas 2012).

As the observer moves to the West the density and visibility of these pro-Russian networks declines, but they do not disappear. There are explicit channels of public diplomacy such as the television channel RT and the recently reorganized news service Sputnik. These services not only provide a vector for Russia's narrative about itself but also for its narrative about the West. Indeed, there has been much comment about the predilection for conspiracy theories and negative stories about Western countries in order to construct a narrative of hypocrisy. This sense of a Russian attempt to counter Western narratives has also been observed on social media where people have not just tried to post material supporting the Russian narrative but also to challenge what they see as pro-Western or pro-Ukrainian narratives. This is a tactic deployed inside Russia, reportedly by paid social media agents (Pomerantsev and Weiss 2014; Reisinger and Golts 2014).

Finally, in the countries surrounding Russia there are networks of individuals who are willing to speak out in favor of the Russian cause or at least in favor of the maintenance of trade relations or against sanctions (Sherr 2013; Szpala 2014).

How then do these networks interact with the narrative? The narrative of the Russian World is in large part the narrative of a nation-state, albeit that of an incomplete nation. It focuses on the identity of the community and is indifferent to the reaction of those that it excludes. It mobilizes rhetorics of culture, language, and religion and uses them to bind its targets to the foreign policy objectives of the state (which can act as a protector of its diaspora). The mobilization of nationalism acts to legitimate the regime within Russia (Pomerantsev and Weiss 2014; NATO 2014; Bogomolov and Lytvynenko 2012).

In the West the negative narrative of media outlets such as RT is constrained by the need to conform to expected norms of Western media and by the need to operate within the regulation of Western media systems. In the United Kingdom, RT has been put on notice of sanctions following breaches of impartiality requirements (Ofcom 2014, 44). Even within these constraints it is able to construct an alternative view, however.

How have the narratives promoted via these networks resonated with broader publics? What is clear here is the interaction between Russian network narratives, events, and counternarratives offered by Ukrainian groups and Western governments and international organizations. The Russian World narrative (and related Slavic world narratives) portrays an opposition between Russia and the West that excludes what is non-Russian. This may be well received within the Russian World and its sympathizers, but it is directly opposed to official Western liberal narratives, which reframe the idea as an unacceptable sphere of influence. Where the narrative has had resonance is among those on the Right or Left that reject the liberal narrative (and the EU) as a threat to traditional values (including the nation) or an imperialist (American) ideology (Pomerantsev and Weiss 2014, 26–28).

Within Ukraine, even among consumers of Russian media and those who participate in Russian networks, it is important to note that their reaction to the narrative is conditioned by events. The presence of armed groups as well as extensive fighting will influence their willingness to express agreement or dissent from the narrative and their overall reaction to the situation. The apparent intervention by Russian forces in Ukraine created a double dynamic. On one hand Russia seems to have successfully created a degree of uncertainty about what was happening, which contributed to Ukrainian government and Western confusion as to the correct course of action, but at the same time allowed the emergence of a view that Russia, despite its denials, was behind the situation in Ukraine (Darczewska 2014; NATO 2014). This was a view that was crystallized by the shooting down of Malaysia Airlines flight MH17 on July 17, 2014.

The MH17 incident illustrates some of the roles of social media in the efforts to buttress and erode the evidence that supports narrative. The preferred Western version of events rapidly came to be that the plane was shot down by a surface-to-air missile fired by separatists who mistook the aircraft for a Ukrainian military flight. The version supported by the Russians and their sympathizers was that the plane had been shot down either by a Ukrainian ground-launched missile or by a Ukrainian fighter. The Western case was supported by recordings of conversations between separatists made by the Ukrainian government and by the circumstantial evidence of previous cases of planes being shot down by these groups. These were supplemented by analysis of the damage to the plane (U.S. Embassy 2014). In a new twist journalists using material posted to social media were able to track the movements of the Russian missile launcher as it traveled from a base in Russia and across Ukraine. Aided by the volume of material available via social media, partisans on both sides subjected the claims of the participants and their supporting evidence to forensic analysis (*Bellingcat.com* 2015). Despite this volume of material, it is less clear what real difference this made to the projection and reception of narratives.

The outcome of the crisis over Ukraine will only become clearer over time, but the evidence at present suggests that the direct Russian effort to project a narrative has gained traction only with existing sympathizers. Opinion polling in Europe suggests a decline in positive opinions of Russia (BBC 2014). The mobilization around the EU/NATO narrative contributes to a concern with Russian intentions. The impact of narrative (as in the earlier case) can more be seen in its ability to generate political pressure through agenda setting and mobilization, not just through direct acceptance.

The Rise of ISIS

If the case of the Russian narrative has a strong resemblance to our earlier case, how does the rise of the Islamic State compare?

What is the Islamic State? ISIS emerges from the welter of groups formed to oppose the American-led occupation of Iraq in 2003. Its narrative is typical of groups emerging from the networks of jihadi-Salafism of which up to this point al Qaeda has been the best known (Meijer 2009). Despite the ideological background, elements of the senior leadership are drawn from former members of the Ba'athist regime. Its major point of differentiation from al Qaeda is its enthusiasm for the creation of a caliphate, a polity of all Muslims. ISIS draws its support from two sources: the transnational community of jihadi-Salafists and local Sunni Muslims opposed to the regimes in Baghdad and Damascus. Although the founder of the group, Abu Musab al-Zarqawi, attracted much attention during the middle of the last decade, his group lost prominence after his death as local tribes turned against its violent methods. As the United States withdrew from Iraq the group rebuilt itself and was then able to exploit the civil war in Syria to gain strength. In January 2014 it captured the Iraqi city of Fallujah without any effective government response, but it did not gain world attention until June when its capture of Mosul was accompanied by the wholesale disintegration of large parts of the Iraqi army. This was followed by the proclamation of the caliphate, when ISIS became a policy problem and a focus for the international community. In the months that followed Western policymakers became obsessed with Muslim citizens traveling to join ISIS, with lurid videos of executions of Iraqi troops and Western hostages, reports of sexual exploitation of female captives, discussion of the permissibility of slavery under Islam, and jihadi groups around the world switching their allegiance from al Qaeda to the new caliph. By the end of the year Western and Arab air forces were attempting to reverse the advance of ISIS (Lister 2014).

Western commentators lamented the advance of the ISIS narrative expressed in a series of videos that far surpassed al Qaeda's in technical quality and in an enormous social media presence (Charai 2014). Yet it was the combination of the fall of Mosul, the proclamation of the caliphate, and the embrace of foreign language media that attracted the attention of Western policymakers and media. This failed to recognize that the foundations of the group were in the carefully constructed organizational networks that had embedded in parts of Iraq. As early as 2005 U.S. intelligence had estimated that the group predominantly drew its resources from extortion within Iraq rather than from gifts from foreign benefactors (Lister 2014, 22). Hence the key narrative-networks were those within Iraq that drew on the experiences of Sunnis under the Shia-dominated Nouri al-Maliki regime rather than those oriented to broader publics. But given the aim of creating a regime that operated in accordance with their version of Islamic law, there was no contradiction between appealing to those in Iraq and Syria and Muslims everywhere. Once the caliphate was proclaimed ISIS placed a greater emphasis on foreign-language campaigns in order to attract foreign Muslims to come and live within the territory of the Caliphate (Lister 2014).

The ISIS narrative was strategic in relation to Muslims and needed to do two things. The first requirement was to show the Islamic basis of the proclamation in the face of other groups (not least al Qaeda) that rejected ISIS and its strategy. The proclamation makes great play on the way in which the creation of Islam brought together the divided tribes of the Arabian Peninsula and gave them dignity and strength. Those that reject unity cannot be true Muslims. The second requirement was to show the strength of the caliphate, and here showing its brutality both demonstrated its sectarian identity and the fact that the proclamation was based on military realities. At the same time this demonstration of power and purity was expressed in the publicity given to violent acts against captives of the group and their accompanying statements (Voltaire Network 2015).

This was a narrative that was firmly planted within the terrain of jihadi-Salafism but at the same time drew a clear line within that field against the perceived authority of al Qaeda (Joscelyn 2015). The public impact of such a narrative within this field was one thing, but beyond it the narrative had little appeal. Regardless of any sympathy for the group's aim or vision of an Islamic society, it was seen as a threat by many governments whether close or far from the region.

Yet the impact of the narrative was closely connected to the course of events. One of the rules of wartime propaganda is that it is much easier to do a good job when you are winning (Lockhart 1947, 160). While Western commentators rushed to warn of the need to counter the high-quality productions of ISIS, the impact of their narrative was a function of its consistency with events in Syria and Iraq

The response to the ISIS narrative was to encourage social media companies to block ISIS accounts, which forced them to retreat from Twitter to other less well-known platforms (al-' Ubaydi et al. 2014, 50–51). The torrent of negative coverage of ISIS in the West was accompanied by images of heroic Kurdish fighters and accounts of suffering and slaughter under the regime. Yet directly countering the projection of the narrative had limited success as long as the group held its position. There remains pessimism about the speed with which the group can be forced to give up its territorial gains.

ISIS exists both in the space of transnational Islam and the territory of the Middle East, and to assess it through its transnational linkages or its existence "on the ground" results in a different perspective on the organization. Such jihadi-Salafi groups have been a regular presence in conflicts that involve Muslims since the 1980s, but there have been reports from different conflicts of them alienating local populations through their insistence on conformity with their norms. The decline of the Islamic State in Iraq from 2006 to 2008 was tied to their alienation from the local community, and their resurgence shows an element of adaptation and integration into local networks. Local integration is the key to their current prominence on the global stage. On the global stage ISIS appears as a narrative, but on the ground the narrative is part of the practices of governance rather than a freely floating rhetoric (Lister 2014, 25–29).

Only time will tell how long the Islamic State will endure. At the time of writing its appeal was confined to the space of jihadi-Salafi groups. While it is tempting to see the Islamic State as a contemporary phenomenon, where a state can materialize from a narrative, it can be argued that the same can be said about the Soviet Union or Czechoslovakia. The former emerged from the transnational network of Marxist revolutionaries while the latter came into being via the tireless promotion of the narrative of a naturally democratic, Westward-leaning republic by Thomas Masaryk and his colleagues to the elites of France, Britain, and the United States during the First World War (Orzoff 2011).

Conclusion

This chapter set out to explore two claims, first that narratives can be used strategically and second that narratives have become more important. It approached the task through an examination of three cases where actors have sought to promote strategic narratives in, as might be expected, contentious cases.

In all three cases the major impact of this strategic use of narrative has been through the political mobilization of preexisting networks of sympathizers rather than through a simple acceptance of the narrative by broader publics. Of course the narrative is an essential element of that mobilization. While the most committed members of a network may be easily moved to action, the less committed require a more persuasive story. This basic finding underlines the point that narrative is part of a political figuration. While established narratives are powerful in shaping international action, establishing influence is a different problem from explaining how they become established.

However, it is important to note that all of these cases were marked by situations of contention where the narratives deployed were met with counternarratives and by efforts to disrupt the propagation of the narratives. Where narratives can be deployed without opposition the effects may be different. For instance, it has been argued that the impact of the BRICS narrative has tended to mask weaknesses in the economies of the countries concerned and to increase their influence, but the impact of this narrative comes from the fact that it was adopted and promoted by the original four countries and by international corporate actors and the media without facing systematic and motivated opposition (Simão et al. 2014; see Miskimmon and O'Loughlin, chapter 11, this volume). Any losses caused by the rise of the narrative were indirect (for instance, through the diversion of potential investments), and for the countries and economic actors concerned the acceptance of the narrative benefited everyone involved, in the short term at least.

Have narratives become more important in a digital era? The history of public diplomacies suggests a cautious response. It seems plausible to acknowledge that the diffusion of digital technologies has some effect on the dynamic of networks through which narratives flow, but the real issue is how much difference. Here there is a danger of overestimating the degree of change on both historical and theoretical grounds. As we saw in the historical case study, even a century ago national leaders were faced with competing campaigns of influence, both from abroad and from domestic pressure groups. The theoretical point is that any persistent social group will have its own narrative and provide a structure through which that and other narratives can flow. The consequence is that a new strategic narrative must gain a footing within a world of networks and other narratives. Social media provides a platform for the creation of new groups, but, as with previous technologies, it also does the same for the maintenance of old groups. Strategic narratives are part of the "webs of significance" that shape the world, but without an understanding of the way that meanings exist in a world that is also social and material, strategic narratives cannot be effective, nor can we understand the sources of success and failure.

NOTES

1. For instance, Richard T. Arndt, *The First Resort of Kings: American Cultural Diplomacy in the Twentieth Century* (Washington, DC: Potomac Books, 2005), strongly differentiates between "culture" and "information." Alan L. Heil, *Voice of America: A History* (New York: Columbia University Press, 2003), argues that broadcasting is a completely different activity from the other two.

REFERENCES

al-' Ubaydi, Muhammad, Nelly Lahoud, Daniel Milton, and Bryan Price. *The Group That Calls Itself a State: Understanding the Evolution and Challenges of the Islamic State*. West Point, NY: Combating Terrorism Center, 2014.

Anderson, Benedict R. O'G. *Imagined Communities: Reflections on the Origin and Spread of Nationalism.* London: Verso, 1983.
Archetti, Cristina. "The Impact of New Media on Diplomatic Practice: An Evolutionary Model of Change." *Hague Journal of Diplomacy* 7, no. 2 (January 1, 2012): 181–206. http://dx.doi.org/10.1163/187119112X625538
BBC. "What Does the World Think of Putin?" *BBC Magazine*, July 12, 2014. Accessed July 12, 2012. http://www.bbc.co.uk/news/magazine-28233825
Bellingcat.com. "Geolocating the MH17 Buk Convoy in Russia." September 24, 2014. Accessed February 16, 2015. https://www.bellingcat.com/resources/case-studies/2014/09/29/geolocating-the-mh17-buk-convoy-in-russia/
Bogomolov, Alexander, and Oleksandr Lytvynenko. *A Ghost in the Mirror: Russian Soft Power in Ukraine.* London: Chatham House, 2012.
Burrows, Mathew. "'Mission Civilisatrice': French Cultural Policy in the Middle East, 1860–1914." *Historical Journal* 29, no. 1 (March 1, 1986): 109–35.
Carr, Edward Hallett. *The Twenty Years' Crisis, 1919–1939: An Introduction to the Study of International Relations.* 2nd ed. London: Macmillan, 1946.
Charai, Ahmed. "The ISIS Challenge Online: When Twitter Becomes Anti-Social Media." *National Interest*, November 14, 2014. Accessed November 20, 2014. http://nationalinterest.org/blog/the-buzz/the-isis-challenge-online-when-twitter-becomes-anti-social-11681
Chaubet, François. *La politique culturelle Française et la diplomatie de la langue: L'Alliance Française (1883–1940).* Paris: L'Harmattan, 2006.
Chickering, Roger. *Imperial Germany and the Great War, 1914–1918.* New York: Cambridge University Press, 1998.
Conrad, Sebastian. *Globalisation and the Nation in Imperial Germany.* Cambridge: Cambridge University Press, 2010.
Cull, Nicholas. *The Cold War and the United States Information Agency: American Propaganda and Public Diplomacy, 1945–1989.* Cambridge: Cambridge University Press, 2008.
Danish Ministry of Foreign Affairs. *Danish Arab Partnership Programme 2013–2016.* Copenhagen: Danish Ministry of Foreign Affairs, 2013.
Darczewska, Jolanta. *The Anatomy of Russian Information Warfare: The Crimean Operation, a Case Study.* Point of View 42. Warsaw: Centre for Eastern Studies, 2014.
Denscheilmann, Heike. *Deutschlandbilder: Ausstellungen im Auftrag Auswärtiger Kulturpolitik.* Wiesbaden: Springer, 2013.
Doenecke, Justus D. *Nothing Less Than War: A New History of America's Entry in World War I.* Lexington: University Press of Kentucky, 2011.
Doerries, Reinhard. "Promoting Kaiser and Reich: German Propaganda in the United States during World War 1." In *Confrontation and Cooperation: Germany and the United States in the Era of World War 1: 1900–1924*, edited by Hans-Jürgen Schroder. Providence, RI: Berg, 1993.
Dubosclard, Alain. *Histoire de la federation des alliances Française aux Etats-Unis: L'alliance au coeur.* Paris: L'Harmattan, 2000.
Düwell, Kurt. *Deutschlands Auswärtige Kulturpolitik 1918–1932: Grundlinien und Dokumente.* Cologne: Böhlau, 1976.

Elias, Norbert. *The Civilizing Process: Sociogenetic and Psychogenetic Investigations*. Rev. ed. Oxford: Blackwell, 2000.

Entman, Robert M. "Theorizing Mediated Public Diplomacy: The U.S. Case." *International Journal of Press/Politics* 13, no. 2 (April 1, 2008): 87–102, http://dx.doi.org/10.1177/1940161208314657

Epstein, Susan B., and Lisa Mages. *Public Diplomacy: A Review of Past Recommendations*. Washington, DC: Congressional Research Service, 2005.

Finkelman, Paul. "The War on German Language and Culture, 1917–1925." In *Confrontation and Cooperation: Germany and the United States in the Era of World War 1: 1900–1924*, edited by Hans-Jürgen Schröder. Providence, RI: Berg, 1993.

Fitzpatrick, Kathy. *The Future of U.S. Public Diplomacy: An Uncertain Fate*. Leiden: Brill, 2010.

Gary, Brett. *The Nervous Liberals: Propaganda Anxieties from World War I to the Cold War*. New York: Columbia University Press, 1999.

Grigas, Agnia. *Legacies, Coercion and Soft Power: Russian Influence in the Baltic States*. London: Chatham House, 2012.

Haglund, David G. "France and the Issue of a 'Usable' Diaspora in (North) America: The Duroselle-Tardieu Thesis Reconsidered." *International History Review* 34, no. 1 (2012): 71–88. http://dx.doi.org/10.1080/07075332.2012.620241

Hauser, Claude, Thomas Loué, Jean-Yves Mollier, and François Vallotton. *La diplomatie par le livre: Réseaux et circulation internationale de l'imprimé de 1880 à nos jours*. Paris: Nouveau Monde Editions, 2011.

Iggers, Georg G. *The German Conception of History: The National Tradition of Historical Thought from Herder to the Present*. Rev. ed. Middletown, CT: Wesleyan University Press, 1983.

Ikegami, Eiko. "A Sociological Theory of Publics: Identity and Culture as Emergent Properties in Networks." *Social Research* 67, no. 4 (Winter 2000): 989–1029.

Jackson, Patrick T., and Daniel H. Nexon. "International Theory in a Post-Paradigmatic Era: From Substantive Wagers to Scientific Ontologies." *European Journal of International Relations* 19, no. 3 (2013): 543–65.

Jansen, Christian. *Exzellenz Weltweit: Die Alexander von Humboldt-Stiftung Zwischen Wissenschaftsfoderung und Auswartiger Kulturpolitik (1953–2003)*. Cologne: Dumont, 2004.

Joscelyn, Thomas. "AQAP Rejects Islamic State's 'Caliphate,' Blasts Group for Sowing Dissent among Jihadists." *Long War Journal*, November 2014." Accessed February 16, 2015. http://www.longwarjournal.org/archives/2014/11/al_qaeda_in_the_arab_1.php

Kahler, Miles. *Networked Politics: Agency, Power, and Governance*. Ithaca: Cornell University Press, 2009.

Keck, Margaret E., and Kathryn Sikkink. *Activists beyond Borders: Advocacy Networks in International Politics*. Ithaca: Cornell University Press, 1998.

Krotz, Ulrich. "Parapublic Underpinnings of International Relations: The Franco-German Construction of Europeanization of a Particular Kind." *European Journal of International Relations* 13, no. 3 (September 1, 2007): 385–417. http://dx.doi.org/10.1177/1354066107080129

Kudors, Andis. "'Russian World': Russia's Soft Power Approach to Compatriots Policy." *Russian Analytical Digest* 81 (June 16, 2010).
Lepenies, Wolf. *The Seduction of Culture in German History*. Princeton: Princeton University Press, 2006.
Lister, Charles. *Profiling the Islamic State*. Doha: Brookings Doha Center, 2014.
Lockhart, R. H. Bruce. *Comes the Reckoning*. London: Putnam, 1947.
MacDonnell, Francis. *Insidious Foes: The Axis Fifth Column and the American Home Front*. Guilford, CT: Lyons Press, 2004.
Magnusdottir, Rosa. "Mission Impossible? Selling Soviet Socialism to Americans, 1955–1958." In *Searching for a Cultural Diplomacy*, edited by Jessica Gienow-Hecht and Mark C. Donfried, 50–72. New York: Berghahn, 2010.
Mann, Michael. *The Sources of Social Power: The Rise of Classes and Nation-States, 1760–1914*. Cambridge: Cambridge University Press, 1993.
Mattelart, Armand. *Mapping World Communication: War, Progress, Culture*. Minneapolis: University of Minnesota Press, 1994.
May, Ernest. *The World War and American Isolation 1914–17*. Cambridge: Harvard University Press, 1959.
Meijer, Roel, ed. *Global Salafism: Islam's New Religious Movement*. London: Hurst & Co, 2009.
Migdal, Joel S. *Strong Societies and Weak States: State-Society Relations and State Capabilities in the Third World*. Princeton: Princeton University Press, 1988.
Mische, Ann. "Relational Sociology, Culture, and Agency." In *The Sage Handbook of Social Network Analysis*, edited by John Scott and Peter J. Carrington, 80–98. Thousand Oaks, CA: Sage, 2011.
Mische, Ann, and Harrison C. White. "Between Conversation and Situation: Public Switching Dynamics across Network Domains." *Social Research* 65, no. 3 (Spring 1998): 695–724.
Miskimmon, Alister, Ben O'Loughlin, and Laura Roselle. *Strategic Narratives: Communication Power and the New World Order*. New York: Routledge, 2013.
Mock, James Robert, and Cedric Larson, *Words That Won the War: The Story of the Committee on Public Information, 1917–1919*. Princeton: Princeton University Press, 1939.
Mutzel, Sophie. "Networks as Culturally Constituted Processes: A Comparison of Relational Sociology and Actor-Network Theory." *Current Sociology* 57, no. 6 (November 1, 2009): 871–87. http://dx.doi.org/10.1177/0011392109342223
NATO Strategic Communication Centre of Excellence. *Analysis of Russia's Information Campaign against Ukraine*. Riga: NATO Stratcom COE, 2014.
Nexon, Daniel H. *The Struggle for Power in Early Modern Europe: Religious Conflict, Dynastic Empires, and International Change*. Princeton Studies in International History and Politics. Princeton: Princeton University Press, 2009.
Ofcom. *Broadcast Bulletin 266*. November 10, 2014. London: Ofcom, 2014.
Orzoff, Andrea. *Battle for the Castle: The Myth of Czechoslovakia in Europe, 1914–1948*. Oxford: Oxford University Press, 2011.
Pachucki, Mark A., and Ronald L. Breiger. "Cultural Holes: Beyond Relationality in Social Networks and Culture." *Annual Review of Sociology* 36, no. 1 (June 2010): 205–24. http://dx.doi.org/10.1146/annurev.soc.012809.102615

Paikert, Geza Charles. "Hungarian Foreign Policy in Intercultural Relations, 1919–1944." *American Slavic and East European Review* 11, no. 1 (February 1, 1952): 42–65.

Paschalidis, Gregory. "Exporting National Culture: Histories of Cultural Institutes Abroad." *International Journal of Cultural Policy* 15 (August 2009): 275–89.

Peterson, Horace Cornelius. *Propaganda for War: The Campaign against American Neutrality, 1914–1917*. Port Washington, NY: Kennikat, 1968.

Pomerantsev, Peter, and Michael Weiss. *The Menace of Unreality: How the Kremlin Weaponizes Information, Culture, and Money*. New York: Institute of Modern Russia, 2014.

Read, Donald. *The Power of News: The History of Reuters, 1849–1989*. Oxford: Oxford University Press, 1992.

Reisinger, Heidi, and Aleksander Golts. *Russia's Hybrid Warfare: Waging War below the Radar of Traditional Collective Defense*. Rome: NATO Defence College, 2014.

Roche, François, and Bernard Pigniau. *Histoires de diplomatie culturelle des origines à 1995*. Paris: ADPF la Documentation française, 1995.

Rosenberg, Emily S., ed. *A World Connecting*. Cambridge: Belknap Press of Harvard University Press, 2012.

Rugh, William A. *American Encounters with Arabs: The "Soft Power" of U.S. Public Diplomacy in the Middle East*. Westport, CT: Praeger, 2005.

Sanders, Michael L., and Philip M. Taylor. *British Propaganda during the First World War, 1914–18*. London: Macmillan, 1982.

Satter, David. *The Last Gasp of Empire: Russia's Attempts to Control the Media in the Former Soviet Republics*. Washington, DC: Center for International Media Assistance, 2014.

Scheuerman, William E. "Carl Schmitt and Hans Morgenthau: Realism and Beyond." In *Realism Reconsidered: The Legacy of Hans Morgenthau in International Relations*, edited by Michael Williams, 62–75. Oxford: Oxford University Press, 2007.

Scott-Smith, Giles. "Searching for the Successor Generation: Public Diplomacy, the US Embassy's International Visitor Program and the Labour Party in the 1980s." *British Journal of Politics and International Relations* 8, no. 2 (May 2006): 214–37. http://dx.doi.org/10.1111/j.1467-856X.2006.00221.x

Sherr, James. *Hard Diplomacy and Soft Coercion: Russian Influence Abroad*. London: Royal Institute of International Affairs, 2013.

Simão, Licinia, Teresa Almeida Cravo, André Barrinha, and Reginaldo Mattar Nasser. *The Discursive Articulation of the Concept of the 'Rising Power': Perceptions, Stances and Interests in Brazil, Russia and Turkey*. Oslo: Norwegian Peacebuilding Resources Centre, 2014.

Sproule, J. Michael. *Propaganda and Democracy: The American Experience of Media and Mass Persuasion*. Cambridge: Cambridge University Press, 2005.

Szondi, Gyorgy. "Central and Eastern European Public Diplomacy: A Transitional Perspective on National Reputation Management." In *Routledge Handbook of Public Diplomacy*, edited by Nancy Snow and Philip M. Taylor, 292–313. New York: Routledge, 2009.

Szpala, Marta. *Russia in Serbia: Soft Power and Hard Interests*. Warsaw: Centre for Eastern Studies, 2014.

Trommler, Frank. *Kulturmacht ohne Kompass: Deutsche Auswärtige Kulturbeziehungen im 20. Jahrhundert*. Cologne: Böhlau-Verlag, 2013.

Trommler, Frank. "Inventing the Enemy: German-American Cultural Relations 1900–1917." In *Confrontation and Cooperation: Germany and the United States in the Era of World War 1: 1900–1924*, edited by Hans-Jürgen Schroder, 99–125. Providence, RI: Berg, 1993.

U.S. Embassy. "United States Assessment of the Downing of Flight MH17 and Its Aftermath." July 20, 2014. http://usembassy.state.gov/statements/asmt-07192014.html

Vaughan, James. *The Failure of American and British Propaganda in the Arab Middle East, 1945–57: Unconquerable Minds*. Basingstoke: Palgrave Macmillan, 2005.

Voltaire Network. "Proclamation of the Caliphate." *Voltaire Network*. July 1, 2014. Accessed February 16, 2015. http://www.voltairenet.org/article184550.html

Volz, Yong Z. "China's Image Management Abroad, 1920s–1940s: Origin, Justification, and Institutionalization." In *Soft Power in China: Public Diplomacy through Communication*, edited by Jian Wang, 157–79. New York: Palgrave Macmillan, 2011.

Weber, Eugen. *Peasants into Frenchmen: The Modernization of Rural France, 1870–1914*. Stanford: Stanford University Press, 1976.

Welch, David. "Mobilizing the Masses: The Organization of German Propaganda during World War One." In *War and the Media: Reportage and Propaganda, 1900–2003*, edited by Mark Connelly and David Welch, 19–46. London: I. B. Tauris, 2005.

White, Harrison C. *Identity and Control: How Social Formations Emerge*. 2nd ed. Princeton: Princeton University Press, 2008.

Wilson, Woodrow. "Speech to Joint Session of Congress, April 2, 1917." Accessed July 20, 2014. http://www.presidency.ucsb.edu/ws/?pid=65366

Young, Robert J. *Marketing Marianne: French Propaganda in America, 1900–1940*. New Brunswick: Rutgers University Press, 2004.

Zaharna, R. S. *Battles to Bridges: US Strategic Communication and Public Diplomacy after 9/11*. Basingstoke: Palgrave Macmillan, 2010.

8 | Strategic Narratives of the Arab Spring and After

Amelia Arsenault, Sun-ha Hong, and Monroe E. Price

Our quondam certainties about what occurred during the 2011 "Arab Spring" have faded.[1] What even to call the series of events in Tunisia, Egypt, and beyond is increasingly problematic, given the less than rosy aftermath to the initial protests (see for example, "Arab Spring" 2013). The struggle over nomenclature underscores the power of stories and their limitations in policy and political change. The uprisings were replete with projected narratives, narratives whose proponents sought to shape current and future events as protestors took to the streets and state actors dug in their heels to retain power. These strategic narratives were constructed externally, by and large, in Western capitals like Washington, London, and Paris—though Beijing, Moscow, and Doha began to play a significant role as the months and complexities unfolded. These were not narratives of the street; they did not originate from social media. These were elite-driven narratives, proposed and agreed upon by heads of state and designed to provide the basis for actions going forward. Often far from concomitant with the force and intention of the protesters, these narratives were designed to create something akin to unity among the external coalitions seeking influence over the short and long-term outcomes of the waves of civil unrest in the Middle East and North African region. Processes of narrative negotiation played out among established and external entities through negotiations within the United Nations, but often without or in lieu of UN Security Council validation. These narratives generally involved calling upon the former dictator, military leader, or authoritarian figure to step down. Some of these pronouncements had a profound effect; others were less successful.

As Ben O'Loughlin noted in 2011, "Nobody has come close to explaining how strategic narratives work in international relations, despite the term being banded about" (O'Loughlin 2011). Works like Alister Miskimmon, Ben O'Loughlin, and Laura Roselle's 2013 *Strategic Narratives: Communication Power and the New World Order* attempt to remedy this gap. Extending such efforts, we seek to engage with the notion of strategic narratives in tandem with the specific case of the Arab Spring. In the Arab Spring, we find a specific type of narrative—elite-driven, oriented toward political change, transnational in its diffusion and effect—clearly at work in the struggle against incumbent regimes. Focusing on Libya as a prototypical case, and Syria as a highly atypical one, in this chapter we suggest that the following five critical components make a narrative strategic: (1) sponsoring agents; (2) narrative structures; (3) strategies of promotion; (4) legitimizing agents, particularly the media; and (5) suggested narrative outcomes. Taken together, we believe that these five components provide a schema for the study of strategic narratives. A comprehensive review of all five elements is beyond the scope of this chapter. Here, we review them briefly, concentrating in particular on sponsorship and narrative themes. We hope that this schema may provide a replicable framework for subsequent case studies, serving as a basis for comparative study that can help expand knowledge and understanding of the evolving role of strategic narratives in international relations.

In this discussion, we can reach no definitive conclusions on the Arab Spring itself, or even exhaust the range of narratives and strategic objectives that populated that conflict. Such a project would, for starters, involve a far greater engagement with Arab-language media and other material. An ongoing spiral change in the Middle East indicates that overprediction is a fool's game. We are primarily interested in the mobilizing of specific strategic narratives that originated from Western elites, were communicated largely through the Western media, and then influenced Middle Eastern geopolitics. In so focusing, our intention is to develop a framework that builds and refines Miskimmon, O'Loughlin, and Roselle's understanding of how and under what conditions a narrative becomes strategic within an event-driven geopolitical crisis like the Arab Spring. Specifically, we examine the role of political, mainstream media, and social media texts generating and contesting narratives; outline conceptual and methodological flaws and challenges; explore the implications of the changing media and communications environment for both the production of strategic narratives and the academic identification of what makes a narrative strategic, as opposed to just another narrative; and suggest future directions in research.

Strategic Narratives as Scripts

There are numerous uses and abuses of the term "strategic narrative," both in and outside of academia (LeCuyer 2011; Zalman 2011). Although fashionable, the concept of a strategic narrative can only be theoretically and operationally meaningful if we identify the point at which narratives become strategic. Precisely because of the many meanings of the term, we believe it is important to identify a threshold or minimal condition for a narrative's ability to operate strategically (as we use the term). We propose the following threshold definition of strategic narratives: *narratives are strategic if and only if they have the purpose of assuring that the story predicted or ordered by the narrative will take place, or threatening severe consequences to relevant actors if it does not*. Strategic narratives thus take the rhetorical form, "X should or must happen, or else." In their implied coercion, strategic narratives are akin to law—or, at least, aspire in that direction. Like scripts in a theater, strategic narratives seek to bind actors to roles and hold those actors to expected ways of behaving. Krebs and Jackson (2007, 36) have previously argued that rhetorical coercion (as opposed to rhetorical persuasion) is the principal mechanism through which rhetorical contestation influences policy outcomes because "rhetorical maneuver can prove critical to success in political contests even when one's opponents have not internalized the promoted values." Such rhetorical coercion is a critical component of understanding what makes a narrative strategic. As we will argue, however, strategic narratives are entangled with institutionalized systems of promotion and legitimation that go beyond rhetorical strategy in determining their fate.

In the following sections, we examine how two states—Libya and Syria—were affected in part by mostly unsuccessful efforts to form strategic narratives about their future. Between December 2010 and March 2011, the initial set of Arab Spring countries—Tunisia, Egypt, and Libya—appeared to follow a clear pattern. There was a spark, a seeming mobilization, a challenge to a long-sitting autocratic leader, and, finally, regime change. Western leaders were swept up in the spirit of the moment—on "what side of history" they would be on, in balancing historical approaches to what seemed to be the inevitability of change. Libya presents what might be called a classic case of Arab Spring rearticulation and response, one that eventuated in seemingly effective strategic narratives. The Western strategic narrative that emerged surrounding Libya in mid-February 2011 inscribed Muammar Gaddafi as a (Western) historical and rhetorical figure of the tyrant. Driven by state leaders in the United States, the United Kingdom, and France, this strategic narrative presented Libya as embodying a universalized struggle between the tyrant and the historical force of freedom and democracy, a moralized teleology of liberation and modernization. However, just weeks later, when Syria seemed likely to follow as a candidate for Arab Spring transformation, the U.S.-European alliance of consensus did not put forward an equivalent strategic narrative with sufficient persuasive force. We argue that this disparity can be traced to reasons such as the nature of the internal opposition; the military and political power of the Bashar al-Assad regime; the more assertive role played by China and Russia; Syria's geopolitical position among the Gulf states; and its strong ties to Iran. Both the design and deployment of strategic narratives differed greatly between these two countries, where one might briefly have expected identical triumphs of the "oppressed" against the "oppressors." Just as these scripts constrain the political realities and the "space of possibles" (Bourdieu 1993) they address, their conditions of production, located in the heart of the state, are also circumscribed by the preceding landscape of *perceived* political positions.

If strategic narratives are scripts, these geopolitical realities are analogous to the scattered stages upon which these scripts are performed. In comparing Syria and Libya, we can begin to observe how strategic narratives are confined by these theatrical stages. The relatively slow movements toward prescribing a binding solution in Syria arose in part from the stark military, geopolitical, and geographic contrasts between the two countries. These geopolitical realities determined what strategic narratives were feasible. In February 2011, Gaddafi commanded a force of around 76,000 ill-equipped and poorly trained troops. In comparison, according to 2011 estimates, Assad had at his disposal 295,000 frontline personnel and 314,000 reserve duty soldiers supported by L-39 and MiG jets and an annual foreign military aid budget of $100 billion (International Institute for Strategic Studies 2011, 320, 330). This is just one of the reasons that NATO would have had a more difficult time enforcing a Syrian no-fly zone. In contrast to Libya's desert terrain, Syria is intensely more urban and densely populated, posing the threat of more collateral damage in any military action by external forces. Perhaps most important, Syria, ruled by the Alawite Assad family since 1970, has also long maintained a strategic political and military alliance with Iran. The future of Syria, therefore, could not be separated from larger Western geopolitical conflicts with Iran, continued unrest in Lebanon, and the implications of intensified Shia-Sunni polarization (Landis 2012; Salloukh 2013). Because there is a strong and explicit connection between strategic narratives and state actors, the states' perceived parameters of political and military action constrain the scope of feasible narratives. The stage in many ways constrains the script, the actors, and the authors. A script can sediment into a stage, of course; the success of the Libyan narrative and its real implications for regional geopolitics fed into, for instance, a more stringent Russian refusal of the possibility of interventionist narratives in Syria.

While this is hardly the whole answer, many of the differences between the Libyan and Syrian cases could be analyzed in terms of the conditions for producing and implementing the narrative itself. We focus now on sponsoring agents in order to differentiate these limited conditions in Libya and Syria and assess how narratives develop, and how they might be evaluated.

Sponsoring Agents

Lawrence Freedman (2006, 22) suggests that narratives "are strategic because they do not arise spontaneously but are deliberately constructed or reinforced out of the ideas and thoughts that are already current." If we equate strategic narratives to theatrical scripts designed to bind outcomes, then we may think of the sponsoring agents as competing playwrights. A first step in analyzing strategic narratives, therefore, involves examining the range of officials who attempted to put forward narrative interpretations of events, that is, the claimants in a bid for narrative dominance. Did different categories of sponsors have different narratives, different processes for legitimating those narratives, and different processes for bringing such narratives forward?

Looking at the cases of Libya and Syria, we identify several potential scenarios of narrative creation. Narratives may (1) reflect the self-conscious efforts of singular actors, (2) be co-created by a coalition with an interest in shared outcomes, or (3) be so diffused in their origin as to lack any identifiable sponsorship. In the case of Libya, the narrative of Gaddafi as tyrant was supported by a broad coalition of actors. The demand for Gaddafi's removal was solidified just two months after the protests began, when U.S. president Barack Obama, U.K. prime minister David Cameron, and French president Nicolas Sarkozy published a joint statement in *Le Figaro,* the *Times of London,* and the *International Herald Tribune* calling for the removal of Gaddafi because it "is unthinkable that someone who has tried to massacre his own people can play a part in their future government" (Cameron, Obama, and Sarkozy 2011).

In the case of Syria in the early months of the crisis, the competition over narratives was much more explicit. On one hand, the United States and the European Union, later joined by Turkey and individual members of the Arab League, put forward a narrative of revolutionary change with Bashar al-Assad cast as tyrant. The only possible resolution to the Syrian conflict, according to this narrative, was Assad's removal, and an open election supported by the members of the opposition—a classic liberal democratic outcome. Russia, the Assad regime itself, Iran, and at certain times the Arab League sought to present a competing narrative by repeatedly characterizing Syria as undergoing a process of "Somalization," or the breakdown of the state into warring factions.[2] These alternatives did not necessarily form a unified consensus as to a future, but they challenged the Arab Spring script of incumbent as tyrant and protestors as heroes. In this telling, the opposition group—or a significant segment—was cast not as heroes of a true and unified Syria, but in part as another kind of threat against the fulfillment of a (better) Syrian nation. This interpretation suggested the only credible outcome could be one of negotiation, which would necessarily include Assad—a "political solution" of the conflict that preserves the Syrian state in some form.[3]

These differences highlight the international and domestic factors that produce an agent's interests vis-à-vis a given event, and in turn the kinds of narratives they are likely to support. These logically dovetail with the general constraints of the "stage." The geopolitical realities of the country or topic of interest invite different complexities. Elites sponsor narratives first and foremost because the resolution of an event, such as a revolution or change in leadership, is important to ongoing arrangements of power and spheres of influence. The Arab Spring offered a classic risk/opportunity situation: extraordinary geopolitical volatility threatened long-term interests, even as it made new narratives and thus political options possible. While China and Russia remained largely silent on the question of Libya, they took a much more active role in Syria. This is not surprising, given the fact that Russian business investments in Syria's energy and tourism industries, along with several major infrastructure projects, amount to nearly $20 billion and Russia has been responsible for approximately 78 percent of all arms sales to Syria since 2007 (Borshchevskaya 2013). Russia, in contrast to the United States, advocated for "dialogue" and offered to broker a "truce" between two disputing parties and was among the most vocal proponents of the 2012 Geneva Communiqué, which advocated dialogue between the Assad regime and opposition leaders (Action Group 2012). It consistently objected to any suggestion of the need for unilateral victory by the opposition over Assad. For example, Foreign Minister Sergei Lavrov, speaking at the General Assembly of the United Nations, lambasted opponents of a "political solution":

> Those who are opposing the implementation of the Geneva communiqué are assuming huge responsibility. By insisting that only the government must cease-fire and encouraging the opposition to step up combat actions, they are in fact pushing Syria further toward the abyss of a bloody strife. ("Russia Argues . . ." 2012)

This and similar statements prescribe a narrative of resolution of domestic discord, not revolution against tyranny (see also "Russia Sees . . ." 2013; Saab 2013). While proving a counterfactual is difficult, if not impossible, we can assume that countries like Russia, which largely remained silent on the question of Gaddafi's fate, would be less likely to challenge the consensus narrative put forward by a coalition of Western actors if they were not worried about access to Syrian resources. In such ways, the matrix of geopolitical interests constrains sponsors as they produce and challenge strategic narratives.

Equally, we cannot underestimate the importance of the domestic conditions of the sponsoring and target countries. While elite narratives of the Arab Spring may have been targeted at the Mubaraks, Gaddafis, and Assads (to facilitate transformation), and to the oppositions and protesters (to reinforce their message), they were also aimed at the home audiences (in Europe and the United States and at the key parties in the United Nations). Narratives sponsored by key Western leaders, we might assume, had clearer direct impact on their own constituencies. Their narratives were privileged by the Western and global press. On the other hand, countries like Russia, who do not conform to traditional Western democratic models, are less likely to champion narratives of change because they may contradict domestic models of governance and destabilize rather than promote domestic solidarity. As Russian foreign minister Sergei Lavrov has stressed repeatedly in talks over Syria, Russia "isn't in the business of regime change" (Statement 2012; Salmi 2012).

Any theory of strategic narratives also has to take into account the internal mode of domestic narrative formation—the "hijacking" of narratives by intense advocacy. For example, in 2009, Save Darfur, a U.S.-based large coalition of religious, political, and human rights organizations, conducted civil disobedience outside of the Sudanese embassy, helped to organize Genocide Prevention Month, and vocally criticized President Obama's special envoy to the Sudan, Maj. Gen. Scott Gration, for his characterization of the genocide. As Cristina Archetti (2012, 126) has pointed out, "The context in which contemporary international relations take place . . . is not characterized by the interaction among states only. Access to global communications has empowered . . . states, NGOs, corporate actors, transnational actors, even private citizens [all of whom] have acquired a voice." This leads to complicated processes of attribution. New dynamics arise when nonstate actors master methods of affecting the environment for narrative production. States and other elite actors may provide funding for "grassroots" activists promoting a certain agenda. Conversely, they may also label these groups as proxies or front organizations for opposing geopolitical powers. These questions surrounded the international recognition of the Libyan National Transition Council and the Syrian Opposition Coalition. Strategic narratives, therefore, are played out in multiple registers of communication and political debate. Between a narrative sponsor and its own domestic public (which must include not only the "public" writ large but pressure groups such as NGOs and religious groups) there is a constant confirmation and negotiation of the narrative as it is being projected on the international stage. Certainly—in the cases of the Arab Spring—the "opposition," the "rebels," NGOs, and diaspora groups strenuously sought to shape narratives and influence the Western leadership, the David Camerons and William Hagues (British foreign secretary), the Barack Obamas and Hillary Clintons of narrative formation.

Sponsorship is key to the operation of strategic narratives because the nature of the sponsor affects elements of the narrative itself. Sponsorship is related to credibility, and credibility leads to effectiveness. In the Arab Spring, Western elites tempered their narrative explanations with obeisance to the role of protests, or to the credibility of the opposition; that is, the sponsors downplayed their own status as the producers of narratives.

Who sponsors were and the extent of their inclusiveness likely made certain narratives more or less credible and more or less likely to become strategic. Moreover, as the next section will illustrate, the characteristics of the sponsoring agents are also directly tied to what narrative themes were credible and thus more likely to become binding.

Narrative Structures

Sponsorship and other geopolitical mechanisms often translate into particular narrative "structures" (i.e., formal dependencies on different machines of narrative production)—the ways in which the script itself unfolds. In the Arab Spring, we can identify (1) consensus based, (2) power based, (3) historically driven, and (4) self-generating narrative structures. We elaborate on these below. Specific outcomes, such as the deposition of Gaddafi or Assad, may be presented as axiomatic according to several mechanisms: the agreement of the global community (consensus-based narrative); the force of the U.S. military behind the rebels (power-based); because Gaddafi and Assad ostensibly employ tactics similar to leaders such as Adolf Hitler (historically driven); because these revolutions are part of the domino effect sweeping the Middle East and North African region (self-generating). These categories are not always mutually exclusive but complementary.

First, consensus-based narratives refer to those that are presented as agreed upon by key international actors, with all the moral and diplomatic authority that carries. Of course, this is partly tautological, as illustrated by the Libyan and Syrian experiences. Consensus in this approximation is geopolitically produced. One of the characteristics that differentiated the Syrian experience was the role of China and Russia (and the Assad regime itself) in constraining the perception of consensus and thus efficacy for both observers and those involved.

Second, power-based narratives refer to those that become effective because of the power held by a sponsoring agent to bind outcomes. Again, we see significant differences between the Libyan and Syria process of narrative-making. As the Arab Spring progressed, the Western coalitions' ability to put forward a power-based narrative was increasingly stymied by a widening array of interested parties. For instance, the escalation of the Syrian conflict coincided with Qatar's ascendency to the presidency of the Arab League, providing the country with a more strategic position in the escalating war of narratives.[4] In the fall of 2011, the fledgling Egyptian government also began to lobby for more active involvement in the future of Syria. Iran, a longtime ally of the Assad regime (which remained largely silent on the fate of Gaddafi), maintained that the conflict in Syria reflected "a mischievous act of Westerners, particularly Americans and Zionists" ("Iran Calls . . ." 2011). The presence of other competing narrative sponsors, with significant if not always equal ability to enforce different geopolitical outcomes, tended to clutter and undermine the credibility of the Western coalition's preferred narrative (Saddiki 2012; Gallup 2012).

The processes of narrative negotiation among this array of parties invested in the future of Syria underscores the fact that power-based narratives are sometimes necessary preconditions of moving toward consensus-based narratives. In other words, strategic narratives often constrain the production and success of future strategic narratives; in this way, narratives as scripts can become a part of the "stage" for new narratives. China and Russia put forward narratives underscoring the importance of their participation in the Syrian peace (power-based narrative). Only when their participation was negotiated would a consensus-based narrative be possible.

This takes us to a third narrative structure. Historically driven narratives sometimes arise because previous events suggest that a particular narrative be adapted to a subsequent event. There is no historical determinism, or a necessary transposition of narratives from one situation to another; there are only possibilities that sponsors may or may not tap into. Narrative interpretations of Libyan and Syrian protests were inextricably tied to narratives of earlier events of the Arab Spring in Tunisia and Egypt, as well as the broader protest movements that began sweeping the globe in late 2010. In 2011, protesters took to the streets in New York, in London, in Madrid, in Athens, in India, and elsewhere. What started as Occupy Wall Street turned into the global occupy movement. *Time* magazine named the "Protester" as their 2011 person of the year (Andersen 2011). We are not suggesting that the Arab Spring was necessarily the inspiration for the protesters themselves, but rather we are outlining what factors international strategic narratives fed upon to achieve a sense of continuity and validity. In this avalanche of protests, the Arab Spring seemed to confirm an overarching global narrative of 2011 as a year of protest. People on the streets of Tripoli emerge as protestors, Libyan Davids fighting the Gaddafi Goliath. Each event, however, is subject to competing historical narratives. For instance, it is notable how Western media made no effort to cover mentions of King Idris of Libya, Gaddafi's predecessor, by rebels in 2011. Syrians could equally invoke narratives of Kurdish independence, of Christian subordination, of a precolonial more federated structure of communities, and of the special role of Alawites; each affords a different configuration of sponsors, narratives, and end objectives.

Although strategic narratives are elite-driven and generally require state power to enforce "or else" clauses, they may arise wholly or partly from nonelite sources. In some cases, narratives have such "aesthetic strength" that they become an (or the) accepted version of what should occur. These narratives might not originate with strategic actors, but may be co-opted by those actors, and in the process become strategic. These we call self-generating narratives. These may serve the interests of political actors even if they were not the initiators, or vice versa. Some narratives have such strength and resonance that they become the accepted version of what can and could be done and what binds the conduct of actors. This illustrates the important fact that these narrative themes are not exclusive; they are temporary configurations of the "stage." Narratives can self-generate and then become consensual, or power-based narratives can draw upon particular historical strands for broader legitimacy.

If strategic narratives are to operate, then the actors must fulfill their roles. In Syria, the opposition's effort to present a unified, cohesive identity to the world was slow and ultimately abortive. In November 2012, nearly a year and a half after the onset of conflict, the National Coalition of Syria was formed under the leadership of Ahmed Mouaz al Khatib, a former geologist and imam of the Damascus Mosque. Although the Friends of Syria met in Doha to recognize the Coalition as the legitimate representative of the Syrian people, uncertainty over its cohesion persisted. Key members of earlier opposition organizations (e.g., the Syrian National Coordination Committee) continued to refuse to recognize the Coalition. In contrast, the Libyan National Transition Council formed on February 27, 2011, just ten days after the protests began. It had a website and was formally recognized by Western partners as early as March 2, 2011. While concerns still resounded about the cohesiveness and the legitimacy of the opposition leadership, the presence of a relatively stable National Transition Council played a critical role—allowing the presence of an identifiable David to Gaddafi's Goliath.

Time plays a key role in the success and failure of these narratives, and the ways in which they might morph into one another. The longer a narrative takes to achieve its self-designated end point the more likely a consensus narrative is to crumble. Gaddafi was captured and killed just over ten months after the initial uprising. In comparison, the Syrian civil war began in March 2011 and continues to the time this chapter goes to publication, fall 2016. Libya's post-Gaddafi transition to democracy has proved to be complex and violent. However, Gaddafi's swift removal solidified the strategic narrative of tyranny under Gaddafi and liberation through revolution. While events like the September 2012 bombing of the U.S. Embassy in Benghazi brought Libya back into the media spotlight, they did not invite a reexamination of the primary narrative, which conformed to the script suggested by previous events in Tunisia and Egypt. Rather, subsequent events invited new strategic narratives bound by a changed theater of geopolitical realities. In contrast, Assad was neither quickly nor easily deposed; the unrest in Syria continued unabated. As the hostilities continued and no clear resolution came to the fore, the nature of sponsorship changed. The previously "effective" mode of Western leadership consensus seemed to lose its capacity. Provisionally, and not necessarily with greater degrees of success, other sponsors (Egypt, Iran, China) emerged. In October–November 2012, China called for a vague four-point peace plan that called for a cease-fire and a negotiated settlement but stopped short of calling for Assad to step down. In a move considered bold at the time, President Mohamed Morsi of Egypt flew to Tehran in August 2012 to enlist the Islamic Republic as a shaper of a new narrative in which Iran would play a central role as peacemaker.

Strategic narratives represent self-conscious attempts at shaping interpretations of events. As such, any examination of strategic narratives and their life "on the ground" must account for their conditions of sponsorship and narrative mechanisms. In the cases of Libya and Syria, these explain how preexisting geopolitical factors enabled and constrained narratives. We find that narratives are vulnerable to and dependent on a range of different actors and events. Rather than a narrative being bound to a specific "type" de facto, we might say that narratives' struggle to survive and persuade under these conditions gradually define them.

Strategies of Promotion

The Arab Spring provides ample evidence of the multiplying means through which different actors seek to promote particular narratives. Promotion means not only persuasion of stakeholders but also the sheer exposure and momentum that may tilt perceptions of validity and potentiality in its favor, and thus compel members to follow the script.

First, we saw the continued relevance of traditional methods of diplomacy and public diplomacy through the use of press releases, press conferences, speeches, and international broadcasts. Throughout the events of the Arab Spring, diplomats and heads of state continued to deliver policy statements in these traditional formats. Until his demise, Gaddafi broadcast defiant messages to the world via Al-Orouba TV and Assad sporadically delivered regular speeches to the Syrian people and the world via Al-Rai media.

Second, we identify the use of promotion by proxy. Promotion by proxy refers to elite support for particular videos and reports that reinforce the narrative of interest. For example, the U.S. Department of State sponsored, supported, or otherwise endorsed multiple activist organizations, not limited to the major opposition parties, throughout the Arab Spring. Secretary of State Hillary Clinton participated in multiple town halls with youth and civil society in the Middle East, which were rebroadcast and promoted through State Department channels.

Third, the multiple uses of social and new media open up their own spaces of narrative communications. The torrent of tweets and Facebook posts were touted as evidence of the strength and reach of the revolutionary movements (Howard et. al. 2011; Hounshell 2011; Vargas 2012). Subsequent analysis has raised serious questions about this relationship (Lim 2012; Howard and Hussain 2011). Regardless of the complexities of social media's role in citizen activism, there is little doubt that it served as a major actor in the narratives surrounding the uprisings. This role was multifaceted. In the case of the Arab Spring, social media was simultaneously a contested space where state actors jockeyed for power, a conduit for narrative promotion, and a narrative in itself. Meanwhile, major state actors dedicated substantial funding for Internet freedom activities, often framed as a sign of solidarity with the Arab Spring protesters (Clinton 2011). In May 2011, the Obama administration announced its "International Strategy for Cyberspace," reflecting America's "core commitments to fundamental freedoms, privacy, and the free flow of information" (Office of the President 2011, 5). Following this policy, it expanded funding for circumvention technologies for activists living in closed regimes such as Syria. In December 2011, the European Commission followed with a "no disconnect strategy," premised on developing circumvention tools, educating activists, monitoring censorship, and building cooperative networks of stakeholders interested in increasing access to information. Discussions about Internet freedom were not limited to the West, but were championed in regional stakeholder meetings such as the Asia Pacific Regional Internet Governance Forum and the European Dialogue on Internet Governance (Kalathil 2010).

Social media also provided a major conduit through which elite actors conveyed strategic narratives. Prior to the Arab Spring, the use of social media by state actors in the region was typically perfunctory. As protests multiplied, so too did initiatives designed to capitalize on these digital transformations. For example, one of the first marquee programs of Hillary Clinton's 21st Century Statecraft initiative was to engage in an open question and answer session with Egyptian bloggers on the Arabic social media platform masrawi.com in the spring of 2011 (U.S. Department of State 2012). At the same time, we also witness several efforts to subdue social media, which itself feeds into the narrative of social media as democracy. As opposition forces took to the streets of Egypt, then Libya, then Syria, each of these regimes leveraged their control over the infrastructure through which social media operate by shutting down Internet service traffic.

The strategies of promotion considered here are not exhaustive. As the following section will demonstrate, these strategies of promotion are inextricably tied to legitimizing agents. Elites may sponsor or support specific narratives. However, their success often depends on the host of interested parties ranging from nonstate actors, to established media organizations, to individual bloggers.

Legitimizing Agents Including Media

A strategic narrative gains momentum—that is, diffusion, normative authority, and a sense of inevitability—through *legitimizing agents*. Since a narrative only exists and grows through the telling, a legitimizing agent is an individual or group that speaks, or is made to speak, in affirmation of the narrative and its strategic goals. In practice, the generation and legitimization of strategic narratives are difficult to separate. One agent might contribute to both, while the processes themselves can occur more or less simultaneously. National elites, mainstream media, alternative and social media, and public opinion can all speak as legitimizing agents. In this section, we focus on the role of the mainstream media. Because the mainstream media simultaneously function as actors that voice particular narratives and as a conduit (and sometimes as a filter) for narratives put forward by a host of actors (including smaller media and new media organizations), they have a special role to play. As James Carey stressed, "reality is a scarce resource . . . the fundamental form of power is the power to define, allocate, and display that resource" (1989, 87).

The media not only act as legitimizing agents but also often contribute to the production of the field of legitimization. Presidents and dissidents, heroes and villains are mobilized through newspaper front pages, in television news hours, and via computer screens; it is in these mediated spaces that narratives are validated, contested, and ultimately made into reality. In general, the media have an entrenched ability to produce a myth of the "center"; what they show, though partial and limited, is the reality that matters (Couldry 2003, 14–19, 30). In the case of international relations, the fact that public interaction with global politics is heavily mediated by logistical necessity, and the elite *perception* that media representation is critical to public opinion, means that the media play a key role as a legitimizing agent.

Regarding the Libyan Uprising, during 2011 the U.S. and U.K. mainstream media in particular lofted the voices of Obama, Cameron, and Sarkozy, giving them opportunities to performatively legitimize their own strategic narratives.[5] In addition, the media coverage mobilized both its own voice (of journalism) and, increasingly, that of the "Libyan People" to stitch together a reality that accentuated the narrative of tyranny, democracy, and freedom. On February 15, 2011, the Arab Spring spread to Libya with popular protests against Colonel Gaddafi's 41-year-old regime. Initially, media descriptions of the protests appeared to retain an "incumbent frame"; that is, a regime-oriented language of "crackdowns," "dissent," and even "civil war," all of which recognized the basic sovereign authority of the Libyan government. But as the regime escalated violence and the rebels emerged as a serious threat, the media quickly developed a schema of tyranny and criminality, and in some cases explicitly called for Western intervention. An example was the reporting of *Daily Mail* correspondent Richard Pendlebury:

> Since last week the streets here have been controlled by civilian militias and soldiers who have mutinied against Gaddafi's often eccentric but always ruthless tyranny. I stood on the peaceful harbour front of Tobruk last night. There was no sound of even distant con-

flict, only that of local dogs. But even in "free" Libya fear still stalks the countryside. . . . These people [Libyans] want the world to be here, to witness and record their struggle and, where necessary, the tyrant's bloody reprisals. No more walls to hide the dark deeds, no more secrecy. (Pendlebury 2011)

This kind of emotive discourse proliferated in the Western mainstream media throughout 2011, depicting Gaddafi and "the People" as morally opposed. Gaddafi was consistently inscribed as a *personally* cruel, megalomaniac, lustful, unhinged, and incompetent ruler, furnishing a specific position of engagement for the reading public. This inscription mobilized a wide range of journalistic armaments. "Hard news" on military and political developments confirmed Gaddafi's cruelty, and implied that his rule was *already* broken, already illegitimate, only waiting for (Western) action to fulfill the course of history. Gaddafi was also covered in many "soft," "human interest" articles that dealt with his apparent proclivities; through them, the media coverage formed a "unified body that exhibits clear themes and patterns" (Bird and Dardenne 1997, 335) about the situation. Western journalists reported on Gaddafi's alleged depravity against his "Amazonian Guards," his "relationship" with the "voluptuous" Ukrainian nurse Halyna Koloynystska, and an apparent romantic obsession with Condoleezza Rice (Clark 2011). But it was insanity and buffoonery that came to define Gaddafi for the Western public's mediated vision. One BBC journalist wrote:

> [Gaddafi] changed personas as other men change their socks. One day he was a Motown backing vocalist with wet-look permed hair and tight pants. The next, a white-suited comic-operetta Latin American admiral, dripping with braid. When I saw him, he had chosen the robes of a Berber tribesman, and what he presumably imagined to be the inscrutable gaze of a desert mystic. . . . It was utterly ludicrous of course, but somehow we did not say so. He was an old-fashioned, theatrical sort of tyrant, whose lineage you can trace from the bombastic ravings of Mussolini, through the kilted debauchery of Idi Amin, to the platform-heeled kleptocracy of Omar Bongo of Gabon. (Connolly 2011)

These reports created a Gaddafi, and, in turn, the Libyan Uprising for the reading public, furnishing a mediated reality within which the strategic narrative of liberation and Western intervention made sense. Eccentricity, insanity, and buffoonery are perhaps the most dominant in Gaddafi's instantiation of the Tyrant figure. Nicknames like the "Mad Dog of the Middle East" or the "Buffoon Dictator" proliferated, especially following Gaddafi's defeat and death. In international obituaries, journalists who had visited Gaddafi in previous years dug out exotic accounts of his paranoia, theatrics, and sheer incomprehensibility; Gaddafi's speeches and media appearances were edited and mistranslated for comedic effect on television programs and YouTube.[6]

Consider, in contrast, the position Syria's Bashar al-Assad was made to occupy in this mediated reality. Throughout 2011, the "incumbent frame" of coverage was more or less retained in the Syrian case, and the relentless characterization of tyrannic vice was spared Assad (*Canberra Times* 2011). Assad was a dentist, the surprise successor; he was the alternative to a potentially harsh and evil uncle. There were international hopes for his evolution and moderation. Even when Turkey and the Arab League began to openly call for Assad's resignation, he was often addressed as a national leader rather than a public enemy. In November 2011, King Abdullah of Jordan gently *recommended* that "if Bashar has the interests of his country he would step down" (BBC News 2011). Whether deliberate or otherwise, Assad's consistent self-presentation as a dour bureaucrat also played into this situational advantage. Whereas Gaddafi, with his flamboyant attire and defiant, rambling discourse, attempted to directly contest the West's narrativization of him and his struggle, Assad, at least initially, was much more subtle in deflecting criticisms.

The civil war in Syria proceeded interminably throughout 2012, and neither Western elite voices nor media depictions provided a clear strategic and preferable *goal*. Whereas Gaddafi's exit was loudly proclaimed as if preordained just weeks into the initial unrest, no such narrative had concretized around Assad as of December 2012 (e.g., Barnard and Saad 2012). In the Libyan case, the Western elites' willingness and ability to organize a diplomatic consensus for intervention was joined by the media legitimization of a tyranny/liberation narrative. As for Syria, the reluctance of numerous nations to rejoin the strategic narrative became well known. For instance, Russia was adamant that the strategic narrative on Libya not be transposed automatically to the Syrian case (e.g., *RT* 2012). The media thus generate a site or field of legitimization that distributes value/credence and visibility not only to specific *claims* (strategic narratives about the situation) but also to *agents* (Gaddafi, Obama, or even the mythical figure of the "Libyan People") and *frameworks* (the general situations about which claims are made).

The cases of Libya and Syria have introduced multiple types of legitimating agents at work. The most obvious example is state actors, often personified by leaders such as Obama and Gaddafi. Their capacity as legitimating agents depends primarily on the structure of the strategic narrative itself: what is the *object* of the strategic narrative, *to whom* must they legitimate the narrative, and *from whence* does their capacity to legitimize originate? The Western strategic narrative on Libya has an international object (the Libyan conflict), which they must legitimate to the domestic and international publics (though primarily "Western," and thus domestically oriented). These state actors derive this capacity from their preexisting positions in the international community as powerful sponsors of narrative. All these factors must be relativized for every agent, influencing that agent's priorities and capacity for legitimization. Gaddafi himself constituted a deprived agent, who was divested of the ability both to provide his own narrative and to contest the legitimacy of the Western one.

Narrative Outcomes

Strategic narratives, by their nature, contain a prescriptive element that is then buttressed by an "or else" clause. In some cases, the desired outcome might be explicitly foregrounded, in other cases the consequences of failure are paramount; the outcome itself may remain vague to allow for various forms of fulfillment, or concretize into a specific political proposal. We return to Libya as a case of a "successful" strategic narrative in which a definite outcome was presented, and then its fulfillment declared and celebrated. We demonstrated earlier that, in February 2011, the initial unrest in the country was covered using a typical "incumbent frame." By early March, however, the Western media was fully engaged in producing a narrative of liberation and democracy. The "Libyan People," conflated with the rebels, were interpellated as innocent, righteous victims of an immoral and inhumane tyrant; the Western public was positioned as *obligated*, morally if not legally, to support intervention. In the United Kingdom, the *Observer* wrote an editorial stating:

But the only response that matters now is a common position which brooks no more argument: not to say in divisive detail what may or may not happen just down the road, but to pledge, with the honest passion we affect to feel that, whether repulsed in time or not, this particular tyranny will not be allowed to stand. Libya is part of freedom's future: it must not be buried by a quavering past. (*Observer* 2011)

While an editorial in the *Sunday Herald* stated:

There are risks, but for once the West is doing the right thing. If leaders like Muammar Gaddafi are allowed to prevail, it will be a dark day for the world. Let tyrants hear the message loud and clear: we are all Benghazians now. (*Sunday Herald* 2011)

The first quotation provides a striking formulation; do not debate the consequences of your actions, *because* tyranny is evil. These journalist voices joined the communiqués of Obama, Cameron, and Sarkozy to push for the Western public to support intervention first in the form of a no-fly zone, enacted in March, and then increased levels of military and political support. The narrative effectively positioned stakeholders as actors with particular roles to play; in a story about an evil oppressor and a heroic People, the choice was simple. The distant suffering of the Libyan people, and of Gaddafi as well (whether he "deserved" his own suffering or not), was aestheticized into cinematic narratives of heroes and villains at the expense of rational deliberation about the causes and responsibilities for Gaddafi's regime and the Arab Spring (Chouliaraki 2006, 8–9). The criminalization of Gaddafi was so effective because it divested the Western public of responsibility for what happened in Libya, or even responsibility to act. Instead, the audience was simply encouraged to agree that Gaddafi was evil incarnate, nod with approval at his deserved execution, and feel unity with the Libyan people.

Notably, many articles published in the mainstream Western press in support of intervention eschewed details of the specific proposal (in March, the no-fly zone) in favor of a generalized, moral commitment to "help the Libyan People." The ultimate outcome—the fall of Gaddafi—was *prescribed*, while the methods were left *axiomatic*; this made the progressive escalation of Western intervention between March and October 2011 relatively unproblematic in public debate. At the same time, interpretations or facts unhelpful to the narrative were variously discarded or foreclosed. In contrast to the American War on Terror, the Libyan intervention was rarely articulated in terms of West and East; American and European soldiers' status as foreigners intervening in civil war was de-emphasized by foregrounding this transhistorical and transnational narrative of tyranny and freedom. Ken McDonald of the London *Times* reminded his readers:

> Not the least of the tragedies of the Iraq war is that it has taught us to turn away from the right thing. We parry and doubt and we worry at the wound; it's an itch that we just have to scratch. . . . It may be too late to arm these brave [rebels], but certainly Gaddafi's planes should not fly free to blast their positions apart; it shames us that the dictator still orders his jets into the skies. So let us have a no-fly zone. (Macdonald 2011)

Comparisons with Afghanistan and Iraq were thus suppressed. Finally, the prescription of Gaddafi's fall was buttressed by an implication that Gaddafi's death was inevitable, or even preordained in some manner. Gaddafi was conflated with the Arab world's old regimes as a whole (all of which were now "tyrannified" by proxy) ("Arab World's Tyrants . . ." 2011), and even with the historical figure of the Tyrant itself. This connection to a transhistorical metanarrative lent authority to the narrativization of Gaddafi and Libya; the rebels' war was a universal struggle that *must* succeed, and in turn Western intervention was "on the right side of history."[7] Take, for example, the following statement by Obama and Cameron:

> Bin Laden's ideology is one that has failed to take hold. Gaddafi's reign represents the region's past. We stand for something different. We see the prospect of democracy and universal rights taking hold in the Arab world, and it fills us with confidence and a renewed commitment to an alliance based not just on interests but on values. (Obama and Cameron 2011)

Thomas Friedman, influential commentator for the *New York Times*, read from the same page:

> With Libya, Yemen, Bahrain and Syria now all embroiled in rebellions, it is not an exaggeration to suggest that the authoritarian lid that has smothered freedom in the Arab world for centuries may be coming off all 350 million Arab peoples at once. Personally, I think

that is exactly what is going to happen over time. Warm up the bus for all the Arab autocrats—and for you, too, Ahmadinejad. (Friedman 2011)

Such discourse, from both leaders and media, peaked on October 20 when Gaddafi's death prompted various triumphant claims of historical progress (Connolly 2011; Tisdall 2011). This was Libya's "Mission Accomplished" moment; the strategic narrative was declared fulfilled, retroactively affirming its legitimacy as part of a transhistorical metanarrative.

In the case of Syria, parallel approaches faced significant limitations. Syrian's air force was a far more complicated target than Libya's for a no-fly zone, and it was impossible to gain sufficient consensus to enforce it. The "or else" aspect of the narrative faced these limitations. The capacity of the Assad regime to impose fatalities—to take steps to assert its control over events, even at great cost to the Syrian people—also rendered the "or else" aspect of a strategic narrative momentarily inconclusive. Indeed, military force on the ground frequently sinks and pushes off course the most painstakingly devised narratives. The word is not law. Nevertheless, analysis of competing strategic narratives is useful. The Syria context was fluid, and the fate of different narratives is one way to diagnose how perceptions of possible action were transforming for different actors. In other words, the unstable environment could be understood in terms of shifting efforts, recurrently unsuccessful, to build new strategic narratives.

Toward a Taxonomy

We have suggested here a potential schema drawn from our discussion of Libya and Syria. Critical components of what makes a narrative strategic include the characteristics of sponsorship, the narrative themes, the strategies of promotion, and legitimizing agents. Each of these items invokes a research agenda: Who and what are the emerging sponsors of narratives and their themes? How do legitimizing agents work, vis-à-vis the ecology of strategies of promotion?

Strategic narratives are amorphous and difficult to identify. Future areas of research include closer analysis on questions of measures and methods. Given that strategic narratives are a collection of factors, measures of effectiveness become difficult. A simple correlation between narrative inputs and strategic risks obscures the important multitude of intervening variables that can support or undermine the utilization of narratives by states. We end with more questions than answers, but hope that these provide a basis for future research. In beginning this path toward understanding the components of strategic narratives we come to several tentative conclusions suggested by the Arab Spring.

First, the mainstream media plays a specific and critical role as the site in which strategic narratives are not only disseminated but gain legitimacy and momentum. Although many strategic narratives originate from elites in one or several states, it is in the codified space of the media that their ultimate success is determined. The Libyan Uprising demonstrates this media-centric production and dissemination of strategic narratives, and their relation to Western states' strategic objectives—in this case, of removing Colonel Gaddafi from the political scene in favor of a liberal democracy, ensuring the retention of Western influence in regional geopolitics, and appearing proactive and principled to their own Western publics. For instance, Obama, Cameron, and Sarkozy's public communiqués constituted a codified and performative production line of discourse that drew on and perpetuated specific normative matrices of truth and knowledge, enjoining the reader, both "host" (Western) and "target" (Western and localized in the Middle East), to accept not only the legitimacy but also the moral necessity of Western guidance or intervention of a specific kind.[8] This discourse interpellated Colonel Gaddafi as a tyrant, calling upon a long history of the figure in *Western* history. The narrative around the Libyan Uprising was a familiar one of simple and essentialized polarities: Us versus Them, Right versus Wrong, Freedom versus Tyranny. What media narratives, or mediated narratives, achieve is that they aggregate such discursive performances over time, space, and different actors. The result becomes an echo chamber that provides the narrative with a sense of generality and authority for the audience. Indexing may also offer new insight into the identification and study of strategic narratives. Developed by Lance Bennett, who drew on earlier work by Daniel Hallin on the Vietnam War, it suggests that media professionals "index" the range of voices and viewpoints in both news and editorials according to the range of views expressed in mainstream government debate about a given topic (Bennett 1990; Hallin 1986). Therefore, media adoption of a particular frame can provide a threshold indication of the emergence of a strategic narrative as espoused by states.

Second, in light of the focus on social media resulting from the Arab Spring or Arab Awakening, it is important to ask whether a new condition is necessary for a narrative to be strategic—and to have a good chance of being binding: namely, whether the proposed international narrative is in harmony or synchronous with dominant perspectives in the social media in the local context where the internationally fashioned narrative is intended to hold sway. Another way to put this is whether new media technologies and social media provide a check on the capacity of elite international players to establish a controlling framework. If social media does perform such a "validating" function, what are the standards—if any—for its approval or acquiescence? If it does not, in what way can it be said to possess agency for political change?

Third, narratives derive their normative efficacy from the way they interpolate people and things into preexisting roles and positions, including the audience. In other words, narratives attempt to cultivate specific perspectives and ranges of opinion in their audience, and delimit the range of what might be considered "true," "right," or convincing within that context. The Western elites' narrative on Libya effectively positioned stakeholders as actors with particular roles to play; and in a story of an evil oppressor and a heroic People, the choice is simple. Potentially problematic arguments or frames, such as the similarities between a Western intervention in Libya and prior "interventions" in Iraq and Afghanistan, were largely de-emphasized by foregrounding this transhistorical and transnational narrative of tyranny and freedom. Such narratives operated both at a microlevel of specific events at hand and as metanarratives on national or transnational scales. In contrast, the Syrian situation was analogized to Somalia, to the breakdown of law and order, to chaos. Given the specter of previous quagmires, interpellation in the Syrian case undermined rather than solidified a unifying strategic narrative.

Fourth, insofar as strategic narratives about specific conflicts or crises (such as those analyzed in this chapter) are defined by their goal-oriented nature, a clear "or else" clause must be identifiable. The narrativization of Gaddafi as soon-to-be-dead tyrant was from the beginning oriented toward a specific, short-term political goal: the successful implementation of a no-fly zone in support of the Libyan Uprising. The "or else" clause was provided in the form of a moral injunction against (a Western conception of) tyranny, which itself drew on the background of both sensational media reports about the violence in the country and the recent history of other Arab Spring uprisings. The geopolitical complexities of the Syrian case precluded such "or else" clauses. Moreover, the ever-expanding array of narrative sponsors precluded any generalized consensus on a specific set of outcomes a coalition or singular actor could credibly put forward in a power-based narrative.

Finally, given the "or else" clause, the effectiveness of strategic narratives must be measured, in part, by their capacity to mobilize a consensual understanding of how things are, what must be done, and by whom. Our hypothesis has been that some narratives were more effective than others. We believe that the answer likely involves a compatibility between script and stage, and the ability and willingness of the actors to play their parts. But here we are only at the beginning: What were the specific characteristics of the strategic narrative surrounding Libya and Gaddafi that yielded prolonged and extensive Western military intervention in the country? Why did other narratives, both real (such as some African media's insistence on Gaddafi's status as an anticolonial, nationalist hero) and hypothetical (such as an extended analogy to the by then highly problematized intervention in Iraq and Afghanistan) not take off? And what is different about other political contexts, such as the Syrian conflict, that disabled seemingly similar strategic narratives? To be sure, more longitudinal and comparative case studies of strategic narratives are needed. Observers can then better articulate and identify determining factors behind conditions of compatibility and willingness. And they can suggest, as well, those conditions where narratives fail to perform the strategic functions intended for them.

NOTES

1. This chapter was completed in the fall of 2013. At the time of writing, the conflict in Syria remained ongoing, as did the ultimate resolution of events in Libya. It does not claim to provide an exhaustive account of the strategic narratives of the Arab Spring.

2. The first high-profile use of the term Somalization to describe Syria was by Nobel Peace Prize laureate José Ramos-Horta in an interview with the Associated Press in October 2012. A week later, the Arab League and UN envoy Lakhdar Brahimi began to use the term, after which it began to appear in Iranian, Russian, and other Middle Eastern press outlets, although less so in the West. See "Ramos-Horta Warns of 'Somalization' of Syria as Airstrikes Leave More Deaths," October 30, 2012. Accessed January 26, 2013. http://english.alarabiya.net/articles/2012/10/30/246621.html

3. Assad has frequently espoused this characterization of opposition forces as "armed gunman." The Arab League as well as Moscow has begun to use the term "political solution" as the only alternative to regime change, which would end in Somalization of the country. See, for example, United Nations News Service, "Transcript of Press Conference by Joint Special Representative for Syria, Lakhdar Brahimi, with Secretary-General of the League of Arab States Dr. Nabil Al Arabi," UN News Centre, December 30, 2012. http://www.un.org/apps/news/infocus/Syria/press.asp?NewsID=1257&sID=45

4. Qatari-owned, international broadcasting heavyweight Al Jazeera also came under fire for covering the violence in Syria in a manner that underscored the official Qatari narrative. See, for example, "The Shameful Arab Silence on Syria," *Daily Star* (Beirut), April 7, 2011. http://www.dailystar.com.lb/Opinion/Columnist/Apr/07/The-shameful-Arab-silence-on-Syria.ashx

5. This point, and subsequent examples, are drawn from one of the authors' analysis of print media coverage on Gaddafi. The data included approximately 200 articles from major online and print news outlets in the West throughout 2011, as well as speeches, non-Western articles, and coverage prior to 2011. The sample was drawn through LexisNexis and prefiltered for relevance.

6. These include preproduced TV skits, such as numerous ones created by *Conan*, hosted by Conan O'Brien (2011; TBS); or amateur adaptations, such as "FUNNY Gaddafi—What's the Question? (original) HQ," *YouTube*, last modified March 2, 2011, http://www.youtube.com/watch?v=i5FNjVdTFlY

7. The refrain itself, or its variants, was used several times in the media.

8. In this sense, the exercise of discourse invokes and is implicated in a game of legitimacy, or what Pierre Bourdieu referred to as a "market of linguistic exchange." See Pierre Bourdieu, "Language and Symbolic Power," in *The Discourse Reader*, edited by Adam Jaworski and Nikolas Coupland (London: Routledge, 2006), 480–82.

REFERENCES

Action Group for Syria. "Final Communiqué, June 30, 2012." http://www.un.org/News/dh/infocus/Syria/FinalCommuniqueActionGroupforSyria.pdf

Andersen, Kurt. "Person of the Year 2011: The Protester." *Time*, December 14, 2011. http://www.time.com/time/specials/packages/article/0,28804,2101745_2102132,00.html

"The Arab Spring: Has It Failed?" *Economist,* July 13–19, 2013, special report.

"Arab World's Tyrants Must Have Gone to the Same School." *Canberra Times*, March 30, 2011.

Archetti, Cristina. *Understanding Terrorism in the Age of Global Media: A Communication Approach*. New York: Palgrave Macmillan, 2012.

Barnard, Anne, and Hwaida Saad. "No Easy Route if Assad Opts to Go, or to Stay, in Syria." *New York Times,* December 24, 2012. http://www.nytimes.com/2012/12/25/world/middleeast/no-easy-route-if-bashar-al-assad-opts-to-go-or-stay.html?ref=world&_r=0

BBC News. "Dozens Killed in Syria as Jordan King Tells Assad to Go." November 15, 2011. http://www.bbc.co.uk/news/world-middle-east-15727325

Bennett, W. Lance. "Toward a Theory of Press-State Relations in the United States." *Journal of Communication* 40, no. 2 (1990): 103–27.

Bird, S. Elizabeth, and Robert W. Dardenne. "Myth, Chronicle, and Story: Exploring the Narrative Qualities of News." In *Social Meanings of News: A Text Editor*, edited by Dan Berkowitz. Thousand Oaks, CA: Sage, 1997.

Borshchevskaya, Anna. "Russia's Many Interests in Syria." Washington Institute, January 24, 2013. http://www.washingtoninstitute.org/policy-analysis/view/russias-many-interests-in-syria

Bourdieu, Pierre. *The Field of Cultural Production: Essays on Art and Literature*. New York: Columbia University Press, 1993.
Cameron, David, Barack Obama, and Nicolas Sarkozy. "The Bombing Continues until Gaddafi Goes." *Times of London*, April 15, 2011, Opinion section. http://www.thetimes.co.uk/tto/opinion/columnists/article2986866.ece
Canberra Times. "Pressure Mounts on Syria." August 20, 2011.
Carey, James. *Communication as Culture: Essays on Media and Society*. New York: Routledge, 1989.
Chouliaraki, Lilie. *The Spectatorship of Suffering*. London: Sage, 2006.
Clark, Neil. "Two Faces of a Tyrant and Both of Them Evil." *Express*, October 21, 2011.
Clinton, Hillary. "Internet Rights and Wrongs: Choices and Challenges in a Networked World." February 15, 2011. http://blogs.state.gov/stories/2011/02/15/internet-rights-and-wrongs-choices-and-challenges-networked-world
Connolly, Kevin. "Colonel Gaddafi: The Last of the Buffoon Dictators?" *BBC News*, October 22, 2011. http://www.bbc.co.uk/news/magazine-15405274
Couldry, Nick. *Media Rituals: A Critical Approach*. London: Routledge, 2003.
Freedman, Lawrence. *The Transformation of Strategic Affairs*. New York: Routledge, 2006.
Friedman, Thomas L. "Hoping for Arab Mandelas." *New York Times*, March 27, 2011.
Gallup. "NATO Intervention in Libya Unpopular in Arab World." Analysis by the Gallup Center for Muslim Studies. July 9, 2012. http://www.gallup.com/poll/154997/Snapshot-NATO-Intervention-Libya-Unpopular-Arab-World.aspx?
Hallin, Daniel C. *The "Uncensored War": The Media and Vietnam*. New York: Oxford University Press, 1986.
Hounshell, Blake. "The Revolution Will Be Tweeted." *Foreign Policy*, June 20, 2011.
Howard, Philip, Aiden Duffy, Deen Freelon, Muzammil M. Hussain, Will Mari, and Marwa Mazaid. "Opening Closed Regimes: What Was the Role of Social Media during the Arab Spring?" Working Paper 2011.1. Seattle: University of Washington, Project on Information Technology and Political Islam, 2011.
Howard, Philip N., and Muzammil M. Hussain. "The Role of Digital Media." *Journal of Democracy* 22, no. 3 (2011): 35–48.
International Institute for Strategic Studies. *The Military Balance 2011: The Annual Assessment of Global Military Capabilities and Defence Economics*. London: ISSI, 2011.
"Iran Calls Syrian Protests a Western Plot." Reuters, April 12, 2011. http://www.reuters.com/article/2011/04/12/us-syria-iran-idUSTRE73B22V20110412
Kalathil, Shanthi. "Internet Freedom: A Background Paper." Prepared for the Aspen Institute International Digital Economy Accords (IDEA) Project, October 2010.
Krebs, Ronald R., and Patrick T. Jackson. "Twisting Tongues and Twisting Arms: The Power of Political Rhetoric." *European Journal of International Relations* 13, no. 1 (2007): 35–66.
Landis, Joshua. "The Syrian Uprising of 2011: Why the Assad Regime Is Likely to Survive to 2013." *Middle East Policy* 19, no. 1 (2012): 72–84.
LeCuyer, Jack A. "Op-Ed: A National Strategic Narrative and Grand Strategy for the 21st Century." United States Army War College Strategic Studies Institute, July 1, 2011. Accessed January 20, 2016. http://www.strategicstudiesinstitute.army.mil/index.cfm/articles/A-National-Strategic-Narrative-and-Grand-Strategy-for-the-21st-Century/2011/7/1#_ednref1

Lim, Merlyna. "Clicks, Cabs, and Coffee Houses: Social Media and Oppositional Movements in Egypt, 2004–2011." *Journal of Communication* 62, no. 2 (2012): 231–48.

Macdonald, Ken. "Don't Let the Scars of Iraq Deny Justice in Libya." *Times* (London), March 16, 2011.

Miskimmon, Alister, Ben O'Loughlin, and Laura Roselle. *Strategic Narratives: Communication Power and the New World Order*. New York: Routledge, 2013.

Obama, Barack, and David Cameron. "Not Just Special, But an Essential Relationship." *Times* (London), May 24, 2011.

Observer (UK). "Libya: The West Can't Let Gaddafi Destroy His People." March 13, 2011.

Office of the President. "International Strategy for Cyberspace: Prosperity, Security, and Openness in a Networked World." May 2011. http://www.whitehouse.gov/sites/default/files/rss_viewer/international_strategy_for_cyberspace.pdf

O'Loughlin, Ben. "Does the Arab Spring Show How Strategic Narratives Work?" London: New Political Communication Unit, Royal Holloway University, 2011. http://newpolcom.rhul.ac.uk/npcu-blog/2011/4/22/does-the-arab-spring-show-how-strategic-narratives-work.html

Pendlebury, Richard. "I Stand in a Libya on the Brink of Liberation, But Fear Still Stalks This Scarred Land." *Daily Mail* (London), February 24, 2011.

RT. "'Syria Is Not Libya'—Lavrov." December 5, 2012. http://rt.com/politics/syria-russia-chemical-weapons-nato-lavrov-314/

"Russia Argues That Geneva Communiqué Opponents in Fact Encouraging Bloodshed in Syria." *Russia Beyond the Headlines*, September 29, 2012. Accessed February 11, 2013. http://rbth.ru/articles/2012/09/29/russia_argues_that_geneva_communique_opponents_in_fact_encouraging_b_18679.html

"Russia Sees No Alternative to Geneva Communiqué on Syria." Xinhua News, January 11, 2013. http://news.xinhuanet.com/english/world/2013-01/11/c_132097183.htm

Saab, Nabil Abi. "UN REPORT: Russian Non-paper on Geneva—2 / Syria." *UN Report*, June 16, 2013. http://un-report.blogspot.com/2013/06/russian-non-paper-on-geneva-2-syria.html

Saddiki, Said. "Arab Public Opinion and NATO after the International Military Operations in Libya." *Turkish Journal of International Relations* 11, no. 2 (2012): 78–89.

Salloukh, Bassel F. "The Arab Uprisings and the Geopolitics of the Middle East." *International Spectator* 48, no. 2 (2013): 32–46.

Salmi, Ismail. "Towards 'Somalization'? Syria Swings between 'Dialogue,' Chaos and Bloodshed." *GlobalResearch.ca*, December 31, 2012. http://www.globalresearch.ca/towards-somalization-syria-swings-between-dialogue-chaos-and-bloodshed/5317471

Statement by Russian Foreign Minister Sergei Lavrov after Talks with Arab League and UN Representative Lakhdar Brahimi in Moscow in December 2012.

Sunday Herald (UK). "Why the West Must Stand Firm against the World's Tyrants." March 20, 2011.

Tisdall, Simon. "The Wheel of History Turned Yesterday: It Won't Turn Back." *Guardian* (London), October 21, 2011.

U.S. Department of State. "The Internet Moment in Foreign Policy." 2012. http://www.state.gov/statecraft/overview/index.htm

Vargas, Jose Antonio. "How an Egyptian Revolution Began on Facebook." *New York Times*, February 17, 2012. Accessed January 20, 2016. http://www.nytimes.com/2012/02/19/books/review/how-an-egyptian-revolution-began-on-facebook.html

Zalman, Amy. "2011: Year of the Protest Narrative." *Strategic Narrative.net*, December 28, 2011. Accessed January 20, 2016. http://strategic-narrative.net/blog/tag/arab-spring/

9 | Narrative Wars

Understanding Terrorism in the Era of Global Interconnectedness

Cristina Archetti

Both in terrorism research and counterterrorism practitioners' circles "narratives" are *en vogue*. Just to illustrate the extent of their ubiquity on both sides of the Atlantic, the U.K. government's 2009 antiterrorism strategy identified the narrative of "oppression and victimhood" promoted by al Qaeda (Home Office 2009, 155)—which portrays Muslims around the world as victims of Western aggressors—as the fuel for homegrown extremism (141). The Dutch National Coordinator for Counterterrorism released a whole collection of contributions by academics and researchers about "Countering Violent Extremist Narratives" in 2010. A White House document about preventing violent extremism has more recently stated that "[r]adicalization that leads to violent extremism includes the diffusion of ideologies and narratives that feed on grievances, assign blame, and legitimize the use of violence against those deemed responsible" (White House 2011, 6). Again in the United Kingdom, the *Prevent* strategy (Home Office 2011, 29) mentions either "narrative" or "counter-narrative" 25 times and further assigns the highest priority in counterterrorism to activity that "challenges the terrorist ideology, for example speakers challenging terrorist narratives."

The interest in narratives stems from the growing realization, in the post-9/11 context, that both terrorism and counterterrorism take place, beyond the material and military dimensions, in the realm of communication, perceptions, and persuasion. For instance, David Betz emphasizes the importance of the informational domain in what is regarded as a "battle of ideas" between Western democracies and al Qaeda:

> The contemporary operations environment . . . in the "Global War on Terror" . . . has two dimensions: the first is the actual tactical field of battle in which bullets fly, bombs explode and blood is shed; the second is the virtual, informational realm in which belligerents contend with words and images to manufacture strategic narratives which are more compelling than those of the other side and better at structuring the responses of others to the development of events. (Betz 2008, 510)

The very idea of progress in counterterrorism appears to be related to both establishing a credible narrative and damaging "their" narrative. William Casebeer and James Russell (2005), in this respect, suggest that the most effective way to counter terrorism is by developing a "better story" to replace the extremists' one. A special communication unit, the Research, Information and Communication Unit, was set up in Whitehall in 2007 with the specific task of using "messaging to disrupt the Al Qa'ida narrative" (Home Office 2009, 153; see also Home Office 2011, 51–52). A U.S. Presidential Task Force (2009) report on how to counter radicalization also argues for "rewriting the narrative" of Islamist extremists.

Despite the continuous repetition of the term, surprisingly little effort has gone into understanding the nature of narratives as well as their role in the phenomenon of contemporary extremism: What are narratives, exactly? How do they support—even supposedly drive—radicalism? Not only that. As will be shown in the following pages, narratives overwhelmingly appear to be regarded as "stories." But through which process does a "sequence of events" or a "tale" acquire the power to turn an apparently law-abiding citizen into a radical ready to engage in murderous violence? How can the shift from "exposure to a message" to "action" be explained? This chapter is a contribution to filling such gaps in our understanding by explaining the role of narratives in the political mobilization of terrorist groups within a globally interconnected media environment.

In addition to this, the following discussion tackles very similar questions to those addressed, at the level of international relations, by Miskimmon, O'Loughlin, and Roselle (2013). While the authors discuss the formation, projection, and reception of *state* narratives within the new media ecology—in other words, they try to unravel the process through which a "story" produced by a government leads to change in the real world—they also point at the emergence on the international arena of new political actors. Through the Internet, social media, and global communication networks these actors—among them we can mention NGOs, citizen activists, transnational social movements, and, importantly for this chapter, terrorist groups—are able to communicate their narratives to (potentially) worldwide audiences. As the authors ask, "If new actors have the opportunities to communicate their own narratives or challenge others, what does this mean for states?" (2013, 11). The analysis here is thus also an examination of the nature and function of narratives by a specific—and increasingly influential—category of nonstate actors in the 21st-century international political environment.

The argument develops in five progressive stages. First, it suggests an understanding of the concept of narrative based on the notion that narratives are socially and relationally constructed rather than merely being "scripted messages." Secondly, the chapter illustrates the analytical benefits of the relationally conceived narrative concept in explaining the process through which prospective terrorists embrace the message of extremist organizations—radicalization. As a third step, the analysis exposes the outdated assumptions that underpin much of current research and policy, particularly the simplistic notion that a narrative is similar to an information "bullet" that produces behavioral effects upon impact. The fourth section illustrates the new insights that a deeper understanding of narratives can bring to the "war of ideas" against radical groups. As a final stage, the conclusions point out further practical implications of a narrative approach to terrorism, not only in the very way we conceive extremism, but also in the practice of countering radicalization.

Not Just a "Story": The Social Construction of Narratives

We all intuitively understand the meaning of "narrative": it is a sequence of events tied together by a plot line. Technically, however, narratives are something deeper and more complex. As Stephanie Lawler (2002, 242, her emphasis) writes, for instance, narratives do not simply "carry" "a set of 'facts'": they are "*social products* produced by people within the context of specific social, historical and cultural locations." They are "interpretive devices through which people represent themselves, both to themselves and to others" (ibid.). In this sense narratives are central to the construction of identity (Somers and Gibson 1994; Benwell and Stokoe 2006, 42).

Narratives are social products in two respects. First, a narrative does not exist independently of individual agency. Narrative is the means through which *people* "connect together past and present" (Lawler 2002, 242). This occurs through a process of "emplotment" through which apparently unrelated events become "episodes" of a coherent thread (245–46). To illustrate this, Hayden White (1973) suggested that historians *emplot* events into histories, rather than simply *find* them. Second, a narrative is a collective construction. As Charlotte Linde points out, even "an individual's life story is not the property of that individual alone, but also belongs to others who have shared the events narrated—or were placed to have opinions about them" (Linde 2009, 4). Dennis Mumby (1993, 5) further underlines that the study of narrative is about understanding the struggle over the construction of social meaning—a struggle that is related to power, politics, and the ability for some actors to "fix" meaning (7).

From the perspective of this analysis, the phenomenon of violent extremism takes place in a social world that is constituted by overlapping networks of relationships.[1] Social relationships shape who we are—our identity. The model is fundamentally based on a tight interrelation among identity, knowledge, and action. In other words, who we are shapes what we know—including the interpretation of incoming information—and this, in turn, shapes our behavior (action). Each single relationship we have exists on the basis of a "story." This means that we are able to provide an account of who the person we have a relationship with is, what the nature of our relationship is, and how it developed. Exchanges of information, goods, and resources might be attached to the relationship. They are part of the story. In fact, they constitute it, and over time can also change it. The combination of all of these stories, together with the view of the world we develop as a result of our constellation of relationships, the interpretation of incoming information through the perspective resulting from our position in the social space at any given time, our account of what we do (including why we do it) as a result, constitute our *individual narrative*. This could be described as the unique perspective that an individual has on the world from his or her "corner" of the social reality (figure 9.1).

Within this perspective communication—as the sharing and transmitting of information, communication technologies, media organizations,

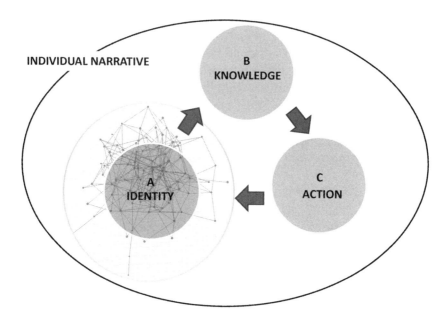

Fig. 9.1. The social construction of the individual narrative

and media coverage—contributes to the formation of identity (figure 9.1, area A). Communication is the very enabler of the formation of any relationship. Social ties do not just exist with people we are in contact with but are also indirect. Craig Calhoun (1991) argues that the proliferation of "indirect relationships" and the production of "imagined communities" are two features that fundamentally characterize modernity. Beyond direct interpersonal relations (face-to-face), he envisages imagined personal connections that can exist, for instance, with political representatives, TV personalities, but also through tradition (96–105). Communication technologies can thus extend our social reach in forming direct relationships (through e-mails, for example, or by having a chat over the phone), but they can also contribute to indirect ties. For instance, an activist can develop an indirect relationship with an admired political figure one comes to know through television or speeches available online.

The imagined communities are based on, in Craig Calhoun's term, the "politics of identification." As Calhoun explains, "People without direct interpersonal relations with each other are led by the mediation of the world of political symbols to imagine themselves as members of communities defined by common ascriptive characteristics, personal tastes, habits, concerns" (Calhoun 1991, 108). In this sense, there can be imagined communities of interest like those constituted by environmental activists, gay marriage campaigners, radical Muslims who aspire to live in a society regulated by sharia law, people with a passion for knitting or tap dancing, communities of consumers of Ikea furniture or Mac cosmetics, Lady Gaga's fans, and so on. Although it is possible for a person belonging to any of these communities to actually know like-minded individuals, the sense of shared identity and "fellow feeling" extends well beyond the direct relationship.

The belonging to an imagined community can be supported in a variety of ways. Media can be directly involved. Benedict Anderson (1983, 29), for instance, explained the rise of nationalism—in other words, the state as "imagined community"—through the daily ritual of reading the newspaper: "The mass ceremony . . . is performed in silent privacy. . . . Yet each communicant is well aware that the ceremony he performs is being replicated simultaneously by thousands (or millions) of others of those whose existence he is confident, yet of whose identity he has not the slightest notion." The same could be said for contemporary viewers and listeners of globally covered events. Daniel Dayan and Elihu Katz (1992, 1) call "media events" those "historic occasions . . . that are televised as they take place and transfix a nation or the world." Among the examples of media events they present are the funeral of Egypt's president Anwar el Sadat and John Fitzgerald Kennedy, and the wedding of Prince Charles and Lady Diana. During media events the barriers to total and unmediated communication normally represented by the fact that there are multiple messages, that audiences are selective, and that diffusion of information takes time, are momentarily overcome. Media events, in the analysis of Dayan and Katz, are able to create communities of vast audiences (15). Their being broadcast live, the ceremony and ritual that accompany them, the focus on a central value, the interruption they bring in daily life contribute to an experience of communion among members of the audience that the authors write "is reminiscent of holy days" (16). The same principle could apply more recently to the witnessing of events like 9/11, the British royal wedding in 2011, and the Paris demonstration following the Islamist attacks against the *Charlie Hebdo* magazine in early 2015. The live coverage of these events, this time on multiple platforms, might have led to a sense (albeit perhaps only fleeting) of connection among global members of the audience who knew other people around the world were experiencing the same scenes at the very same moment. In the case of the 2015 Paris demonstration the sense of connection was made even more tangible—expressed not only visually but also materially—by the simultaneous display across the world of the same "*Je suis Charlie*"—I am Charlie—white writing on a black background on placards and signs.

A community, in fact, can be supported both by material artifacts—placards, as we have seen, but also buildings, like a temple in the case of a religious community (Calhoun 1991, 112)—but also by immaterial objects, such as memories of events. An example of the latter is the very name chosen by the Greek terrorist organisation 17 November (Council on Foreign Relations n.d.). The date, evoking the authorities' bloody repression of student protests that took place in 1973 at the Athens Polytechnic, also serves as a powerful reminder of the common ideological commitment of the group's members both within the organization and externally.

Face-to-face communication, communication technologies, and media coverage, however, occupy another place in the social map (figure 9.1, area B). They allow the acquisition of new information (through conversation, surfing on the Internet, reading the newspaper, watching TV, and so forth), which will be interpreted through the individual's relational perspective at any specific time. It is at this point that an individual can come into contact with other narratives. These might be other actors' individual narratives (belonging to our friends and acquaintances, for instance), but also collective narratives (related to the sense of belonging of a democratic society, for example, or sustained by the traditions of an ethnic minority, the rituals of a religious group, and so on). The collective narratives might be promoted, as in the case of political movements (as also terrorist organizations) for specific mobilization purposes. I will come back to this in discussing collective narratives.

Any incoming information, including other actors' narratives, will never be absorbed as it is but filtered and appropriated through the prism of the individual narrative. This might, over time, lead to a change in the vision of the world of the individual, reflected in his or her changing patterns of social relationships, development of a revised identity, individual narrative, behavior, and so forth in a continuous cycle. Partly as a result of our action, partly as the outcome of the simultaneous action by all the actors within our networks, the relationships' maps are constantly changing. This leads to our identity continuously evolving, together with the way we interpret the world around us and the way we act. The change in our interpretation of the world, in turn, involves a continuous reworking of the

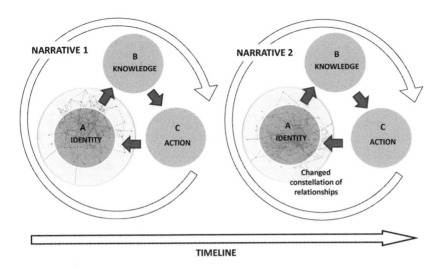

Fig. 9.2. Evolution of the individual narrative over time

past, as well as of our projections of future action trajectories (Emirbayer and Mische 1998). This is reflected in a continuously and progressively transforming individual narrative. Figure 9.2 shows the way in which different networks lead to different identities, interpretations of the world, and consequent behavior.

As identities exist at both individual and collective levels, so do narratives. Collective identities are at the same time constructed out of individual identities and constitute the context within which such individual identities are formed (Sciolla 1983, 14).

Being a member of a group means sharing a common collective narrative while simultaneously having an individual narrative that is compatible with it (figure 9.3, narratives of individual 1 and 3).

In this perspective, according to Alberto Melucci, social movements (as also terrorist groups) "offer individuals the collective possibility of affirming themselves as actors and of finding an equilibrium between self-recognition and hetero-recognition" (Melucci 1982, 72). If, over time, the collective and individual narratives, in their continuous evolution, come to diverge, the dissonance between them will lead the individual not to identify any longer with the group (figure 9.3, narrative of individual 2).

Those who develop an individual politically extremist narrative as a

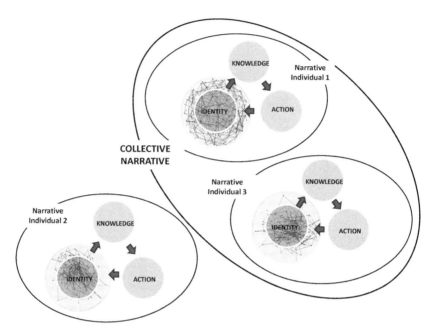

Fig. 9.3. Changing membership of a group over time: Compatibility/dissonance of individual narratives with a collective narrative

result of a time- and place-specific constellation of relationships can either interact face-to-face in a group or indirectly through the phone or the Internet. Alternatively, or in addition to that, they might feel part of a broader community of extremists they have never met and which coalesces around political symbols. It is important to understand that sharing a common collective narrative within a group does not mean deleting the peculiar features that uniquely characterize the individual narrative of each of the members of the group. In this respect, Anna Cento Bull (2009), in analyzing the self-narratives of three Italian neofascists in the 1960s and 1970s, demonstrates that the narratives of the three individuals maintain their own uniqueness, even if they embrace the same radical ideology—which we might think of as a collective narrative. She points out, for example, the differences between the self-narratives of Vincenzo Vinciguerra and Luigi Ciavardini. Vinciguerra's narrative is highly idealistic and characterized by three "myths": "the myth of the hero overcoming adversity; the myth of the martyr, ready to die in defence of his faith; and finally, the myth of Christ, who was betrayed by his disciples and died to show the way to the whole humankind" (191). Ciavardini, instead, strongly downplays idealistic aspirations as a motivation for engaging in terrorist activity:

> We [Ciavardini and Vale, another neofascist] did not have a political project. . . . we are [sic] taking the distance from politics. I was getting close to being spontaneous [*spontaneismo*]. To get armed, to attack, to steal. Living my own way against all and everybody. (Semprini 2003, in Cento Bull 2009, 193, my translation)

The same applies to individuals who have more recently joined al Qaeda or the Islamic State of Iraq and Syria (ISIS). While they all share a feeling of belonging to an Islamist extremist group, the specific motivation of each individual is shaped by one's unique narrative. A report by the Institute for Strategic Dialogue (Hoyle, Bradford, and Frenett 2015, 38) about the causes of female migration to the Islamic State, for example, concludes that women tend to share motives similar to those of male fighters—an urge to defend the Ummah under attack, a religious duty to "do something," a search for comradeship and meaning in life—but also present further distinctive reasons. On the basis of the analysis of the accounts provided on social media by the female recruits themselves, they also appear to embrace more strongly the state-building mission of ISIS (11–14, 38). Each woman also experiences a different personal journey that might involve a sense of empowerment, self-realization, and the achievement of greater independence from the family (38; Saltman 2014). In addition to this, anthropologist Scott Atran (2014), discussing the motivations of Western ISIS teenage recruits, suggests that they have very different reasons than the political ideology that might drive older generations: "what inspires the most lethal terrorists in the world today is not so much the Qur'an or religious teachings as a thrilling cause and call to action that promises glory and esteem in the eyes of friends." As he further elaborates, younger recruits "are self-seekers who have found their way to jihad in myriad ways: through barbecues or on the web; because they were perhaps uncomfortable with binge-drinking or casual sex; or because their parents were humiliated by form-checking bureaucrats or their sisters insulted for wearing a headscarf."

Narratives, Communication, and Radicalization in a Global Media Environment

The relational understanding of narrative that has been illustrated helps make sense of the social and political impact of communication in the 21st century. Particularly, it both complements and improves explanations of the way individuals become radicalized,[2] especially those analyses that envisage a dynamic relationship between individual agency and social-structural facilitating conditions (Neumann and Rogers 2007; Neumann 2008) rather than reducing radicalization mainly to exposure to radical ideas (see Bergin et al. 2009, for instance). As an example of the former literature, Peter Neumann and Brooke Rogers (2007) describe the process through which individuals come to join terrorist organizations through the lens of social movement theory. Terrorist organizations, according to the authors, are engaged in a mobilization effort that involves the communication of messages ("frames") to audiences, but also a "frame alignment" (16). This is "the convergence between the movement narrative and the views of the recruits" (ibid). Frame alignment, or the sharing of the same view of the world, however, is "rarely sufficient" in persuading people to engage in acts of extreme violence. A process of "socialization" should also take place in which the individual "alters the perceptions of self-interest and increases the values of group loyalties and personal ties" (ibid). The authors suggest that there is a message (frame); that this message is embraced by individuals (frame alignment); and that the difference between sharing an extremist view of the world and translating it into action is made by intense interaction within a group. My argument, as illustrated in the previous section, is that the concept of narrative, relationally constructed and changeable over time, is more effective in explaining this process. The individual narrative is a social actor's account of his or her identity as shaped by a constellation of relationships at any given time, resulting in a vision of the world and corresponding action. In this perspective joining an extremist group is not the result of an external narrative being received and internalized by the individual, as if the collective narrative of the group substituted for the individual one. Becoming part of an extremist group means rather having developed, as a result of shifting patterns of relationships, an individual narrative that is compatible with the collective narrative of the group. Individual and collective narratives coexist.

This explanation of radicalization emphasizes the active role of the individual. Although the position within the set of relationships that constitutes the social space defines who we are, what we know, the way we think, and how we act, this is not meant in deterministic terms. It is, in fact, the individual who ultimately manages the social ties. Additionally, any incoming information is not flowing straight into one's mind, but is always selected and read through the prism of the individual narrative.

Such uniqueness of both the selection and interpretation of incoming information supported by the individual narrative challenges the widespread rhetoric about strategic communication, particularly the idea that it is possible to target selected audiences with the "right" messages to achieve a predefined set of objectives. Instead, no firm assumptions can be made about the kind of information an individual or a target audience will be exposed to. Although this has to some extent always been true, the fact that, for instance, 80 years ago within a country there could have been one national radio station, or a few decades later a couple of national TV channels, could have led to the reasonable expectation that a substantial proportion of a national audience had been exposed to the content of the same evening news bulletin. The interpretation of the information conveyed through that bulletin would have still been unique to each individual. So would have been the way each member of the audience could have discussed that information with family members, friends, and work colleagues. This would have further contributed to the evolution of the personal reading of the initial "message." So no certain prediction could have legitimately been made about its effects. The mainstream media sources of information, however, were fairly limited and at least identifiable. Today, instead, countless sources of information are available through the Internet, cable TV, satellite dishes, mobile phones, and social media platforms. The possibility of sharing text, images, videos, and links with potentially a far broader circle of individuals than would have been possible in the past fatally undermines planning that certain messages are going to be consumed by desired audiences. The availability of information and connectivity are, of course, not limitless. It is true that, even if hundreds of newspapers are available on the Internet, no one is going to consult them all. Even if citizen journalists around the world tell us what's happening in their respective neighborhood, we simply do not have the time to read many of their accounts and we still refer to mainstream newspapers. That is why we still need journalists and editors, as well and foreign correspondents from abroad, to tell us what we should pay attention to. Consumption is limited by the time we have at our disposal to sort through the information tide and by the amount of attention we can devote to it. Professional communicators do indeed exploit the fact that information does not flow randomly. We are all familiar with the feeling of being spied upon when ads about products we have recently researched online start popping up in the corner of our computer screens. Nonetheless, the range of information an individual will be exposed to every day is increasingly unpredictable.[3]

The simultaneous communication and construction of narratives by each individual social actor in a global and potentially transparent information environment could be compared, in its complexity, to the overlapping reflections in a hall of mirrors. Figure 9.4 graphically represents the way narratives are socially constructed in a global communication environment. It builds on the points presented in the previous section. The elaboration of narratives takes place in a relationally constituted social space. The overlapping networks of relationships every social actor is enmeshed in is purposely *not* represented in the figure to avoid thinking that narratives are being transmitted across the social links as if they were bits of data sent through fiber optic cables. Instead, the obligations, information, demands, and expectations that are attached to any relationship should be rather conceived as the pulling forces of a gravitational field. Every actor (A, B, C, D, and so on) could be seen as a mirror, and the information each individual receives from the outside could be thought of as light. In a global and transparent information environment, light comes from virtually all directions. The image each mirror (each individual) will reflect will depend on the individual's position within his or her constellation of relationships. As Lawler (2002, 253), talking about the relationship between narratives and the social context in which they are produced, phrases it: "different social positioning is reflected in the kinds of stories people tell." The position affects the "amount of light" reflected—in other words, the selection of information made by the individual within the available data deluge.

In this communication environment, messages are not simply transmitted, but are constantly reinterpreted. Continuing with the hall of mirrors metaphor, the position within the social field will affect the orientation of each individual's mirror, its surface (whether it will be smooth or rough), and whether the mirror will be straight, concave, or convex (emphasizing a part of an image much more than the rest or leading to an upside-down

Narrative Wars | 231

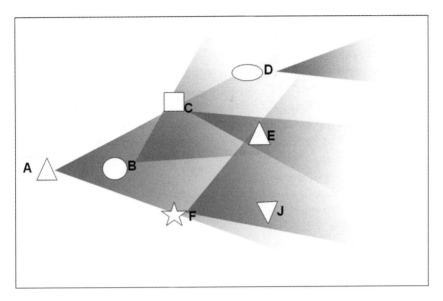

Fig. 9.4. Simultaneous coexistence of multiple individual narratives in the global communication environment

reflection: an opposite reading perhaps). The position also affects where (to which people) the image is going to be further reflected to. Some actors might plan to convey specific images/messages, but the image they will ultimately reflect is itself shaped by their own position in the set of relationships. The planned image or narrative an individual might intentionally convey is being reinterpreted at each stage of the communication process. The image is being reflected further, and the way it looks at every stage depends on the position of each mirror and on the nature of the mirror's surface. There is no guarantee that the image will keep the same shape. For example, actor A in the figure might want to promote a specific narrative (represented by the triangle) in an attempt to mobilize other individuals around a political cause. Other actors who are exposed to that "message," such as B, C, D, F, however, might read it in completely different terms. Only E might read it in similar terms. Not because E has somehow "absorbed" that narrative, but because E's relational setting facilitates a reading that closely matches E's narrative. J, while "listening" to what A is arguing, might entirely disagree and, contrary to what A is hoping for, develop an entirely oppositional reading (the inverted triangle).

The concept of narrative helps us understand how the terrorist "story" is constructed by the organization's leaders, and how it manages to keep on existing over time through the retelling of sympathizers, engaged supporters, and new recruits. The terrorists' narrative, as any narrative, is the result of a collective construction. It is certainly promoted by specific actors, in the case of al Qaeda or ISIS by terrorist leaders, but there is evidence that it is being appropriated, most notably in what is mistakenly referred to as "self-radicalisation" (Jenkins 2007, 5–6) by individuals and local groups. The retelling of these narratives is made by a range of different actors with varying agendas and very diverse intended audiences. Each of them potentially sees a different "story." As David Betz describes this process in relation to al Qaeda in the early days of the "War on Terror":

> Bin Laden and his associates do not appear endlessly on the British Broadcasting Corporation, or Cable News Network or even Al-Jazeera defending these talking points [basic elements of their strategic narrative]: this work is done (very effectively) by largely voluntary networks which have open access, share material, work collectively, and have a diversity of motives. Not everybody in the network needs to be a committed Jihadi, they may or may not like the idea of living under a restored Caliphate, they may indeed in some circumstances not be Muslim at all because the mindset of sullen resentment, which is what animates the movement, is shared by diverse groups from anti-globalists to anti-vivisectionists. (Betz 2008, 521)

This dynamic and multilayered reality of the construction of narratives contrasts sharply with the way narratives are approached in connection to extremism. This aspect is further discussed next.

20th Century Views: Outdated Approaches to Extremism

The concept of narrative as it is mostly used within current research on extremism and in counterterrorism presents two main shortcomings. The first is the tendency to overlook the sociological depth of the narrative and, instead, take strategic narrative as a synonym for a "story." Literature on the role of the Internet in promoting the radicalization of extremists, for example, identifies "an effective *tale* of an imaginary 'clash of civilizations' in which, supposedly, a monolithic West has been engaged in an aggressive struggle against a monolithic Islam for centuries, since the time of the Crusades" (HSPI/CIAG 2007, 2, my emphasis). The implication is a reification of the narrative, the belief that it has an objective existence outside the mind of audiences—a notion that clashes with the understanding of narrative as a social product that only exists through its continuous retelling. Such understanding is arguably the legacy of outdated communication models related to the successful distribution of propaganda messages being applied to the current ideational conflict between extremism and liberal democracy. It particularly appears to resemble some aspects of the hypodermic needle model of communication (Rogers 2003, 303). This was developed in the early 20th century and posited powerful, immediate, and direct effects of mass media on audiences (ibid). It was based on the idea that audiences could be inoculated with a message, which would then trigger predictable and homogenous behavioral change.

A modification of this linear model of communication, to illustrate the differences with the previous and more complex process through which narratives are socially constructed (figure 9.4), is represented in figure 9.5. The idea is that a message (represented by the triangle), once crafted by an actor A, exists independently of individual agency and can be "sent" to other actors (actor B, for example). B can then either pass the message on or not (C, for instance, does not pass the message on to E). An actor might pass on just part of the message (the smaller triangle passed from B on to C).

The fact that this model informs most works about extremism is supported by frequent statements in the literature about the power of the terrorist narrative to "spread" (Gupta 2011; Presidential Task Force 2009), by the use of terms like "infected" (Speckhard 2011, 172), or the very idea that the effectiveness of "our" counternarratives can be assessed by measuring the reach of our message, such as by counting the visits, clicks, and downloads on a media product (such as a video) that contains "our" message (Lemieux and Nill 2011; Speckhard 2011, 171–72). This linear model, however, is misleading: the narrative is not a "message" to be sent out to an audience in order to trigger certain expected (and predictable) behaviors. Communication is crucial, but more emphasis is needed on the differentiated ways in which the narrative is appropriated, interpreted, and retold by individuals.

The understanding of the narrative as a message or a story leads to a second problem: a tendency to concentrate on the contents of the narra-

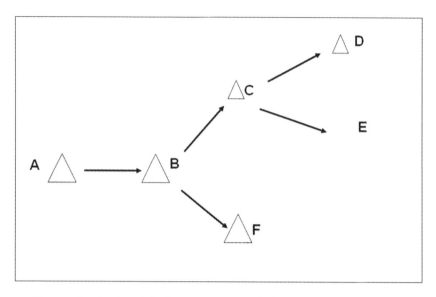

Fig. 9.5. Outdated models of communication: The linear transmission of a message

tive, particularly on how to craft the "right" message, and how it can best be delivered to a target audience. The emphasis is on achieving a successful transmission. Steven Corman (2009b), in this respect, points out that U.S. public diplomacy efforts, which should communicate American values and contribute to "winning hearts and minds" in the global fight against terrorism, are based on oversimplified models of communication. According to him, the way in which U.S. officials attempt communicating with foreign publics to curb extremism is based on the notion that "messages" are transmitted by an "Information Source" through a "Transmitter" (via a "Signal") to a "Receiver," which will then convey the message to the desired "Destination." The implications are that communication occurs only when messages are sent, and that successful communication can be achieved by improving the skill of the communicator, by reducing the "noise" in the system, by carefully planning the content of the message, and by carefully transmitting it (ibid.). This model was developed by David Berlo in the 1960s and was based on the study of telephone communication systems. Corman explains its current role in shaping official thinking through the fact that, having being taught across communication and public relations courses over decades, it has become part of the way public diplomacy practitioners in the United States read the reality of international communications (Corman 2010). Yet, this model of communication, as he puts it, was "cutting-edge at the time of Eisenhower" (Corman 2009b). Its continued existence is nonetheless confirmed by a whole range of statements contained in a "Report on Strategic Communications" issued by the U.S. Department of Defense in 2009. Indeed, the fact that the model appears in the *Information Operations Primer: Fundamentals of Information Operations* of the U.S. Army War College (2011) shows that that it is still part of the training curriculum.

Especially the last link between Berlo's model and information operations suggests the influence of information warfare doctrine on current approaches to counterterrorism. The doctrine of information operations developed out of the integration of command and control warfare and information warfare in the 1990s and is based on the acknowledgment that information is "an element of power across the spectrum of peace, conflict, and war" (3). The purpose of information operations is "to influence the *behavior* of target audiences by changing their ability to make decisions, while simultaneously defending the friendly capability to make proper decisions. This is no different from the exercise of the other forms of national power. In this instance the means is information, but the resulting outcome is the same" (ibid.). The notion that information can replace bullets to fight war underpins the whole discourse of strategic communication and messaging.

The messaging model, however, does not fit the complexity of current global communications. There is no longer the possibility, as when propaganda studies developed at the time of the diffusion of radio and TV, that a message could be targeted at a specific audience (as, in its crudest form, by physically dropping leaflets behind enemy lines, for instance). The feature of the current information environment that makes it radically different from the past is its transparency. It is true that information does not flow randomly, and that there are blind spots represented by areas where communication infrastructures are either underdeveloped (issues of access in African countries, for example) or controlled (as in China). Nonetheless, information is far less constrained by state borders and through its digital format can travel almost seamlessly across communication platforms like the Internet, TV, and mobile phones (de Waal 2007). As Corman writes elsewhere:

> Communication is not a process of transmission of messages but of dialogue with an audience. Modern media systems make exclusively targeting narrow audiences difficult or impossible. Communication systems are so complex that planning is of limited use. You can't straightforwardly assess results and tweak your tactics, as if you were a strategic communication version of a forward artillery spotter. (Corman 2009a)

Realizing that in the 21st century environment, despite the myriad technological gadgets available, it is neither possible to "fire" messages at selected audiences nor expect them to necessarily respond in the desired manner is key in understanding the role of narratives in countering radicalism.

Understanding Narratives and the "War of Ideas" against Extremism

Recognizing that strategic narratives are collectively constructed affects the assessment of what can and cannot be achieved in the ideological fight against extremists: while it is not possible to stop either al Qaeda's or ISIS's narrative[4] from being communicated, and it is not feasible to rewrite "their" narrative, the best way forward is being consistent with one's own. These points will now be illustrated in turn.

A narrative is not just a story. It is a story that is being continuously retold. The idea that the spreading of an extremist group's narrative can be arrested by interfering with that group's communication channels is based on the idea that the story is being told through a one-way process: the "message" is being sent by extremists to audiences. While the extremists have an interest in promoting that narrative, this is a reductive understanding not only of communication processes but also of the way they take place in the 21st century media-saturated environment. There are too many channels to stop the narrative from being communicated. Beyond the Internet, the "old technologies" are still there: Carl Björkman (2010, 242–43), for instance, in talking about jihadi-Salafi terrorism in Italy, writes that military manuals and jihadi documents from prominent thinkers have over the last decade "spread . . . on CD-ROMs, videos and audiocassettes." In countries with poor literacy levels, as in Afghanistan, face-to-face interaction is still the most widely used form of communication between radicals and the wider population (Johnson 2007). Besides, disrupting communications—for example, by taking down websites—leads to a loss in terms of sources of information (International Crisis Group 2006, 2). In addition to this, the narrative is only partly actively promoted by a terrorist group's leadership. The reason why the narrative keeps on existing is that it is constantly retold and reevoked by wider audiences. They do not just involve terrorist sympathizers. The extremists' narrative might be contained in a journalistic report about the ISIS or al Qaeda leadership's latest message, in a critique of the terrorist organization, or in an academic study about it.

Replacing "their" narrative with a "better story," as Casebeer and Russell (2005, 9) suggest especially in relation to al Qaeda's founding myth, is unrealistic, at least for Western governments. The myth is part of the group's identity and is constantly constructed and reconstructed by the members of the group. The myth is itself a narrative that can be changed, through collective reconstruction over time. Any contribution that appears to be coming from the West, however, lacks credibility. As Betz (2008, 511) points out, the debate about the correct interpretation and implementation of the meaning of jihad is an intra-Muslim debate, "not one which we as outsiders can contribute to in a sophisticated and convincing way." A better way to go about it would be encouraging public debate in the Muslim world.

Attempting to target radicalized individuals with the "right" message, to put it bluntly, is a waste of time. The influence of ideas based in information warfare doctrine implies that bites can replace bullets. The logic is that, instead of physically killing opponents, we can affect their behavior by changing their minds through the appropriate message. This is, again, completely unrealistic. Terrorists are already listening to what Western governments, think thanks, and media are saying. The *Al Fajr* Centre, the media hub that coordinates the distribution of online communiqués, videos, and statements by al Qaeda and other jihadi groups (Iraqi insurgency groups, Palestinian, Somali, Saudi jihadi groups, and so on) also has an "intelligence brigade" (Elihu Katz's term, cited in Committee on Homeland Security 2007, 18) in charge of monitoring the websites and output of organizations like the White House, the U.S. Army, the RAND corporation, the Jamestown Foundation, and *Time* magazine (see also Geltzer 2010, 22–23). ISIS clearly monitors cyberspace closely: to the point that the group responded with a 5,000-word statement to the release of a two-minute animation video, "Five Considerations for a Muslim on Syria," on *YouTube* in March 2014. The video was part of the cartoon series *Abdul-*

lah-X (2014), designed by a former extremist to invite young audiences to question ISIS's narrative of violence.[5]

Most of those involved in terrorist plots, additionally, live in Western societies where they are constantly exposed to potential counternarratives. Both public discourse and media coverage are overwhelmingly filled with the notion that terrorism and violence are deplorable, as are both ISIS and al Qaeda. The reason why "our" narrative is not having any effect on the extremist mind-set is that "our message" is filtered through a very different personal narrative, grounded in a specific constellation of relationships. In this perspective communication, counterintuitively, is most effective not directed at the terrorists or violent extremists, but *around* them.

While Western democracies can't stop the continuous reconstruction of narratives, they can stop assisting the terrorists' narrative by being consistent about what they claim to represent and what they actually do. Ultimately, competing with the mobilizing power of an opponent's narrative involves increasing one's own appeal. A better understanding of Islamist groups' narrative, especially of how it portrays Western democracies, as well as of the way it is appropriated by audiences, can certainly help avoid words and deeds that might help confirm that identity perception in the Muslim world. The use of torture and extraordinary rendition are at odds with the respect for human rights that should be at the core of Western democracies' identity. They serve to reinforce the idea promoted by Islamists that the West is morally corrupt and engaged in a crusade against Islam. The way forward lies therefore in a consistency between rhetoric and deeds—what Betz (2008, 530) calls "narrative alignment"—and in being consistent with one's own values.

Conclusions: Narratives' Contribution to Countering Radicalization

A narrative approach to explaining extremism can support an alternative way of conceiving the process of becoming a violent radical. In turn, this leads to four practical implications in countering radicalization.

The first is that the availability of extremist content—as also the existence of a terrorist "narrative"—is not the problem per se. The fact that jihadi videos or terrorist websites are potentially available to worldwide audiences does not mean that these publics are necessarily going to access them, let alone embrace the radical ideas such outlets advocate: reach is not impact. Even if extremist messages are accessed, the key issue is the individual *appropriation* of those contents through the interpretative prism of the beliefs and worldview resulting from the individual's constellation of relationships—the individual narrative. This explains, among the rest, why many readers of this paragraph might have watched terrorist propaganda videos or consulted extremist manifestos without having become radicalized. The proposed narrative-based explanation of radicalization offers an insight into how social ties shape the way individuals will interpret external information and events, for example the extent to which they will either appropriate, reinterpret, or reject extremist ideas they might have come across on the Internet, by watching the news, or reading a book. This point leads to a second implication.

What is "extremist" is relative. The very understanding of what constitutes an "extremist" idea or content in the first place depends on the parameters established by the individual narrative at any given time. What law-abiding citizens of a democratic country might normally regard as excessively violent and extremist might appear entirely acceptable within a social setting that regards violence as legitimate. Conversely, even ideas that are not regarded as a threat to society can be used as a rationale for violence. The case of the Norwegian Anders Breivik—responsible for the bombing of the Oslo city center, which caused eight fatalities, and the shooting of 68 young political activists on Utøya Island in the summer of 2011—is a telling example in relation to this point. In his manifesto of over 1,500 pages (Breivik 2011) he discusses at length his ideological reasons for the killings. The sources he cites, particularly "the cultural Marxists" who gathered around the "Frankfurt School"—he specifically mentions Georg Lukacs, Antonio Gramsci, Wilhelm Reich, Erich Fromm, Herbert Marcuse, and Theodor Adorno (26–30, 40–45 for "Further Readings on the Frankfurt School")—produced texts that are not normally regarded as "extremist" and that are widely available in ordinary libraries.

This shows, as a third aspect, that focusing on eliminating extremist online content is not the best use of resources in countering violent extremism. Beyond the fact that this practice only has limited effectiveness—given that the material can easily be copied and transferred elsewhere before being removed by censors (Theohary and Rollins 2011, 14)—it also targets what Western counterterrorists see as "extremist" from the perspective of *their own* network of relationships. In principle, any content (text, video, image, audio recording) across any communication platform (the Internet, VHS tape, mobile phone, audio cassette, photocopied leaflet, wall graffiti, and so forth) could be contributing to reinforcing a violent extremist interpretation of the world. What should "we" be doing about that, then?

The time- and context-specific combination of circumstances that leads to the development of violent extremist action makes community-based and local approaches the most effective in dealing with radicalization. Trying to identify the individual characteristics, such as personality traits, and structural conditions that lead to radicalization in general and abstract terms (most existing literature talks about radicalization as if it occurred in the same way on a national, even international level) is meaningless for two reasons. One is that individual characteristics and structural factors do not exist independently from each other. The second is that, in the social world, timing and sequence are of the essence, as well as the continuous rearrangement and renegotiation of relationships that comes from responding to unfolding events. Reality never sits still. Police forces engaging with local communities on a regular basis are the best assessors of whether radical ideas that could sustain violent action are developing in their respective contexts because they are part of the same networks in which radical individuals are also enmeshed. As much as violent extremists might want to avoid contact with the external world, in fact they are still living in somebody else's neighborhood, buying food, paying bills, renting accommodation. As Robert Lambert, former head of the Muslim Contact Unit in the Metropolitan Police in London, pointed out, the most useful intelligence is gathered in the United Kingdom through collaboration with community members who volunteer information as part of what they see as their civic duty (Lambert 2011). The fact that in the United Kingdom 40 plots have been foiled since 7/7, the July 7, 2005, bombings in London (Eleftheriou-Smith 2014), while in the United States 50 terrorist operations were disrupted between 9/11 and 2012 (Carafano, Bucci, and Zuckerman 2012)—not to count the successful minor antiterrorist operations—should be seen as a confirmation of the fact that information related to terrorist activities does circulate and, in doing so, gets systematically picked up along the law enforcers' networks.

NOTES

1. The argument develops on the basis of a theoretical framework that combines relational sociology (White 2008), actor network theory (Latour 2005), and social

movement theory (Tarrow 1998; Tilly 2002). It is part of a broader multidisciplinary research program that uses the insights offered by the study of communication to develop a greater understanding of extremism in the age of global interconnectedness (Archetti 2012).

2. A report by the International Centre for the Study of Radicalisation and Political Violence defines radicalization as "the process (or processes) whereby individuals or groups come to approve of and (ultimately) participate in the use of violence for political aims" (Stevens and Neumann 2009, 10). Some authors refer to "violent radicalization" to emphasize the violent outcome and distinguish the process "from non-violent forms of 'radical' thinking" (ibid.).

3. This point is also made, particularly in relation to the reception of narratives by state actors in the new media ecology, by Miskimmon, O'Loughlin, and Roselle (2013).

4. Although counterextremism discourse tends to use the blanket term "single narrative" (Schmid 2014) when referring to Islamist ideology, one could argue that there are indeed multiple narratives. Not only is ISIS, through its public beheadings, for example, projecting a more radical narrative to potential recruits than al Qaeda did in the past (Archetti 2014)—the al Qaeda leadership famously criticized al Zarqawi's beheadings in Iraq in 2005 because such brutality might alienate Muslim audiences (Bergen 2006). It is also questionable, when analysis is conducted at a deep enough level, whether al Qaeda ever had a single narrative to start with (Stenersen 2009).

5. Presentation by the creator of the cartoon character, who wishes to remain anonymous, CVE (Countering Violent Extremism) Expo, Abu Dhabi, December 9, 2014. More on Abdullah-X can be found on the character's website: http://www.abdullahx.com/what-i-do/

REFERENCES

Abdullah-X. "Five Considerations for a Muslim on Syria." *YouTube*, March 7, 2014. https://www.youtube.com/watch?v=tKKbydB4scA

Anderson, Benedict. *Imagined Communities: Reflections on the Origin and Spread of Nationalism*. London: New Left Books, 1983.

Antonello, Pierpaolo, and Alan O'Leary, eds. *Imagining Terrorism: The Rhetoric and Representation of Political Violence in Italy 1969–2009*. Oxford: Modern Humanities Research Association and Maney Publishing, 2009.

Archetti, Cristina. *Understanding Terrorism in the Age of Global Media: A Communication Approach*. Basingstoke: Palgrave, 2012.

Archetti, Cristina. Interview on "The World Tonight." *BBC Radio 4*, October 7, 2014.

Atran, Scott. "Jihad's Fatal Attraction." *Guardian*, September 4, 2014. Accessed August 3, 2016. https://www.theguardian.com/commentisfree/2014/sep/04/jihad-fatal-attraction-challenge-democracies-isis-barbarism

Benwell, Bethan, and Elizabeth Stokoe. *Discourse and Identity*. Edinburgh: Edinburgh University Press, 2006.

Bergen, Peter. "Bin Laden Might Find Relief in al-Zarqawi's Death." *CNN Anderson Cooper Blog 360°*, June 8, 2006. Accessed June 9, 2006. http://edition.cnn.com/CNN/

Programs/anderson.cooper.360/blog/2006/06/bin-laden-might-find-relief-in-al.html

Bergin, Anthony, Sulastri Osman, Carl Ungerer, and Nur Azlin Mohamed Yasin. "Countering Internet Radicalisation in Southeast Asia." RSIS-ASPI Special Joint Report Issue 22, March 2009. Accessed January 24, 2016. https://www.rsis.edu.sg/staff-publication/1010-countering-internet-radical/#.VqTlJjZIiRs

Betz, David. "The Virtual Dimension of Contemporary Insurgency and Counterinsurgency." *Small Wars & Insurgencies* 19, no. 4 (2008): 510–40.

Björkman, Carl. "Salafi-Jihadi Terrorism in Italy." In *Understanding Violent Radicalisation: Terrorist and Jihadist Movements in Europe,* edited by Magnus Ranstorp, 231–55. London: Routledge, 2010.

Boje, David. M. "The Storytelling Organization: A Study of Story Performance in an Office-Supply Firm." *Administrative Science Quarterly* 36, no. 1 (1991): 106–26.

Bourdieu, Pierre, and James Samuel Coleman, eds. *Social Theory for a Changing Society.* Oxford: Westview Press, 1991.

Breivik, Anders. "2083: A European Declaration of Independence." 2011. http://www.slideshare.net/darkandgreen/2083-a-european-declaration-of-independence-by-andrew-berwick

Calhoun, Craig. "Indirect Relationships and Imagined Communities: Large-Scale Social Integration and the Transformation of Everyday Life." In *Social Theory for a Changing Society,* edited by Pierre Bourdieu and James Samuel Coleman, 95–121. Oxford: Westview Press, 1991.

Calhoun, Craig, ed. *Social Theory and the Politics of Identity.* Oxford: Blackwell, 1994.

Carafano, James Jay, Steven Bucci, and Jessica Zuckerman. "Fifty Terror Plots Foiled since 9/11: The Homegrown Threat and the Long War on Terrorism." Heritage Foundation, Backgrounder #2682, April 25, 2012. Accessed Aril 26, 2012. http://www.heritage.org/research/reports/2012/04/fifty-terror-plots-foiled-since-9-11-the-homegrown-threat-and-the-long-war-on-terrorism

Casebeer, William D., and James A. Russell. "Storytelling and Terrorism: Towards a Comprehensive 'Counter-Narrative Strategy.'" *Strategic Insights* 4, no. 3 (2005). Accessed July 1, 2012. http://0-www.ciaonet.org.wam.leeds.ac.uk/olj/si/si_4_3/si_4_3_caw01.pdf

Cento Bull, Anna. "Political Violence, *Stragismo* and 'Civil War': An Analysis of the Self-Narratives of Three Neofascist Protagonists." In *Imagining Terrorism: The Rhetoric and Representation of Political Violence in Italy 1969–2009,* edited by Pierpaolo Antonello and Alan O'Leary, 183–99. Oxford: Modern Humanities Research Association and Maney Publishing, 2009.

Clandinin, D Jean, ed. *Handbook of Narrative Enquiry: Mapping a Methodology.* London: Sage, 2007.

Committee on Homeland Security. "Using the Web as a Weapon: The Internet as a Tool for Violent Radicalization and Homegrown Terrorism." Hearing before the Subcommittee on Intelligence, Information Sharing, and Terrorism Risk Assessment of the Committee on Homeland Security, House of Representatives, November 6, 2007. Serial No. 110–83. http://www.fas.org/irp/congress/2007_hr/web.pdf

Corman, Steven R. "Same Old Song from GAO on Strategic Communication." *CO-*

MOPS Journal, June 3, 2009a. Accessed July 1, 2012. http://comops.org/jour nal/2009/06/03/same-old-song-from-gao-on-strategic-communication/

Corman, Steven R. "What Power Needs to Be Smart." Paper presented at the Digital Media and Security Workshop, University of Warwick, May 21, 2009b. Not publicly available.

Corman, Steven R. "Public Diplomacy as Narrative." Paper presented at the Annual Convention of the International Studies Association, New Orleans, February 20, 2010.

Cortazzi, Martin. *Narrative Analysis*. London: Falmer Press, 1993.

Council on Foreign Relations. "November 17, Revolutionary People's Struggle, Revolutionary Struggle." N.d. http://www.cfr.org/greece/november-17-revolutionary-peo ples-struggle-revolutionary-struggle-greece-leftists/p9275

Dayan, Daniel, and Elihu Katz. *Media Events: The Live Broadcasting of History*. Cambridge: Harvard University Press, 1992.

De Waal, M. "From Media Landscape to Media Ecology: The Cultural Implications of Web 2.0." *Open* 13 (2007): 20–33.

Eleftheriou-Smith, Loulla-Mae. "Theresa May: British Security Services Foiled 40 Terror Plots since 7/7 Attacks." *Independent*, November 24, 2014.

Emirbayer, Mustafa, and Ann Mische. "What Is Agency?" *American Journal of Sociology* 103, no. 4 (1998): 962–1023.

Fenstermacher, Laurie, and Todd Leventhal, eds. *Countering Violent Extremism: Scientific Methods and Strategies*. Wright-Patterson Air Force Base, OH: Air Force Research Laboratory, 2011. http://www.nsiteam.com/pubs/U_Counter%20Violent%20 Extremism%20Final_Approved%20for%20Public%20Release_28Oct11v3.pdf

Geltzer, Joshua. A. *US Counter-Terrorism Strategy and al-Qaeda: Signalling and the Terrorist World-View*. London: Routledge, 2010.

Gupta, Dipak. "Tracking the Spread of Violent Extremism." In *Countering Violent Extremism: Scientific Methods and Strategies*, edited by Laurie Fenstermacher and Todd Leventhal, 44–55. Wright-Patterson Air Force Base, OH: Air Force Research Laboratory, 2011.

Home Office. *Pursue Prevent Protect Prepare: The United Kingdom's Strategy for Countering International Terrorism*. London: Cabinet Office, 2009. http://www.northants. police.uk/files/linked/terrorism/The%20Goverments%20Counter%20Terror ism%20Strategy.pdf

Home Office. *Prevent Strategy*. London: Cabinet Office, 2011.

Homeland Security Policy Institute and the University of Virginia Critical Incident Analysis Group. *NETworked Radicalization: A Counter-Strategy*. 2007. http://www. gwumc.edu/hspi/policy/NETworkedRadicalization.pdf

Hoyle, Carolyn, Alexandra Bradford, and Ross Frenett. *Becoming Mulan? Female Western Migrants to ISIS*. London: Institute for Strategic Dialogue, 2015. http://www.stra tegicdialogue.org/ISDJ2969_Becoming_Mulan_01.15_WEB.PDF

International Crisis Group. *In Their Own Words: Reading the Iraqi Insurgency*. Middle East Report No. 50, 2006. http://www.c4ads.org/files/ICG_report_021506_iraqi_in surgency.pdf

Jenkins, Brian Michael. *Building an Army of Believers: Jihadist Radicalization and Re-*

cruitment. Testimony presented before the House Homeland Security Committee, Subcommittee on Intelligence, Information Sharing and Terrorism Risk Assessment on April 5, 2007, Rand Corporation. Accessed January 24, 2016. http://www.rand.org/pubs/testimonies/2007/RAND_CT278-1.pdf

Johnson, Thomas H. "The Taliban Insurgency and an Analysis of Shabnamah (Night Letters)." *Small Wars & Insurgencies* 18, no. 3 (2007): 317–44.

Kohler Riessman, Catherine. *Narrative Analysis*. London: Sage, 1993.

Lambert, Robert. "Police and Muslims in Partnership." Paper presented at "Radicalisation and Extremism: A Symposium for Researcher and Practitioners," Lancashire Constabulary, Hutton, December 1, 2011.

Latour, Bruno. *Reassembling the Social: An Introduction to Actor-Network-Theory*. Oxford: Oxford University Press, 2005.

Lawler, Stephanie. "Narrative in Social Research." In *Qualitative Research in Action*, edited by Tim May, 242–58. London: Sage, 2002.

Lemieux, Anthony, and Robert Nill. "The Role and Impact of Music in Promoting (and Countering) Violent Extremism." In *Countering Violent Extremism: Scientific Methods and Strategies*, edited by Laurie Fenstermacher and Todd Leventhal, 143–52. Wright-Patterson Air Force Base, OH: Air Force Research Laboratory, 2011.

Linde, Charlotte. *Working the Past: Narrative and Institutional Memory*. Oxford: Oxford University Press, 2009.

May, Tim, ed. *Qualitative Research in Action*. London: Sage, 2002.

Melucci, Alberto. *L'Invenzione del Presente: Movimenti, Identità, Bisogni Individuali*. Bologna: il Mulino, 1982.

Miskimmon, Alister, Ben O'Loughlin, and Laura Roselle. *Strategic Narratives: Communication Power and the New World Order*. New York: Routledge, 2013.

Mitroff, Ian I., and Ralph H. Kilmann. "Stories Managers Tell: A New Tool for Organizational Problem Solving." *Management Review* 64, no.7 (1975): 18–28.

Mumby, Dennis K. *Narrative and Social Control: Critical Perspectives*. London: Sage, 1993.

National Coordinator for Counterterrorism, ed. *Countering Violent Extremist Narratives*. The Hague: National Coordinator for Counterterrorism, 2010.

Neumann, Peter R. *Joining al-Qaeda: Jihadist Recruitment in Europe*. Adelphi Paper 399. London: International Institute for Strategic Studies, 2008.

Neumann, Peter R., and Brooke Rogers. *Recruitment and Mobilisation for the Islamist Militant Movement in Europe*. London: ICSR, 2007.

Presidential Task Force. *Rewriting the Narrative: An Integrated Strategy for Counterradicalization*. Washington, DC: Washington Institute for Near East Policy, 2009.

Rogers, Everett M. *Diffusion of Innovations*. 5th ed. London: Free Press, 2003.

Saltman, E. Interview on "Today" Program. *BBC Radio 4*, January 28, 2014.

Schmid, Alex P. *Al-Qaeda's "Single Narrative" and Attempts to Develop Counter-Narratives: The State of Knowledge*. The Hague: International Centre for Counter-Terrorism, 2014.

Sciolla, Loredana, ed. *Identità: Percorsi di analisi in sociologia*. Turín: Rosenberg & Sellier, 1983.

Somers, Margaret R., and Gloria D. Gibson. "Reclaiming the Epistemological 'Other':

Narrative and the Social Constitution of Identity." In *Social Theory and the Politics of Identity*, edited by Craig Calhoun, 37–99. Oxford: Blackwell, 1994.

Speckhard, Anne. "Battling the 'University of Jihad': An Evidence-Based Ideological Program to Counter Militant Jihadi Groups Active on the Internet." In *Countering Violent Extremism: Scientific Methods and Strategies*, edited by Laurie Fenstermacher and Todd Leventhal, 164–74. Wright-Patterson Air Force Base, OH: Air Force Research Laboratory, 2011.

Stenersen, Anne. "Blood Brothers or a Marriage of Convenience? The Ideological Relationship between al-Qaida and the Taliban." Paper presented at 50th Annual Convention of the International Studies Association, New York, February 15–18, 2009.

Stevens, Tim, and Peter R. Neumann. "Countering Online Radicalization: A Strategy for Action." London: ICSR/Community Security Trust, 2009.

Tarrow, Sidney. *Power in Movement: Social Movements and Contentious Politics*. 2nd ed. Cambridge: Cambridge University Press, 1998.

Theohary, Catherine A., and John Rollins. *Terrorist Use of the Internet: Information Operations in Cyberspace*. Congressional Research Service Report for Congress, R41674, 2011. http://www.fas.org/sgp/crs/terror/R41674.pdf

Tilly, Charles. *Stories, Identities, and Political Change*. Oxford: Rowman and Littlefield, 2002.

U.S. Army War College. *Information Operations Primer: Fundamentals of Information Operations*. Philadelphia: Army War College, 2011. http://www.au.af.mil/au/awc/awcgate/army-usawc/info_ops_primer.pdf

U.S. Department of Defense. "Report on Strategic Communication." Washington, DC: U.S. Department of Defense, 2009. http://www.carlisle.army.mil/dime/documents/DoD%20report%20on%20Strategic%20Communication%20Dec%2009.pdf

White, Harrison, C. *Identity and Control: How Social Formations Emerge*. Princeton: Princeton University Press, 2008.

White, Hayden. "Interpretation in History." *New Literary History* 4, no. 2 (1973): 281–314.

White House. "Empowering Local Partners to Prevent Violent Extremism in the United States." August. Washington, DC: Government Printing Office, 2011. http://info.publicintelligence.net/WH-HomegrownTerror.pdf

10 | Filling the Narrative Vacuum in a Global Crisis

Japan's Triple Disaster

Ben O'Loughlin

The silhouette of the triple disasters striking Japan in March 2011 had loomed large for several decades in Japan (cf. Kittler 2010, 25). The country is regularly beset with natural disasters, while the iconography of nuclear energy and disaster is embedded in Japanese culture through the mushroom clouds of Hiroshima, the films of Godzilla (Kirby 2011), and Katsuhiro Otomo's 2005 film *Steamboy* (see Sotinel 2011). Its material infrastructure is as prepared as any for earthquakes (Kingston 2012, 2). Risk was known and anticipated. On March 11 the fourth largest earthquake reported globally since 1900 hit in the sea just east of Japan, creating a tsunami that devastated Fukushima Prefecture. These two natural disasters damaged several nuclear plants and created the largest nuclear disaster since the 1986 Chernobyl crisis. A year later, the Japanese police counted the human death toll at 15,854 from the earthquake and tsunami (Leflar et al. 2012), and while fewer died immediately in the nuclear disaster the eventual death toll from radiation poisoning cannot be predicted. Approximately 80,000 people were evacuated and a region with a relatively weak economy and elderly population faced bleak prospects for long-term recovery. Striking images from the tsunami and nuclear reactor explosions enabled the triple disaster to become a "global crisis" event (Cottle 2011, 2014), one whose arrival and consequences were visually premediated (Grusin 2010; cf. Jacobs 2010) through decades of Japanese popular culture.

One might expect the Japanese government to have had a strong strategic narrative to project when disaster struck. Strategic narratives are a means for political actors to construct a shared meaning of the past, present, and future of international politics to shape the behavior of domestic and international actors (Miskimmon, O'Loughlin, and Roselle 2013; Freedman 2006). Around short-term events and long-term transitions, competing political actors form and project rival narratives in an attempt to make others see problems and solutions their way (Hajer 1995, 53). A major crisis event would afford the Japanese government the opportunity to articulate a narrative about its resilience and ability to recover, and project it in a way that would reassure and mobilize domestic publics. This is something other governments have tried to do: for example, the British government prepared a narrative to articulate its response to the London 7/7 bombings of July 2005. Given the nature of such a crisis, it would also enable the Japanese government to narrate to other states its future approach to energy security, economic interdependence, critical infrastructure, and climate change. This study explores the failure of the Japanese government to project such a narrative, and how the gap in sense-making around the event was filled by citizens themselves and by international agencies and commentators.

Why did the Japanese state and media fail to offer a coherent strategic narrative in circumstances that were on the cultural and scientific horizon? The content and parameters of strategic narratives that a state can draw upon are shaped by expectations from domestic and international audiences about that state's history, identity, and interests, but also by expectations about when, how, and to whom the state should speak (Miskimmon et al. 2011). The failure explored here marks the crystallization of a gradual internal collapse of a domestic social compact and the legitimacy and functioning of the Japanese state as a directing force. In the postwar years, the Japanese state successfully managed what Perkins (2011) calls a "commonsense consensus" through three mechanisms: (1) the state managed the economy; (2) a sense of national identity was established that set expectations about work, gender, and saving; (3) the promise that hard work would bring rising living standards. This strategic narrative was nonthreatening to those outside Japan and legitimated the Japanese state internally. It depended on concepts of harmony and balance that informed internal and external arguments about Japanese uniqueness, which had instrumental purpose. The idea of Japan-as-unique was expressed through many popular books:

> [T]hese texts were not just about describing Japanese national identity, they were also texts used in the active management of Japanese national subjectivity. In producing a certain form of commonsense about "being and performing" Japaneseness, these texts actively contributed to the alignment of the individual with the economic goals of the state. (Perkins 2011, 5)

In the 1970s the relation between state and citizen in this social compact changed. Responsibility for economic progress was devolved from state to citizen under the label "self-responsibility," a concept in turn linked to economic productivity. The responsible, productive citizen best served the state. Risk was transferred (cf. Shaw 2005).

Did the 2011 triple disaster highlight the collapse of the pre-1970s social compact that had been building since the 1970s? Perkins makes the astute argument that being able to cope with risk depends on knowledge and information. To be self-responsible entails acting in a way in which desired results are expected. Whether in the workplace, as a citizen, or as a parent, we need a basis upon which to act. This puts a responsibility on the state and national media to provide relevant information so that individuals can act accordingly. If it does, the state is legitimate, media are credible, and everyday life can function:

> The significance of Fukushima is as a final breach in these structures and processes of legitimacy. Actions of politicians, the evident close structural links between the nuclear industry and the state, the complicity of academics, and the lack of serious questioning of state policy in the mainstream media has further eroded that trust in the processes that produce safe knowledge to act upon in Japan. (Perkins 2011, 7)

For one resident of Fukushima this translated into a series of unsolvable questions:

> Every day, without break we are forced to make decisions. Evacuate or not to evacuate? Eat or not to eat? To make our children wear masks or not? To hang out our washing or not? To plant or not to plant? To speak out or to stay silent? We have options, all of them distressing. (Perkins 2011, 9)

These questions are distressing because, like radiation itself, the consequences of all these decisions are unknowable (ibid). Such a crisis, crosscutting from individual to state, was exacerbated by the controversial status of nuclear energy in Japan. Japan's nuclear strategy had two elements. First, Japan had agreed in 1960 to the United States stationing nuclear weapons in Japan, culminating in public protests. Second, Japan's energy policy promoted a nuclear state, as nuclear power generation grew from 3 percent in 1973 to 26 percent of energy supplies in 2008. Both of these policies embed nuclear energy in a society that suffered from nuclear attacks on the cities of Nagasaki and Hiroshima in 1945. Japan's nuclear policy could be associated with an identifiable set of "villains": the Tokyo Electric Power Company (TEPCO), Prime Minister Naoto Kan's cabinet, and the Nuclear and Industrial Safety Agency (NISA) (Duus 2012)—an elite group known in Japan as the "nuclear village."

Analysis of responses to the triple disaster allows us to address five important research questions. **First**, what information did the Japanese government select to present to its citizens and to international audiences? The narrative theorist Tzvetan Todorov (1988, 160) distinguishes between *story* and *plot*: "the story is what happened in life, the plot is the way the author presents it to us." The practice of international political communication involves constructing plots from the raw material of ongoing political history, filtering (strategically) as the situation demands to present audiences with a compelling narrative. The triple disaster resulted in agencies in Japan and abroad producing different types of informational raw materials—medical, seismic, radiological, economic, psephological—which political leaders could craft into narratives to use to reassure, inspire, or produce some other political effect.

A **second** question follows: How does the information infrastructure constrain and enable strategic narrative "work" or action by different actors? Japan's triple disaster is a good case study of the effect that information infrastructure has as the condition within which states communicate around a breaking international event. The disasters involved all media—not just publicly available civilian media like the Internet, TV, and phones, but scientific and security systems that also constitute the information infrastructure but which are often ignored in media studies (Kittler 2010, 32). Indeed, this study goes further to explore how civilian and private media interacted as the Japanese authorities sought to control the release of information. Historical analysis of empires, the formation of the state system, and more recent work on globalization and network societies show that technology enables certain communication patterns with particular affordances that allow for new forms of political organization and power relations.[1] The terrorists in Mumbai in 2008 and the Nairobi shopping center in Kenya in 2012, citizen-dissenters in the 2011 Arab Spring, and counterterrorist agencies across the world have used Google Earth, Google Maps, and Twitter to follow and participate in unfolding events (Bratton 2009; Sullivan 2014). Jay Blumler (2015) argues that we need new forms of holistic analysis to understand political communication. This case study addresses traditional questions about the interdependence of political, media, and scientific institutions, and allows renewed conceptual and theoretical definition delivered through the holistic perspective advocated by Kittler and Blumler and extends the author's work on media ecologies (Awan, Hoskins, and O'Loughlin 2011; Hoskins and O'Loughlin 2010, 2011, 2015; Miskimmon et al. 2013; cf. Fuller 2005; Postman 1970).

Third, this study addresses how actors conceptualize and act in circumstances of uncertainty and risk. One reason Japan's nuclear village failed to project a convincing strategic narrative to domestic or international audiences was that they lacked full data on how the crisis was developing or a framework to evaluate the short-term and long-term risks involved. The study of global risk, communication, and IR has grown in recent years, addressing war (Williams 2008; Coker 2009; Hoskins and O'Loughlin 2010), terrorism (Croft 2012; Awan, Hoskins, and O'Loughlin 2011), financial crises (Chakravarty and Downing 2010; Boy, Burgess, and Leander 2011), pandemics (Ungar 2008), and climate change (Cottle 2009b). All of these explore ways in which the objective character of risks is changing under conditions of globalization and technological change. According to Ulrich Beck's risk society thesis, human scientific and technological progress has created global financial risk, ecological risk, and terrorism risk, which are beyond our control. Crucially, they are beyond our understanding and create a problem of knowledge:

> Contemporary risks are fiendishly complex, involving chains of causation that are uncertain but potentially rapid. For instance, new communication technologies enable quicker financial market transaction, making regulation of markets more difficult, making a crash more likely, which then has knock-on effects on housing, social welfare, jobs. (Awan, Hoskins, and O'Loughlin 2011, 7)

Such a chain reaction befell Japan: an earthquake caused a tsunami that together knocked out electricity, which prevented cooling systems in nuclear power stations and led to a meltdown. This is why the shorthand "Fukushima" is also sometimes called the triple disaster or tripartite disaster. This study documents how the crisis was made knowable through different scientific and communications technologies in varied and not always trustworthy ways, and how actors tried to formulate tactics and strategies in conditions of limited information and high stress.

Fourth, this study explores how citizens used new media technologies to cope amid crisis and uncertainty. Social theorists of "liquid modernity" (Zygmunt Bauman), "reflexive individuation" (Anthony Giddens), network society (Manuel Castells), and risk society (Beck) draw our attention to the uneven opportunities, unequal value, and differentiated capacities of individuals and organizations to communicate. Some have mobility, are able to plot out a successful life course, and achieve some satisfactory degree of agency and security; but many are not able to do so. However, it's unclear how globally these theories apply (Lee 2011). Similarly, studies of online participation often take the critical position that individual users' activity is wholly conducted through corporate-created templates that harness users' activity for profit, create archives subject to state surveillance, and create subjectivities aligned to capitalist logics (e.g., Bauman 2012, 146–47; Fuller 2012; Goldberg 2010; Gehl 2011). Uses of social media in Japan following the triple disaster offer a useful test case for European theories of modernity about how individuals and institutions are expected to respond to crises under these conditions, and how everyday online spaces and activities respond to disruption and urgent needs for assistance.

Fifth, and finally, this study responds to Simon Cottle's (2011, 2014) call to investigate how media constitute global crises. Cottle is not simply reasserting the CNN effect, namely the hypothesis that media and journalism enter into crises, driving public and policy responses to the extent that media and journalism could be considered to be causal or determinative of whether policymakers intervene. Instead, media constitute crises through several mechanisms. The global reach of media and their capacity to trigger global recognition, opinion, and response creates a condition of global surveillance. Indeed, the power of computing technology today compared to the Chernobyl disaster of 1986 allows for the global plotting of patterns of radiation, clouds, and sea movement. The information infrastructure affords new layers of visibility that create different modalities of spectacle and the spectacular, which in turn can make a crisis be seen and understood *as* global and responded to as a "global focusing event" (Cottle 2011, 89), one that national governments and international organizations feel compelled to address. However, Cottle writes, "scholars and students of media and journalism have yet, it seems, to concertedly examine how proliferating and interpenetrating global crises are now elaborated and enacted within the complex glows and formations of journalism around the globe and, importantly, with what further globalizing impacts" (2011, 78). International Relations scholars have not provided systematic understanding of these dynamics either. The study presented here provides a new case for comparative analysis with Cottle's (2009a) studies of the 2004 Asian tsunami, 2005 Hurricane Katrina, the 2005–6 Make Poverty History campaign, and other global focusing events. More important, through the analysis of narrative work by a range of actors this study develops Cottle's agenda by studying the interaction of citizens' "everyday" media use with the formation of national-level energy strategy and international economic and security policies.

Having set out the historical domestic and international context of the disaster and the questions this study will address, the analysis that follows focuses on four phases of the triple disaster: the immediate responses and manner in which citizens and international media compensated for a strategic narrative vacuum from the nuclear village; the buildup of international and local criticisms of the nuclear village; the opening up of elite political contestation alongside citizen counternarratives; and, in the months that followed, attempts by official committees and citizens themselves to verify the effects of the disaster and overcome a lack of imagination when preparing for risks. Analysis draws on a mix of data: statements of political leaders and—through social media—local officials and citizens; domestic and international news reports; scientific and official reports; and secondary scholarly and think tank studies that have emerged rapidly since the events. Together these data enable the tracing of the formation, projection, and reception or interpretation of strategic narratives, including attention to individual experience and the role of narrative in the way people make sense of events. The triple disaster was also an opportunity to examine how strategic narrative work can be done through action as well as rhetoric. "The assessment of government responses came from expectations about what such a tragedy necessitated from government," Mary McCarthy (2012, 5) writes. "Whether or not these expectations were being met was answered in part by the media as it related government policies and actions, but also by the experiences of individuals." This study brings together the study of strategic action and communication through domestic and international media ecologies in ways that link information infrastructure, institutions, and experience.

Immediate Responses and the Compensation Effect

The earthquake struck on March 11 with its epicenter 130 kilometers east of the coast of Miyagi Prefecture. It was the fourth largest recorded earthquake on Earth since 1900, of magnitude 9. There have been hundreds of aftershocks since the main earthquake, many greater than magnitude 6 (UNESCO 2011). The first tsunami wave arrived at the coastline within about 15 minutes of the earthquake. Waves of up to 10 meters high followed in the ensuring hours. Whole communities were washed away and much infrastructure was destroyed. Phone networks and electricity for Internet and television were struck down.

The Pacific Tsunami Warning and Mitigation System initially issued widespread tsunami warning bulletins for most Pacific Ocean countries. The seismic detection systems were able to identify the location and magnitude of the earthquake within minutes, allowing for timely regional warnings to be issued to the Pacific Ocean countries. The Deep-ocean Assessment and Reporting of Tsunami buoys and sea-level monitoring stations worked well and the communications systems allowed for near real-time monitoring of the event (UNESCO 2011). However, given the mere 15-minute warning, such communication did not help those communities destroyed.

One immediate effect of this destruction was uncertainty. Radiation measurement instruments were damaged (Kotsev 2011). This meant local authorities lacked data as the crisis developed (*Japan Times* 2011a). Robots would eventually be sent in to monitor radiation levels (BBC News 2011). The robots were not Japanese. On March 17, six days after the disaster, Japan sent a request to the United States for robots. This signaled first, a cultural-economic malaise—Japan once led the world in robotics—and, second, poor strategy by the nuclear regulatory nexus of TEPCO, the Nuclear Industry Safety Agency, and the Japanese government, which had failed to invest in disaster-relief robotics because this would have contradicted a public discourse that nuclear power was safe (Yasuyuki 2011).

Prime Minister Kan failed to *form* or *project* a coherent strategic narrative and met a negative *reception*. As a result, Kan became "a lightening rod for widespread frustration and dissatisfaction" (Kingston 2012, 7). This shows an expectation about what political leaders should offer in moments of crisis. He did not offer reassurance, hope, or confidence (Curtis 2012). Rather than appoint a reconstruction minister or offer his own plan, on April 14 Kan created a commission, the Reconstruction Design Council, which would produce an interim report in June and whose final report was not due until the end of 2011. This Council was constructed to produce a consensus view from what Kan called "diverse public views" (cited in Curtis 2012, 26). It must be added that no other Japanese political leader offered a plan or vision. Such paralysis illustrates the difficulty of acting in a situation of uncertainty as well as the post-1970s Japanese political discourse of citizen self-reliance rather than social direction through the state. The result was that the projection of any strategic narrative was deferred.

However, the immediate goal was to stabilize the situation: to "ensure that nuclear fall-out is averted or mitigated, and secure shelter, food, heating and clean water for the thousands of people made homeless" (Duraiappah et al. 2011). Kan was swift to appoint leaders to coordinate volunteers and donations, and a well-organized operation began. Government liaised with business and civil society within a single structure, whose basic framework had been put in place after the perceived inadequate response to the 1995 Kobe earthquake. Indeed, this typified the minimal state described by Perkins (2011), since the operation was so dependent on the resources and energies of civil society (Avenall 2012). However, civil society's role was to volunteer and donate, not to challenge government energy policy in the first place. Yuko, Pekkanen, and Tsujinaka (2012) ask whether a more advocacy-focused civil society might have performed the policy scrutiny that might have led to better safety at the nuclear plants and thus limited the crisis in the first place.

Communication was forthcoming from multiple official channels; the problem was its content. The Japanese government immediately imposed tight control of media reporting. From March 11 the prime minister or Chief Cabinet Secretary Edano Yukio held press conferences for Japanese mainstream media twice per day. Internet media and foreign media were excluded from all bar one press conference per week. They were briefed instead by lower ranking administrative staff (Segawa 2011). The journalist Makiko Segawa argues that since TEPCO was a major advertiser in Japanese mainstream media outlets, only foreign reporters could ask critical questions. The Prime Minister's Office and TEPCO also managed public discourse through Twitter, which was used by 20 percent of Japanese by May 2011. They set up their own accounts and issued guidelines to local authorities on using Twitter for public communication (Akimoto 2011). On March 16 one former overseas official noted that the "government's statements are too general in tone and light on content to offer the reassurances a tense and devastated Japanese public needs" (Choate 2011). There was also a problem of reach: paradoxically, those closest to the disaster received the least information, because the information infrastructure was damaged in the disaster. As one survivor put it, "With only the radio as our contact to the outside world, almost everyone else across the planet knew more about what was happening to us than we ourselves" (Morris 2012, 36). The Tohoku region was relatively poor, its population elderly, so Internet and smartphone penetration were low (Slater, Nishimura, and Kindstrand 2012).

A divergence soon emerged between the information held by the Japanese government and what was being communicated to the public. In terms of narrative theory, the story—what is actually happening over time—diverged from the plot—the series of events the audience is presented with (Todorov 1988). As early as March 17, the Ministry of Education, Culture, Sports, Science, and Technology (MEXT) read the nuclear crisis as equivalent to Chernobyl, yet on March 25 NISA's public position was that the crisis was of a lower order, with "10,000 times less release of radioactivity than what was actually measured," creating a "different reality" (Ikegami 2011). It was noticeable, for instance, that an official 20 kilometer evacuation zone was set up for citizens, but journalists were not allowed inside a 50 kilometer zone (Liscutin 2011). People were told to evacuate, but not told where to go. People were given iodine tablets, but not told whether to take them (Liscutin 2012).

How was the Japanese government's response received and interpreted? In the first days and weeks, the Japanese government was not heavily criticized by national media, but public approval of its response was low. On March 18 the newspaper *Asahi Shimbun*'s public opinion poll showed 73 percent of those polled finding the government's job to be unsatisfactory; a poll two weeks later by *Yomiuri Shimbun* found 70 percent feeling dissatisfied with the prime minister's leadership in the crisis (McCarthy 2012). McCarthy's analysis of newspaper editorials in that first month shows an editorial attempt to create calm and warn against rumors, but also some criticism: calls for leadership that were an implicit suggestion it was lacking, calls for more and quicker public information, and calls for parties and factions to put aside differences and cooperate in this time of emergency (McCarthy 2012).

In the absence of reliable information or a compelling strategic narrative from authorities or mainstream media, citizens circulated information and generated meaning through horizontal networks. From the first hours, social media were critical for gathering and exchanging information about the disasters. Slater, Nishimura, and Kindstrand (2012) argue that social media use went through three phases. The first 48 hours involved firsthand information generation, since professional journalists could not access the area and because user-generated content had a visceral quality that has become almost a genre of contemporary disaster reporting. This was followed, second, by weeks of consolidation of information into useful archives and streams through blogs, Facebook, and Mixi, and the formation of audio/visual/textual mashups for appeals for volunteers and donors. For instance, a Canadian alumni of a Japanese exchange and teaching program set up a Facebook page from his Calgary base that other alumni used to try to trace people they had met while on the program in Japan. It soon became clear that Facebook was ill-suited to this purpose, so a searchable wiki linked to Google Maps was set up instead (Jacobsen, 2011). The third stage saw social media being used for the mobilization of criticism and, by May, protest, explored below. These uses of social media show how numerous small acts of recording, witnessing, and sharing (Liscutin 2011) contribute to the global surveillance function critical to Cottle's argument about how media constitute global crises events.

These spontaneous efforts led Slater, Nishimura, and Kindstrand (2012, 96) to argue that social media's "tactical rise [w]as a way to compensate for, or move in alternative directions to, official statements and mainstream media." If strategic narratives involve the construction of the meaning of events in time, then this meaning-making function was devolved from state to citizen-users and civil society groups. For example, Liscutin (2011) documents the role of the Citizens' Nuclear Information Center (CNIC), a Tokyo-based nonprofit organization established in 1975. Until the March 2011 disasters CNIC had simply maintained a website offering nuclear safety information and research and some online "public education seminars." However, after March 11 they were overwhelmed with requests for information by phone and e-mail. CNIC set up its own rolling "news" channel on UStream. It held daily press conferences in Japanese and in English, and then began to incorporate expert guests for discussions. Liscutin argues that efforts like these met a demand and created increased literacy among the Japanese citizenry about nuclear energy.

To some extent, citizens' horizontal communications were seen as a threat by authorities. The Japanese government was wary of rumors and false information hampering relief efforts, and shut down certain websites. It sent "letters of request"[2] to phone, Internet, and cable companies asking them to quash rumors (Segawa 2011). In China, too, rumors that radiation from Japan had leaked into the sea triggered panic buying of salt. A man in Zhejiang Province was charged for "spreading salt rumors" (Shieber 2011). Xinhua, the Chinese news agency, reported that the episode was used by the Chinese government to "spread scientific knowledge about radiation, such as its definition and impact on people's health" (Xinhuanet.com 2011).

It was notable too that an internal critique formed among Japanese social media users about their own medial exchanges: with lives at stake, users began to discuss "responsible" use of social media, particularly as iterations of retweets lose the context of the original post (Slater, Nishimura, and Kindstrand 2012, 104). Parents faced the difficult choice of voicing concern about radiation affecting their children and being accused of scaremongering (Liscutin 2011). The information infrastructure is itself a condition for emergent dynamics that interrupt any ordered, institutionalized model of communication. However, there is also a reflexivity at work. People reflect on the fact of mediation and their media participation. This is part of how narratives are experienced—through reflection on how they form in a media ecology.

International and Local Criticism of the Nuclear Village Grows

Noriko Murai suggests the watershed moment was the March 28 issue of the newspaper *AERA* (published by Asahi). Its cover headline was "Nuclear Radiation Is Coming." Murai notes that while the newspaper was criticized for sensationalism, that issue began to end "the widespread practice of *jishuku* [self-restraint] in the media. From the same week onward, a wider range of representations, including more-sensationalist pieces . . . began to appear in the popular media" (Murai 2011, 118).

By then, ordinary citizens had begun to collect their own radiation readings through "crowdsourcing": "a Tokyo hacker collective built Internet-connected Geiger counters and drove along the perimeters of the evacuation zone, plotting their findings to a free map service. . . . Local citizens' groups followed suit and procured Geiger counters to take their own measurements to be posted on shared sites" (Slater, Nishimura, and Kindstrand 2012, 105). Even in Tokyo people were buying these devices (Belson 2011). Citizens were following the Japanese national identity of self-responsibility, but in a way that demonstrated their distrust of official information, or lack of information, and this formed a critique of official discourse.

However, March 17 might have been a more important date. Until then, domestic Japanese news had framed the disaster in terms of the earthquake and tsunami, whereas international news looked to frame it in nuclear terms, with comparisons to Chernobyl and Three Mile Island commonplace. On March 17 the U.S. Nuclear Regulatory Commission informed its citizens in Japan that they should keep at least 80 kilometers away from the Fukushima nuclear plant. *Asahi Shimbun* reported this announcement by suggesting it indicated doubts on the U.S. government's part about the quality of information coming from the Japanese government and TEPCO (Tkach-Kawasaki 2012, 121). On March 14 the International Atomic Energy Agency (IAEA) also criticized the Japanese government for releasing insufficient information, while adding, however, that "[w]e will not try to second-guess the people on the ground" (Amano 2011a). The Nuclear Regulatory Commission and the IAEA were later vindicated, as the 20 kilometer evacuation zone recommended by the Japanese government proved inadequate (Karamoskos 2011).

Japanese social media users were also noticing international reporting and on March 22 the French Institute for Radiation Protection and Nuclear Safety began publishing bulletins in Japanese (Slater, Nishimura, and Kindstrand 2012). International scientific institutes openly contested TEPCO information and called for greater translation from Japanese and for a pooling of data (*Asia Pacific Journal* 2011a). Into April, the Japanese government was discussing how decontamination and the lifting of evacuation zones would begin once nuclear reactors had achieved "cold shutdown." However, it had not defined cold shutdown, leaving the situation ambiguous (Asahi.com 2011). The 20km exclusion zone was expanded to 30–50km on April 12 as the government publicly reclassified the radiation event magnitude from level 5 (Three Mile Island) to level 7 (Chernobyl) (Segawa 2011). The U.S. Council on Foreign Relations' journal *Foreign Policy* immediately posted a photo essay entitled "Japan's Chernobyl" showing scenes suggesting that, as one caption said, "parts of Japan are starting to be reminiscent of Pripyat, the Ukranian city reduced to a ghost town after the 1986 disaster" (*Foreign Policy* 2011).

Further public uncertainty became apparent in April as a controversy emerged concerning safe radiation levels for schoolchildren. On April 19, the Ministry of Education, Culture, Sports, Science, and Technology set the radiation safety standard for schools under the Fukushima Board of Education. MEXT stated it sought to balance safety with the social good of continued education. The "safe" radiation level was set at 3.8 microsieverts per hour outdoors, or 20 millisieverts per year, even though the Japanese Labor Standards Act prohibits those aged under 18 from working in conditions in which they will be exposed to 3.8 microsieverts per hour (Hitomi and Field 2011). The next day, a booklet was sent out to all schools, putting schoolteachers at ease (Fukushima Network for Saving Children from Radiation 2011). However, a number of experts were unsettled. The chair of the Japan Federation of Bar Associations, Kenji Utsunomiya (2011), made a public statement questioning MEXT's safety level. A University of Tokyo Graduate School professor specializing in radiation safety, Kosako Toshiso, resigned his post as a nuclear advisor to the Cabinet (Hitomi and Field 2011). On May 2 a group of citizens and NGOs met with MEXT officials. MEXT conceded the safe level was not "fine" and offered no clear scientific basis for the level.

Local political leaders began to use social media to challenge central authorities' communication and action. On April 6, Sakurai Katsunobu, the mayor of the city of Minami-Soma, just 25km from the Fukushima Daiichi plant, posted an 11-minute YouTube video in which he appealed for help.[3] Sitting in the boiler suit he had been wearing while managing the cleanup, he said, "With the scarce information we can gather from the government or TEPCO, we are left isolated. I beg you to help us" (quoted in McNeill 2011). He posted a second video to YouTube the next day.[4] He said, "Many businesses had started operating. But, there is no reliable information on the nuclear reactor" (quoted in Segawa 2011). The videos were watched hundreds of thousands of times; by April 21 Mayor Katsunobo had become one of *Time* magazine's 100 most influential people in the world during 2011 (Beech 2011).

Questions of risk, responsibility, and who would pay for the effects of the triple disaster were present in media discourse in April. This question became increasingly acute once it became clear that the cost of paying for the effects of the nuclear disaster would extend beyond TEPCO. Indeed, in the *Asia Times*, journalist Victor Kotsev speculated that fallout could reach the United States and the European Union, leading to "a worst case scenario . . . [the disaster] could threaten global financial stability." The failure of the Ministry of Economy, Trade and Industry to regulate TEPCO made it a "man-made disaster," argued the former governor of Fukushima Prefecture, Sato Eisaku (quoted in Satoko 2011). In the *Japan Times*, researchers Bogi Tóth, Hiroi Megumi, and Georg Zachmann (2011) considered whether the disaster counted as a "black swan" event, drawing on Nassim Taleb's theory that humanity is beset by occasional one-off events of great magnitude that seem unpredictable but can be rationalized with hindsight.[5] Humans cannot evaluate the risk or regulate for such events because they cannot grasp the complexity of social or natural processes. Like the 2008 financial crisis, Tóth, Megumi, and Zachmann observed how the costs would be largely "socialised." Neither banks and financial regulators nor energy companies and their regulators could fully compensate societies for the losses generated. They recommended that risk-generators should take on insurance against the full catastrophic potential of their industries, but argued it was not feasible because of the impossibility of calculating this potential and because of the political interests against such a policy.

Nevertheless, there was still little open debate about the future of nuclear power and national energy strategy in Japan. For other countries, this was not the case. The week prior to the G8 summit in France on May 26, 2011 was instructive. Some major powers used the occasion of the summit to set out a clear energy strategy and strategic narrative. The United States, the United Kingdom, France, and Russia affirmed their commitment to nuclear power, while Germany, Italy, and Sweden announced that they would freeze or diminish their reliance on it (Martin 2011; Duus 2012). In Japan, Prime Minister Kan was under pressure simply to have an energy policy at all, amid fears that he would not be able to explain Japan's response to the crisis. A leading figure in Kan's Democratic Party, Nishioka Takeo, called for Kan's resignation (*Asia Pacific Journal* 2011b).

Elite Political Contestation and Citizen Counternarratives

After the G8 summit in France, elite political contestation about energy policy began in Japan. This happened for two reasons. First, Kan had finally articulated a clear policy in France, stating that nuclear power would remain one of the "pillars" of Japan's energy policy (Martin 2011). Second, TEPCO announced it had misled the Japanese public about the nature and scale of the disaster by not informing them that there had been three meltdowns. This was followed by a public rebuke by the IAEA for not providing timely, accurate information (Kingston 2012). It was not until May that the word "meltdown" appeared in the Japanese national press, despite being a key term in international news reporting (Tkach-Kawasaki 2012). On May 29 it was reported that 81 percent of the Japanese public did not trust government information about the nuclear crisis (Krieger 2011). Staggeringly, on June 6 the Nuclear and Industrial Safety Agency announced that its latest estimate of the radioactive release from the Fukushima Daiichi plant was over double its prior estimate (Tabuchi 2011a).

There followed a month of intense debate about the future of nuclear energy in Japan. On June 7 the minister for energy, Banri Kaieda, argued that nuclear power should remain a core energy source for Japan (*Japan Times* 2011b). However, an advisory panel in the Fukushima Prefecture reported on June 16 that Fukushima should create a "safe, secure and sustainable society" *not* dependent on nuclear energy (*Japan Times* 2011c). The IAEA suggested that whatever level of reliance on nuclear energy Japan took, it ensure that its regulatory bodies were independent of the nuclear industry (Amano 2011b). Critically, the commission set up by government back in March provided a response that supports Perkin's thesis regarding the state-society compact in post-1970s Japan. In their June 25 report to the prime minister, the 16-member Reconstruction Design Council indicated that it was not for the state to lead. Reconstruction and recovery could not be led by the prime minister and a government's strategic narrative. While it was not the remit of the Council to address overall energy policy, it did prescribe how Japan would recover and find direction: through social participation and a bottom-up revival of hope. Citizens should not look to their state to set direction:

> [I]n such situations we must uphold a spirit of "self-aid" . . . to find yourself tethered to others before you even notice it is a cause of sadness. It is exactly in the trials and tribulations towards reconstruction that people regain their independence and seek out "hope" from that independence. (Reconstruction Design Council 2011, 49)

Kan arrived at a position that reflected the Reconstruction Design Council's perspective. On July 13 he said that he would prefer a society that was not dependent on nuclear energy, a position supported by 77 percent of public opinion (Kingston 2012). For Kan, it was a matter of balancing risk, and "I have realized that nuclear accidents cannot be prevented completely with the conventional safety measures we have at present" (quoted in *Daily Yomiuri* 2011). However, he added that this was a *personal* and not an official position. In other words, the government could not take a clear position. Kansei Nakano, head of the National Public Safety Commission, immediately said Kan's remarks were "causing confusion" (*Japan Times* 2011d). The risk dilemma highlighted by Kan entrenched the policy paralysis. The government was unable to prove the safety of nuclear plants so it could not restart them. This resulted in power shortages, and the government depended on citizens willingly reducing their energy usage (*Japan Times* 2011e).

If TEPCO became one of the villains of the story in this period, it was not clear who counted as a victim. Certainly the immediate victims were identifiable and categorizable: 60 percent of those killed by the earthquake and tsunami were aged 60 or over (Kennedy and Luthra 2011). Among survivors, those who stayed in relief centers became televisual victims; those who returned to what was left of their homes forfeited official recognition and support as victims (Morris 2012). Given the uncertainty and duration of the effects of radiation, it will be impossible for a definitive set of victims of the nuclear disaster to be known even decades later. This was a crisis without narrative resolution or a clear ending.

After Hiroshima, Japan developed the world's longest longitudinal study of radiation poisoning, and has methods as advanced as any country to monitor long- and short-term effects (Kennedy and Luthra 2011). However, Japanese studies of radiation exposure effects are based on large one-off doses delivered quickly through atomic bombs, not small regular doses over decades from steady power plant leaks and contaminated food and water (Wald 2011). According to nuclear radiologist Peter Karamoskos, "Even though risk models of cancer induction can be used to predict the likely cancers over the next six decades, it is possible that we will never know the true number of actual excess cancers in the general population due to inherent statistical limitations and large uncertainties, even several decades after the event. This is particularly so at very low doses" (2011, 19). One expert, Checchi, suggested that Japan invest in reinforcing cancer and birth defect registries and commission cohort studies (Kennedy and Luthra 2011). It was also impossible to predict who and how many people would suffer mental health problems because of the disaster. The rate of suicides increased after the 1995 Kobe earthquake (Glionna 2011), so Japanese authorities might have expected a similar rise after March 2011. Telling the empirical story of the disaster, with victims and the physical and mental effects known, would depend on the construction of medical, scientific infrastructure.

The Japanese taxpayer also became a victim. The 1961 Act on Compensation for Nuclear Damage places no cap on damages that can be paid out to victims. Given that large compensation would bankrupt firms, liability would pass to the taxpayer (Karamoskos 2011). On August 3, Japan passed a law to allow use of public funds to pay compensation, thereby keeping TEPCO operational (Tabuchi 2011b).

By now social media and mainstream media had been reconfigured through activist practices into new hybrids that revealed the constructed nature of news. Social media circulated mainstream media reports, while mainstream media reported on social media activity, creating a reinforcing dynamic. More significantly, mainstream media reports, when remediated through social media, were annotated: users added subtitles to mainstream media reports, saying, for instance, "TEPCO is lying . . . again" (Slater, Nishimura, and Kindstrand 2012, 99).

This creates a new condition within which strategic narratives must operate. If news consumers are reflecting on news' arbitrary character, then how officials use mainstream media to project their narratives involves new questions of credibility. This is illustrated by Liscutin's (2012) analysis of social media responses in Japan. She highlights a YouTube video[6] posted in February 2012 entitled "A Letter to Lady Gaga." The woman in the video thanks the pop superstar for visiting Japan in the aftermath of the triple disaster, and asks if Lady Gaga could help publicize that the event should not be forgotten; or rather, that the accident is not "over" but rather is an indefinite presence. She argues that the people of Japan feel abandoned. Although the video's claims are consistent with those of antinuclear groups, the media mix employed is important. The video points to the "masking" effect of mainstream media by presenting fabricated newspaper front pages with headlines such as "Invisible, Radiation Causes Unease," "Incoherent Management of Crisis," and "What Is Going On?" Scientific visualizations of the spread of radiation, news clips of the explosion at the Fukushima Daiichi plant, and press conferences by the prime minister are juxtaposed to suggest the duplicity of the nuclear village—the gap between the ongoing story and the plot presented to the Japanese people.

Digital information infrastructure allows for more data and, often, greater availability of evidence to validate claims (Mor 2012a, 2). Ben Mor identifies this as a tendency: "the importance of validation tactics is only expected to grow with technological advances, rising transparency, and the level of contestation they generate in the system" (2011, 4). If the nuclear village sought to control the plot presented to citizens and journalists, "A letter to Lady Gaga" shows how easily a young person can reassemble the same raw materials of plot to articulate a counternarrative.

Soteigai: A Failure of Imagination

Ultimately, the Japanese government failed to offer any kind of vision for the future—not even more of the same, just a blank. "Gripped by a sense of powerlessness, we feel uncertainty about the future of our country," said the novelist Haruki Murakami at an acceptance speech at a literary prize ceremony in Barcelona on June 9, 2011. Murakami explicitly connected the 3/11 disaster to Hiroshima and Nagasaki, and to questions of national identity and the nation's future:

> [N]ow, today, sixty-six years after the dropping of the atomic bombs, the Fukushima Daiichi nuclear power plant has been spewing out radiation continuously for three months, polluting the ground, the ocean and the atmosphere around the plant. And no one knows when and how this spewing of radiation will be stopped. This is a historic experience for us Japanese: our second massive nuclear disaster. But this time no one dropped a bomb on us. We set the stage, we committed the crime with our own hands, we are destroying our own lands, and we are destroying our own lives. (Murakami 2011)

Part of this "crime" was a lack of imagination when evaluating risk, according to the December report presented by the Investigation Committee of TEPCO, set up by the Cabinet in May (ICANPS 2011). The report criticized TEPCO staff for saying that the events of 3/11 were *soteigai*, or "outside our imagination" (Kageyama 2011). The repeated use of this term indicated a shirking of responsibility, the report said. While the report also criticized TEPCO's decision making, operational procedures, and public communications, it highlighted quotes from TEPCO staff indicating they had not considered what would happen should an "external" force hit its power plants. This would explain why they did not create contingency plans for such events. The report stated that "the excuse that nothing could be done in the face of an extraordinary situation involving the onslaught of a tsunami beyond all assumptions is not convincing—rather, the only conclusion is that there existed major problems in nuclear emergency preparedness" (ICANPS 2011, 602). The report urged planning for low probability "multidimensional" disasters, which would involve expanding TEPCO's assumptions about what events are possible. How could TEPCO establish the boundaries or parameter of what can be assumed? The report was entirely ambiguous on this:

> How, then, do we establish that parameter? That decision is influenced by various limitations. There are economic limitations, of course, and social limitations, limitations imposed by the past, regional limitations, and so on. The parameter is established by satisfying the demands of those limitations. Those limitations are not necessarily clearly identified. They may not be spelled out in writing. We must be careful to realize that *some limitations may exist as a premise that is implicitly understood among those involved, but not verbalized.* (ICANPS 2011, 603, italics added)

The difficulty of calculating risk appears to come down to a hunch, a sense, a feeling that cannot be put into words. This statement exemplifies the difficulty contemporary policymakers have in evaluating risk.

There is also the question of whether this incident will force Japan to improve its nuclear safety procedures. The Japanese state has now witnessed how global transparency operates, and the loss of credibility caused by attempts to hide information; hence the information infrastructure should drive policy in a certain direction, and Japan's energy narrative will have to account for this. The lack of a Japanese strategic narrative of recovery and for the future of its energy policy challenged Japan's position in the "hierarchy of prestige" in the international system of states (Gilpin 1981, 30). Despite other major powers suffering nuclear disasters since the 1970s, major international figures openly questioned the Japanese political elite (Suzuki 2011). The founding president of the European Bank for Reconstruction and Development, Jacques Attali, said, "A mixture of pride and arrogance—along with a penchant for secrecy and lack of transparency—has led the public and private authorities in Japan to refuse international aid while hiding the scope of the disaster, both from their own people and from the international community" (2011). Suzuki (2011) argues that such statements present a view of Japan as culturally unique, within a "hierarchy of cultures" where others must be superior; Japan as a nation whose unique deficiencies require international intervention. Indeed, Attali called for an international consortium of experts to lead an intervention, and argued that the Japanese must accept this.

Conclusions

Japan's government failed to form a strategic narrative after the triple disaster. The priority of the Japanese state and national media was to avoid panic and maintain national reputation at a time of economic slowdown. However, too many institutions spoke, information was too general, and it was later proven wrong. This highlights how information infrastructure both conditions and is the condition for action around global crisis events. The volume, speed, and diversity of sources in the new media ecology creates a perpetual "risk of credibility loss" (Mor 2006, 165) and a loss of dignity and reputation in the international "hierarchy of prestige" (Gilpin 1981; Mor 2012b).

Infrastructure matters: "If you want power in a networked society, you need to orchestrate control over the ecosystem," dana boyd writes (2012, n.p.). The Japanese government tried to create a national media "container" space by providing mainstream domestic journalists with access to political and TEPCO leaders at daily press conferences. However, the information infrastructure made this container permeable: overseas media was available in Japan; overseas scientific reports were picked up by Japanese journalists; Japanese citizens could interact with citizens, NGOs, and others in other countries. As soon as powerful actors like the IAEA and the United States began to openly refute the claims of the Japanese state, Japanese mainstream media began to follow. As space for legitimate dissensus was formed, which social media had already been constituting, but they had been ignored by mainstream journalists. These findings support power indexing theory: that when actors with the power to determine a situation are in agreement, mainstream media will follow (Entman and Page 1994; Nacos et al. 2000). But these findings also show how the conditions for indexing, namely a well-ordered "mainstream" political-media system, are transformed by the new media ecology.

Even if the Japanese government was more skilled at using the information infrastructure, its strategic narrative work was hampered by the raw materials of the narrative: evidence of risks and their effects. Narratives of global risk must have a particular character: they must account for risk being both "instantaneous" and "glacial" in its temporalities—Fukushima was both now and will last decades (Urry 2000, 158). Risk narratives must acknowledge the contingency of unexpected chains of causation, the likelihood of unknown unknowns, and create expectations about how much knowledge is required to act. As the ICANPS report argued, Japanese authorities did not recognize or acknowledge these; such notions were *soteigai*, beyond the imagination—and responsibility.

Japanese authorities must be aware how global transparency operates now, and the loss of credibility that attempts to hide information brings. The information infrastructure should drive policy in a certain direction, and Japan's energy narrative will have to account for this. Japanese authorities are not responding to media images, but to global information and global media as a system and condition. This is made up of machines gathering, reading, and interpreting data, telling each other their findings (and telling us if we can turn them into visualizations). Unlike previous media ecologies based around writing or broadcast, this is characterized by interoperability, the transfer of information at the speed of light. Techniques of "sending, saving and calculating" have merged in digital computing (Peters 2010, 12). NGOs, scientific institutes, local officials, and citizens can form credible or compelling narratives through digital media, for instance the "Letter to Lady Gaga" or Mayor Katsunobu's appeal for help, an appeal that instantly made him a *Time* magazine person of the year.

Nevertheless, the Reconstruction Design Council report instructed that Japan's future depended not on government direction and a compelling narrative but on citizens' "self-aid" and independence. *Soteigai* is not a problem. This fits a longer term discourse about self-responsibility that has underpinned a social compact between the Japanese state and citizens since the 1970s (Perkins 2011). Fukushima pushed that compact to its limit, as citizens were forced to fend for themselves, from informing one another through social media to taking their own radiation readings. There was a compensation effect that only highlighted the lack of action and direction from the state.

This analysis raises a number of questions. Media representation of the disaster involved a mix of modalities, featuring scientific diagrams, phone footage, news reporting, and so on. This expands the raw material for strategic narratives, but it becomes hard to control the meanings these generate or predict the variegated distribution of affective responses. For instance, in years to come, visual images of the nuclear disaster may create increasing affective significance for people in Fukushima Prefecture, since those images rekindle the feelings of panic or solidarity formed in the event (Liscutin 2011). For international audiences, however, such images may become just another news template (Hoskins 2006) in a string of post–Cold War, 24-hour news disasters, a visual shorthand for a generic event-type, thereby containing and nullifying affective connections to Japan.

Crafting the sequence of a credible narrative amid uncertainty is not easy; leaders face pressure to say something knowing they will in all likelihood be contradicted by subsequent events and findings. As this case shows, however, to say nothing, deferring judgment for a sunnier day, may be even worse.

NOTES

I am indebted to Chris Perkins for his ideas and encouragement for this chapter, and for the service of the Harvard University's Digital Archive of Japan's 2011 Disasters, available at http://jdarchive.org/

1. For authoritative histories of world systems that account for the role of communication in the management of power relations, see Barry Buzan and Richard Little, *International Systems in World History* (Oxford: Oxford University Press, 2000); Manual Castells, *The Rise of the Network Society*, vol. 1 of *The Information Age: Economy, Society and Culture* (Malden, MA: Blackwell, 1996); Daniel H. Deudney, *Bounding Power: Republican Security Theory from the Polis to the Global Village* (Princeton: Princeton University Press, 2010); Marshall McLuhan and Quentin Fiore, *War and Peace in the Global Village: An Inventory of Some of the Current Spastic Situations That Could Be Eliminated by More Feedforward* (New York: Bantam Books, 1989). For accounts examining how contemporary political systems depend on information infrastructures, see Luciano Floridi, *The Fourth Revolution: How the Infosphere Is Reshaping Human Reality* (Oxford: Oxford University Press, 2014); Matthew Fuller and Andrew Goffey, *Evil Media* (Cambridge, MA: MIT Press, 2012); Taylor Owen, *Disruptive Power: The Crisis of the State in the Digital Age* (New York: Oxford University Press, 2015).

2. Available on the Ministry of Internal Affairs and Communications website, http://www.soumu.go.jp/menu_news/s-news/01kiban08_01000023.html (accessed June 6, 2012).

3. www.youtube.com/watch?v=R6URqs9kb20 (accessed June 6, 2012).

4. http://www.youtube.com/watch?v=VBcnhghD1wQ (accessed June 6, 2012).

5. Nassim Nicholas Taleb, *The Black Swan: The Impact of the Highly Improbable Fragility* (New York: Random House, 2010).
6. "A Letter to Lady Gaga," http://www.youtube.com/watch?v=q_cf5k0iYLc (accessed June 7, 2012).

REFERENCES

Akimoto, Akky. "Japan, the Twitter Nation." *Japan Times*, May 18, 2011. Accessed June 6, 2012. http://www.japantimes.co.jp/text/nc20110518aa.html
Amano, Yukiya. "IAEA Director General Launches Daily Briefing on Nuclear Safety in Earthquake-Stricken Japan." Statement, International Atomic Energy Agency, April 14, 2011a. Accessed June 6, 2012. http://www.iaea.org/newscenter/statements/2011/amsp2011n006.html
Amano, Yukiya. "IAEA Ministerial Conference on Nuclear Safety: Introductory Statement." International Atomic Energy Agency, Vienna, June 20, 2011b. Accessed June 6, 2012. http://www.meti.go.jp/english/earthquake/nuclear/iaea/iaea20110620b.pdf
Asahi.com. "Government Reveals Timeline for Decommissioning Reactors." July 21, 2011. Accessed June 6, 2012. http://www.asahi.com/english/TKY201107200277.html
Asia Pacific Journal. "'Long Since Passed the Level of Three Mile Island'—the Fukushima Crisis in Comparative Perspective." May 25, 2011a. Accessed June 6, 2012. http://japanfocus.org/events/view/59
Asia Pacific Journal. "Resign Now, Prime Minister Kan." May 25, 2011b. Accessed June 6, 2012. http://japanfocus.org/events/view/90
Attali, Jaques. "The International Community Must Intervene—in Japan." *Huffington Post*, March 30, 2011. Accessed June 7, 2012. http://www.huffingtonpost.com/jacques-attali/the-international-communi_1_b_842630.html
Avenall, Simon. "From Kobe to Tohoku: The Potential and Peril of a Volunteer Infrastructure." In *Natural Disaster and Nuclear Crisis in Japan: Response and Recovery after Japan's 3/11*, edited by Jeff Kingston. London: Routledge, 2012.
Awan, Akil, Andrew Hoskins, and Ben O'Loughlin. *Radicalisation and Media: Terrorism and Connectivity in the New Media Ecology*. London: Routledge, 2011.
Bauman, Zygmunt. *This Is Not a Diary*. Cambridge: Polity, 2012.
BBC News. "Robots Record High Radiation Levels at Japan Reactors." April 18, 2011. Accessed June 6, 2012. http://www.bbc.co.uk/news/world-asia-pacific-13112444
Beck, Ulrich. *World at Risk*. Cambridge: Polity, 2009.
Beech, Hannah. "Katsunobu Sakura: Boat Rocker." *Time*, April 21, 2011. Accessed June 6, 2012. http://www.time.com/time/specials/packages/article/0,28804,2066367_2066369_2066461,00.html
Belson, Ken. "Doubting Assurances, Japanese Find Radioactivity on Their Own." *New York Times*, July 31, 2011. Accessed June 6, 2012. http://www.nytimes.com/2011/08/01/world/asia/01radiation.html?pagewanted=all
Blumler, Jay G. "The Shape of Political Communication." In *The Oxford Handbook of Political Communication*, edited by Kate Kenski and Kathleen Hall Jamieson. Oxford: Oxford University Press, 2015. http://dx.doi.org/10.1093/oxfordhb/9780199793471.013.78

Boy, Nina, J. Peter Burgess, and Anna Leander. "The Global Governance of Security and Finance: Introduction to the Special Issue." *Security Dialogue* 42, no.2 (2011): 115–22.

boyd, danah. "The Power of Fear in Networked Publics." *SXSW*. Austin, Texas, March 10, 2012. Accessed June 6, 2012. http://www.danah.org/papers/talks/2012/SXSW2012.html

Bratton, Benjamin H. "On Geoscapes and the Google Caliphate: Reflections on the Mumbai Attacks." *Theory, Culture & Society* 26, nos. 7–8 (2009): 329–42.

Chakravartty, Paula, and John D. Downing. "Media, Technology, and the Global Financial Crisis." *International Journal of Communication* 5 (2010): 693–95.

Choate, Allen. "In Face of Disaster, Japanese Citizens and Government Pull from Lessons Learned." *In Asia*, March 16, 2011. Accessed June 6, 2012. http://asiafoundation.org/in-asia/2011/03/16/in-face-of-disaster-japanese-citizens-and-government-pull-from-lessons-learned/

Coker, Christopher. *War in an Age of Risk*. Cambridge: Polity, 2009.

Cottle, Simon. *Global Crisis Reporting: Journalism in the Global Age*. Maidenhead, UK: Open University Press, 2009a.

Cottle, Simon. "Global Crises in the News: Staging New Wars, Disasters and Climate Change." *International Journal of Communication* 3 (2009b): 494–516.

Cottle, Simon. "Taking Global Crises in the News Seriously: Notes from the Dark Side of Globalization." *Global Media and Communication* 7, no. 2 (2011): 77–95.

Cottle, Simon. "Rethinking Media and Disasters in a Global Age: What's Changed and Why It Matters." *Media, War & Conflict* 7, no. 1 (2014): 3–22.

Croft, Stuart. *Securitizing Islam: Identity and the Search for Security*. Cambridge: Cambridge University Press, 2012.

Curtis, Gerald L. "Tohoku Diary: Reportage of the Tohoku Disaster." In *Natural Disaster and Nuclear Crisis in Japan: Response and Recovery after Japan's 3/11*, edited by Jeff Kingston. London: Routledge, 2012.

Daily Yomiuri. "Kan Wants to Phase Out N-Power." July 14, 2011. Accessed June 6, 2012. http://www.yomiuri.co.jp/dy/national/T110713005486.htm

Duraiappah, Anantha Kumar, Kazuhiko Takeuchi, and Carmen Scherkenbach. "As Japan Rebuilds, It Should Look to Satoyama and Satoumi for Inspiration." United Nations University, May 3, 2011. Accessed January 24, 2016. http://unu.edu/publications/articles/as-japan-rebuilds-it-should-look-to-satoyama-and-satoumi-for-inspiration.html#info

Duus, Peter. "Dealing with Disaster." In *Natural Disaster and Nuclear Crisis in Japan: Response and Recovery after Japan's 3/11*, edited by Jeff Kingston. London: Routledge, 2012.

Entman, Robert M., and Benjamin Page. "The News before the Storm." In *Taken by Storm: The Media, Public Opinion, and US Foreign Policy in the Gulf War*, edited by W. Lance Bennett and David L. Paletz, 82–101. Chicago: University of Chicago Press, 1994.

Foreign Policy. "Japan's Chernobyl—an FP Slideshow." April 12, 2011. Accessed June 6, 2012. http://www.foreignpolicy.com/articles/2011/04/12/japans_chernobyl

Freedman, Lawrence. "Networks, Culture and Narratives." *Adelphi Papers Series* 45, no. 379 (January 2006): 11–26. Accessed June 6, 2012. http://dx.doi.org/10.1080/05679320600661640

Fukushima Network for Saving Children from Radiation. "Violation of the Human

Rights of the Children of Fukushima." August 17, 2011. Accessed June 6, 2012. http://greenaction-japan.org/internal/110817_Fukushima_human_rights_UN_submission.pdf

Fuller, Matthew. *Media Ecologies: Materialist Energies in Art and Technoculture.* Cambridge, MA: MIT Press, 2005.

Gehl, Robert W. "The Archive and the Processor: The Internal Logic of Web 2.0." *New Media & Society* 13, no. 8 (2011): 1228–44.

Gilpin, Robert. *War and Change in World Politics.* Cambridge: Cambridge University Press, 1981.

Glionna, John M. "Japan Fears Post-Quake Rise in Suicides." *Los Angeles Times*, April 24, 2011. Accessed June 7, 2012. http://articles.latimes.com/2011/apr/24/world/la-fg-japan-suicides-20110424

Goldberg, Greg. "Rethinking the Public/Virtual Sphere: The Problem with Participation." *New Media & Society* 13, no. 5 (2010): 739–54.

Grusin, Richard. *Premediation: Affect and Mediality after 9/11.* New York: Palgrave, 2010.

Hajer, Maarten A. *The Politics of Environmental Discourse: Ecological Modernization and the Policy Process.* Oxford: Oxford University Press, 1995.

Hitomi, Kamanaka, and Norma Field. "Complicity and Victimization: Director Kamanaka Hitomi's Nuclear Warnings." *Asia-Pacific Journal* 9, issue 18, no. 4 (May 2, 2011). Accessed June 6, 2012. http://www.japanfocus.org/-Norma-Field/3524

Hoskins, Andrew, and Ben O'Loughlin. *War and Media: The Emergence of Diffused War.* Cambridge: Polity, 2010.

Hoskins, Andrew, and Ben O'Loughlin. "Remediating *Jihad* for Western News Audiences: The Renewal of Gatekeeping?" *Journalism: Theory, Practice & Criticism* 12, no. 2 (2011): 199–216.

Hoskins, Andrew, and Ben O'Loughlin. "Arrested War: The Third Phase of Mediatization." *Information, Communication & Society* 18, no. 11 (2015): 1320–38.

Ikegami, Eiko. "Three Realities: Cultural Capital, Scientific Measurements, Political Denial." *Edge*, Special Event: What We Can't Predict, March 25, 2011. Accessed June 6, 2012. http://edge.org/documents/archive/edge341.html#ikegami

Investigation Committee on the Accident at the Fukushima Nuclear Power Stations (ICANPS). "Interim Report." December 26, 2011. Accessed June 7, 2012. http://icanps.go.jp/eng/interim-report.html

Jacobs, Robert A. *The Dragon's Tale: Americans Face the Atomic Age.* Amherst: University of Massachusetts Press, 2010.

Jacobsen, David. "The JET Program's Finest Hour." *Chin Music Press*, July 9, 2011. Accessed June 6, 2012. http://chinmusicpress.com/blog.php?action=display&entryID=13

Japan Times. "Power Outages, Downed Communication Lines Knocked Out Most Radiation Monitoring Systems in Disaster Areas." May 29, 2011a. Accessed June 6, 2012. http://www.japantimes.co.jp/text/nn20110529a4.html

Japan Times. "Despite Crisis, Nuclear to Remain Core Energy Source: Kaieda." June 15, 2011b. Accessed June 6, 2012. http://www.japantimes.co.jp/text/nn20110615a5.html

Japan Times. "Fukushima Urged to Stop Relying on Nuke Power." June 16, 2011c. Accessed June 6, 2012. http://www.japantimes.co.jp/text/nn20110616a8.html

Japan Times. "Fukushima to Scrap Nuclear Plants." July 16, 2011d. Accessed June 6, 2012. http://www.japantimes.co.jp/text/nn20110716a4.html

Japan Times. "Energy Policy Drift Deepens Shortages Fears." July 23, 2011e. Accessed June 6, 2012. http://www.japantimes.co.jp/text/nn20110723f2.html

Kageyama, Y. "Japan Probe: Nuclear Crisis Response Failed." *Time*, December 26, 2011. http://www.time.com/time/world/article/0,8599,2103120,00.html?xid=rss-most-popular (no longer accessible).

Karamoskos, Peter. "Fukushima Burning: Anatomy of a Nuclear Disaster." *Physician Life* (May/June 2011): 14–19. Accessed June 7, 2012. http://issuu.com/medicallife/docs/physicianlife_final_v1

Kennedy, Rebecca, and Karuna Luthra. "Looking to the Future: Healthcare Reform and Disaster Preparedness Planning in Japan." National Bureau of Asian Research, May 26, 2011. Accessed June 7, 2012. http://www.nbr.org/downloads/pdfs/CHA/NBR_Interview_MakotoAoki.pdf

Kingston, Jeff. "Introduction." In *Natural Disaster and Nuclear Crisis in Japan: Response and Recovery after Japan's 3/11*, edited by Jeff Kingston. London: Routledge, 2012.

Kirby, Peter Wynn. "Japan's Long Nuclear Disaster Film." *New York Times*, March 14, 2011. Accessed June 6, 2012. http://opinionator.blogs.nytimes.com/2011/03/14/japans-long-nuclear-disaster-film/#

Kittler, Friedrich. *Optical Media*. Cambridge: Polity, 2010.

Kotsev, Victor. "Japan Nuclear Crisis Goes Global." *Asia Times Online*, April 16, 2011. Accessed June 6, 2012. http://www.atimes.com/atimes/Japan/MD16Dh01.html

Krieger, Daniel. "Monitoring the Monitors." *Slate*, June 16, 2011. Accessed June 6, 2012. http://www.slate.com/articles/health_and_science/green_room/2011/06/monitoring_the_monitors.html

Lee, Raymond L. M. "Modernity, Solidity and Agency: Liquidity Reconsidered." *Sociology* 45, no. 4 (2011): 650–64.

Leflar, Robert B., Ayato Hirata, Masayuki Murayama, and Shozo Ota. "Human Flotsam, Legal Fallout: Japan's Tsunami and Nuclear Meltdown." *Journal of Environmental Law & Litigation* 27 (2012): 107–24. Accessed June 7, 2012. http://ssrn.com/abstract=2025761

Liscutin, Nicola. "Indignez-Vous! 'Fukushima,' New Media and Anti-Nuclear Activism in Japan." *Asia-Pacific Journal* 9, issue 47, no. 1 (November 21, 2011). Accessed June 6, 2012. http://www.japanfocus.org/-Nicola-Liscutin/3649

Liscutin, Nicola. "Beyond Indignation: New Media, Anti-Nuclear Activism, and the 'Abandoned People of Fukushima.'" London Asia Pacific Cultural Studies Forum Special Talk, London, March 1, 2012.

Martin, Alex. "G-8 Differ in Reactions to Fukushima." *Japan Times*, May 29, 2011. Accessed June 6, 2012. http://www.japantimes.co.jp/text/nn20110529a2.html

McCarthy, M. M. "Japanese Media Assessments of the Governmental Response to the 2011 Crisis." Paper presented at the Annual Convention of the International Studies Association, San Diego, April 1–4, 2012.

McNeill, David. "Back from the Brink: A City in Ruins Looks to the Future." *Asia-Pacific Journal* 9, issue 16, no. 1 (April 18, 2011). Accessed June 6, 2012. http://www.japanfocus.org/site/view/3515

Miskimmon, Alister, Ben O'Loughlin, and Laura Roselle. "Forging the World: Strategic Narratives and International Relations." Working Paper. Accessed June 6, 2012.

http://newpolcom.rhul.ac.uk/storage/Forging%20the%20World%20Working%20Paper%202012.pdf

Mor, Ben D. "Public Diplomacy in Grand Strategy." *Foreign Policy Analysis* 2 (2006): 157–76.

Mor, Ben D. "Credibility Talk in Public Diplomacy." *Review of International Studies* 38, no. 2 (2012a): 393–422.

Mor, Ben D. (2012b). "Using Force to Save Face: The Performative Side of War." *Peace & Change* 37, no. 1 (2012b): 95–121.

Morris, John F. "Recovery in Tohoku." In *Natural Disaster and Nuclear Crisis in Japan: Response and Recovery after Japan's 3/11*, edited by Jeff Kingston. London: Routledge, 2012.

Murai, Noriko. "'But Is It Not in Fact Leaking a Little?'" In *Tsunami: Japan's Post-Fukushima Future*, edited by Jeff Kingston. Washington, DC: Foreign Policy, 2011. Accessed June 6, 2012. http://www.foreignpolicy.com/files/tutEkfeUr4fOa3v/06282011_Tsunami.pdf

Murakami, Haruki. "Speaking as an Unrealistic Dreamer." Translated by Emanuel Pastreich. Speech, International Catalunya Prize, Barcelona, July 18, 2011. Accessed June 7, 2012. http://circlesandsquares.asia/2011/07/19/translation-of-murakami-harukis-speech-at-barcelona-in-japan-focus/

Perkins, Chris. "Aftermath of the Japanese Earthquake—Rethinking the Use of Nuclear Power, Reconstruction and the National Character of the Japanese People." Warwick and Hong Kong Public Affairs and Social Service Society Asia Summit 2011, Warwick University.

Peters, John D. "Introduction: Friedrich Kittler's Light Shows." In *Optical Media*, by Friedrich Kittler. Cambridge: Polity, 2010.

Postman, Neil. "The Reformed English Curriculum." In *High School 1980: The Shape of the Future in American Secondary Education*, edited by A. C. Eurich, 160–68. New York: Pitman, 1970.

Reconstruction Design Council. "Towards Reconstruction: 'Hope beyond the Disaster.'" Report to the Prime Minister, June 25, 2011. Accessed June 6, 2012. http://www.cas.go.jp/jp/fukkou/english/pdf/report20110625.pdf

Satoko, Onuki. "Former Fukushima Governor Sato Eisaku Blasts METI–TEPCO Alliance: 'Government Must Accept Responsibility for Defrauding the People.'" *Asia-Pacific Journal* 9, issue 15, no. 4 (April 11, 2011). Accessed June 6, 2012. http://japanfocus.org/-Onuki-Satoko/3514

Segawa, Makiko. "Fukushima Residents Seek Answers amid Mixed Signals from Media, TEPCO and Government." *Asia-Pacific Journal* 9, issue 16, no. 2 (April 18, 2011). Accessed June 6, 2012. http://japanfocus.org/-makiko-segawa/3516

Shaw, Martin. *The New Western Way of War: Risk-Transfer War and Its Crisis in Iraq*. Cambridge: Polity, 2005.

Shieber, Jonathan. "Despite Arrest, Wounds Still Fester in China over Japan Radiation Salt Panic." *Wall Street Journal*, March 22, 2011. Accessed June 6, 2012. http://blogs.wsj.com/chinarealtime/2011/03/22/debate-continues-after-china-arrests-japan-radiation-salt-panic-culprit/

Slater, David H., Keiko Nishimura, and Love Kindstrand. "Social Media in Disaster Japan." In *Natural Disaster and Nuclear Crisis in Japan: Response and Recovery after Japan's 3/11,* edited by Jeff Kingston. London: Routledge, 2012.

Sotinel, Thomas. "Tsunamis, Meltdowns and Japan's Disaster Movie Obsession." *Le Monde/Worldcrunch.* March 21, 2011. Accessed June 6, 2012. http://worldcrunch.com/tsunamis-meltdowns-and-japans-disaster-movie-obsession/2778

Sullivan, Rachel. "Live-Tweeting Terror: A Rhetorical Analysis of @HSMPress_ Twitter Updates during the 2013 Nairobi Hostage Crisis." *Critical Studies on Terrorism* 7, no. 3 (2014): 422–33.

Suzuki, Shogo. "Fukushima and Cultural Superiority." *Diplomat,* July 15, 2011. Accessed June 7, 2012. http://the-diplomat.com/2011/07/15/fukushima-and-cultural-superiority/

Tabuchi, Hiroko. "Radiation Understated after Quake, Japan Says." *New York Times,* June 6, 2011a. Accessed June 6, 2012. www.nytimes.com/2011/06/07/world/asia/07japan.html.

Tabuchi, Hiroko. "Japan Passes Law Supporting Stricken Nuclear Plant's Operator." *New York Times,* August 3, 2011b. Accessed June 6, 2012. http://www.nytimes.com/2011/08/04/world/asia/04japan.html

Tkach-Kawasaki, Leslie M. "March 11, 2011 Online: Comparing Japanese Newspapers Websites and International News Websites." In *Natural Disaster and Nuclear Crisis in Japan: Response and Recovery after Japan's 3/11,* edited by Jeff Kingston. London: Routledge, 2012.

Todorov, Tzvetan. "The Typology of Detective Fiction." In *Modern Criticism and Theory: A Reader,* edited by David Lodge, 158–65. London: Longman, 1988.

Tóth, Bogi, Hiroi Megumi, and Georg Zachmann. "Fallout of Nuclear and Financial Meltdowns." *Japan Times,* April 7, 2011. Accessed June 6, 2012. http://www.japantimes.co.jp/text/eo20110407a1.html

UNESCO. "3 Days after the 11 March 2011 Earthquake off the Pacific Coast of Tohoku, Japan." Intergovernmental Oceanographic Commission, March 15, 2011. Accessed June 7, 2012. http://www.unesco.org/new/en/natural-sciences/ioc-oceans/single-view-oceans/news/3_days_after_the_11_march_2011_earthquake_off_the_pacific_coast_of_tohoku_japan/

Ungar, Sheldon. "Global Bird Flu Communication: Hot Crisis and Media Reassurance." *Science Communication* 29, no. 4 (2008): 472–97.

Urry, John. *Sociology beyond Societies: Mobilities for the Twenty-First Century.* London: Routledge, 2000.

Utsunomiya, Kenji. "Statement concerning the Government's 'Provisional Guideline for the Utilization of School Buildings, Grounds, and Related Facilities in Fukushima Prefecture.'" Japanese Federation of Bar Associations, April 22, 2011. Accessed January 24, 2016. http://www.nichibenren.or.jp/en/document/statements/year/2011/20110422.html

Wald, Matthew L. "Radiation's Unknowns Weigh on Japan." *New York Times,* June 6, 2011. Accessed June 7, 2012. http://www.nytimes.com/2011/06/07/business/energy-environment/07radiation.html

Williams, Michael J. "(In)Security Studies, Reflexive Modernization and the Risk Society." *Cooperation and Conflict* 43, no. 1 (2008): 57–79.

Xinhuanet.com. "China Races against Radiation-Triggered Salt Rush." March 18, 2011. Accessed June 6, 2012. http://news.xinhuanet.com/english2010/china/2011-03/18/c_13786594_2.htm

Yasuyuki, Sakai. "Japan's Decline as a Robotics Superpower: Lessons from Fukushima." *Asia-Pacific Journal* 9, issue 24, no. 2 (June 13, 2011). Accessed June 6, 2012. http://japanfocus.org/-Sakai-Yasuyuki/3546

Yuko, Kawato, Robert Pekkanen, and Yutaka Tsujinaka. "Civil Society and the Triple Disasters: Revealed Strengths and Weaknesses." In *Natural Disaster and Nuclear Crisis in Japan: Response and Recovery after Japan's 3/11*, edited by Jeff Kingston. London: Routledge, 2012.

11 | Understanding International Order and Power Transition

A Strategic Narrative Approach

Alister Miskimmon and Ben O'Loughlin

> Only by pushing the envelope of what we assume to be natural or inherent can we hope to envision and create a genuinely new world order.
> —Anne-Marie Slaughter (2004, 35)

Understanding continuity and change in international order is a central question in the study of International Relations. IR theories conceptualize order in different ways. Each theory underpins a narrative about how an effective resolution to obstacles or tensions in the international system can be reached and stability secured. Neorealists conceive order as the result of power balances in the international system between dominant states (Waltz 1979). The English school conceives order being built on a "society of states" (Bull 2002; Linklater and Suganami 2006; Linklater 2007). Koivisto and Dunne (2010, 615) suggest that "for English School internationalists, the problem with international order is that its institutions are "deformed" because of a failure to legitimise power and institutions." This signals how this school conceive what a coherent order would look like. Studies on governance focus on how institutions and multilateral agreements between state and nonstate actors define the order (Barnett and Finnemore 2004; Slaughter 2004). Constructivist studies deconstruct the normative underpinnings of order that shape the behavior of actors and analyze how norms become intersubjectively held or contested (Wendt 1999). Gramscians analyze how orders rest on institutionalized relations of coercion and consent (Cox 1981, 1987; Cox and Sinclair 1996). During the Cold War, interactions between great powers were largely viewed from within the prism of realism (Kennedy 1988) and neorealism (Waltz 1979). According to Waltz's theory, stability and peace within the international system was best achieved through the balancing of power between the world's leading nations. Bipolarity between the United States and the Soviet Union was considered to be a largely stable condition with such writers as John Lewis Gaddis describing the Cold War period as "the Long Peace" (1987). Yet even here, narratives were vital to making sense of world order. While the Cold War's end appeared to usher in a US-led order or "unipolar moment" (Krauthammer 1990–91), recent analysis has been directed toward predicting and charting the rise of challengers to American dominance in the international system. Goldman Sachs's prediction that Brazil, Russia, China, and India (the so-called BRICS, now joined by South Africa) would come to exert significant geopolitical influence on the basis of economic power by 2050 captured the imagination of scholars and policymakers (Wilson and Purushothaman 2003).

It is striking that even U.S. realist scholars are pointing to the need for a new narrative framework through which actors can make sense of the world. Randall Schweller (2014, 1) writes, "The future hinges on what the present anticipates, on how established and emerging powers portray the coming world and how they intend to act on their present understandings." He sees no clear narrative that different societies and regions can buy into:

> Profound dislocations throughout the global system are causing the narrative of world politics to become an increasingly fragmented and disjointed story. Like a postmodern novel, the plot features a wild menagerie of wildly incongruent themes and unlikely protagonists, as if divinely plucked from different historical ages and placed in a time machine set for the third millennium. (Schweller 2014, 9)

The increasing prominence, confidence, and material power of rising powers (Taylor 2006; Whitney and Shambaugh 2008; Tharoor 2012) appears to put more issues, identities, experiences, grievances, and memories on the table to be taken into account in any future world order.

There is a structural dimension to some of these dynamics, not least a shift of the center of gravity of the global economy from West to East, which has been accentuated by the 2008 financial crisis. But there is also something unusual about the nature of this emerging wave of great power politics itself. This new wave does not seem to present a direct challenge to the predominant position of the United States in world politics, nor lead to a period of hegemonic antagonisms and wars (see Gilpin 1981; Organski and Kugler 1980). That is, the emerging great powers do not seem to act as traditional challengers in a race for global dominance/hegemony (Gilpin 1981; Mearsheimer 2001; Pape 2005). In contrast, what seems to be at issue is *recognition* rather than *domination* or *redistribution*.[1] The aim of the emerging powers seems to be to "register" their status as great powers in world politics, rather than to implement their own global hegemony (Layne 2009; Hurrell 2005; Tharoor 2012). Their aim therefore is not to take the place of the existing sole superpower, but rather to change the context in which this superpower operates, thus expanding their influence and playing a shaping role in an emerging order. Ultimately, they are trying to create a new kind of international system.

As a result, the study of material power is in itself not sufficient to understand the emerging international order. In this vein, Buzan argues that

> loss of material capability is probably not going to be the main factor moving the US away from sole superpower status. The key factors in this move will be social, and they are working both within the US, where the will to support a superpower role may well be waning and outside it, where the US is likely to find ever fewer followers, whether it wants to lead or not. . . . Changes in social support on either the domestic or international level could thus quite quickly shift the US from superpower to great power status. (Buzan 2011, 6)

In international society, the United States—at least under the Obama administrations—did not want to assume the role and material cost of being universal leader.

We offer an original theory of power transition because it is the first to account for the role of communication in a serious way. We must take communication into account because the 21st century media ecology leaves states with no choice but to project and contest strategic narratives in constructing a new order. Previously, diplomacy and state interaction was conducted by transnational elites—figures such as Viscount Castlereagh, Klemens von Metternich, Otto von Bismarck, or Henry Kissinger

(Kissinger 1994; Rothkopf 2009). Today this no longer holds. G8 summits are as much about what happens outside the negotiation room as within it. Suspicions about the Bilderberg meetings are a reflection that acceptance of an order defined by elites without negotiation with domestic and international polities has become contested. The new media ecology[2] increases the participation of a range of actors, including citizens, in international affairs—what Miliband (cited in Bright and Kampfner 2008) calls the "civilian surge" and Anne-Marie Slaughter, Moises Naim, and others call the rise of "the people" as a major force (O'Loughlin 2015). This media ecology also increases the transparency of international interactions. While, strictly speaking, states created the Internet and many states have been part of the rise of satellite television, states are now in a position of reacting to and adapting to the global media ecology.

This changes the nature or constitution of "order." Analysis of power transition helps illuminate this. We argue that there is a change in order (who shapes the international system) and a change of order (how influence or power operate and thus how order is constituted). Strategic narratives are integral to this. We follow Hurrell (2005), Bially Mattern (2005), and others in arguing that how order functions depends on how order is understood: on the underlying common sense of what order is and how it works. Without this shared meaning, actors cannot consent to the legitimacy of an order. States try to construct these meanings or understandings by projecting strategic narratives. Hence, by analyzing how states project and contest strategic narratives we see how rising and established powers try to impose a common sense of how the international system does and should work, including what would be a legitimate legal and institutional basis for order.

Media ecologies enable and constrain state action. Attention to how states communicate narratives in and across national, regional, and transnational media ecologies sheds new light on power transition dynamics. For instance, from the Habermasian perspective of Risse (2000), Lynch (2002), and others, if international relations is conducted under increasing transparency then more states and other actors should be able to communicate more narratives, take into account others' narratives and claims, and rationally determine through dialogue the most compelling narrative. This will have an educating, rationalizing effect on newcomers to the international community; notwithstanding the varying power of different states to project their narratives (the United States, the United Kingdom, Germany, China, Russia, France, and Qatar have multilingual transnational TV stations; Benin, Chad, and Luxembourg do not), states and other actors should become socialized into a new way of carrying out arguments about the future of world order. Or, we might expect increased disruption to order. Transparency makes it very easy to identify a society's sensitivities, its sacred symbols, and social antagonisms. These can then be targeted, as al Qaeda has done in many countries around the world in the past two decades, which has been taken to new levels by the Islamic State. As Fiercke (2013, 12) argues, "The development of a global media has . . . meant . . . that states have greater difficulty excluding alternative narratives or blocking images from view." These dynamics shape and constrain how states form and project their strategic narratives and hence how they try to define the meaning of international order.

By taking into account the changing nature of order and power transition, our thesis presents a strong refutation of universal theories of IR. The positions of G. John Ikenberry and Kenneth Waltz, for instance, seem to rule out any change in how order works and how power transitions will unfold. Indeed, Ikenberry's work offers little scope for even imagining any future power transition, since he presents an inevitable unfolding and expanding of liberal institutions—a vision not far removed from Fukuyama's (1992) "End of History" thesis. Instead, we argue *it is the case not only that there will be future power transitions, but that future power transitions will be different*. Charles Kupchan argues the following:

> [E]merging powers will want to revise, not consolidate, the international order erected during the West's watch. They have different views about the foundation of political legitimacy, the nature of sovereignty, the rules of international trade, and the relationship between the state and society. As their material power increases, they will seek to recast the international order in ways that advantage their interests and ideological preferences. The developmental paths followed by the rising rest represent alternatives to the Western way, not temporary detours on the road to global homogeneity. (Kupchan 2012, 7)

The aim of this chapter is to show how the strategic narrative concept helps explain the views and paths to which Kupchan points. The study of strategic narratives offers us a means to understand and chart the process of recasting the international order. In the chapter that follows we first set out the limitations of the principle scholarship on the question of changing international order, namely power transition theory and neorealism. We argue that they fail to take into account the social, nonmaterial dynamics of international relations through which states negotiate their relative status and ascribe legitimacy to order. In the second part of the chapter we evaluate the work of those who have tried to incorporate these social dynamics into their analysis, for instance work on prestige, socialization, and soft power. A focus on strategic narrative complements and enhances this work by offering an analytical framework to capture how interstate and state-public communications operate. Much International Relations scholarship treats such communication as entirely straightforward, whereas strategic narrative analysis sheds light on the conditions required for communication to actually succeed in creating the intended meaning among audiences. Finally, we demonstrate our arguments by examining the BRICs narrative advanced by Goldman Sachs in the early 2000s, and evaluating how China in particular has responded to its position and role as an emerging great power. We explore the formation of China's narrative about itself and the international system, and the difficulties China has had projecting and managing overseas interpretations of its narrative. China has formed what to Chinese policy elites and publics might seem a coherent narrative about its peaceful rise and the transition to a multipolar order, and it has invested large sums in a range of diplomatic and public diplomacy initiatives to project this narrative. However, once we examine how this narrative is received by different audiences around the world it becomes clear how difficult it is to generate legitimacy for a different vision of international order.

The Limitations of Neorealism and Power Transition Theory

> The world is now interactive and interdependent.
> —Zbigniew Brzezinski (2013)

How power transition is viewed varies markedly depending on which theoretical lens we hold up to the empirical evidence. Neorealism's contention is that the world is moving toward a multipolar order in which the United States and emerging great powers will balance each other and maintain stability. Similarly, Mearsheimer (2001) asserts that in order to maintain their position in the international system, major nations will seek to maximize their power vis-à-vis challengers. Power is defined in terms of economic and military strength. However, Pape (2005) argues that in the face of significant American dominance in military affairs, rising powers will "soft balance," that is, challenge United States' dominance in all areas of interaction, barring defense (see also Paul 2005).[3] Despite studies that contest the existence of soft balancing behavior by emerging states toward the United States (Brooks and Wohlforth 2005; Howorth and Menon 2009; Lieber and Alexander 2005), there are numerous studies debating whether America's influence, particularly under George W. Bush, began to wane (cf. Brooks and Wohlforth 2005; Ikenberry 2003; Layne 2009). Evidence exists to support the idea of American relative material decline (for a review, see Acharya 2014), even if potential rivals are not energetically rushing to challenge Washington's dominance.

Power transition theory counters neorealism's claims that stability is produced through balancing. Abramo Organski claimed that rather than states aiming to balance power in the system, asymmetric power distribution played a greater role in maintaining peace and stability (Organski and Kugler 1980; Kugler and Organski 1989; Dicicco and Levy 1999; Chan 2005; see also Kupchan, Davidson, and Sucharov 2001). The existence of a dominant power, therefore, is a precondition for stability in the system.[4] The dominant power outlines the rules that define the system that other states adhere to. It is only in cases where a dominant power is surpassed by a challenger who is unhappy with the status quo that the conditions exist for the potential of violence in the system. Organski and Kugler (1989) make the following claims about power transition in the international system. The world is not anarchical—rather, it is defined by hierarchies of dominant powers. International and domestic politics are defined by the same dynamics—the competition for scarce resources in the system. Competition in the system is not fundamentally about power accretion—rather, it is about obtaining net gains in the system. Internal economic growth within a country will determine its ability to rise to challenge the status quo. Parity of material power between the dominant and challenger state, combined with a sense of dissatisfaction in the challenger state with the order imposed by the dominant power will—according to Organski— prove the major factor in determining the conditions in which war may occur. Power transition theory, therefore, focuses on quantifying power resources to ascertain tipping points in history when dominant states are challenged by rapidly developing powers (Chan 2005, 2007; Lemke 1997; Kim 1991). Quantifying internal growth in emerging states relative to dominant states is the key focus, although writers such as Woosang Kim (1991) have also pointed to the importance of forging alliances. Houweling and Siccama (1991) also stress the importance of "critical points" in power transitions as key determinants of peaceful or violent transition when opportunities for emerging states are most conducive (see also Doran 1991).

The idea of cyclic development of international orders based on material strength and development is central to power transition theory, to Robert Gilpin's work on war and change and Michael Mann's work.[5] Mann, for instance, argues that for all political systems power is institutionalized. However, as economic, military, ideology, and technology develop, this creates uneven development among polities and groups to the extent that some fall between the institutional cracks and feel disenfranchised within the system. Eventually they unite and "outflank" the existing institutions, and consolidate the new institutional arrangement. This process repeats itself, endlessly. However, neither Gilpin nor Mann examines *how* actors come to understand their interests and opportunities at these junctures. These are taken as transparent and given. That there is competition to frame one's own interests and claims as having definitional primacy over those of others is not accounted for.

Much of the literature on the United States and potential challenges to its dominance in the international system focuses on the potential impact of the transition of power to the East and, in particular, the emerging roles of China and India as foreign policy actors (Acharya 2014, 59–78; Breslin 2010; Chan 2007; Christensen 2006; Fenby 2014; Friedberg 2005, 2015; Grinter 2006; Khong 2014; Kissinger 2014a; Kugler 2006; Pouliot and Thérien 2015; Shambaugh 2005; Zeng, Xiao, and Breslin 2015). Christensen (2006) argues that relations between China and the United States are characterized by positive-sum thinking on developing closer institutional contacts and economic cooperation and negative-sum dynamics on a number of intractable issues such as the status of Taiwan. Relations between the dominant state and potential challengers are characterized not by black-and-white assertions of satisfaction and dissatisfaction, but by a mixture of the two, which further complicates the predictive qualities of power transition theory. It is not that China is fully supportive of the international system or existing wholly in the interstices or cracks between institutions. It has an ambivalent relationship to the existing international order.

"Even those who accept that China's power is growing," argues Friedberg (2005), "and believe that rising powers tend to be dissatisfied, do not necessarily believe that China will behave in an especially assertive or aggressive fashion. This may not simply be a function of China's capabilities but a reflection of its underlying intentions." China has become more active in foreign policy in an attempt to be a more influential player in international affairs, particular within its own region (Medeiros and Fravel 2003). Yet, as Medeiros and Fravel correctly point out, the development of a more engaged foreign policy has significant domestic reverberations within China, at a time of significant adaptation within the country. With such rapid change taking place domestically, Medeiros and Fravel argue that this will limit China's ability to project its foreign policy and go through substantial change in the domestic self-perception of China's role in international affairs. In other words, what kind of foreign policy actor China becomes will have a significant bearing on both China's domestic politics and its national identity. This is evident in Ning's chapter in this volume, which argues that national identity narratives affect Chinese narratives about the emerging system. Developing these ideas further, Friedberg (2005) contends that "[r]ising powers seek not only to secure their frontiers but to reach out beyond them, taking steps to secure access to markets, materials, and transportation routes; to protect their citizens far from home, defend their foreign friends and allies, and promulgate their values; *and, in general, to have what they consider to be their legitimate say in the affairs of their region and of the wider world*" (emphasis added). On this basis it can be argued that a key limitation of power transition theory is its tendency to focus only on material capabilities and the struggle for domination and international hegemony. It thus fails to capture key aspects of the new great power politics (e.g., identity politics), as well as great power politics that is not just about global domination.

From the Material to the Social

Strategic narratives are a means for political actors to construct a shared meaning of the past, present, and future of international politics to shape the behavior of domestic and international actors. We argue and demonstrate in this chapter that great powers do considerable narrative work, not only to gain a voice in shaping power transition, but as a vital component of understanding power in all its elements. As Andrew Hurrell argues,

> To understand power in international relations we must place it side by side with other quintessentially social concepts such as prestige, authority, and legitimacy. A great deal of the struggle for political power is the quest for authoritative control that avoids costly and dangerous reliance on brute force and coercion. It is one of the great paradoxes that, because it so resolutely neglects the social dimensions of power, realism is unable to give a full or convincing account of its own proclaimed central category. (Hurrell 2005, 49)

We argue that by looking at the BRICS' narrative work we can see their attempts to gain prestige, authority, and legitimacy. Interaction is at the center of power transition and international affairs (Lynch 2002). Chafetz et al. argue that

> [e]conomic strength, culture, and ideology lack significance in the international context without international interaction. Without histories of hostility and friendship states lack the experiential basis for developing images of what kinds of states are more likely to be friendly and what kind are likely to be adversarial. (Chafetz, Spirtas, and Frankel 1999, xi)

This presents us with the task of tracing international interactions over time to explain the strategic narratives circulating, being projected, and being contested. This makes communication central to the field of international relations.

Emerging powers try to resolve domestic conflicts or participate in the making of world politics, or both, by articulating and projecting narratives that are based on (counter or new) identity claims. These narratives are both about the identity of these states themselves and their place and stance in world politics. Representations (communications) and the act of projecting a political representation (communicating) have *constitutive* effects, *making* identities and understandings. For example, states projecting a notion of "the West" are successful insofar as nation-states identified as part of the West "*live the experience* of the . . . identity," thinking and acting as if this identity definitely obtained (Bially Mattern 2005, 14). In this way, through "language-power," international order becomes possible.

With regard to the international order this raises the question of which actors have the language-power to shape international order and which do not. While material power can buy TV stations and public relations experts—as we see later in the chapter when we examine China's strategic narrative—it is not decisive here. What Bially Mattern calls "representational force" is a matter of rhetorical, argumentative, and narrative skill, pointing to the "intolerable incongruities and inconsistencies" in rivals' identities and actions (48). Bially Mattern argues that communication is mediated but does not investigate what difference media systems make. We also understand narrative as strategic, but for Bially Mattern's insights to fully "pay out" there is a need to take into account the rich literature in political communication that helps identity how mediation works. Mediation is not a given. This is the contribution we are trying to make.

The soft power debate has addressed the social role of communications in international affairs, but runs into both conceptual and methodological problems. Much focus on the social dimension of power has centered on Joseph Nye's conception of soft power, the idea that actors can achieve influence in international affairs through attraction rather than coercion or payment (Nye 1990). To assert dominance in an international order, material power is not enough (Finnemore 2009; van Ham 2010). The skilled leader blends hard and soft power as best fits the context—what Nye more recently called "smart power," which he describes as the "ability to combine hard and soft power into an effective strategy" (Nye 2008, 43; see also Nye 2011, xiii; Nye 2015, 60). Certainly, this conceptualization allows for public discussion about influence and power-through-communication, and a few studies have tried to explore how states try to harness soft power assets to fulfill some strategic interaction with overseas actors (Bially Mattern 2005). Nevertheless, the concept remains too imprecise for scholarly analysis. It is not clear whether attraction just happens or must be cultivated, at what moment attraction has occurred, and at what moment attraction translates into behavioral change in the targeted actor. "Soft power is a natural by-product of one's values, principles, and behaviour (at home and abroad). It cannot be strategised" (Gary Rawnsley, cited in House of Lords 2014, 133n820). An actor's attempts to promote its soft power run the risk of diminishing the actor's own credibility and the attractiveness of its identity to others. Nor have analysts explored whether audiences find orders, or the states that manage international order, attractive. Due to these conceptual ambiguities, it is extremely difficult to measure or evaluate the presence or effectiveness of soft power (Burchell et al. 2015; Gillespie and O'Loughlin 2015). A number of soft power indexes and league tables exist, but these are based either on experts' subjective assessment of the attractiveness of countries' "assets," such as cultural or sporting institutions, or else based upon surveys of public attitudes toward countries. Such measures become detached from our core concern: power. We argue that influence can be more accurately conceptualized and traced by identifying the narratives through which publics or elites understand their country, others, and the system as a whole (Roselle et al. 2014; others are following our move, for instance, Hartig 2015).

The study of communication of strategic narratives offers the bridge between studies of ideas and social identities, which is so central to mainstream International Relations now (Finnemore 2009; Katzenstein 1996; van Ham 2010), and questions of effects.

If we accept that states are acting strategically to achieve certain ends, how do we know that norm diffusion or socialization has had the intended effects? And how do we identify how the exercise of such power and the unfolding of these social dynamics is shaped by the media systems they work within? Not enough attention has been given to the context in which this power is exercised, nor indeed under what conditions such power proves telling. We turn now to an important recent system narrative, the rise of the BRICS, and then analyze the formation, projection, and reception of one BRICS member, China, to illustrate how this works.

The BRICS Narrative

In 2001 Jim O'Neill (2001) of Goldman Sachs coined the term "BRICs" in a paper that argued that the growing proportion of global economic activity of the four emerging powers Brazil, Russia, India, and China hinted that they should take an increasing role in international organizations responsible for the coordination of global economic policy. This increased role should be at the expense of EU countries. O'Neill effectively provided justification for a narrative of influence passing from "old" to "new" powers. In another Goldman Sachs paper two years later a projection of economic and demographic trends to 2050 presented an even more explicit narrative of a changing international system (Wilson and Purushothaman 2003). It suggested the transition to a multipolar world in which the United States is superseded as the largest economy. Goldman Sachs's purpose was to identify shifting areas of opportunity for economic development and its target audience was private sector investors who looked to Goldman Sachs for such insights. Indeed, many financial firms set up BRICs funds, offering high returns if at a high risk (Shaw, Antkiewicz, and Cooper 2008, 36). Indeed, the term BRICs is significant but not necessarily *analytically* useful in International Relations: there is little to unify these four countries (Stuenkel 2011), and in the last decade of diplomacy and international organization discussions we find changing constellations of emerging powers acting together. The term's significance is *political*: it signifies the prospects of a changing international order in which power and influence are redistributed and the nature of the order may be up for grabs. The report possesses narrativity: it describes a past, present, and future, an obstacle or challenge to be overcome, a cast of actors with different characters, reputations, and interests, and—for investors—a potential happy ending.

The political importance of the BRICs narrative lies to some extent in its performativity: if actors believe the narrative and begin to experience international relations as if that narrative is real, then they may perform it into actuality. Countries may act on the assumption that a multipolar order is definitely emerging, even if in fact the United States retains its economic and military advantages. The Goldman Sachs papers expressed some caution. Their projections rested upon the assumption that the four countries would continue with progrowth policies and institutional change and that each would adapt to any major disruptions (Wilson and Purushothaman 2003). Nevertheless, the analysis operated to shore up a narrative with a past, present, and future, one that would surely excite investors: "The projection of a substantial shift in the generation of growth towards the BRICs is *dramatic*" (10, emphasis added). Indeed, the authors represented their analysis as an automobile race.

According to Goldman Sachs's visualization, the Chinese economic racing car has already overtaken those of the United Kingdom and Germany, and will race on ahead of the United States after 2041. The BRICs team's four cars will already be ahead of the G6 team, overtaking them by 2037. Translated back into International Relations, if it is the "leader" that defines the international order, then China and a BRICs alliance should be challenging for hegemony in the forthcoming decades.

The race metaphor underpins much analysis in a number of recent books seeking to explain China's increasing power. For instance, in *Will China Dominate the 21st Century?* Jonathan Fenby writes:

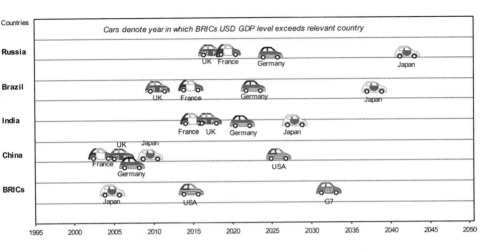

Fig. 11.1. Overtaking the G6: When BRICs' US$GDP would exceed G6

After the woes it suffered between the mid-19th century and the death of Mao in 1976, China has been coming from a long way back, and the more it progresses, the less the incremental effort of each advance and the greater complications that envelop it. (Fenby 2014, 102)

As China surges forward, domestic political and economic tensions develop. Yet in Goldman Sachs's diagram the grid is fixed. States move across a surface that is given and will not change. There are no bends or potholes, such as the 2008 global financial crises. We can infer that the cars are propelled forward by the engine of economic growth, the fuel of industry, rather than due to alliances or regional blocs. There is no need for a winning line or checkered flag for the metaphor to make sense. Fundamental to human cognition is the notion that space can stand for time. Cognitive linguists George Lakoff and Mark Johnson note that we ask for ourselves and for our nations "what's *up ahead of us* in the next century" (1999, 153). The metaphor is grounded in our common, basic experience of having a body that moves and that we experience time passing as we move.[6] In this way, using the car race metaphor gives intuitive sense to the future of the global economy. One did not need to read O'Neill's text: just look at the picture and feel a sense that the BRICs will get ahead.

What happens when the drivers begin to act as if the winners of the race are preordained? Nye (2010) argued that the race was wide open, that the Goldman Sachs analysis did not tell the whole story, and hence policymakers should not act as if matters had been settled. In his analysis of Chinese and American responses to the 2008 financial crisis as the U.S. mortgage and banking industries imploded, Nye notes how voices in both countries assumed this signaled U.S. decline and the confirmation of Goldman Sachs's prediction of Chinese economic supremacy in the 2020s. Nye was writing in the context of a fraught interdependence between the two economies, as China held U.S. dollars but relied on exports to U.S. markets, such that "[i]f it dumped its dollars, China would bring the United States to its knees, but might also bring itself to its ankles" (148). Nye argued that while China's GDP may catch up with that of the United States, its level of technological, societal, and political development will not in the foreseeable future: China lacks cutting-edge science, its rural population is not integrated into the national economy, and the regime lacks political legitimacy, he suggested. Nye was, in effect, putting forth arguments about the meaning of objective structural changes (cf. Nye 2015, 29, 52). If Nye is correct in his diagnosis, this would put limits on the kind of narrative and ambitions China could credibly form and project. His concern was that U.S. policymakers who accepted a narrative of U.S. relative decline would offer concessions they otherwise would not, while Chinese policymakers convinced of that same narrative would make demands they otherwise would not. That narrative itself has effects, hence Nye cautioned:

> China's current reputation for power benefits from projections about the future. Some young Chinese use these projections to demand a greater share of power now. Feeling stronger, they demand greater accommodation of what they consider their "core interests" in Taiwan, Tibet, and the South China Sea. . . . Extrapolating the wrong long-term projections from short-term cyclical events like the recent financial crisis can lead to policy miscalculations. (Nye 2010, 149, 151)

The BRICs narrative becomes one strategically suited to China, which can use its projections of the future to justify advancing its interests today. Where neorealism takes interests as given, we see here how narrative constructions of the *meaning* of changing international relations create altered understandings of interests. We might speculate that, as a commentator close to the U.S. administration, Nye's analysis tacitly reached conclusions that would advance U.S. interests today. He was critiquing the BRICs narrative, identifying how such narratives have effects, but also projecting an alternative narrative, one of sustained U.S. primacy.

But, in fact, the BRICs' own interpretations of this situation are far from straightforward. Based on interviews with Brazilian and Indian foreign policy makers and academics and analysis of public statements, Oliver Stuenkel (2011) concluded that Brazil and India hold ambiguous positions regarding power transition. Here we see how important it is to account for how states make sense of the international system (Hurrell 2005). Brazil and India each position their policies and identities in relation to their particular conception of "the West." Traditionally, their foreign policy elites have been opposed to the West and the Western order, but now that Brazil and India are becoming major powers in that order, they are in an awkward position. Each has formulated a narrative to express their experience of power transition; as Stuenkel (2011, 180) writes, "In both societies, there is a predominant assumption that their nation has a destiny that has yet to be fulfilled." This destiny may require the reform of the international system, yet it is this very system—and its associated processes of globalization—that have enabled the two countries to emerge as major powers. Domestic audiences demand a degree of criticism of the United States and "the West" and solidarity with the global South or developing countries, or both, yet the policy elites of each country are beginning to see from the perspective of those maintaining the current international order. This shows the pragmatics of negotiating power transition in terms of both concrete policy and overarching, strategic narrative.

In the context of the BRICs narrative—and BRICS narrative once South Africa became accepted as part of the group—and these contestations and ambivalences around it, let us look closely at how the biggest of the emerging powers, China, has formed and projected a strategic narrative about power transition.

China's Strategic Narrative in the Context of the BRICS Narrative: Formation

A prevailing assumption in debates about order is that the rising powers will have more voice (e.g., Acharya 2014, 6–9). Greater relative material power will bring positions in international institutions and greater capacity to communicate a rising power's perspective through global television stations and the funding of NGOs. Much attention is therefore given to existing and emerging powers and whether emerging powers will accept or reject the current ideational basis of the international system. What would they use their increased voice for? What order do they want? John Ikenberry (2009), Charles Kupchan (1990), Jeff Legro (2005), and Alistair Ian Johnston (2008) are just some of the scholars dealing with this issue. Explicit in the work of Ikenberry is the role of material incentives for accepting a hegemonic ideational order—that is, emerging powers will be satisfied with existing ideational orders if they stand to gain materially from the existing order (Ikenberry 2009). Ikenberry argues that the principles of the first British and then American-sponsored liberal order are so embedded, or sticky, as Mead (2004) puts it, that even if supervision of the order passes from being an exclusively American responsibility, rising powers will operate within its norms (Ikenberry 2011). In this way Ikenberry is mirroring Gilpin's (1981, 40) distinction between systems change (when fundamental change of the system occurs) and systemic change (when an existing system changes its governance structures). Acceptance of the existing order, we argue, cannot be seen as a given under conditions of power transition. As Legro (2005) argues, crises can often lead to consolidation of existing ideas or their rejection, which results in reinforcement of an order or its replacement (see also Nau 2003, 2011). Legro suggests that "events that contradict the expectations generated by dominant states and their ideas will nurture opportunities for critics of the dominant ideas to attempt to alter the content of structure" (2005, 365). Charting the narratives of emerging powers—how they are formed, projected, and received—offers a chance to chart change and continuity in this period of power transition. The new media ecology provides ample incentive—and competition—for states to seek influence through the use of strategic narratives, moving this process away from the traditional exclusive remit of career diplomats (Kissinger 1994). It will also enable us to assess whether emerging powers can be characterized as challenger or status-quo states (Johnston 2003, 2008). Transition also may be messy and incomplete, neither reflecting a completely new order nor a copy of the existing rules and principles, as Shashi Tharoor argues:

> Global policy makers will have to cope with a growing demand for multilateral cooperation when the international system will be

stressed by the incomplete transition from the old to the new order. And the new players will not want to cooperate under the old rules. (Tharoor 2012, e-book version, 251)

Similarly, Martin Jacques argues that China's response to the liberal order will be one of partial engagement and partial rejection:

In the long term, though, China is likely to operate both within and outside the existing international system, seeking to transform that system while at the same time, in effect, sponsoring a new China-centric international system which will exist alongside the present system and probably slowly begin to usurp it. (Jacques 2009, 362)

The rise of the BRICS and China in particular presents a situation of ambiguity. On the one hand, Ikenberry argues that the liberal international order created and led by the United States after 1945 is now sufficiently embedded in different regions of the world that the United States no longer needs to unilaterally lead it. On issues of security and economy, emerging powers such as China and India are on the whole integrating into the existing order, reproducing it, and extending it. They are not even soft-balancing against the United States.

On the other hand, the BRICS countries themselves hold ambiguous positions vis-à-vis that existing U.S.-created order. They are emerging as great powers within that order, hence to an extent their material interests are being served by it. As they host global sporting events and launch global media organizations, the BRICS countries seek the social status symbols associated with the great powers in the existing order, and yet they may use these to narrate a change *of* order. Their increased material power, and the divergent values, concepts, and perspectives each holds about international order, means they may seek to reform the institutions, rules, and conceptual underpinnings of the existing order.

This ambiguity creates divisions among scholars. Robert Kagan (2009, 2012) suggests that Russia and China integrate selectively on some issues to be able to reassert status, with Russia in particular viewing the world through the lens of 19th-century great power politics. As both countries assert a return to multipolarity, this threatens the West because it indicates not just multiple poles of material power but also multiple value systems and ideas (2009, 71), threatening the U.S. liberal order. Against this, Drezner's (2014) more empirically grounded study of China's role in the aftermath of the 2008 global financial crisis supports a more integrationist narrative. His analysis shows that China acted as a responsible stakeholder in the U.S.-led system (19 and 184). The G20, including China, took steps to manage domestic public pressures and balance currencies for some years after the main 2010 stabilization operations. China abided by WTO and IMF rules even when it had incentives not to. In short, Drezner concludes that the crisis was managed by a "hegemonic coalition" of the United States, the European Union, and China (140).

Understanding how these emerging powers conceive of the emergent system requires a focus on the domestic and international constraints facing both the ability of the United States to accommodate and how the BRICS seek to fashion a new order. Colin Dueck highlights how national cultural reference points limit not only how policy is communicated but also the range of policy options available to policymakers:

> [P]ublic and presidential references to liberal foreign policy goals within the United States are not inconsequential. Such language is used for a reason. At a minimum, policymakers appeal to cultural symbols in order to legitimize their authority as well as their chosen policies. References to common ideals function as a form of communication between policymakers and the public, so that grand strategy takes on a meaning that is intelligible in terms of the national creed. More to the point, the cultural content of policy framing has practical consequences for policy outcomes, in that decision-makers (1) have to tailor their policies to fit their rhetoric in order to maintain public support, and/or (2) actually come to believe their own public statements and therefore follow a different policy than they would have otherwise. (Dueck 2006, 24; see also Layne 2014 and Snyder 2015)

We are not yet seeing a concerted effort by existing and emerging great powers to shape a collective new world order. Rather, with the creation of new institutions such as the Asian Infrastructure Investment Bank, we are witnessing emerging centers of power (Kissinger 2014a, 2014b; Layne 2014; Soros 2015).

This ambiguous situation brings into stark relief why existing theories of power transition are inadequate and why a focus on strategic narratives can help us understand how each actor is seeking to negotiate their way through this transition. The ambivalence of the BRICS to the existing order shows why an account based on material factors and tipping points cannot explain how today's power transition is unfolding. However, simply incorporating "social" or "communication" processes into analysis is not easy, especially when all countries are to some extent projecting their own strategic narrative. For instance, Ramo (2004, 28) argues that "[i]f China wants to achieve Peaceful Rise, it is crucially important that it gets other nations to buy into the world view it proposes." However, such "buy-in" depends on China's narrative being commensurable with the narratives and understandings of the state and international system held by those other nations. As we find below, China is likely to have difficulties achieving this buy-in.

A nation's "image" is tied to images of the international system itself, and the narrative a nation projects must accept associations with narratives of the system. India's situation exemplifies this. As a nuclear weapons power with sometimes awkward relations to regional neighbors Pakistan and China, how India balances its use of military and economic resources against the softer methods of diplomacy or intangible cultural "influence" is important, both for local conflicts (Burma, Afghanistan, Kashmir) and the broader transition this century to a multipolar or nonpolar order (O'Loughlin 2011). India must find a strategic narrative both of itself and as part of the BRICS. It will be interpreted by the United States and the European Union as a stand-alone country but also as part of the trend toward multipolarity identified by Goldman Sachs in 2003. It must craft a narrative that expresses that it is part of a group of powers entitled to a greater say in how the international system is structured and governed. But it must also take advantage of the sense of momentum intrinsic to the BRICS narrative; as Nye said earlier, young Chinese are "feeling stronger" today in international affairs. We would expect the same to be true, then, for young Indians. This points again to the importance of sense-making in international relations, which narratives contribute to. This is vital to how strategic narratives contribute to identities and order.

Narrating a power transition and the "rise" of one's country is risky. Crafting a narrative that sets out a direction of travel without obfuscating internal contradictions and potential pitfalls is very difficult for policymakers to achieve (Snyder 2015). Take the staging of global sporting events. This is something the BRICS have all undertaken since 2000. Brazil hosted the 2014 soccer World Cup and the 2016 Summer Olympics. Russia hosted the 2014 Winter Olympics[7] and will host the 2018 soccer World Cup. India hosted the 2010 Commonwealth Games. When China hosted the 2008 Olympics, it experienced human rights scrutiny as well as protests at torch events leading up to the games (Ding 2011). India experienced similar difficulties for its national prestige and narrative hosting the 2010 Commonwealth Games. Mishra (2012, 883) has documented how news media in Australia, Canada, New Zealand, and the United Kingdom focused on problems in the event preparations in ways that reinforced stereotypes "of India as a third world country that is poor, backward, corrupt and fraught with problems, and thereby challenged its rising status in the world." She cites a *New York Times* report that begins:

> The Commonwealth Games, which opened 12 days ago with the world bracing for the worst, managed to conclude on Thursday without any of the predicted embarrassment or disaster. Stadiums did not collapse. Terrorists did not strike. Fears of disease went *mostly* unrealized. And the closing ceremony was a stirring success. (Yardley 2010, emphasis added)

Such damning with faint praise undercuts any Indian narrative of being an international power with a globalizing economy by reconstructing difference between India and the West, reminding readers of the basis of that difference, and not so subtly pointing out that development has not reached the stage where one can visit India without risk of disease. Hence, even if India has a coherent strategic narrative for its future in the international system, the success of that narrative depends on others. Power is relational (Hurrell 2005).

Sporting events highlight the broader point that even if a state has a clear narrative to project about its rising power and attractive identity, others within the international system will receive and interpret it in unintended ways. We have already established the ambiguous relationship that China, of all the rising powers, has to the existing international system. In the following section we begin to explore China's narrative projection and reception in more detail. In this context, it soon becomes clear that this projection is no guarantee that overseas audiences receive and interpret the strategic narrative in the terms China intended.

China's Problems of Projection and Reception

Since introduction of its "open door" economic policy in the 1970s, China has integrated into the international system in terms of trade and investment flows and membership in international organizations. Nevertheless, it is unclear the extent to which China's integration "involves mutual *acceptance* and *identification*" of and with the system (Wang 2010, 204). At a domestic level, Chinese public opinion of regional and great powers is not favorable: of Chinese citizens surveyed in 2008, 38 percent saw Japan not just negatively but as "an enemy," 34 percent saw the United States as an enemy, and 24 percent saw India that way. When Chinese and U.S. or European citizens disagree on policy it is often because of a more fundamental disagreement on values, reflected in policy choices (Wang 2010). At an elite level, it is not simply that Chinese foreign policy is underpinned by different conceptions of the international system to those held in the EU and the United States. It is that Chinese foreign policy is framed by conceptions *actively and deliberately eschewing* EU and U.S. conceptions of international order. The Chinese leadership is constrained by a need to satisfy domestic constituencies who expect an assertive nationalism; not doing so may lead to audience costs (Fearon 1994), hence the Chinese state continually monitors public opinion to ensure a degree of alignment, as Ning Liao illustrates in chapter 5, this volume.

Chinese foreign policy is underpinned today by three narratives that have emerged historically over centuries as different regimes have responded to both international structures and events and to internal historical and cultural changes. Feng Zhang's (2011) excellent analysis of Chinese scholarly and foreign policy international relations documents makes clear how these three concepts provide the foundations for a coherent Chinese vision of the world. First, China is not just a great power, it is a *Chinese* great power. Western great powers have achieved dominance through zero-sum power politics, according to this analysis. For China to follow such a path to hegemony would be to betray its distinctive moral qualities. An international order featuring this new kind of great power would be a different kind of international order. The second concept is benevolent pacifism. Based on a reading of imperial China that mythologizes its history by suggesting China went to war only as a last resort and when provoked, China today claims to be a benign presence in international relations. This allows for public statements about a "peaceful rise" that have been articulated most clearly, according to Zhang, by the official Zheng Bijan (2005) and two government White Papers (PRC State Council 2005, 2011). The third concept is harmonious inclusion. Until the early 2000s this referred to "harmony with difference," namely an international order characterized by diverse perspectives through which mutual understanding could be reached. All states' views hold legitimacy and the system should seek to include them all. From around 2005 this was redefined to "harmonious world" in official speeches. This concept differs from the "imperial inclusionism" of China's past, namely "China's magnanimous admission of other polities into the family of the Chinese civilization *under* the influence, leadership, or even perhaps domination of the Chinese empire" (Zhang 2011, 8). Rather, no state today should dominate a harmoniously inclusive international order. These three concepts add up to an alternative, multipolar world order—as Buzan argued earlier. This cluster of concepts can underpin a Chinese strategic narrative that aligns closely with the BRICS narrative presented by Goldman Sachs.

How has China projected this narrative in public? After the global media spectacle of the Tiananmen Square crackdown in 1989, the Chinese leadership has renewed its methods to target international as well as domestic audiences (Ding 2011). Institutional change saw the creation of the International Communication Office of the Chinese Communist Party in 1991, and the publication of white papers designed to explain China's position on issues such Tibet, national defense, intellectual property, and climate change. China has used U.S. PR firms such as Hill and Knowlton and Weber Shandwick to help craft its narrative. The numbers of tourists, international students, and people learning Chinese has exploded since the 1980s. It has spent large sums on cultural diplomacy initiatives (Nye 2010), including the 2008 Olympic Games in Beijing; funded a proliferation of Confucius Institutes around the world; and launched cultural diplomacy exchanges with numerous countries' museums and exhibit spaces. China has transformed its international broadcasting capacity as Xinhua News Agency has become a rival to the Associated Press and Reuters among news wire services. CCTV has entered the market of global television channels, offering news in multiple languages, following Al-Jazeera, Russia Today, France 24, CNN, and the BBC. If the motto of the BBC's 2012 Olympic coverage was "bringing the UK to the world and the world to the UK" (Mosey 2008), China is certainly promoting China to the world, though how much of the world is brought to China is certainly a matter of tight control. Narratives of minority ethnic groups within China are suppressed and there are continued efforts to control communication concerning Tibet. China has taken on the media adornments of a great power and is using these to project its distinct great power narrative and status.

China has also understood media as both infrastructure and content (Reuters 2015; *Washington Post* 2014). China limits access for foreign investors seeking to invest in Chinese media firms while investing itself in overseas media or by ensuring business ties between overseas media firms and Chinese businesses (Ding 2011). China is fairly explicit about its "great firewall,"—the fact that bloggers must register with the state, and the fact that people are paid to make pro-China comments on social media sites—China's "50-cent party" (King, Pan, and Roberts 2013). In Africa, China has contributed to the creation of media organizations, thereby providing jobs and infrastructure, but it has also used media to try to shape how events are understood there (Franks and Ribet 2009). Just as with its attempts at media control at home, such efforts in Africa are inevitably political. It is difficult for China to avoid negotiating its contribution to media systems with the host government, which has an interest in constructing a media system that keeps them in power. This jeopardizes China's broader strategic narrative of offering developing countries an apolitical, benevolent hand. The tension could be exploited by counter-narratives, what Bially Mattern earlier called the "intolerable ambiguities" in a state's identity. If it appears willing to work with dictators in Africa, China risks behaving in the manner of Western powers despite claiming to be a unique, *Chinese* great power (Zhang 2011). Equally, China is in a position where it is hard not to be seen to be controlling things. It has the reputation of an authoritarian country. So even if its actions to manage debate at home or abroad are no more controlling, repressive, or invasive the actions taken by the United States or the EU, it will still confirm suspicions outside China.

Another tension concerns China's reluctance to proselytize. Unlike the United States and the EU, Chinese leaders are less forthcoming with universalist new rights and doctrines, nor are they clear that their success is a model for others given that it rests on a unique convergence of circumstances (Drezner 2014). Chinese leaders and intellectuals support a multipolar world of diverse values—on this Kagan is correct. Its expansion into Africa opens up a "say-do gap," the appearance of hypocritically talking of respect but acting as an imperialist. This is indeed an intolerable ambiguity, with which all great powers must contend.

How do audiences around the world make sense of China? When we compare the narrative China actually projects and how it is interpreted, we see how difficult it is for China to achieve the meaning it seeks among its intended audiences. Hongying Wang (2003) analyzed two regular official publications aimed at both foreign and domestic readers, the *Peking Review* (later *Beijing Review*) and the Government Work Reports (*Zhengfu Gongzuo Baogao*). Over the period 1952–2002 Wang found the Chinese government has continually projected China as a peace-loving, developing nation, a victim of foreign aggression and an opponent of global hegemony. Since the end of the Maoist era in the 1970s, the government has projected China less as a socialist, revolutionary state and instead as a major power and international cooperator. In other words, the narrative it has projected reflects the concepts of unique great power, benevolent pacifism, and harmonious inclusion identified by Zhang (2011). The problem is that overseas audiences do not interpret the narrative in those terms. Wang analyzed U.S. public opinion data over almost the same period (1954–2002) and found some shifts in parallel with China's own changing narrative, but some contradictory shifts. Americans agree that China is both a developing country and a major power, but disagree with China's self-image of a peace-loving, cooperative actor. The former attributes are relatively objective—GDP figures justify such opinions—but cooperation can be measured too: China has become a far more active and cooperative participant on many international issues. Wang explains U.S. public perceptions in terms of identity. As an anticommunist, hegemonic developed state, it is easy for U.S. publics to view China as a developing, antihegemonic, aggressive, and uncooperative state. What China projects as positive values are interpreted in the United States as confirming prior suspicions. China has in effect confirmed a stereotype. At the same time, U.S. and other international media draw attention to aspects of Chinese life that are underplayed in Chinese media, namely corruption, inequality, lack of political rights, and environmental degradation (Ding 2011). China cannot control its "image" in the new media ecology. Not only do stories leak out, but any attempt to tighten control of journalists or information flows only reinforces China's reputation. It affects the credibility of China as a narrator of its own and the international system's future.

States must also manage the simple fact that many processes in international affairs are being narrated, for instance narratives of globalization, nature and climate change, different regions or constellations of actors (the BRICS, the global South), or the clash of religions. The effect of strategic narratives depends upon how their audiences interpret these many dimensions and multiple narratives of international order. Consider how Europeans view the competing claims of the United States and China. Kim, Meunier, and Nyiri's (2011) analysis of 2010 survey data showed European attitudes toward China and the United States are positively correlated: those who resent U.S. power feel equally negative about China, while those who welcome U.S. power welcome the rise of China. However, these attitudes reflected individuals' wider feelings toward globalization. Broadly speaking, European publics are divided between "cosmopolitans" "confident of their place in the world" who associate globalization with positive change, and "protectionists" who fear that competition will harm their welfare. For protectionists, a world in which the United States or China, or both, were strong would be a world of threat and insecurity—the EU would lose out, and their livelihoods with it. This poses problems for U.S. or Chinese diplomats and leaders trying to craft a strategic narrative of a 21st-century power transition: what reassures their domestic audiences may unsettle half of Europe. Similarly, Natalia Chaban has found that EU-U.S. relations are evaluated by countries in ways that bear upon specific attitudes toward each (Chaban, Bain, and Stats 2007; Holland and Chaban 2011). Consequently, even if the EU thought its narrative was persuasive to U.S. audiences, it might be simultaneously offending or antagonizing audiences elsewhere.

This shows there are clear, analytically defined reasons why a Chinese strategic narrative of itself or of international order faces problems; indeed, this applies to any state. Creating a narrative of inclusive change is difficult.

In sum, China has a fairly coherent strategic narrative and it has been extremely active in constructing the tools to project its narrative. However, it has no control over how its narrative is received and interpreted around the world, and domestic interests will continue to compete to shape the development of this narrative over time (Hameiri and Jones 2015). China wants to offer an alternative form of international order based upon different, non-Western concepts. For that order to have legitimacy requires other states and populations to consent to it or even endorse it; legitimacy is relational—it is conferred, not intrinsic. China's growing material power puts it in a position to be heard, but that does not entail that other countries will "buy into the world view it proposes" (Ramo 2004, 28).

Conclusion: The Many-Layered Narratives of International Order

Understandings of international order bring together a host of processes, each of which has particular meanings to different leaders, countries, and populations. The BRICS narrative proposed by Goldman Sachs may have been primarily an economic one, but it resonated with existing geopolitical, military, and cultural diagnoses about the rise of China and U.S. relative decline present in those countries in the 1990s (Lynch 2002). The plausibility of the BRICS narrative depended on understandings of contemporary globalization, the likelihood that the United States would allow or preempt challenges, and the skill of these countries to shape international institutions and governance across issue areas. Ultimately, the BRICS narrative of shifting material power reignites the question of "what kind of order we want." It is no surprise that the United States, the EU, and the BRICS countries have all responded in the early 21st century with their competing narratives of the present and future of international order. These narratives are strategic insofar as they describe and prescribe versions of order that serve their particular interests.

There is great uncertainty about both the future of global order and about the nature of the power transition that will get us there. In this chapter we have seen Schweller's unease with a world characterized by "an increasingly fragmented and disjointed story ... the plot features a wild menagerie of wildly incongruent themes and unlikely protagonists" (2014, 9)—this is an order he struggles to make sense of. On the other hand, while Acharya (2014) similarly concludes that any prognosis about the future of order will be speculative, he is at least more comfortable with what he describes as the transition to a "multiplex" order, which, like the cinema, hosts both major blockbusters, art house world cinema from all regions, and a range of mixtures in between, offering audiences a world of perspectives in a contingent but still-present hierarchy. What this collision of plots, novels, and movie analogies expresses is a striving toward the key arguments we have made in this chapter. First, that in a new media ecology, the way power and order are constituted will continue to change. Second, that means we should not ask who is power transitioning to (to China or staying with the United States) but *what kind* of power transition is unfolding.

We can reach a nuanced understanding of how actors are negotiating the current power transition—and the transition-in-the-type-of-power transition—through careful attention to what narratives are and are not projected, what preexisting discourses and alliances constrain those narratives, and how narratives are perceived and understood by others.[8] For this is our ultimate argument. In the context of communication's constitutive role in contemporary order, the study of strategic narratives is heir to Organski and Gilpin because it offers a framework that allows us to analyze the mechanisms driving the general shifts described by Kupchan and Legro, Ikenberry and Nye, thereby containing the anxieties and uncertainties of Schweller and Acharya.

NOTES

1. For the problematic "recognition vs. redistribution," see Fraser (1995).
2. In the introduction to this volume we state that by media ecology "we refer to the simple idea that media technologies can be understood and studied like organic lifeforms. They exist in a complex set of relationships within a specific balanced environment. Rapid developments or a disruptive new technology can upset the existing balance. This impacts upon the entire 'ecology.' Since this ecology is the condition that shapes how information flows and knowledge is spread through a society, a changing ecology impacts upon the distribution and form of authority, legitimacy, and—ultimately—power."
3. Brooks and Wohlforth (2005) and Lieber and Alexander (2005) argue that there is little evidence to support to idea of "soft balancing" as contenders to the United States' preeminent position are largely satisfied with present conditions.
4. Countering this assumption, Monteiro suggests that for the United States to maintain its dominant position through military projection, it will run the risk of regular conflict with emerging powers such as China.
5. Mann (1986, 3), drawing on Ernest Gellner's definition, describes this as neoepisodic.
6. For a discussion of how this has a causal effect on our thinking, see Lakoff and Johnson 1999, 170–211.
7. For analysis of how Russia managed its competing narratives during the Sochi 2014 Winter Games as global attention turned toward coverage of the Ukraine conflict, see Burchell (2015) and Hutchings et al. (2015). On *Russia Today*'s particular role, read Yablokov 2015.
8. Johnston (2013) also raises concerns that if certain unqualified assumptions about Chinese intentions become embedded, it runs the danger of preventing a nuanced response to China's emerging role.

REFERENCES

Acharya, Amitav. *The End of American World Order*. Cambridge: Polity, 2014.
Barnett, Michael, and Martha Finnemore. *Rules for the World: International Organizations in Global Politics*. Ithaca: Cornell University Press, 2004.
Bially Mattern, Janice. *Ordering International Politics: Identity, Crisis and Representational Force*. London: Routledge, 2005.
Bull, Hedley. *The Anarchical Society: A Study of Order in World Politics*. 3rd ed. Basingstoke: Palgrave, 2002.
Breslin, Shaun. "China's Emerging Global Role: Dissatisfied Responsible Great Power." *Politics* 30, no. 1 (2010): 52–62.

Bright, Martin, and John Kampfner. "Interview: David Miliband." *The New Statesman*, January 17, 2008. Accessed August 3, 2016. http://www.newstatesman.com/politics/2008/01/interview-miliband-progressive

Brooks, Stephen G., and William C. Wohlforth. "Hard Times for Soft Balancing." *International Security* 30, no. 1 (2005): 72–108.

Brzezinski, Zbigniew. *Strategic Vision: America and the Crisis of Global Power*. New York: Basic Books, 2013.

Burchell, Kenzie. "Infiltrating the Space, Hijacking the Platform: Pussy Riot, Sochi Protests, and Media Events." *Participations: Journal of Audience and Reception Studies* 12, no. 1 (2015): 659–76.

Burchell, Kenzie, Ben O'Loughlin, Marie Gillespie, and Eva Nieto McAvoy. "Soft Power and Its Audiences: Tweeting the Olympics from London 2012 to Sochi 2014." *Participations: Journal of Audience and Reception Studies* 12, no. 1 (2015): 413–37. http://www.participations.org/Volume%2012/Issue%201/27.pdf

Buzan, Barry. "The Inaugural Kenneth N. Waltz Annual Lecture: A World Order without Superpowers Decentred Globalism." *International Relations* 25, no. 1 (2011): 3–25.

Chaban, Natalia, Jessica Bain, and Katrina Stats. "'Frenemies'? Images of the US-EU Relations in Asia-Pacific Media." *Critical Policy Analysis* 1, no. 1 (2007): 62–96.

Chafetz, Glenn R., Michael Spirtas, and Benjamin Frankel. *The Origins of National Interests*. London: Frank Cass, 1999.

Chan, Steve. "Is There a Power Transition between the US and China? The Different Faces of National Power." *Asian Survey* 45, no. 5 (2005): 687–701.

Chan, Steve. *China, the US and the Power-Transition Theory: A Critique*. London: Routledge, 2007.

Christensen, Thomas J. "Fostering Stability or Creating a Monster? The Rise of China and US Policy toward East Asia." *International Security* 31, no. 1 (2006): 81–126.

Cox, Robert W. "Social Forces, State and the World Order: Beyond International Theory." *Millennium* 10, no. 2 (1981): 116–55.

Cox, Robert W. *Production, Power, and World Order: Social Forces in the Making of History*. Vol. 1. New York: Columbia University Press, 1987.

Cox, Robert W., and Timothy J. Sinclair. *Approaches to World Order*. Cambridge: Cambridge University Press, 1996.

DiCicco, Jonathan M., and Jack S. Levy. "Power Shifts and Problem Shifts: The Evolution of the Power Transition Research Program." *Journal of Conflict Resolution* 43, no. 6 (1999): 675–704.

Ding, Sheng. "Branding a Rising China: An Analysis of Beijing's National Image Management in the Age of China's Rise." *Journal of Asian and African Studies* 46, no. 3 (2011): 293–306.

Doran, Charles F. *Systems in Crisis: New Imperatives of High Politics at Century's End*. Cambridge: Cambridge University Press, 1991.

Drezner, Daniel W. *The System Worked: How the World Stopped Another Great Depression*. New York: Oxford University Press, 2014.

Dueck, Colin. *Reluctant Crusaders: Power, Culture, and Change in American Grand Strategy*. Princeton: Princeton University Press, 2006.

Fearon, James D. "Domestic Political Audiences and the Escalation of International Disputes." *American Political Science Review* 88, no. 3 (1994): 577–92.

Fenby, Jonathan. *Will China Dominate the 21st Century?* Cambridge: Polity, 2014.
Finnemore, Martha. "Legitimacy, Hypocrisy, and the Social Structure of Unipolarity." *World Politics* 61, no. 1 (2009): 58–85.
Franks, Suzanne, and Kate Ribet. "China–Africa Media Relations." *Global Media and Communication* 5, no. 1 (2009): 129–36.
Fraser, Nancy. "From Redistribution to Recognition? Dilemmas of Justice in a 'Post-Socialist' Age." *New Left Review* (1995): 68–68.
Friedberg, Aaron L. "The Future of US-China Relations: Is Conflict Inevitable?" *International Security* 30, no. 2 (2005): 7–45.
Friedberg, Aaron L. "The Debate over US China Strategy." *Survival* 57, no. 3 (2015): 89–110.
Fukuyama, Francis. *The End of History and the Last Man*. New York: Basic Books, 1992.
Gaddis, John Lewis. *The Long Peace: Inquiries into the History of the Cold War*. Oxford: Oxford University Press, 1987.
Gillespie, Marie, and Ben O'Loughlin. "Editorial Introduction: International News, Social Media and Soft Power: The London and Sochi Olympics as Global Media Events." *Participations: Journal of Audience and Reception Studies* 12, no. 1 (2015): 388–412.
Gilpin, Robert. *War and Change in the International System*. Princeton: Princeton University Press, 1981.
Grinter, Lawrence E. "China, the United States, and Mainland Southeast Asia: Opportunism and the Limits of Power." *Contemporary Southeast Asia: A Journal of International and Strategic Affairs* 28, no. 3 (2006): 447–65.
Hameiri, Shahar, and Lee Jones. "Rising Powers and State Transformation: The Case of China." *European Journal of International Relations* (2015). Online first. http://dx.doi.org/10.1177/1354066115578952
Hartig, Falk. "Communicating China to the World: Confucius Institutes and China's Strategic Narratives." *Politics* (2015). Online first. http://dx.doi.org/10.1111/1467 9256.12093
Holland, Martin, and Natalia Chaban. "The EU as an Agent for Democracy: Images of the EU in the Pacific Media 'Mirror.'" *Journal of European Integration* 33, no. 3 (2011): 285–302.
House of Lords. *Power and Persuasion in the Modern World*. London: HM Stationary Office, 2014.
Houweling, Henk W., and Jan G. Siccama. "Power Transitions and Critical Points as Predictors of Great Power War: Toward a Synthesis." *Journal of Conflict Resolution* 35, no. 4 (1991): 642–58.
Howorth, Jolyon, and Anand Menon. "Still Not Pushing Back: Why the European Union Is Not Balancing the United States." *Journal of Conflict Resolution* 53, no. 5 (2009): 727–44.
Hurrell, Andrew. "Power, Institutions, and the Production of Inequality." In *Power in Global Governance,* edited by Michael Barnett and Raymond Duvall, 33–58. Cambridge: Cambridge University Press, 2005.
Hutchings, Stephen, Marie Gillespie, Ilya Yablokov, Ilia Lvov, and Alexander Voss. "Staging the Sochi Winter Olympics 2014 on Russia Today and BBC World News: From Soft Power to Geopolitical Crisis." *Participations: Journal of Audience and Reception Studies* 12, no. 1 (2015): 630–55.

Ikenberry, G. John. "Is American Multilateralism in Decline?" *Perspectives on Politics* 1, no. 3 (2003): 533–50.

Ikenberry, G. John. "Liberal Internationalism 3.0: America and the Dilemmas of Liberal World Order." *Perspectives on Politics* 7, no. 1 (2009): 71–87.

Ikenberry, G. John. "The Future of the Liberal World Order." *Foreign Affairs* 90, no. 3 (2011): 56–68.

Ikenberry, G. John. *Liberal Leviathan: The Origins, Crisis, and Transformation of the American World Order*. Princeton: Princeton University Press, 2012.

Ikenberry, G. John, and Charles A. Kupchan. "Socialization and Hegemonic Power." *International Organization* 44, no. 3 (1990): 283–315.

Jacques, Martin. *When China Rules the World: The End of the Western World and the Birth of a New Global Order*. London: Penguin, 2009.

Johnston, Alastair Iain. "Is China a Status Quo Power?" *International Security* 27, no. 4 (2003): 5–56.

Johnston, Alastair Iain. *Social States: China in International Relations, 1980–2000*. Princeton: Princeton University Press, 2008.

Johnston, Alastair Iain. "How New and Assertive Is China's New Assertiveness?" *International Security* 37, no. 4 (2013): 7–48.

Kagan, Robert. *The Return of History and the End of Dreams*. New York: Vintage, 2009.

Kagan, Robert. *The World America Made*. New York: Alfred Knopf, 2013.

Katzenstein, Peter J., ed. *The Culture of National Security: Norms and Identity in World Politics*. New York: Columbia University Press, 1996.

Kennedy, Paul. *The Rise and Fall of Great Powers*. New York: Random House, 1988.

Khong, Yuen Foong. "Primacy or World Order? The United States and China's Rise—a Review Essay." *International Security* 38, no. 3 (2014): 153–75.

Kim, Soo Teon, Sophie Meunier, and Zsolt Nyiri. "Yin and Yank: Relations between Public Opinion towards China and the U.S. in Europe." Paper prepared for the workshop "The Politics of Anti-Americanism," Princeton, May 13, 2011. Accessed August 12, 2012. http://www.princeton.edu/~smeunier/KimMeunierNyiri%20Final%20January%202012.pdf

Kim, Woosang. "Alliance Transitions and Great Power War." *American Journal of Political Science* 35, no. 4 (1991): 833–50.

King, Gary, Jennifer Pan, and Margaret E. Roberts. "How Censorship in China Allows Government Criticism but Silences Collective Expression." *American Political Science Review* 107, no. 2 (2013): 326–43.

Kissinger, Henry. *Diplomacy*. New York: Pocket Books, 1994.

Kissinger, Henry. *World Order: Reflections on the Character of Nations and the Course of History*. London: Penguin UK, 2014a.

Kissinger, Henry. "Henry Kissinger on the Assembly of a New World Order: The Concept That Has Underpinned the Modern Geopolitical Era Is in Crisis." *Wall Street Journal*, August 29, 2014b. Accessed August 30, 2014. http://online.wsj.com/articles/henry-kissinger-on-the-assembly-of-a-new-world-order-1409328075

Koivisto, Marjo, and Tim Dunne. "Crisis, What Crisis? Liberal Order Building and World Order Conventions." *Millennium–Journal of International Studies* 38 (2010): 615–40.

Krauthammer, Charles. "The Unipolar Moment." *Foreign Affairs* 70, no. 1 (1990–91): 23–33.

Kugler, Jacek. "The Asian Ascent: Opportunity for Peace or Precondition for War?" *International Studies Perspectives* 7, no. 1 (2006): 36–42.
Kugler, Jacek, and A. F. K. Organski. "The End of Hegemony?" *International Interactions* 15, no. 2 (1989): 113–28.
Kupchan, Charles A. *No One's World*. Oxford: Oxford University Press, 2012.
Kupchan, Charles, Jason Davidson, and Mira Sucharov, eds. *Power in Transition: The Peaceful Change of International Order*. Tokyo and New York: United Nations University Press, 2001.
Lakoff, George, and Mark Johnson. *Philosophy in the Flesh: The Embodied Mind and Its Challenge to Western Thought*. New York: Basic Books, 1999.
Layne, Christopher. "The Waning of US Hegemony—Myth or Reality? A Review Essay." *International Security* 34, no. 1 (2009): 147–72.
Layne, Christopher. "America's View of China Is Fogged by Liberal Ideas." *Financial Times*, August 13, 2014. Accessed August 14, 2014. https://next.ft.com/content/6971dec4-22d3-11e4-8dae-00144feabdc0
Legro, Jeffrey. *Rethinking the World: Great Power Strategies and International Order*. Ithaca: Cornell University Press, 2005.
Lemke, Douglas. "The Continuation of History: Power Transition Theory and the End of the Cold War." *Journal of Peace Research* 34, no. 1 (1997): 23–36.
Lieber, Keir A., and Gerard Alexander. "Waiting for Balancing: Why the World Is Not Pushing Back." *International Security* 30, no. 1 (2005): 109–39.
Linklater, Andrew. *Critical Theory and World Politics: Citizenship, Sovereignty and Humanity*. London: Routledge, 2007.
Linklater, Andrew, and Hidemi Suganami. *The English School of International Relations: A Contemporary Reassessment*. Cambridge: Cambridge University Press, 2006.
Lynch, Marc. "Why Engage? China and the Logic of Communicative Engagement." *European Journal of International Relations* 8, no. 2 (2002): 187–230.
Mann, Michael. *The Sources of Social Power*. Vol. 1, *A History of Power from the Beginning to AD 1760*. Cambridge: Cambridge University Press, 1986.
Mead, Walter Russell. "America's Sticky Power." *Foreign Policy* 141, no. 1 (March 2004): 46–53.
Mearsheimer, John J. *The Tragedy of Great Power Politics*. New York: W. W. Norton, 2001.
Medeiros, Evan S., and M. Taylor Fravel. "China's New Diplomacy." *Foreign Affairs* 82, no. 6 (2003): 22–35.
Mishra, Suman. "'The Shame Games': A Textual Analysis of Western Press Coverage of the Commonwealth Games in India." *Third World Quarterly* 33, no. 5 (2012): 871–86.
Miskimmon, Alister. "German Foreign Policy and the Libya Crisis." *German Politics* 21, no. 4 (2012): 392–410.
Miskimmon, Alister, Ben O'Loughlin, and Laura Roselle. *Strategic Narratives: Communication Power and the New World Order*. New York: Routledge, 2013.
Monteiro, Nuno P. *Theory of Unipolar Politics*. Cambridge: Cambridge University Press, 2014.
Mosey, Roger. "London 2012: The Biggest Event, the Biggest Challenge." BBC Sport, December 3, 2008. Accessed March 26, 2015. http://www.bbc.co.uk/blogs/legacy/sport editors/2008/12/london_2012_the_biggest_event.html
Nau, Henry R. "Identity and the Balance of Power in Asia." In *International Relations*

Theory and the Asia-Pacific, edited by G. John Ikenberry and Michael Mastanduno, 224–30. New York: Columbia University Press, 2003.

Nau, Henry R. "Ideas Have Consequences: The Cold War and Today." *International Politics* 48, no. 4 (2011): 460–81.

Nye, Joseph S. "Soft Power." *Foreign Policy* No. 80 (1990): 153–71.

Nye, Joseph S. *Soft Power: The Means to Success in World Politics*. New York: Public Affairs, 2004.

Nye, Joseph S., Jr. *The Power to Lead*. New York: Oxford University Press, 2008.

Nye, Joseph S., Jr. "American and Chinese Power after the Financial Crisis." *Washington Quarterly* 33, no. 4 (2010): 143–53.

Nye, Joseph S. *The Future of Power*. New York: Public Affairs, 2011.

Nye, Joseph S. *Is the American Century Over?* Cambridge: Polity, 2015.

O'Loughlin, Ben. "India's Soft Power Is Unclear." *Duck of Minerva* blog, February 20, 2011. Accessed August, 12 2012. http://duckofminerva.blogspot.co.uk/2011/02/indias-soft-power-is-unclear.html

O'Loughlin, Ben. "The Shadow People." Keynote presentation, 8th International Conference on Communication and Reality, "Negotiating (In)Visibility: Managing Attention in the Digital Sphere," Blanquerna, University Ramon Llull, Barcelona, June 4–5, 2015.

O'Neill, Jim. "Building Better Global Economic BRICs." Goldman Sachs Global Economics Paper 66. New York, 2001. Accessed August 16, 2012. http://www.goldmansachs.com/our-thinking/topics/brics/brics-reports-pdfs/build-better-brics.pdf

O'Neill, Jim. "How Solid Are the BRICs?" Goldman Sachs Global Economics Paper 134. New York, 2005. Accessed August 16, 2012. http://www.goldmansachs.com/our-thinking/topics/brics/brics-reports-pdfs/how-solid.pdf

Organski, Abramo F. K. *World Politics*. New York: Knopf, 1958.

Organski, Abramo F. K., and Jacek Kugler. *The War Ledger*. Chicago: University of Chicago Press, 1980.

Pape, Robert A. "Soft Balancing against the United States." *International Security* 30, no. 1 (2005): 7–45.

Paul, Thazha V. "Soft Balancing in the Age of US Primacy." *International Security* 30, no. 1 (2005): 46–71.

Pouliot, Vincent, and Jean-Philippe Therien. "The Politics of Inclusion: Changing Patterns in the Governance of International Security." *Review of International Studies* 41, no. 2 (2015): 211–37.

PRC State Council. "*China's Peaceful Development Road*." Beijing, 2005. Accessed August 16, 2012. http://www.gov.cn/zwgk/2005-12/22/content_134060.htm

PRC State Council. *China's Peaceful Development*. Beijing, 2011. Accessed August 16, 2012. http://www.gov.cn/zwgk/2011-09/06/content_1941258.htm

Ramo, Joshua Cooper. *The Beijing Consensus*. London: Foreign Policy Centre, 2004.

Reuters. "China's Xi Urges Young, New Media Workers to Lead Rejuvenation of Nation." May 21, 2015. Accessed May 21, 2015. http://www.reuters.com/article/2015/05/21/us-china-xi-media-idUSKBN0O60C420150521

Risse, Thomas. "'Let's Argue!': Communicative Action in World Politics." *International Organization* 54, no. 1 (2000): 1–39.

Roselle, Laura, Alister Miskimmon, and Ben O'Loughlin. "Strategic Narrative: A New Means to Understand Soft Power." *Media, War and Conflict* 7, no. 1 (2014): 70–84.

Rothkopf, David. *Running the World: The Inside Story of the National Security Council and the Architects of American Power.* New York: PublicAffairs, 2009.

Schweller, Randall L. *Maxwell's Demon and the Golden Apple: Global Discord in the New Millennium.* Baltimore: Johns Hopkins University Press, 2014.

Shambaugh, David L., ed. *Power Shift: China and Asia's New Dynamics.* Berkeley: University of California Press, 2005.

Shaw, Timothy M., Agata Antkiewicz, and Andrew F. Cooper. "The Logic of the B(R) ICSAM Model for Global Governance." In *Emerging Powers in Global Governance: Lessons from the Heiligendamm Process,* edited by Andrew F. Cooper and Agata Antkiewicz. Toronto: Wilfrid Laurier University Press, 2008.

Slaughter, Anne-Marie. *A New World Order.* Princeton: Princeton University Press, 2004.

Snyder, Jack. "Dueling Security Stories: Wilson and Lodge Talk Strategy." *Security Studies* 24, no. 1 (2015): 171–97.

Soros, George. "A Partnership with China to Avoid World War." *New York Review of Books,* July 9, 2015. Accessed June 23, 2015. http://www.nybooks.com/articles/archives/2015/jul/09/partnership-china-avoid-world-war/

Stuenkel, Oliver. "Identity and the Concept of the West: The Case of Brazil and India." *Revista Brasileira de Política Internacional* 54, no. 1 (2011): 178–95.

Taylor, Ian. "China's Oil Diplomacy in Africa." *International Affairs* 82, no. 5 (2006): 937–59.

Tharoor, Shashi. *Pax Indica: India and the World in the 21st Century.* New Delhi and New York: Allen Lane, 2012.

Van Ham, Peter. *Social Power in International Politics.* London: Routledge, 2010.

Waltz, Kenneth N. *Theory of International Politics.* London: McGraw-Hill, 1979.

Wang, Hongying. "National Image Building and Chinese Foreign Policy." *China: An International Journal* 1, no. 1 (2003): 46–72.

Wang, Hongying. "Understanding the Intangible in International Relations: The Cultural Dimension of China's Integration with the International Community." In *China and International Relations: The Chinese View and the Contribution of Wang Gungwu,* edited by Yongnian Zheng. New York: Routledge, 2010.

Washington Post. "Chinese President Xi Jinping Takes Charge of New Cyber Effort." February 29, 2014. Accessed February 29, 2014. https://www.washingtonpost.com/world/chinese-president-takes-charge-of-new-cyber-effort/2014/02/27/a4bffaac-9fc9-11e3-b8d8-94577ff66b28_story.html

Wendt, Alexander. *Social Theory of International Politics.* Cambridge: Cambridge University Press, 1999.

Whitney, Christopher B., and David Shambaugh. "Soft Power in Asia." Chicago Council on Global Affairs and East Asia Institute (2008): 1–45.

Wilson, Dominic, and Roopa Purushothaman. "Dreaming with BRICs: The Path to 2050." New York: Goldman Sachs Global Economics Paper 99, 2003. Accessed August 12, 2012. http://www.ucema.edu.ar/u/rfl03/Preferred_papers/gs-BRICs.pdf

Yablokov, Ilya. "Conspiracy Theories as a Russian Public Diplomacy Tool: The Case of

Russia Today (RT)." Politics (2015). Online first. http://dx.doi.org/10.1111/1467 9256.12097

Yardley, Jim. "India Declares Commonwealth Games a Success." *New York Times*, October 14, 2010. August 12, 2012. http://www.nytimes.com/2010/10/15/world/asia/15india.html?_r=1&hpw

Zeng, Jinghan, Yuefan Xiao, and Shaun Breslin. "Securing China's Core Interests: The State of the Debate in China." *International Affairs* 91, no. 2 (2015): 245–66.

Zhang, Feng. "The Rise of Chinese Exceptionalism in International Relations." *European Journal of International Relations* 19, no. 2 (2011): 305–28.

Zheng, Bijan. "China's 'Peaceful Rise' to Great Power Status." *Foreign Affairs* 84, no. 5 (2005): 18–24.

12 | Conclusions

Alister Miskimmon, Ben O'Loughlin, and Laura Roselle

This volume has made three advances in the study of international relations and communication. First, the chapters show the *durability* of the strategic narrative concept. They demonstrate how the dynamics of formation, projection, and reception and our three narrative types operate across a range of case studies. Second, the volume illustrates the *inclusivity* of the strategic narrative approach. Authors explored different points on the spectrum of persuasion without guidance from the editors, in ways that enrich our understanding of how influence works. Third, the volume shows the continued *potential* of the strategic narrative approach. All authors added ideas beyond what we, the editors, expected and developed aspects of the original framework in different ways. The chapters add significantly to the study of strategic narratives and provide insight into methodological issues associated with the study of strategic narratives. All of the chapter authors were asked to take on big issues in international relations today, as the chart below outlines.

Conceptually, the result of these engagements with the concept of strategic narrative was to expand insights and suggest future research paths for students and analysts of international relations and communication. Below, we also draw out the methodological insights generated by the authors and practical lessons for policymakers, activists, and others doing politics. Finally, we offer areas for future research and some final thoughts on strategic narrative as an emerging field of study.

TABLE 12.1. Chapter Summaries

Chapter and Author	Issue	Conceptual Insights
Chapter 3 Roselle	Great powers (United States and Russia)	Identity narratives can undermine attempted changes in international system narratives
Chapter 4 Miskimmon	European Union	The EU's narrative of an emerging cosmopolitan supranationalism conflicts with views of citizenship based on the nation-state. Who narrates matters.
Chapter 5 Liao	China	Narratives can trap political leaders, e.g., victimization narrative conflicts with peaceful rising power narrative.
Chapter 6 Singh	International development	Organization/institutional structures and personnel affect the formation and projection of strategic narratives.
Chapter 7 Brown	Public diplomacy	There is an interdependent relationship between relationships (networks) and narratives.
Chapter 8 Arsenault, Hong, and Price	Arab Uprising and after	Strategic narratives are entangled with institutionalized systems of promotion and legitimation that go beyond rhetorical strategy in determining their fate.
Chapter 9 Archetti	Terrorism	Narratives are not simply transmitted, but are constantly reinterpreted.
Chapter 10 O'Loughlin	Uncertainty and risk	The information infrastructure affects how states communicate around a breaking international event/crisis, raising new questions about credibility.
Chapter 11 Miskimmon and O'Loughlin	Transition and order	Power transitions now occur in the conditions of a global media ecology in which states must narrate to multiple audiences; this more transparent order affects how states achieve legitimacy for their narrative.

Conceptual Insights

A number of chapters engaged with the concept of the international system itself and the ongoing process of narrativization associated with transition after the Cold War. Roselle's chapter showed that domestic political considerations associated with the projection of military force in the 1990s and 2000s undermined the formation and projection of a new system narrative or new world order. Both in the United States and in the Russian Federation, identity narratives setting out expectations about how superpowers "should" behave hindered the ability to project resonant system narratives. Miskimmon and O'Loughlin's chapter on transitions and order suggests that the study of material power is in itself not sufficient to understand the emerging international order—we must understand strategic narratives. As they note, "by analyzing how states project and contest strategic narratives we see how rising and established powers try to impose a common sense of how the international system does and should work, including what would be a legitimate legal and institutional basis for order." Add to this a new media ecology that affects how states achieve legitimacy for their narrative. An analysis of strategic narratives shows us that there is a change in order (who dominates the international system) and a change of order (how power operates and thus how order is constituted).

A second conceptual issue addressed by a number of chapters is the importance of understanding the relationship between system, identity, and policy or issue narratives. This is clear in Liao's discussion of the conflict between China's identity narrative of victimhood, which appeals to a domestic audience, and its system narrative of a peaceful rising power. Victimhood overrelies on "othering" and suggests the need for vigilance and the reassertion of strength, which may undermine the credibility of a peaceful rise to an international audience. Likewise, leaders in the United States and Russia asserted a great power identity narrative about war that clashed with a more cooperative and horizontal international system order. Miskimmon's analysis of the European Union adds to this conceptualization the idea of multiple identity narratives that are difficult to reconcile. National or state identity narratives may challenge a European identity narrative, for example.

Not only is it important to understand how system and identity narratives resonate or clash, but the contestation of narratives across and within states and international organizations is a fruitful area for study. This is demonstrated by a number of contributions to this book. Miskimmon's EU chapter stresses this, as does Singh's chapter on narratives of international development. Singh points to the importance of understanding the role of technocrats within international organizations in constructing strategic narratives, for example.

While some authors focus on system and identity narratives, other authors concentrate more squarely on policy narratives. Arsenault, Hong, and Price, for example, address behavioral power and strategic narratives. They focus on strategic narratives about the Arab Uprising. This is not to say that they, too, do not bring in other narratives as they argue that "narratives derive their normative efficacy from the way they interpolate people and things into preexisting roles and positions, including the audience."

Although many of the chapters analyze the formation of strategic narratives, new insights on their projection are found here too. Brown's rich discussion of networks and strategic narrative projection in the realm of public diplomacy is important because it highlights the role of relationships in the communicative process. He notes that "[t]here is an interdependent relationship between relationships and narratives" as relationships provide a conduit for the projection of narratives *and* narratives can give meaning to networks. Also, Brown points out that political actors operate within multiple networks and this, too, affects the projection of strategic narratives. Archetti develops an important argument suggesting that "narratives are socially and relationally constructed rather than merely being 'scripted messages.'"

Many of the authors engaged with the important idea—central to the strategic narrative framework—that the communicative process matters, and the new media ecology has important implications for the projection and reception of strategic narratives. Miskimmon and O'Loughlin argue that power transition itself now occurs in the conditions of a global media ecology in which states must narrate to multiple audiences; this more transparent order affects how states achieve legitimacy in the international system. O'Loughlin concludes that the objective character of risks is changing under conditions of globalization and technological change. As many authors note, there are many more channels through which narratives can move, more chances for narratives to be disrupted, and yet political elites still have the upper hand in communicating their own narratives in many cases. Liao shows this in the case of China, even as commercialized media plays a role in the projection of narratives.

Finally, conceptually all of this is wrapped up in understanding how strategic narratives are received. The authors included here advance our understanding of reception by looking at it from different angles. Arsenault, Hong, and Price, for example, focus on the "effectiveness" of narratives, arguing that effectiveness depends (in part) on the nature of the internal opposition, the military and political power of the target, the strength of contesting narratives, and geopolitical considerations. Archetti focuses more directly on the role of the individual human being and strategic narrative, and suggests that understanding individual agency is central to understanding the effects of strategic narratives. She argues that

> an extremist group is not the result of an external narrative being received and internalized by the individual, as if the collective narrative of the group substituted for the individual one. Becoming part of an extremist group means rather having developed, as a result of shifting patterns of relationships, an individual narrative that is compatible with the collective narrative of the group. Individual and collective narratives coexist.

The important point here is that narratives are not received as most notably depicted in the old (and discredited) hypodermic model. Narratives are important to human beings because of how human beings live with those narratives. Roselle makes this point as well. Formation, projection, and reception are inextricably linked and iterative in nature. Narratives are collectively constructed.

Methodological Insights

The discussion of conceptual insights offered by the works included here brings us to important methodological insights related to the study of strategic narratives. Case study selection is important, as are methods for assessing the formation, projection, and reception of narratives.

Most of the authors developed case studies to explore strategic narratives in a particular international relations realm or issue. Roselle, for example, chose to look at two great powers, the United States and the Russian Federation, and then examined how specific wars affected the formation and projection of new system narratives. She broke down the categories of formation, projection, and reception quite starkly even as she recognizes that these conceptual categories overlap and may affect one another. This is one of the challenges of research in this area. The communication process is complicated. We would argue that this is why case studies are particularly important for teasing out how, when, and why strategic narratives matter.

Some authors chose to analyze two or more cases so that comparisons could be made and conclusions drawn:

- Arsenault, Hong, and Price studied strategic narratives related to Libya and Syria;
- Roselle studied the United States (First Iraq War and Second Iraq War) and Russia (First Chechen War and Second Chechen War);
- Singh's analysis within and across the World Bank, the World Trade Organization, the United Nations Development Program, and UNESCO as the Millennium Development Goals were developed focused on three substantive areas and strategic narratives:
  - institutions,
  - poverty and human development, and
  - participatory development;
- Miskimmon's chapter on specific political actors during the Eurozone crisis: Mario Draghi, president of the European Central Bank, and Angela Merkel, the German chancellor;
- Brown's study of the efforts to influence American policy prior to the U.S. entry into the First World War in the cases of Germany, France, and the United Kingdom.

Comparative case studies provide insight into how strategic narratives are formed by different political actors and in different contexts.

Other authors focused on single-case studies, emphasizing the importance of understanding strategic narrative processes within one country over time:

- O'Loughlin's study of Japan;
- Brown's separate analyses of the campaign by Russia to

influence Western policy during the 2013–14 Ukraine Crisis and the information activities of the Islamic State organization in 2014;
- Miskimmon and O'Loughlin's separate cases on the BRICS and China.

Both state and nonstate actors may develop and project strategic narratives as the cases demonstrate. In addition, cases may be used as illustrative, as the BRICS case is, or as in-depth analyses of multiple processes associated with strategic narratives, as is O'Loughlin's Japan case.

Case selection is important, but so is choice of methods used for analysis of strategic narratives within those cases. Most of the authors, when assessing how political elites form and project strategic narratives, study how speeches and other types of communication are constructed and disseminated. Miskimmon, for example, analyzes European Security Strategy documents as well as the public pronouncements of particular leaders. Roselle studies a set of speeches for leaders in her cases. O'Loughlin notes, however, that it is important to recognize that political leaders do not develop strategic narratives in isolation. In his case study of Japan he uses a mix of data: "statements of political leaders and—through social media—local officials and citizens; domestic and international news reports; scientific and official reports; and secondary scholarly and think tank studies that have emerged rapidly since the events." All of the authors identify narratives within these texts, distinguishing actors, setting, conflict or action, behavior, and (desired) resolution or goals. In most cases this is not done in a rote or strict way. Interestingly, many of the authors suggest that phrases, images, or metaphors can stand in for, or trigger, narratives. This is an area that would benefit from further study.

Included in an analysis of the projection of strategic narrative is how communication works, often with special attention to the world's new media ecology. Analyzing media content to see how narratives are depicted is tied to methodologies of content analysis and framing analysis. Roselle's analysis of media coverage of the Iraq and Chechen wars is traditional in that way. But O'Loughlin and Arsenault, Hong, and Price, among others, point out that tracing narratives across different types of media is important as well. Brown notes that narratives can be traced in organizations as well as within media.

Areas for Future Research

A first area for strategic narrative research to explore is whether narratives can be used to overcome tensions between self and mutual interests in international relations. We started writing about strategic narratives because we thought that if actors could share an experience of the world then conflict between them would become less likely (Miskimmon, O'Loughlin, and Roselle 2013, ix). It is not that a shared narrative would lead to shared interests, but at least if states, regions, and peoples could agree on the common features of the world, the dilemmas coming up, and how they might be addressed, then a common sense of past, present, and future might emerge. Within this horizon, conflicts of interest could be negotiated. This question brings up two acute theoretical and political problems.

First, can we agree on what exists in the common world? Who sets the terms of what counts as "the conversation" in international relations and what is a valid item to take into account in the conversation (Latour 1993, 2004, 2010)? Which gods, which events, whose histories, whose grievances? The realist International Relations scholar Randall Schweller writes:

> Profound dislocations throughout the global system are causing the narrative of world politics to become an increasingly fragmented and disjointed story. Like a postmodern novel, the plot features a wild menagerie of wildly incongruent themes and unlikely protagonists, as if divinely plucked from different historical ages and placed in a time machine set for the third millennium. (Schweller 2014, 9)

Will the range of valid items up for debate in international affairs be limited to those that can be represented in narrative communication? What seems a legitimate historical memory to some may seem "divinely plucked" to others.

The second problem concerns how to reconcile different interests. The "new" public diplomacy has emerged in recent years to advocate that states seek to manage relationships with overseas publics in a positive-sum manner (Gilboa 2008; Melissen 2005; Pamment 2012; Zaharna, Arsenault, and Fisher 2013). States should understand that their narratives and interests are always in relation to others', so that engagement and dialogue become more effective forms of statecraft than simply projecting one's values. It is a strand of research that our strategic narrative studies draw upon because it is concerned with international communication between political actors including states and societies. From the new public diplomacy perspective, Kathy Fitzpatrick writes, "A truly relational public diplomacy requires a worldview that sees public diplomacy as a means for achieving *mutual* understanding and advancing *shared* interests among nations and peoples" (2013, 30, italics in original). Fitzpatrick makes the excellent point that states cannot start from realist principles and then tack on some warm and fuzzy relational rhetoric about engagement. Public diplomacy cannot be a means to gain power at others' expense. But this creates a dichotomy between self-interest on the one hand and dialogue and "mutuality" on the other. With self-interested foreign policy, the actor is not willing to change. With foreign policy based on mutuality, all parties are open to change. Fitzpatrick writes that mutuality and reciprocity "does not mean that national self-interest should be subordinated to other interests" (35). This simply puts national interest first. Can we overcome this trap?

Can media help create narrative alignment? News media in individual countries often create settled narratives of events, anchoring breaking events within that trajectory of a meaning of history in a way that makes the new events resonant for audiences. There are narrative-bites such as "recovering from the financial crisis" or "the rise of the BRICS" used by journalists. To the extent that these are used by journalists in many countries, this may help form an international shared common sense of how the world is changing. For example, when Barack Obama won the U.S. presidency in 2008, news media around the world contained reports asking whether Obama would align U.S. interests with those of other countries to a greater degree than his predecessor George W. Bush. Hayden (2011, 788) observed that Obama's "rhetoric [seemed to be] resonating with a kind of global norm." It was no surprise to find statements such as those by Wanh Jisi, dean at Beijing University, who said Obama's presidency indicates "America's adoption to the 'trend' of the world" (ibid.). While such statements express the assumption that such a global norm or trend-of-the-world exists, we can see in such moments how narrative alignment might be crafted. News media gave a platform to such statements and thereby contributed to such alignment.

Networks are a second area for future strategic narrative research. Brown's chapter makes a powerful case that the key to tracing influence is to take into account how social networks function. During World War I,

Britain and France were able to short-circuit the communications of Germany with German Americans, allowing their narrative to gain greater uncontested exposure. This success depended on understanding how the German diaspora functioned. Similarly, Russia is able to communicate effectively in social networks already and historically committed to Russian interests, but Russian communications outside those networks have little purchase. The result is that few in the West have been persuaded by Russia's narrative of the 2013–14 Ukraine Crisis.

This suggests that political context shapes whether narratives have much impact. If two countries are already close, then a new narrative will make little difference to their reciprocal behavior. Their identity relations are routinized and embedded. These are hypotheses that require further testing. Zaharna (2013) asks how networks interact and how narratives move through these overlapping webs of relations. Arsenault (2013) asks how infrastructure shapes those network interactions. Zhang (2013) suggests that while interactions are often routinized, as Brown's chapter illustrates, there are moments of surprise and chaos that offer opportunity to inject a narrative. An ambassador can make an unexpected gesture that journalists—and citizens on Twitter—can narrativize themselves before officials can respond. But for all the attention to virality and memes in contemporary public debate, based on Brown's analysis we would hypothesize that these make little difference to the circulation and persuasiveness of strategic narratives. And let us not forget that actors rarely achieve their goals in foreign policy (Smith 2002, 6) and influence through communication is a particularly difficult goal to achieve (Miskimmon, O'Loughlin, and Roselle 2013).

A second aspect of networks concerns how they acquire actor-ness in order to communicate a narrative. How do international organizations made up of nation-state members formulate and project a coherent narrative? The chapters by Miskimmon on the European Union and Singh on development show how difficult it can be for policy networks and institutions to appear as a coherent actor capable of projecting a single narrative: "Actorness logically precedes effectiveness" (Niemann and Bretherton 2013, 267). Hence, to explain how networks and multilateral organizations and networks communicate, we must first explain how they can operate as authors or narrators in the first place. If, when the European Union speaks, it speaks as more than the sum of its parts, how is this organized and put into effect? Is behind-the-scenes negotiation and contestation masked from the final narrative, or is this plurality made public in order to project unity-in-diversity and thus a kind of democratic authority? Can we compare the actor-ness of the European Union with either its superpower rivals the United States (one state), the BRICS (many states), or other regional bodies like the North American Free Trade Agreement or the Association of Southeast Asian Nations? And if this is possible, how then do we explain what difference this actor-ness can make to effective communication and influence? What comparative frameworks of analysis could allow us both to conceptualize and operationalize these questions (Niemann and Bretherton 2013)? Finally, how do multilateral organizations and networks function alongside NGOs and individual states to craft shared narratives about particular issues such as climate change or global finance? Singh's chapter begins to hint at the conditions needed. What explanatory factors can account for their success in doing this?

A third area for strategic narrative research is the role of media in contributing to the meaning of events. The Arab Spring and conflicts in Syria and Ukraine have focused attention on the role narratives play in fomenting crises, during the event itself, and afterward in periods of consolidation. How do these events come to possess narrativity for audiences? What historical precedents or comparable crises do audiences think about to make sense of breaking events and how do journalists and political leaders guide this sense-making process?

Media researchers have long argued that broadcasting, the press, and now the Internet are not merely mediums through which events are communicated, but that media help constitute events. During a war, a summit, or the Olympic Games, media construct the space of shared experience by linking different sites and places and by reporting on audience reactions around the world (Silverstone 2007; Robertson 2013; Cottle 2009). Strategic narratives are then projected and contested within that space of shared experience. Do media enable or limit the circulation of plural narratives? Strategic narratives are not projected into a vacuum, but onto terrain that has shape and texture in part constituted by media. Researchers need to investigate how this terrain intersects with and conditions the work leaders do to project narratives. Under what circumstances does media construction of history or geography tacitly endorse a narrative, for instance about shared global problems? Do political leaders try to exert power over media systems in order to influence how they construct a sense of history or geography, and is this a precondition to long-term narrative success?

This takes us to a final area for strategic narrative research, the role of audiences. In chapter 2 we wrote that, analytically, audiences are the elephant in the room. Scholars and policymakers alike find it easier to ignore audiences because they are so hard to research. And yet the likelihood of persuasion rests with the audience's interpretation. Understanding reception can present challenging methodological issues. Archetti's argument that individuals have agency and (re)interpret narratives points to the need for a sophisticated and multifaceted approach to reception. Polling data is not sufficient to understand how people receive and make sense of narratives. Roselle's use of focus groups is important because these data allow a more nuanced understanding of individual narratives and how individuals remix official and media narratives (Roselle, Miskimmon, and O'Loughlin 2015; Spray and Roselle 2012). In these groups she has used Q-sort methods in which participants are asked to assess the component parts of narratives. Factor analysis is used to look for patterns in how new narratives are constructed (Capdevila and Rogers 2000). Using this innovative approach in the study of international affairs in a cross-national study would show how audiences in different societies narrate the same events in different ways. Researchers could establish what difference is made by the presence of plural narratives, by visual coverage of events, and by the capacity of more participatory media to allow audiences to interact and project their own narratives and interpretations. It is not good enough to rely on polls based on simple questions about whether individuals feel positively or negatively about a policy or a country. Strategic narrative research must research narratives, not attitudes; otherwise, it is not narrative research.

The field must get to grips with the narratives through which individuals understand the past, present, and future of each conflict. Narrative analysis allows us to identify what individuals understand as the starting point of each conflict, the dilemma or tension at stake in the conflict, the cast of characters who play a role in sustaining or potentially resolving the conflict, and the range of possible resolutions. It provides a sense of how individuals situate current events within history, and therefore a more powerful explanation of their expectations and aspirations for the future course of events.

Final Thoughts

The work presented here shows that the study of material power is in itself not sufficient to understand the emerging international order and that communicative processes matter. In addition, communication is not straightforward. We hope this book provides further encouragement for students of International Relations to take communication more seriously. As we have demonstrated, analyzing communication across borders, between a plethora of political actors and audiences, is difficult. Nevertheless, understanding the impact of narratives in international affairs gets to the heart of demonstrating how influence occurs within the constantly evolving and shifting media ecology. Narratives forge the world.

REFERENCES

Arsenault, Amelia. "Networks of Freedom, Networks of Control: Internet Policy as a Platform for and an Impediment to Relational Public Diplomacy." In *Relational, Networked and Collaborative Approaches to Public Diplomacy: The Connective Mindshift*, edited by Rhonda S. Zaharna, Amelia Arsenault, and Ali Fisher, 192–208. New York: Routledge, 2014.

Capdevila, Roger, and R. Stainton Rogers. "If You Go Down to the Woods Today . . . Narratives of Newbury." In *Social Discourse and Environmental Policy: An Application of Q Methodology*, edited by Helen Addams and John Propps, 152–73. Cheltenham: Edward Elgar, 2000.

Cottle, Simon. *Global Crisis Reporting: Journalism in the Global Age*. Maidenhead: Open University Press, 2009.

Fitzpatrick, Kathy. "Public Diplomacy and Ethics: From Soft Power to Social Conscience." In *Relational, Networked and Collaborative Approaches to Public Diplomacy: The Connective Mindshift*, edited by Rhonda S. Zaharna, Amelia Arsenault, and Ali Fisher, 29–43. New York: Routledge, 2013.

Gilboa, Eytan. "Searching for a Theory of Public Diplomacy." *ANNALS of the American Academy of Political and Social Science* 616, no. 1 (2008): 55–77.

Hayden, Craig. "Beyond the 'Obama Effect': Refining the Instruments of Engagement through US Public Diplomacy." *American Behavioral Scientist* 55, no. 6 (2011): 784–802.

Latour, Bruno. *We Have Never Been Modern*. Cambridge: Harvard University Press, 1993.

Latour, Bruno. "Whose Cosmos, Whose Cosmopolitics? Comments on the Peace Terms of Ulrich Beck." *Common Knowledge* 10, no. 3 (2004): 450–92.

Latour, Bruno. *On the Modern Cult of the Factish Gods*. Durham, NC: Duke University Press, 2010.

Melissen, Jan, ed. *The New Public Diplomacy: Soft Power in International Relations*. Basingstoke: Palgrave Macmillan, 2005.

Miskimmon, Alister, Ben O'Loughlin, and Laura Roselle. *Strategic Narratives: Communication Power and the New World Order*. New York: Routledge, 2013.

Niemann, Arne, and Charlotte Bretherton. "EU External Policy at the Crossroads: The Challenge of Actorness and Effectiveness." *International Relations* 27, no. 3 (2013): 261–75.

Pamment, James. *New Public Diplomacy in the 21st Century*. London: Routledge, 2012.

Robertson, Alexa. "Connecting in Crisis: 'Old' and 'New' Media and the Arab Spring." *International Journal of Press/Politics* 18, no. 3 (2013): 325–41.

Roselle, Laura, Alister Miskimmon, and Ben O'Loughlin. "Public Narratives about Syria: A Q-Sort Analysis of UK and US Students." Paper presented at the Annual Convention of the International Studies Association, New Orleans, February 18–21, 2015.

Schweller, Randall L. *Maxwell's Demon and the Golden Apple: Global Discord in the New Millennium*. Baltimore: Johns Hopkins University Press, 2014.

Silverstone, Roger. *Media and Morality*. Cambridge: Polity, 2007.

Smith, Hazel. *European Union Foreign Policy: What It Is and What it Does*. London: Pluto, 2002.

Spray, Sharon, and Laura Roselle. "Understanding Communication about the Environment: Narratives of Climate Change and Foreign Policy." Paper prepared for the Annual Convention of the International Studies Association, San Diego, April 1–4, 2012.

Wang, Yiwei. "Relational Dimensions of a Chinese Model of Public Diplomacy." In *Relational, Networked and Collaborative Approaches to Public Diplomacy: The Connective Mindshift*, edited by Rhonda S. Zaharna, Amelia Arsenault, and Ali Fisher, 86–99. New York: Routledge, 2013.

Zaharna, Rhonda S. "Network Purpose, Network Design: Dimensions of Network and Collaborative Public Diplomacy." In *Relational, Networked and Collaborative Approaches to Public Diplomacy: The Connective Mindshift*, edited by Rhonda S. Zaharna, Amelia Arsenault, and Ali Fisher, 173–91. New York: Routledge, 2013.

Zaharna, Rhonda S., Amelia Arsenault, and Ali Fisher, eds. *Relational, Networked and Collaborative Approaches to Public Diplomacy: The Connective Mindshift*. New York: Routledge, 2013.

Zhang, Juyan. "A Strategic Issue Management (SIM) Approach to Social Media Use in Public Diplomacy." *American Behavioral Scientist* 57, no. 9 (Sept. 2013): 1312–31. http://dx.doi.org/10.1177/0002764213487734

Contributors

EDITORS

Alister Miskimmon is Reader in European Politics and International Relations and Co-Director of the Centre for European Politics at Royal Holloway, University of London. He has published widely on German politics, European security, and strategic narratives. His current research on British and Polish defense policy after the 2016 NATO summit in Warsaw is funded by the Noble Foundation. He and Ben O'Loughlin are part of an EU-funded Jean Monnet Network conducting research on crisis narratives in Ukraine and Israel/Palestine. He, Ben O'Loughlin, and Laura Roselle won the 2016 Best Book in International Communication from the International Studies Association for their book *Strategic Narratives: Communication Power and the New World Order.*

Ben O'Loughlin is Professor of International Relations and Co-Director of the New Political Communication Unit at Royal Holloway, University of London. He holds degrees from the University of Northumbria at Newcastle (BA), University of Warwick (MA), and the University of Oxford (MSc, DPhil). He is coeditor of the Sage journal *Media, War & Conflict.* His books include *Radicalisation and Media: Terrorism and Connectivity in the New Media Ecology* (Routledge, 2011), *War and Media: The Emergence of Diffused War* (Polity, 2010), and *Television and Terror: Conflicting Times and the Crisis of News Discourse* (Palgrave, 2007). His projects on media and international security have been funded by the Economic and Social Research Council, Technology Strategy Board, and the UK's Centre for the Protection of National Infrastructure). See newpolcom.rhul.ac.uk/npcu-blog

Laura Roselle is Professor of Political Science and International Studies at Elon University. She has served as president of the International Communication Section of the International Studies Association and president of the Internet Technology and Politics Section of the American Political Science Association. She has published articles and book reviews in leading journals, including the *Harvard International Journal of Press/Politics* and the *American Behavioral Scientist*. Her edited volumes include books on media and democracy and media and elections. She is the author of *Media and the Politics of Failure: Great Powers, Communication Strategies, and Military Defeats* (Palgrave, 2006 and 2011). She is coeditor of the Routledge series in Global Information, Politics and Society. Laura holds degrees from Emory University (BA) and Stanford University (MA; PhD).

ADDITIONAL CONTRIBUTORS

Cristina Archetti is Professor in Political Communication and Journalism at the University of Oslo. She is author, among other works, of *Understanding Terrorism in the Age of Global Media: A Communication Approach* (Palgrave, 2012). Her research interests span the many aspects of communication in politics: strategic communication, political spin and media management, the role of the media in the process of radicalization, public diplomacy 2.0. Cristina received the 2009 Denis McQuail prize for innovating communication theory. She is codirector of Archetti Brown Associates, a consultancy specializing in networks and narratives, and regularly delivers training in countering violent extremism for Hedayah and the United States Institute of Peace.

Amelia Arsenault is an Assistant Professor of Communication at Georgia State University. She also serves as the co-Managing Editor of the open access, peer-reviewed journal *Media Industries* and as a research advisor to the U.S. Advisory Commission on Public Diplomacy in the Department of State. Her scholarly work has appeared in the *International Journal of Communication, International Sociology,* the*ANNALS of the American Academy of Political and Social Science,* and *Information, Communication, and Society*. She is coeditor (with Rhonda Zaharna and Ali Fischer) of *The Connective Mindshift: Relational, Networked and Collaborative Approaches to Public Diplomacy* (Routledge, 2013). She holds a BA in Film and History from Dartmouth College, an MSc in Global Media and Communication from the London School of Economics and Political Science, and a PhD from the University of Southern California Annenberg School.

Robin Brown is a director at Archetti Brown Associates, a consultancy specializing in networks and narratives. Previously he was a Senior Lecturer in International Communications at the University of Leeds. He has published widely on the interface between international politics and media. He is currently completing *Public Diplomacies: Politics, Organizations and Influence*, the first general attempt to understand how countries have used engagement with foreign publics as a mode of influence in international politics.

Sun-ha Hong is a Mellon postdoctoral fellow at MIT, with a PhD from the Annenberg School for Communication, University of Pennsylvania. His work analyzes how new media and its data become invested with ideals of precision, objectivity and truth. Specifically: how do relationships between data and knowledge become legitimized—especially through aesthetic, cultural, imaginative, and otherwise apparently nonrational means? He seeks critical, historically informed diagnoses of the contemporary faith in 'raw' data, sensing machines and algorithmic decision-making, and of their public promotion as the next great leap toward objective knowledge.

Monroe Price serves as Director of the Center for Global Communication Studies of the Annenberg School for Communication and Journalism at the University of Pennsylvania. Professor Price was founding director of the Program in Comparative Media Law and Policy at the University of Oxford. Among his books are *Free Expression, Globalism, and the New Strategic Communication* (2015); *Media and Sovereignty* (2003); *Television, the Public Sphere and National Identity* (1995); *Routledge Handbook of Media Law* (2012); and a treatise on cable television.

Ning Liao is Assistant Professor of Political Science at New Jersey City University. He received his PhD in International Studies from Old Dominion University. His current teaching field is international relations. His research interests include international relations in the Asia Pacific. Ning Liao's dissertation project investigates the construction of collective memory and national identity in the context of Chinese domestic and foreign policy interaction. His research has appeared in such refereed journals as *Asian Politics & Policy*, *East Asia: An International Quarterly*, and *Asian Profile*.

J. P. Singh is the Director of the Centre for Cultural Relations (CCR) and Chaired Professor of Culture and Political Economy at the University of Edinburgh. Singh has authored four monographs, edited three books, and published dozens of scholarly articles. He specializes in global governance and development, specifically exploring issues of information technologies, service industries, global deliberations and diplomacy, and cultural identity. His books analyze the evolution of economic rules (property rights) at the global level, transformational understandings of technology and diplomacy, and the formation of cultural identity in highly interactive circumstances.

Index

Abdullah II of Jordan, 206
Abu Ghraib, 29
Academy Awards, 67
Acharya, Amitav, 282, 283, 292, 302–3
Aday, Sean, 58, 66
Adler-Nissen, Rebecca, 32–33, 42
affect, 33, 39, 43, 116–17, 119, 129, 208, 268
Afghanistan, 29, 34, 36, 73–74, 164, 209, 212, 213, 236, 295
Africa, 61, 134, 139
Ahmadinejad, Mahmoud, 209
Akimoto, Akky, 255
Al-Arabi, Nabil, 213n3
Al-Assad, Bashar, 193, 195, 198, 201, 206, 213n3
Al-Jazeera, 214n4, 232, 298
Al-Orouba TV, 202
Al-Qaeda, 34, 218–19, 232, 236–38, 241n4, 280
Al-Rai, 202
Alawites, 200
Alexander, Gerard, 282, 303n3
alliances, 30, 65, 283
Alliance Française, 172
Altheide, David, 35, 65
Amin, Idi, 205
Amin, Samir, 144
Amnesty International, 149
anarchy, 11, 27, 42, 282
Anderson, Benedict, 223
Annan, Kofi, 155, 159
Antkiewicz, Agata, 288
Arab League, 61, 195, 198, 206, 213n2, 213n3

Arab Spring, 16, 79, 190–213, 250, 321
Archetti, Cristina, 197, 312, 314
Argentina, 140
Arizpe, Lourdes, 153
Arsenault, Amelia H., 35, 42, 190–217, 312, 314, 315, 316, 317, 318, 320
Asahi Shimbun, 255, 258
Asia, 61, 139
Asia Times, 260
Asian Infrastructure Investment Bank, 294
Asia Pacific Regional Internet Governance Forum, 202
Association of Southeast Asian Nations, 321
Attali, Jacques, 265
Atran, Scott, 226
audience. *See* Narrative reception
audience research, 45, 47
Avenall, Simon, 254
Awan, Akil, 250

Baghdad, 63
Bahrain, 209
Bain, Jessica, 301
Baltics, 78
Banerjee, Abhijit V., 160
Barnard, Anne, 206
Barnett, Michael, 276
Baumann, Zygmunt, 251
BBC, 46, 68, 253, 298
Beck, Ulrich, 250–51
Belassa, Bela A., 140
Belin, Laura, 58, 77

329

Belsen, Ken, 258
Benghazi, 201
Benin, 280
Bennett, Andrew, 70, 71, 74
Bennett, Lance, 211
Benwell, Bethan, 221
Bergen, Peter, 241n4
Berlin Wall, 57
Berlo, David, 234–35
Betz, David, 218–19, 232, 237–38
Bhagwati, Jagdish, 146
Bially Mattern, Janice, 279, 285–86, 299
Biersteker, Thomas, 142–43
Big Data, 24, 26, 41
Bilko, Steve, 153
Bird, S. Elizabeth, 205
Bismarck, Otto von, 278
Bjorkman, Carl, 236
Blair, Tony, 156
Blumler, Jay G., 250
Bongo, Omar, 205
Borshchevskaya, Anna, 196
Bourdieu, Pierre, 193, 214n8
Boutros-Ghali, Boutros, 152
Boy, Nina J., 250
boyd, danah, 266
Brahimi, Lakhdar, 213n2, 213n3
Bratton, Benjamin H., 250
Brazil, 45, 93, 134, 140, 141, 147, 150, 277, 287, 291, 295. *See also* BRICS
Breivik, Anders, 239
Breslin, Shaun, 283
Bretherton, Charlotte, 320, 321
Bretton Woods, 142
BRICS, 93, 134, 164, 183, 277, 285, 287–91, 293, 300–302, 317, 319, 321
British Broadcasting Corporation (BBC), x, 46, 68, 205, 232, 298
British Council, x, xi, 46
Brooks, Stephen G., 282, 303n3
Brown, Robin, 312, 314, 316–17, 319–20
Brzezinski, Zbigniew, 281
Bucci, Steven, 240
Bull, Hedley, 276
Bundesbank, 98–100
Burchell, Kenzie, 286, 303n7

Burgess, Peter, 250
Burma, 295
Bush doctrine, 65
Bush, George H. W., 56, 60–62, 79
Bush, George W., 64–66, 68, 282, 319
Buzan, Barry, 268n1, 278, 298

Cable News Network (CNN), 232, 251, 298
Cabral, Amilcar, 153
Calhoun, Craig, 222–23, 224
Calleo, David, 52n2
Cameron, David, 195, 197, 204, 208, 209, 211
Campbell, David, 37
Capdevila, Roger, 322
Carafano, James J., 240
Cardoso, Fernando Henrique, 144
Carey, James, 204
Carlson, Timothy, 66
Casebeer, William D., 219, 237
Castells, Manuel, 251, 268n1
causation, 25, 27–28, 29, 31, 36, 44, 232–33
CCTV, 298
censorship, 76
Center for Advanced Studies and Research for Latin America, 150–51
Center for Journalism in Extreme Situations, 76
Cento Bull, Anna, 226–27
Central Asia, 78
Central Intelligence Agency (CIA), 29
central planning, 143
Cerny, Philip, 52n1
Cesaire, Aimé, 153
Chaban, Natalia, 301
Chad, 280
Chadwick, Andrew, 49
Chafetz, Glenn R., 385
Chakravarty, Paula, 250
Chan, Steve, 282, 283
Charlie Hebdo, 223
Chechnya, 8, 56–60, 69–79, 316, 317
Checkel, Jeffrey T., 31
Chernobyl, 246, 251, 258–59
child health, 155

Index | 331

China, 25, 30–31, 134, 138, 147, 158, 193, 195, 198, 199, 201, 235, 257, 279, 283–84, 287–301, 312, 313, 317
Chinese Communist Party, 122, 298
Choate, Allen, 255
Chouliaraki, Lilie, 38–39, 42, 208
Christensen, Thomas J., 283
Clark, Helen, 148
Clark, Neil, 205
climate change, 38, 247
Clinton, Hillary Rodham, 32, 197, 202–3
Clinton, William Jefferson, 30–31, 156
Clunan, Anne L., 71
CNN effect, 251
Coalition Provisional Authority, 66
Coase, Ronald, 144
Coker, Christopher, 250
Cold War, 4, 8, 13, 14, 15, 24, 31–32, 33, 36, 37, 42, 56–79, 276–77
Colombia, 71
Common Foreign and Security Policy, 92–93
Commonwealth Games, 295–96
Community Action Programs, 141
connectivity, 35, 39
Connolly, Kevin, 205, 210
constructivism, 48, 93, 276
Cooper, Andrew F., 288
cooperation, 65
Copenhagen Declaration, 156
Corman, Steven R., 234–36
Cottle, Simon, 246, 250–52, 321
Couldry, Nick, 204
Cox, Robert W., 277
credibility, 197–98
Crimea, 3, 56–57, 177
Croft, Stuart, 250
Cullather, Nick, 141
Cupples, Julie, 139

Dardenne, Robert W., 205
Davidson, Jason, 282
Dayan, Daniel, 223
de Almagro Iniesta, María Martín, 27
Deaton, Angus, 137, 138
Decade for Culture and Development, 152

de Graaf, Beatrice, 27, 28–29
Denmark, 29
deregulation, 141
Deudney, Daniel H., 268n1
development. *See* international development
de Waal, Monica, 235
dialogic communication, 150
dialogue, 25, 31
Dicicco, Jonathan M., 282
Dimitriu, George, 27, 28–29
Ding, Sheng, 296, 298–300
diplomacy, 29, 31–32, 278, 288
discourse, 36–39
Doha Round, 146–47, 157
Doran, Charles F., 283
Downing, John H., 250
Draghi, Mario, 97–99, 101, 316
Dreher, Tanja, 25
Drezner, Daniel W., 293–94, 299
Dueck, Colin, 294
Duflo, Esther, 160
Durariappah, Anantha K., 254
Dunne, Tim, 276
Duus, Peter, 260

East Asian miracle, 143
Eastern Europe, 143
Economic Opportunity Action, 1964, U.S., 141
education, universal, 155
Egypt, 36, 140, 190, 192, 199, 201, 203, 223
Eleftheriou-Smith, Loulla-Mae, 240
embedding, 66–67
Emirbayer, Mustafa, 225
English School, 276
Entman, Robert, 58, 66, 70, 266
environmental sustainability, 155
Escobar, Arturo, 137–38, 151
Epstein, Charlotte, 38, 42
ethics, 25–26, 52
Europe, 61, 70, 79, 136–37
European Central Bank (ECB), 96–97, 316
European Commission, 202
European Dialogue on Internet Governance, 202

European External Action Service (EEAS), 89–90
European Union (EU), 4, 6, 15, 38, 85–102, 177, 195, 260, 287, 294–95, 297, 299–301, 312, 313, 320–21

Facebook, 9, 35, 202, 256
Faletto, Enzo, 144
Fanon, Frantz, 153
Fearon, James D., 297
Fenby, Jonathan, 283, 288–89
Ferguson, James, 138, 144
Field, Norma, 259
Finnemore, Martha, 156, 276, 286–87
Fiore, Quentin, 268n1
Fisher, Ali, 318
Fitzpatrick, Kathy, 319
Floridi, Luciano, 268n1
focus group, 67–69, 78
Foreign Policy, 259
framing, 28, 34, 228
France, 29, 32, 94, 165–83, 193, 223, 260–61, 279, 316, 320
France 24, 298
Franks, Suzanne, 299
Frankel, Benjamin, 285
Fraser, Nancy, 303n1
Fravel, M. Taylor, 284
Freedman, Sir Lawrence, 194, 247
Freire, Paulo, 150–51, 153
Friedberg, Aaron L., 283–84
Friedman, Thomas, 209
Friends of Syria, 200
Fukishima, 246–69
Fukuda-Parr, Sakiko, 156, 157
Fukuyama, Francis, 280
Fuller, Matthew, 251, 268n1

Gabon, 205
Gaddafi, Muammar, 193–214
Gaddis, John L., 277
Gaidar, Yegor, 71
game theory, 28
Gandhi, Rajiv, 141, 143
Gaynor, Niamh, 151
Gehl, Robert W., 251

Geltzer, Joshua, 237
gender equality, 154
Gerber, Theodore P., 80n18
Germany, 29, 31–32, 260, 279, 288–89, 316, 320
Gibson, Gloria D., 221
Giddens, Lord Anthony, 251
Gilboa, Eytan, 318
Gillespie, Marie G., 286
Gilpin, Robert, 265, 278, 283, 292
Glasnost, 57
global order, 56
Global financial crisis of 2008 (GFC), 278, 289, 294
global partnerships, 155
globalization, 300–302
Godzilla, 246
Goffey, Andrew, 268n1
Goldberg, Greg, 251
Golden triangle, 71
Goldman Sachs, 134, 157, 281, 287–91, 295
Goldsmith, Benjamin E., 29, 32, 42
Gorbachev, Mikhail, 31–32, 61
Grant, Jim, 156
Gration, Maj. Gen. Scott, 197
great power narratives, 13–14, 56–80, 177, 278, 281, 284, 293, 297, 299, 313
Greece, 223
Greenwood, Lee, 63
Greif, Avner, 145
Grinter, Lawrence E., 283
Group of 77 (G-77), 152
Grusin, Richard, 246
Gulf Strike, 64
Gulf War, 56
Gupta, Dipak, 233
Guyer, Jane, 144

Habermas, Jürgen, 30, 279
Hague, William, 197
Hajer, Maarten A., 247
Hall, Ian, 25
Hallin, Daniel, 211
Hameiri, Shahar, 301
Hariman, Robert, 26
Hart, Shilpa A., 151

Hartig, Falk, 287
Harvey, David, 143
Hayden, Craig, 34, 319
Hebert, Maeve, 58, 66
hierarchy, 118, 265–66, 302
Hill, Polly, 138, 144
Hiroshima, 246, 249, 262, 276
Hirschman, Albert O., 137
Hirsh, Michael, 65
Hitler, Adolf, 198
Hitomi, Kamanka, 259
HIV/AIDS, 155
Hjarvard, Stig, 35
Holland, 29, 218
Holland, Martin, 301
Hong, Sun-ha, 190–217, 312, 314, 315, 316, 317
Horiuchi, Yusaku, 29, 32, 42
Hoskins, Andrew, 58, 63, 65, 250, 268
Hounshell, Blake, 202
Houweling, Henk W., 283
Howard, Philip N., 202
Howorth, Jolyon, 282
Huesca, Robert, 150–51
Hulme, David, 156, 157
Human Development, 147–49
Human Development Index, 148
Human Development Reports, 153
Huntingdon, Samuel, 48, 151, 153
Hurrell, Andrew, 278, 279, 284–85, 291, 296
Hussein, Muzammil M., 202
Hussein, Saddam, 61–62, 64, 75
Hutchings, Stephen, 303n7
Hybrid media system, 49
hypocrisy, 25, 29, 299

India, 137, 139, 140, 141, 143, 147, 158
identity, 33, 34, 36, 39, 56–79, 221–27, 247–48, 258, 277, 284, 299–300
Ikea, 223
Ikegami, Eiko, 255
Ikenberry, G. John, 52n1, 280, 282, 292–93, 303
images, 26
Import substitution industrialization (ISI), 138–41, 142, 143, 144, 145, 147

indexing, 211
India, 33, 134, 250, 293, 295–96. *See also* BRICS
industrialization, 134–60
Industrial Policy Resolution (India), 137
information infrastructure, 12, 17, 170, 203, 235, 246, 249, 253–57, 264–67, 268n1, 298–99, 312, 320
influence, 25, 51
Institute for Strategic Dialogue, 227
institutional economics, 152
Interdependence, 65
International Atomic Energy Agency (IAEA), 258, 261, 266
International Conference on Financing for Development, 156
International Crisis Group, 237
international development, 134–63, 312, 314
International Monetary Fund (IMF), 141, 142, 146–47, 151, 294
International Telecommunication Union, 157
International Women's Health Coalition, 156
Iran, vii, 12, 36, 42, 79, 193–95, 199, 201
Iraq, 209
Iraq War (2003–14), 29, 34, 56–57, 60–69, 316, 317
Islamic State (ISIS/ISIL), 171, 182–83, 227, 232, 236–38, 280, 317
Israel, 36, 42, 168
Italy, 29, 226, 236, 260

Jackson, Patrick T., 24, 28, 32, 40, 42, 192
Jacobs, Robert A., 246
Jacques, Martin, 293
Jamestown Foundation, 237
Japan, 9, 17, 112, 114–16, 119–29, 246–69, 297, 316
Japan Times, 253, 260–62
Jenkins, Brian M., 232
"Je Suis Charlie," 224
Jisi, Wanh, 319
Johnson, Alastair I., 282, 303n8
Johnson, Lyndon, 140, 141

Johnson, Mark, 289, 303n6
Johnson, Thomas H., 236
Jones, Gareth Steadman, 135
Jones, Lee, 301

Kagan, Robert, 293, 299
Kahler, Miles, 142
Kalathil, Shanthi, 203
Kan, Nobuko, 254, 260–62
Karamoskos, Peter, 262–63
Karpf, David, 49–50
Kashmir, 295
Katovsky, Bill, 66
Katz, Eliu, 223
Katzenstein, Peter, 27, 48, 287
Kennan, George, 37
Kennedy Paul, 277
Kennedy, Rebecca, 262
Kenya, 250
Kerry, John, 68
Khong, Yuen F., 283
Kim, Jennie, 58, 66
Kim, Jim Yong, 152
Kim, Woosang, 282
Kindstrand, Love, 255–58, 263
King, Gary, 299
King Idris, 200
Kingston, Jeff, 261
Kirby, Peter W., 246
Kissinger, Henry, 278–79, 283, 292, 294
Kittler, Friedrich, 246, 249
Knox, David, 41
Kobe earthquake, 254, 263
Kohl, Helmut, 98–99
Kohut, Andrew, 62
Koivisto, Marjo, 276
Kolmer, Christian, 66
Koloynystska, Halyna, 205
Kolsova, Elena, 58
Kosovo, 76
Kotsev, Victor, 253
Kozyrev, Andrei, 71
Kramer, Mark, 75, 77
Krauthammer, Charles, 277
Krebs, Ronald, 28, 32, 42, 192
Krieger, Daniel, 261

Kugler, Jacek, 278, 282, 283
Kuhn, Thomas, 40
Kumar, Anup, 38
Kuomintang (KMT), 114, 116
Kupchan, Charles, 280, 282, 292, 303
Kurds, 200
Kuwait, 61–62, 75

Laclau, Ernesto, 37
Lady Gaga, 223, 263–64, 267
Lakoff, George, 289, 303n6
Lambert, Robert, 240
Landes, David, 137
Landis, Joshua, 194
Latin America, 139, 151
Latour, Bruno, 240n1, 318
Lavrov, Sergie, 196–97
Law, John, 48, 50
Lawler, Stephanie, 220–21, 229
Layne, Christopher, 278, 282, 294
Leander, Anna, 250
Lebanon, 194
LeCuyer, Jack A., 192
Lee, Raymond L. M., 251
Leflar, Robert B., 246
legitimizing agents, 203–7
Legro, Jeffrey, 292, 303
Lemieux, Anthony, 233
Lemke, Douglas, 282
Levy, Jack S., 282
Liao, Ning, 312, 313, 314
liberalism, 30–31, 51, 70, 135, 137, 140, 141, 143, 145, 148, 175, 177, 179, 195, 280, 292–94
Liberation Daily (*Jiefang ribao*), 128
Libya, 16, 32, 42, 94, 190–213, 316
Libyan National Transition Council, 197, 200
Lieber, Keir A., 282, 303n3
Lim, Merlyna, 202
Linde, Charlotte, 221
Linklater, Andrew, 276
Liscutin, Nicola, 255–57, 263–64, 268
Little, Richard, 268n1
Livingston, Steven, 58, 66
Lucaites John L., 26
Luther, Catherine A., 58
Luthra, Karuna, 262

Luxembourg, 280
Lynch, Marc, 30, 42, 285, 302
Lyotard, Jean-François, 157

Malashenko, Igor, 73
Malaysia, 146
Malaysia Airlines flight MH17, 179
Malinkova, Olga V., 73
Malloch Brown, Mark, 156
Mankoff, Jeffrey, 70
Mann, Michael, 283, 303n6
Mansuri, Ghazala, 151
Martin, Alex, 260–61
masrawi.com, 203
maternal health, 155
Matwiczak, Kenneth, 41
Mayor, Federico, 152
McCarthy, Mary, 252, 255–56
McDonald, Ken, 209
McLeod, Douglas M., 73
McLuhan, Marshall, 268n1
McNamara, Robert, 140
McNeill, Desmond, 149
Mead, Walter Russell, 292
Mearsheimer, John G., 278, 281–82
Medeiros, Evan S., 284
Medellin cartel, 71
media ecology, 27, 30, 33, 36, 49, 51, 219, 229–30, 257, 266, 278–79, 292
  defined, 303n2
media events, 223
media logics, 35, 36
  social media logics, 35
mediatization, 35
Melissen, Jan, 318
Melucci, Alberto, 225
Mendelson, Sarah E., 80n18
Menon, Anand, 282
Mereu, Francesca, 73, 77
Merkel, Angela, 97, 99–101, 316
Merrin, William, 48–49
metaphor, 288–91, 303n6
Methmann, Chris P., 38
methodology, 24, 33, 34, 40–52, 315–17
Metternick, Klemens von, 278
Mexico, 139, 140, 143

Mickiewiciz, Ellen, 58, 72–73
Miliband, David, 279
Millennium Development Goals (MDGs), 15–16, 135–36, 155–59, 316
Miller, M. Mark, 58
Mische, Ann, 225
Mishra, Suman, 296
Miskimmon, Alister, 2–5, 14–15, 18, 25, 27, 32, 37, 42, 52, 57, 66, 85–109, 110, 111, 118, 136, 164, 184, 191, 219, 241n3, 247, 250, 287, 312, 313, 314, 316, 317–18, 320, 322
mission accomplished, 64, 65
Modernization narrative, 138
Mondiacult. *See* World Conference on Cultural Policies
Monteiro, Nuno P., 303n4
Monterrey Consensus, 156
Mor, Ben D., 36, 42, 264
Moran, Terence P., 65
Morris, John F., 255, 262
Morsi, Mohamed, 201
Mouaz al Khatib, Ahmed, 200
Mouffe, Chantal, 37
Moynihan, Daniel P., 141
Mubarak, Hosni, 36, 196
multipolarity, 37, 281, 287–88, 293, 295, 298–99
Mumby, Dennis, 221
Murai, Noriko, 257
Murphy, Craig N., 148, 149
Murukami, Haruki, 264
Mussolini, Benito, 205
Myrdal, Gunnar, 149

Nacos, Brigitte, 266
Nagasaki, 249, 264
Naim, Moises, 279
Narayan, Deepa, 152
narrative
  alignment, 238
  consensus-based, 198
  contestation, 136, 191, 313–14
  definitions, 220–21, 249
  formation, 28, 40–46, 64–66, 70–71, 74–76, 136, 159, 219, 222, 252, 281, 287, 291–96, 311, 315–17

336 | Index

narrative (*continued*)
   historically driven narrative, 199
   Identity narrative, 74, 79, 313
   Policy narrative, 314
   power-based, 198
   projection, 23–25, 29, 40–44, 51, 66–67, 71–73, 76–77, 136, 159, 219, 225, 241n4, 252, 254, 279–81, 285, 287–88, 290–91, 295–301, 303n4, 311, 314, 315–17
   reception, 39–41, 43–48, 51, 52n1, 67–69, 73–74, 77–78, 136, 219, 221, 224–25, 229–33, 239, 241n3, 252, 254, 281, 287, 295–301, 311, 314–17, 322
   self-generating narratives, 200
   System narrative, 69, 79, 137, 313
National Coalition of Syria, 200
Nau, Henry R., 292
NBC, 59, 62–63, 67
near abroad, 70
Nehru, Jawaharlal, 137
Nelson, Joan M., 151
"Neoliberalism," 141–44
networks, 12, 14, 16, 46, 164–84, 202, 221, 224, 225, 230, 232, 240, 253, 256, 314, 319–20
Neumann, Peter, 228, 241n2
new world order, 56, 61
New Zealand, 148
Niemann, Arne, 320, 321
Nill, Robert, 233
9/11. *See* September 11, 2001
Nishimura, Keiko, 255–58, 263
Nongovernmental organizations (NGOs), 27, 38, 149, 156, 197, 220, 259, 266
norms, 30, 35, 37, 276
North American Free Trade Agreement, 321
North Atlantic Treaty Organisation (NATO), x, 4, 29, 31, 76, 164, 177, 180, 193
North, Douglass, 144, 145, 152
North Korea, 77
NTV, 59, 72–73, 76, 77
Nye, Joseph S., ix, 286, 290–91, 295, 298, 303

Oates, Sarah, 58, 79n1, 76, 77, 78, 80n17, 80n20
Obama, Barack, viii, 32, 37, 152, 195, 197, 202, 204, 206–11, 278, 319
O'Brien, Conan, 214n6
Occupy Wall Street, 199
O'Loughlin, Ben, 2–5, 9, 10–11, 14, 17–18, 25, 27, 32, 37, 52, 57–58, 65, 66, 88, 110–11, 118, 136, 164, 184, 191, 219, 241n3, 246–75, 279, 286, 287, 295, 312–14, 316–18, 320, 322
Olson, Mancur, 145
Olympics, 41, 295–96, 321
O'Neill, Jim, 134, 287, 289
order, 37, 276–303
Organization for Security and Co-operation in Europe, 74
Organski, Abramo F. K., 278
Orientalism, 138, 153
ORT, 59, 72
Ostankino, 72–73
Our Creative Diversity, 152, 153, 154
Owen, Taylor, 268n1

Page, Benjamin, 266
Paletz, David L., 58, 63
Palmer, Jerry, 65, 66
Pamment, James, 41, 44–45, 52, 318
Pan, Jennifer, 299
Panfilov, Oleg, 76–77
Pape, Robert A., 278, 282
participatory action research (PAR), 150–51
participatory development, 150–54, 316
patriotism, 67, 76
Paul, Thazha, 282
Peaceful rise (heping jueqi), 120, 281, 295, 297, 313
Pekannen, Robert, 254
Pendlebury, Richard, 204–5
People's Daily (*Renmin ribao*), 117, 122, 126
Perestroika, 57
Perez de Cuellar, Javier, 152–53
performativity, 48, 288–91
Perkins, Christopher, 247–48, 254, 261
Persian Gulf War. *See* Iraq War

persuasion, 27, 30–31, 32
  spectrum of, 23–24, 27–43, 46, 47, 51
Peters, John Durham, 25, 267
Petrova, A., 74, 77–78
Pew Center, 67
Philippines, 140
Poell, Thomas, 35
Pogge, Thomas, 149
Poku, Nana, 158
Politkovskaya, Anna, 75
Pouliot, Vincent, 32–33, 42, 283
poverty reduction, 154
Poverty Reduction Strategy Papers (PRSPs), 151
power, 26, 27, 34, 36, 282, 287, 294, 296
  balancing, 282, 303n3
  "Language-power," 285
  See also soft power
power transition, 56, 276–303
prestige, 33, 74, 265–66, 281, 285, 296
Prevent Strategy, 218
Price, Monroe, 24, 35, 36, 42, 190–217, 312, 314, 315, 316, 317
privatization, 141
property rights, 144–47
public diplomacy, 29, 34, 45, 52, 202, 234, 312, 318–19
public relations, 298
Purushothothaman, Roopa, 277, 287–88
Putin, Vladimir, 59, 74–77, 79

Qatar, 198, 214n4, 279
Q-methodology, 52n1, 322

radicalization, 219, 220, 227, 228–40, 241n1
Ramo, Joshua C., 295, 301
Ramos-Horta, Jose, 213n2
RAND Corporation, 237
Rao, Vijayendra, 151, 152
Reagan, Ronald, 80n10, 142
realism, 18, 87, 276–77, 281–85, 290, 318, 319
recognition, 18, 30, 33, 91, 197, 225, 251, 278, 303n1
rhetorical coercion, 192

Ribet, Kate, 299
Rice, Condoleezza, 205
RICU (Research, Information and Communication Unit), 219
Rietbergen-McCracken, Jennifer, 152
Ringsmose, Jens, 27, 28–29, 42
risk, 248, 250–51, 260, 264–67
Risse, Thomas, 31, 33, 42, 279
Roberts, Margaret E., 299
Robertson, Alexa, 321
Rockefeller Foundation, 141
Rogers, Brooke, 228, 233
Rogers, James, 38
Rollins, John, 239
Rosamond, Ben, 38
Roselle, Laura, 2–3, 5, 8, 14, 27, 32, 36, 37, 52n1, 56–79, 88, 110, 164, 191, 219, 241n3, 247, 287, 312, 313, 315–18, 320, 322
Rostow, Walt W., 137
Rothkopf, David, 279
Rudd, Kevin, viii, 3
Ruppert, Evelyn, 48, 50
Russell, James A., 219, 237
Russia, 8, 11, 14, 56–79, 89, 134, 165, 171, 174, 176, 177–80, 193–213, 260, 279, 293, 295, 303n7, 312–13, 316–17, 320. *See also* BRICS
Russia Today / RT, 298, 303n7

Saab, Nabil Abi, 196
Saad, Hwaida, 206
Sachs, Jeffrey, 144
Saddiki, Said, 199
Sadik, Nafi, 156
Said, Edward, 138, 153
Salinas, Carlos, 143
Salloukh, Bassel F., 194
Saltman, E., 227
Sané, Pierre, 149
Saradzhyan, Simon, 73, 76
Sarkozy, Nicholas, 96, 195, 204, 208, 211
Savage, Mike, 26, 48, 50
Save Darfur, 197
Schmid, Alex P., 241n4
Schweller, Randall, 277, 302–3, 318
Sciolla, Loredana, 225

Scott, James C., 138
Scowcroft, Brent, 62
scripts, 192–94, 220
Secunda, Eugene, 65
Segawa, Makiko, 254, 257, 259
Selznick, Philip, 141
Semetko, Holli, 66
Sen, Amartya, 147
Senghor, Léopold, 153
September 11, 2001, 34, 38, 64, 65, 79, 223
Sevodnya, 77
Shambaugh, David, 277, 283
Shaw, Martin, 248
Shaw, Timothy M., 288
Shepherd, Laura, 37
Siccama, Jan G., 283
Sikkink, Kathryn, 156
Silverstone, Roger, 321
Simpson, Emile, 25
Sinclair, Timothy, 277
Singh, J. P., 134–63, 312, 314, 316, 320, 321
Slater, David H., 255–58, 263
Slaughter, Anne-Marie, 276, 279
Smith, Frank, 25
Smith, Hazel, 320
Snow, Nancy, 35
Snyder, Jack, 294–95
socialization, 30–31, 279–80, 287
social media, 9, 11–12, 17, 35–36, 41, 50, 178, 179–82, 184, 190, 191, 202–3, 211–12, 220, 227, 229, 251–52, 256–59, 263, 266, 267, 299, 317
Social power, 3, 88, 103n3
soft power, 33, 281, 286–87
Somalia, 212
Somalization, 195, 213n2
Somers, Margaret R., 221
Soros, George, 294
soteigai, 264–67
South Africa, 134, 147, 151
South Korea, 125, 146
Speckhard, Anne, 233
Spirtas, Michael, 285
Spray, Sharon, 52n1, 322
Stats, Katrina, 301
status, 33, 57, 61–62, 68, 74–75, 79, 86–87, 98, 101, 118, 120, 153, 213, 278, 281–82, 283, 293, 296, 298
St. Clair, Asunción Lira, 149
Steamboy, 246
Steele, Brent, 27, 34, 42
Stenersen, Anne, 241n4
Stevens, Tim, 241n2
Stockholm Intergovernmental Conference on Cultural Policies for Sustainable Development, 154
Stokoe, Elizabeth, 221
strategy, 25, 37, 287, 301
structural adjustment policies, 142, 146
Stuenkel, Oliver, 288, 291
Sucharov, Mira, 282
Suganami, Hidemi, 276
Sullivan, Rachel, 250
Sustainable Development Goals (SDGs), 158
Suzuki, Shogo, 265
Sweden, 45–47, 260
Syria, xi, 16, 79, 171, 177, 181, 182, 191, 192–213, 237, 316, 321
Syrian National Coordination Committee, 200
Syrian Opposition Coalition, 197

Tabuchi, Hiroko, 261, 263
Taiwan, 140
Taleb, Nassim, 260
Taliban, 164
Tarrow, Sidney, 241n1
Taylor, Ian, 277
Tennessee Valley Authority (TVA), 141
terrorism, 65–66, 74–75, 76–77, 79, 218–41, 296
Tharoor, Shashi, 33, 277, 278, 292–93
Thatcher, Margaret, 142
Theohary, Catherine A., 239
Thérien, Jean-Philippe, 283
"Third World," 134
Third World Network, 156
Thomas, Robert P., 144
Thomas, Timothy L., 76
Tilly, Charles, 241n1
Time, 237, 259, 267

Tisdall, Simon, 210
Tkach-Kawasaki, Leslie M., 261
Todorov, Tzvetan, 248
Tokyo Electric Power Company (TEPCO), 248, 255, 258, 260–64, 266
Toth, Robert C., 62
Tsujinika, Yutaka, 254
Tsygankov, Andrei, 75, 80n14
Tumber, Howard, 65, 66
Tunisia, 190, 192, 199, 201
Turkey, 195, 206
Twitter, 35, 250, 255

Ukraine, xi, 3, 8, 56, 79, 89, 165, 171, 176–80, 317, 320, 321
ul Haq, Mahbub, 147, 148
Ungar, Sheldon, 250
United Kingdom, 29, 32, 45–47, 80n20, 142, 193, 218, 240, 247, 260, 279, 288–89, 316
United Nations, ix, 61–62, 64–65, 125, 136, 137, 153, 155, 157, 158, 190
United Nations Children's Fund (UNICEF), 148, 156, 157
United Nations Development Program (UNDP), 135, 147–49, 153, 155, 156, 316
United Nations Educational, Scientific and Cultural Organization (UNESCO), 135, 149, 152–59, 253, 316
United Nations Fund for Population Activities, 157
United Nations Population Fund, 156
United Nations Security Council, 190
United Russia party, 77
United States, 29, 30–31, 32, 34, 36, 37–38, 45–47, 56–79, 136, 142, 193, 196, 218, 234–35, 240, 249, 253, 260, 266, 278, 279, 281–83, 287–91, 297, 299–301, 312, 313, 316, 321
United States Agency for International Development (USAID), 141
United States Department of State, 202
United States Treasury Department, 141
Urry, John, 267
USSR (Soviet Union), 31–32, 36, 37, 56–79, 138, 143

Van Dijck, José, 35
van Ham, Peter, ix, 3, 88, 103n3, 286–87
Vargas, Jose Antonio, 202
Vasquez-Arroyo, Antonio Y., 38
Vernon, Raymond, 139
Vietnam, 36
Vietnam War, 63, 211
Vinter, Louise, 41
Vremya, 72, 77, 80n17

Wald, Matthew L., 262
Walton, Michael, 152
Waltz, Kenneth N., 276, 280
Wang, Hongying, 297, 299–300
war on poverty, 140, 141
war on terror, 208, 232
Washington Consensus, 135, 136, 141, 156
weapons of mass destruction, 66
Weber Shandwick, 298
Weibo, 35
Weidmann, Jens, 98, 100
Weir, Fred, 77
Wendt, Alexander, 276
White, Hayden, 221, 240n1
Whitman, Jim, 158
Whitney, Christopher B., 277
Williams, Michael J., 250
Williamson, John, 141
Wilson, Dominic, 277, 287–88
Wohlforth, William C., 282, 303n3
World Bank, 135, 137, 139, 140, 141, 142, 143, 146, 147, 148, 149, 151, 152, 155, 157, 160, 316
World Commission on Culture and Development, 152, 153, 154
World Conference on Cultural Policies, 152
World Culture Reports, 154
World Cup, 295
World Decade for Cultural Development, 154
World Development Report (HDR), 148
World Heritage program (UNESCO program), 152
World Social Forum, 159
World Summit for Children (1990), 156

World Trade Organization (WTO), 31, 135, 146, 155, 157, 294, 316
World War I, 316, 319–20
World War II, 76, 134

Xiao, Yuefan, 283
Xinhua, 257, 298

Yasuyuki, Sakai, 253
Yeltsin, Boris, 59, 70–71, 74
Yemen, 209

Yomiuri Shimbun, 255
YouTube, 206, 214n6, 237, 259, 263
Yuko, Kawato, 254
Yusuf, Shahid, 137, 138

Zaharna, Rhonda S., 318, 320
Zalman, Amy, 192
Zeng, Jinghan, 283
Zhang, Feng, 297–300
Zhang, Juyan, 25, 320
Zuckerman, Jessica, 240